30 YEARS
OF HURT

30 YEARS OF HURT

THE HISTORY OF ENGLAND'S HOOLIGAN ARMY

CASS PENNANT & ANDY NICHOLLS

First published in paperback 2007
By Pennant Books
www.pennantbooks.com

Text copyright © Andy Nicholls & Cass Pennant

The moral right of the author has been asserted.

British Library Cataloguing-in-Publication Data:
A catalogue record for this book is available from
The British Library

ISBN 978-1-906015-12-1

Design & Typeset by Envy Design Ltd

Printed and bound by 🦁 Grafica Veneta S.p.A., Trebaseleghe (PD) - Italy

Pictures reproduced with kind permission of PA Photos, Action Images,
Lorne Brown/www.acasuallook.co.uk, Michael G Williams.
1, 2, 4,5,18, 19, 30, 31, 36, 37 Action Images;
2,8,9,10,11,12,13,14,15,16,17,20,21,22,23,24,25,26,27,28,29,32,33,34,35,39
PA Photos 6, 7, 38 Lorne Brown/www.acasuallook.co.uk

Cover photograph: front © PA Photos

*Every reasonable effort has been made to acknowledge the ownership of copyright
material included in this book. Any errors that have inadvertently occurred will be
corrected in subsequent editions provided notification is sent to the publisher.*

Pennant Books
A division of Pennant Publishing Ltd
PO Box 5675
London W1A 3FB
www.pennantbooks.com

ACKNOWLEDGEMENTS

We would especially like to acknowledge and thank Carl H Spiers for the book's research, plus all the usual suspects, including some who were the most unlikely sources of information who either paved the way or made contributions to this book, which we believe is the real story of a period of social history that characterises this type of football fan culture.

We would also like to take time out to actually dedicate this book to the mystery drummer who played on in the midst of the Marseille beach battle who showed that, no matter where you are in the world, you will find somewhere either an eccentric or crazy Englishman. When we heard the tale of this man's courage, stubbornness and non-violent stance in the middle of what could be described as total mayhem, it not only stirred us but also became the inspiration to develop and deliver the whole history of why it is some English act barking mad when abroad, particular if it involves following the national football team.

Fascination here should never really overlook or ignore the fact there will always be a serious note and another side.

RIP Stephen Smith.

In memory of my grandfather Wing Commander Richard Nicholls. A proud Englishman who fought during two World Wars for King and Country!

CASS PENNANT

The leading voice on the subject of terrace culture for film, TV, radio and print. He has written seven bestsellers and been name-checked in many others. His first book was his autobiography *Cass*. This was followed by the hugely successful *Congratulations, You Have Just Met the ICF*, *Want Some Aggro?*, *Rolling With The 6.57 Crew*, *Terrace Legends*, *Top Boys* and *Good Afternoon Gentlemen, The Name's Bill Gardner*. Cass's life story is now a major film.

WWW.CASSPENNANT.COM

ANDY NICHOLLS

An Evertonian that more than knows the score – when he wrote best-selling book *Scally*, it was from his confessions as a former category-C football hooligan. In a short time he has become the writer of his genre and his expert knowledge has often been sought by many film documentary makers. Andy did the Everton entry in the best-selling *Terrace Legends*, and followed this by co-authoring *Hooligans, The A-Z of Britain's Football Hooligan Gangs*.

WWW.ANDY-NICHOLLS.CO.UK

CONTENTS

INTRODUCTION

By the mid-70s, football hooliganism in England was spiralling out of control. Grounds and town centres were being wrecked, hundreds were arrested every weekend and there were calls from disgruntled MPs to bring back National Service and corporal punishment to deter offenders.

Domestically, the game was on its knees, due to the trouble that had been growing for a decade, but at this time hooliganism was also being exported by club sides and so-called supporters from Leeds, Man United, Tottenham Hotspur and Liverpool had all been involved in wide-scale disorder abroad while following their clubs in various European competitions.

The cream of the First Division, as it was then called, were an elite bunch and thousands of fans from the less successful and smaller clubs watched in envy as English club sides played in Europe, while many also enjoyed the footage of rioting as the likes of Paris, St Etienne and Rome were conquered by mobs of rampaging thugs from England.

With little or no chance of these clubs getting into the three UEFA tournaments, it was only a matter of time before a couple of hundred latched on to England games abroad for their European fix, and within a few years a couple of hundred became a few thousand, as England games guaranteed violence and opportunities to earn money through the rioting, thieving and looting which went hand in hand with every trip abroad.

Thirty years later, the problem has still not gone away and today England fans are hated and despised all over the world due to the problems they have caused since they began exporting the 'English disease'.

This book is not one man's story of how he took on all-comers as he rampaged through Europe, it is a story told by dozens of hooligans and fans who have travelled with England since 1976. Many of these contributors have been responsible for horrendous acts of violence and thuggery, many have been victims and many have been scapegoats, jailed without trials quite simply because somebody had to take the blame!

Over 15 hooligan authors have contributed to *30 Years of Hurt*, over 30 clubs are represented and scores of press quotes have been sought to give this story an unbiased account of what it was like to follow England all over the world.

This is not a sociologist's view or an attempt to jump on the hooligan-book bandwagon; it is an untold story, from the people who were in the thick of everything that comes from following England. It is social history, not through the eyes of the slanted press or boffins in universities; it's from the people who made that history, the people who for 30 years have gained this country's football reputation … off the pitch!

CHAPTER ONE
NEVER AGAIN
SCOTLAND '77

'The Tartan Army are travelling supporters of the Scottish national football team and they are the "World's Friendliest Fans", as awarded in France during the 1998 World Cup and have won numerous awards over the years from both FIFA and UEFA for their combination of rabid support and friendly nature.'

This quote, taken from the *World Football Encyclopaedia*, makes interesting reading! Many who have met the Tartan Army will agree with it, although many who had the misfortune of meeting them during the 70s will cringe at the statement. None more so than any England fan unfortunate enough to be at Wembley on 4 June 1977. In fact, thousands who were simply unfortunate enough to be in London over that weekend will disagree strongly with that assessment of the Tartan Army, who they see as little more than marauding thugs, drunks and bullies. A drunken mob who terrorised the capital and left in their wake victims who are still affected by the memory to this day.

Most people who were at home that day watching the game on television will probably remember it for the broken crossbar and the good-natured Jocks collecting clumps of turf to plant in window-boxes outside their high-rise Glasgow flats. Mick from Bolton has other memories of the weekend and his opinion of the famous Tartan Army is vastly different to the one portrayed in the *World Football Encyclopaedia*!

MICK, BOLTON:

I have had a few dodgy wedding anniversaries over the years, ones when you forget altogether and come back from the pub pissed to find steak and chips burned in the oven, others when you do remember and take her out only to spend the night arguing because you got her the wrong fucking bracelet from Argos!

Nothing could compare to the weekend of my first wedding anniversary though, when I thought I was a clever cunt and booked us a weekend trip to London. I arranged for her to go shopping on the Saturday with her sister, while me and the brother-in-law went to the England v Scotland game that day at Wembley.

We got on at Manchester and should have got straight off, as seats were limited and the train was three-quarters full of pissed-up Jocks, most claiming their love for 'Bonny Scotland' and hatred for all things English, which was strange as, if the homeland was so fucking rosy, why were they all working locally? I managed to get a couple of seats on the dated British Rail carriage and it was obvious that these pricks had been expected to travel as the train was the kind that we were thrown on for the football specials; the difference was that the price was not reduced like it was for the football and, as it pulled out of Manchester, the look on my wife's face was one of horror not excitement.

Don't get me wrong, I'm no prude and I have a laugh with the best of them but, when a group of kilted twats walk past your wife and show her their cocks at half-twelve on a Friday afternoon, it doesn't seem as funny as it does late at night when you can appreciate the joke after a few pints have been downed. I told them half-heartedly to behave and was spat at by one of the older lot who looked like he had died and been dug up, and then I had to sit back and watch in disgust as one of his offspring had a piss against the back of our seats. It was no place for heroes; the cunts were all drinking out of Newcastle Brown or cheap whiskey bottles and they made it clear they were happy to use them if any threat was made to them.

That set the tone for the complete journey.

I was sorry I had bought tickets, as the only time the collector came near, he was told to fuck off and his hat and one shoe were slung out of the window, as he scampered back to the safety of the guard's room. By Stafford, the train was awash with piss and sick, normal passengers were getting off but, give my missus credit, she was adamant that the twats were not going to beat us, and even more than me she was determined to get to London in time to meet her sister.

The buffet bar had been ransacked and at every station more and more Jocks were getting on and the invasion was in full flow, a bit like the piss lake that was making its way through every carriage. There was the odd police show at the stations but it seemed that, even 24 hours before the match kicked off, the police were shit-scared of the Jocks and their reputation.

As we pulled into Euston, I told my missus to sit tight while I went to collect our bags. Stupidly, we had put them in the rack like all the other thick twats and, when I got there, I saw straight away that mine had been opened; a quick scout revealed that a pair of jeans and trainers were missing but they had left my toilet bag and towel, which summed up the dirty scruffy bastards. My missus's travel bag was still there, though, and, thinking of it then, that alone was a bonus.

The train slowed down but already scores of Jocks had opened the doors and they were jumping off and some were seen running past the train as their momentum took them at speed to their destination. A few jumped too soon and I hoped and prayed that one clown I saw crash into the luggage trolleys and looked like he would be spending the weekend in the London Royal was the cunt who had had my gear away.

The chant of 'We fucking hate England, we fucking hate England, we fucking hate England, we fucking hate England' (Why work and live here then, you cunts?) echoed through the concourse. Terrified passengers waiting to leave and head North were horrified as the Tartan Army landed. We let them all go ahead before getting off and, as we did, the carnage was clear to see – any male over the age of about 13 had been attacked and assaulted. This was not a football thing and, although it did happen in those days at grounds all over the country, this was a Friday afternoon in the summer and the sight of blokes in their fifties with blood pissing out of their noses sickened me.

I often wondered why we were sometimes called animals and it hit home to me that day at Euston why – these Jocks *were* animals, and they were wild animals at that. Bewildered staff were attempting to put the train back into some sort of state that would allow it to make the return journey. What a waste of time – the train wasn't even fit for animals, only the stinking Jocks who had left it would feel any sort of comfort on it.

One hour later, we were in my sister-in-law's, telling them of the journey from hell we had just endured. We agreed it would be better to stay local that night, as central London was under siege and we wanted no part of what was going on there.

As you do when the women go to make themselves beautiful, me and the brother-in-law, Jake, decided to nip to his local for a swift couple but, before we left the house, I heard my missus scream from upstairs. We legged it up to find her in the bedroom, travel bag open, displaying an 8in turd mixed in with her nightie and weekend summer wear. No doubt, some filthy Jock thought it was hilarious at the time but, if I could have one wish, it would be that the twat responsible has since died a slow and horrific death.

Night over, takeaway ordered, a couple of bottles of cheap wine and the hope that we get the chance to team up with a few of Jake's mates the next day while the girls are shopping and fucking muller a few of the Scottish twats who were turning our first wedding anniversary into a complete and utter nightmare.

We were up and about early doors, the girls went one way and we went the other – different agendas but, as it happened, the same outcome.

As soon as we got on the tube, it was the same as the day before, the stink of stale ale and piss was wretched and the sound of anti-English chanting went unchallenged by the few brave souls who had the balls to travel with the kilted bastards who were becoming one major pain in the arse.

In our carriage were three girls, about 18 and tidy, not tartish or scrubbers, just nice and minding their own business. It was years before the 'Get yer tits out for the lads' chant was heard, but what these kids put up with was far worse. At every bend in the track, a load of Jocks would pretend to fall across them and grope their tits and, every time we entered a tunnel, they would scream as some dirty bastard forced his hand up their skirts. Basically, they were being sexually assaulted and there was fuck all anyone could do about it. We pulled in at some station and about 10 Cockneys got on and things took a turn for the better. One girl was crying and, as soon as we pulled off, the Jocks were across them again, taking their sly gropes and no doubt coming in their soiled Y-fronts.

As soon as these Cockney blokes clocked what was happening, they were off. In minutes, they had cleaned the carriage and I don't mean swept it clean; they cleansed the place of the vermin who thought they were above the law. What the Jocks didn't realise was that these blokes were in a different league to their drunken loutishness, but, after an initial headbutt that knocked one Scot clean out, they soon saw that they were out of their league. A couple tried a token bottle-throwing gesture but the Londoners basically wiped the floor with the rammy bastards. By the next stop, the girls were taken off by some of London's finest who disappeared before the police came to see what the commotion was. No one knew if they were West Ham, Chelsea, Millwall or if they were even football fans, but whoever they were I wouldn't like to cross them, but everyone on that tube apart from the Jocks nursing bust noses and with teeth missing wanted to shake their hands and buy them a beer.

That tube trip was the highlight of the day. At Wembley, the place was overrun with the Scottish hordes; it would be unfair to class them all the same but the bad were in the majority. There were a few good-natured blokes singing and dancing about but most I saw were either pissing or taking the piss.

What sickened me was that anyone was deemed fair game. Without sounding like an old bastard, in those days the blokes selling the flags, rosettes and programmes were not the spivs of today who are out to make a quick fortune, they were the old-type blokes who sold the *Evening Standard* or the *Football Pink*. Today, the Mancs and Scousers piss me off at every game and concert with their cheap shite making a killing – if they get turned over today, tough shit. But to see old fellas getting turned over pissed me off. I despise touts, they are the dregs of football, but I even felt sorry for a couple of old timers trying to make money who were given a slap and robbed of their tickets, such was my hatred for the Jocks that day.

In the ground, it was embarrassing, the place was awash with them. I know we lost 2–1 but remember very little about the game apart from Trevor Cherry warming up and being told to hurry up and get on quick by a copper, as the Jocks were lobbing empty bottles at him. When we scored with a penalty, anyone daft enough to cheer or celebrate was either whacked or covered in spit. I think McQueen got the winner for them and at the end the whole ground seemed to empty on to the pitch, and the rest as they say is history!

What people saw on the television, though, is only a fraction of the tale, a few Jocks on the crossbar, the turf getting ripped up, light-hearted jinks. Bollocks! They never saw the women in the tea bars getting robbed, the kids selling programmes in tears as grown men took their money, the one or two stewards who tried to keep them off the pitch getting kicked to fuck or that 8in turd in my missus's travel bag.

We got off sharpish after the game and no doubt were lucky. I have no shame in admitting on the way out me and Jake bought a Scotland scarf each from a Jock who had just robbed another old seller of his wares. Later that night, a minibus from Sheffield stopped off in Jake's local – every window was smashed and most of the blokes on it had taken a hiding. They told us that they were driving out of the coach park and a Jock had jumped on the bonnet, the driver sounded his horn to get him off and the whole crowd turned on them, but for a few brave police officers they said the Jocks would have overturned the minibus with them in it.

The *Evening Standard* was full of tales about the loutish antics of the Tartan Army, yet Joe Public was still led to believe that they were the salt of the earth football fans who just liked a drink. We stayed local again that night, central London was a no-go, as the fountain and main tourist spots were taken by the Jocks.

The following day, we returned home and still they were in our faces; all the way home Jocks were wandering up the train being a pain in the arse, pissed and asking anyone who looked an easy target for spare change. A few students got on and had a few cans of lager, Skol or whatever was the cheapest then, and this bloke sat by them, introduced himself as Cameron and bullied them into giving him the ale. He then took money from them saying he was going to the buffet, never to return.

I was glad when the train pulled into Piccadilly and so was my missus; what should have been a great weekend was nothing more than a nightmare and it was the first – and worst – wedding anniversary we ever had.

We went across Piccadilly Gardens to the bus stop and went into the café while we waited for the number 8 to Bolton. As we were sitting there in the smoke-filled greasy spoon, I couldn't believe my eyes as across the road was the bully Cameron, who was either an exiled Jock working in Manchester or who had decided to go on the piss rather than annoy anyone else on the train. He walked over to the Portland Bars and in he went. I said to my missus that I was going to buy the *Manchester Evening News* and nipped into the pub. The Portland was split into two, a decent bar and a drunks' bar, the Mancs all called it the Dive Bar and the Jock was at home in the latter. I didn't have to wait long for Cameron to go to the gents. I followed him down with one of those chunky pint pots wrapped up in my Scotland scarf.

He was pissing away as I went behind him and, although I am not a hard case, I thought of offering him out, as I also was not a sly bastard. I changed my mind and, as he shook his cock, belted him over the head with the pint pot. He flew into the wall and screamed, so I gave him another couple then smashed his face into the porcelain urinal. Blood spewed out of his wounds and covered the Armitage Shanks piss-pot.

He looked bemused as I booted him across the floor – that's for the girls on the tube, that's for the old blokes at Euston, that's for the rosette sellers, here's another for those students you robbed, you bullying Jock twat. I was going to drop my Levi's and shit on his bloodied head and say that's for my missus's travel bag but thought better of it and fucked off sharpish.

I got back to the café and was shaking, and my missus knew something had happened. She knew I got in a few scrapes home and away with Wanderers and always said if ever I got nicked I would be out on my ear, but she knew this was personal and she even gave me a kiss when I told her the bloke I had done was the twat off the train. We jumped a cab rather than wait for the bus, and I was glad to get home and get in the bath and cleanse myself of the smell of that bloodied bully who I hoped was still lying in his own piss and blood in the Dive Bar.

Even now, I am not proud of what I did to that Jock, but I never lost much sleep about it and I doubt if many of those drunken bastards did either, as some of the stunts they pulled that weekend were much worse than mine.

Many of the smaller violent incidents that occurred that weekend failed to make the papers, yet, if it had been the English doing the rioting, would the media have taken the same stance and just concentrated on the after-match celebrations?

It was only when the true facts came to the surface that the English press condemned the Scots' antics as anything other than high spirits, and by the Monday attitudes towards the Tartan Army were changing, as the *Mirror* reported: 'Scotland's football fans didn't celebrate their team's victory over England at Wembley – they mutilated it!'

The paper went on to say, 'There was nothing good-natured about how they [the Scots] ripped the hallowed turf, or the way they spread broken glass and pressed sharp ring caps from cans into the grass, it was downright destruction and dangerous.'

Wembley groundsman Don Gallagher was distraught and was quoted as saying, 'It is a disaster, I have never seen anything like it; we'll have to work around the clock to sort this lot out. The glass is the most serious problem. We will have to go over the whole pitch inch by inch as just a sliver could seriously gash somebody's leg.'

Sports Minister Dennis Howell claimed there was massive gatecrashing at the match and was told on good authority that: 'Hundreds of these Scottish chaps actually got into Wembley without paying, after a gate was forced opened by their chums from inside the ground.'

'Chaps' and 'chums' were not the names many used to describe the Scottish hordes, and days after the game Howell announced that security for future events would be stepped up and that by the next time Scotland played at Wembley all the chaps and their chums would be caged in.

The *Mirror* took a historical view and in one article said, 'In the long history of battles between the two countries, the Wembley fences will be the equivalent of Hadrian's Wall and they will need to be just as effective. Not so much to keep the sods in but to keep the clots out!'

Despite the deteriorating mood towards Scotland fans, BBC Scotland reporter Les Anderson still managed to see the incident through tartan-tinted glasses and in a somewhat biased report stated, 'Scottish football fans have always travelled down to Wembley en masse in high spirits and jinks and earned a reputation for their fondness for alcohol. In those heady days of the 60s and 70s, drinking large amounts of alcohol was as common as the half-time pie and Bovril. The remarkable scenes from Wembley in May 1977 in a resounding 2–1 victory over the hated Auld Enemy England for Bonny Scotland was reason enough for thousands of jubilant Scottish fans to invade the pitch following the final whistle. Helpless Metropolitan Police watched as the celebrating Scottish football fans brought the goalposts crashing to the ground during the fun and frolics. Though such activities were not violent in nature, they marked the beginning of a period in which many English supporters' behaviour became increasingly moronic, with every Old Firm fixture bringing fresh fears of running battles between the English thugs and the high-spirited fun-loving Scottish supporters.'

So it's fun and frolics when the Jocks play up and plain old thuggery when the English have a go back!

Harry was a member of the Tartan Army that day and his report is slightly less biased than Mr Anderson's.

HARRY, SCOTLAND:
The whole thing, was, shall we say, a protest against the way London treated us up North at the time. I say up North because in those days there was as much hatred of the capital from the English who resided in the likes of Yorkshire and Newcastle, never mind the Scottish! We were treated like second-class citizens so maybe that is why we acted like them. That weekend, we were in a pub in Edinburgh on the Friday at teatime and there were lads coming in rallying the troops to catch the last train down to watch the game. It didn't take

much persuasion and everyone was on to it. There was no way we had to pay and the trip down was just an extension of the drinking hours, which were not what they are today.

I recall at the time that the government was spending hundreds of thousands of pounds relocating Scottish industry in the capital and then the English workers would complain that there were hundreds of Scots working over the border. How blind are they to the fact that, if development money was spent in Scotland, we would all have fucking stayed there? One example was Crawford's the biscuit makers, a massive source of employment to locals up here, it needed money spending on it but it was a profitable industry. Then, the next minute, it was a case of investment is needed, 'So let's build a plant in fucking London making Scottish shortbread biscuits!

Once in London, of course, we took the piss, but we were not the only ones – how about the twats who doubled their prices, the same twats who were crying when we told them they were getting nothing for their cheek. Yes, we rampaged and stole and, of course, with that kind of following, there will be the odd few who go over the top and there were plenty of goings-on that the Scots were not proud of. In the main, though, it was drunkenness and had we been treated with any kind of respect some of the problems would have been avoided.

I remember one incident when we were all herded down the tube near Covent Garden where we had been drinking all afternoon; they forced us on to the tube, then carried on forcing more and more on until you could not move. People were passing out, so on the way to Wembley everyone started smashing the windows and the roof to get some air into the carriages. One carriage lost half of its roof; they smashed it so much it peeled off like a sardine can. If they hadn't forced everyone on the tube, that would never have happened, and anyone will tell you that in the mid-70s football fans were treated like the shit on people's shoes, and we were treated worse, which maybe made us act up a little more than normal.

The game – well, what can you say? We had no tickets and the gates were always going to go in; we won; there were very few English in there and we took the ground apart. Outside was the same, drunken rowdiness, police brutality and a long trip home with a sore head. It was fantastic!

After reading Harry's account, it is interesting to read the *World Football Encyclopaedia*'s piece on the Tartan Army which goes on to say: 'Some say that the amicability of the Tartan Army is due to the high volumes of alcohol imbibed before, during and after a game, a fact that few members would dispute. Countries drawn against Scotland look forward to the arrival of the fans, and events, such as concerts, are put on to keep them occupied.

'These are generally accompanied by a low level of policing due to their good behaviour over the years. Allegations have been made against the Tartan Army that they carry a strong anti-English sentiment, often being highly vociferous in their support of England's opponents. They do, however, assert that there is nothing unusual in bitter rivals wishing to see one another defeated and it occurs the world over.'

What they don't say is that over the years the Tartan Army have been guilty of some of the vilest behaviour ever witnessed at football grounds, and after the game in 1977 England fans were united in their determination that they would not be allowed to take liberties again at Wembley. It would not happen overnight but the foundations had been laid and for their next visit things would be different.

CHAPTER TWO

THE ENGLISH DISEASE
EARLY YEARS

The trail of destruction left by the Scots hurt. Domestically, football violence was out of control and every weekend thousands of hooligans were rampaging the length and breadth of the county, yet Scotland had basically come into the English capital and taken it.

Thousands had watched the events unfold on television and many vowed to join the cause but it would be two years before the Jocks revisited, so payback would have to wait. In the meantime, there were other matches to attend and, soon after the embarrassing scenes at Wembley, a few thousand England fans left their own trail of destruction across Europe after crashing out of the World Cup, having failed to beat Luxembourg by enough goals to make the finals in Argentina. A statistic made so much worse by the fact Scotland had qualified in a blaze of glory!

A trip to Denmark in 1978 saw the English engage in behaviour that to this day is still looked upon as their trademark. Steve, a veteran Charlton and England fan, was one of the early exporters of the 'English disease'.

STEVE, CHARLTON:
We met up at Liverpool Street Station about 15-handed, a few West Ham, and a couple of Chelsea but mainly Charlton, and we all got boozing in the bar. Within an hour and a half, we

had done that many beers we were collared by the Old Bill and told to get out the bar. I thought that was a bad start, but we all got down to Harwich and made it on to the ferry for the old boat-train to Denmark and Copenhagen. The ferry journey was more or less peaceful – there were a few little skirmishes but nothing to write home about. But we were told that, if there was any more trouble, they were going to turn the boat back, so that sort of calmed everyone down. We got over to Denmark nice and early in the evening, which would be our first night, so we done the usual and trawled a few bars. There were a couple of spats with the locals but nothing major and certainly no problems with the Old Bill.

As became the England trademark in the early days, we hung out around the main station where the majority of the England fans were in the bars on the booze, apart from a few Scousers, who were out on the thieve. Late into the night, everyone started hitting the clubs and people seemed to get through that all right, one or two arguments with the bouncers but nothing serious and no sign of what was to come over the next 24 hours.

We had an early start next day and immediately went on the booze again and, as it got nearer and nearer to match-time, we worked our way closer to the ground and we started to get into a few rows with different little firms of Danish lads. I've got to say, they were game but didn't have a clue how to firm up properly, so really when they were starting with us they were coming unstuck every time.

We got down to the ground and the noise from inside just hit you, the game hadn't even started but the noise was unbelievable; it was obvious to us what was going on inside the ground. The England fans outside were saying that it was going off and urging everyone to get in. When we did, what you saw was unbelievable and, without a doubt, for me, it was the worst violence I have ever seen inside a football ground.

England fans were in mixed areas of the ground and there were geezers there just walking through getting whacked over the head with chair legs and lumps of wood, and because they were all blond-looking blokes it probably looked twice as bad as they were getting carried out with their heads covered in claret. A vodka bottle went flying through the air and into the Danes and that was another stretcher job where one of them was taken out covered in claret.

All game, it was continually kicking off because the Danes were trying to have a go but were just getting overwhelmed. Being mixed in like that meant the Danes had nowhere to go and I clearly remember them trying to mob up at the start of the second half to give it a right go, but once the English went into them they didn't have a chance. The Old Bill didn't have a clue and, as much as they tried to hold the England fans back, the boys were going round them and at times through them.

I will always remember the crowd kept up this incessant chanting for about a quarter of an hour. We got talking with this Danish geezer and asked him what the crowd were saying and he simply said, 'Get them out, get them out!'

The whole ground was shouting it, while we were just laughing because obviously they couldn't. I'd met a few geezers out there from Welling and Eltham, who were West Ham and Millwall, and even they were saying they couldn't believe it and that they had seen nothing like it. The levels of aggression shown towards the Danes were unreal but I don't recall any English even getting dragged out or nicked, and so at the end of the game we all made our way outside and back to have a night out in Copenhagen as if nothing had happened!

Every step of the way, it was going off with battles with the police and everyone and anyone. The clubs were refusing to let the English in but we just steamed the club and their doormen. There was a NATO exercise on out there at the time, and it kicked of with a load of American sailors who were game and were right lumps too, but I don't think they were prepared for what we were hitting them with and the lot went into them and they got battered.

Another big row was in this club with a load of bikers over something serious – a game of pinball! That triggered off the greasers who started throwing punches and it really kicked off in there. Even the old women greasers were having a go, trying to throw bottles, and some were getting proper involved, so they were getting right-handers and it turned into a big free-for-all. It only really stopped when the Military Police turned up.

Somehow, all our lads made it through the day and we all got back to the hotel with no more than a few cuts and bruises. I will always say that was the worst I've seen anywhere. I really don't know the reason, maybe it was because you could get over there so easy from everywhere, but it was the first proper big England firm and there was none of the club rivalry, as there were Mancs, Scousers and everyone together on that trip. It changed within a few years but that was never my take on things. It was better to be all together because I've been places and seen a few people come unstuck where the firms have not been all together, with that 'I don't wanna talk to the Northerners' bollocks. I've made mates with Northerners on the England scene that I've kept in touch with for years. To me, England was England, but plenty didn't see it that way and it was a shame as good lads stopped going because of it.

The following year saw England fans clash in Austria, albeit unspectacularly, with locals and police, as more and more fans got the travel bug. Long before the flag of St George was reintroduced, the sight of hundreds of Union Jacks, as they were called before political correctness got out of control, were spotted at most away games.

1979 saw Scotland arrive back in London en masse and again they were untouchable. England were getting their act together but in-house squabbling between London's top firms and the refusal by the Southern mobs to accept any Northern help meant that the Auld Enemy game, for the time being at least, was a mismatch off the field.

As the 70s fizzled out and flared trousers and bovver boots were replaced by tight-fitting jeans and Adidas trainers, the Casuals jumped on the England bandwagon and, although it would be a couple of years before they really made their mark on the international scene, the 80s would see a new-style England following.

The press had been sensationalising hooliganism at home for years, yet it was not until the European Championships in Italy in 1980 that the hooligans made the headlines abroad.

An estimated 15,000 England supporters travelled to Turin for the first game against Belgium and, when fighting broke out with Italians who were allowed entry to the English section of the ground, police were forced to fire tear gas into the crowd to quell the disturbance. It was an unprecedented move by the police and something the English had not faced before. While the gas had the desired effect on the terrace violence, the police did not take into consideration which way the wind was blowing, and the game was stopped when the grey cloud spread across the pitch.

Kevin Keegan was the worst affected and was still in tears after the game when he took time out to tell the watching millions how disgusted he was by the English fans' behaviour. He failed to mention that for days Italian knife gangs had been slashing away at his fellow countrymen.

Not surprisingly, the national newspapers were quick to point the blame at the travelling support and the *Daily Mirror* reported, 'England's travelling soccer thugs once again dragged our name and nation into the depths of disgrace here last night.'

The paper went on to say that play was stopped after Belgium had equalised in the 29th minute, as police tear gas drifted across the pitch and began affecting the players, causing manager Ron Greenwood to ask the referee to stop play. As the hooligans battled and charged across the terraces, both Ron Greenwood and Ted Croker appealed to the fans: 'Please behave yourselves, you are doing the chances of the team and our reputation no good at all, please stay calm for the rest of the game.'

Greenwood blasted later, 'I am ashamed of people like that, they shouldn't be allowed at a football match. Italian people must think we are idiots!'

Ted Croker, who at the time was FA secretary, feared that there would be reprisals because in his own words: 'The rest of the world has had enough of English aggro.'

It didn't help matters that the next game in the group was England v Italy! The press, for once, were worried about the England supporters' safety and even advised them accordingly, with one paper's headline reading: 'HIDE YOUR COLOURS. BACKLASH THREAT AT BIG MATCH V ITALY.'

A chilling message came from the Italian authorities who warned the English fans: 'Wear your red, white and blue colours at your peril!'

In fact, the game passed off relatively quietly and there was little trouble inside the ground, as the 5,000 English fans, who for once were probably glad of the police presence, were kept safely away from 10 times as many home supporters.

It was a dismal tournament for England, as on the field they crashed out during the first stages and they were then fined £8,000 by UEFA for the poor behaviour of their fans, a penalty which the *Mirror* called 'soft' amid claims that England had got away lightly.

Another person who was disgusted by the hooligan following was TV funny man Larry Grayson who found himself being verbally abused in an Italian restaurant by a drunken gang of English yobs, while enjoying a quiet meal with his manager. Mr Grayson was quoted in the *Mirror* saying, 'We were having a lovely meal and a nice chat when all of a sudden this uncouth gang of football yobs recognised me and began hurling insults, calling me a faggot and a poof. I was vexed, and fuming, it was deeply embarrassing. We eventually had to leave the premises and we were showered with beer and spittle. I was deeply ashamed to be English, I can tell you; they should bring back National Service to show them some discipline!'

Larry declined to say if the lads had shouted 'Shut that door' when he left the restaurant!

Phil from Leeds was over in Turin and he painted a slightly different picture to the one that came via the press.

PHIL, LEEDS UNITED:

I used to save up all year round to follow England. There would be about six of us who supported Leeds and were from York, and we would get ourselves down to Dover, stopping in London on the way. At the time, you had to be careful what you said to other England fans, as Leeds had a reputation, but very few of our lads were bothered with the international side and Leeds as a club were not that popular, so people definitely wanted you.

I went to Italy for the 1980 European Championships a couple of years after leaving school; we were not thugs, just young lads out for a laugh and what I saw there opened my eyes a bit. On the way to the ground for the first game against Belgium, my mate pinched a gateaux cake from a bakery – it was just one of those daft things you do at that age when you have had a bit too much Stella. Nobody wanted it so he threw it at a car and the driver obviously took umbrage, got out the car and complained. We were laughing and arguing the toss about it, nothing serious, when from nowhere some England fan ran up and hit this Italian bloke straight round the back of the head with a big lump of wood. It was crazy, the bloke was only having a moan about a load of cake being over his car and ended up getting knocked out! It was a bit out of order really.

When we got into the ground, you could tell all the other England fans had had a good bevy just like ourselves and from the off there were bits of trouble, and soon the tear gas went off. I remember getting carried up to the back of the ground by two West Ham fans and puking my guts up. After the game, there was lots of trouble outside with Italians waiting in the little local bars. People were going in and chasing them out and, as they ran out, the England lads were going straight into them; they were getting kicked all over the place and again I was a bit shocked by the scale of violence, but later lads were telling us how gangs of Italians had been running around and stabbing England fans who were just out there having a good drink.

It was a quick learning curve and we realised that you had to stick with the main lads or you were in danger, so that's what we did, and soon we saw what made them behave so badly because, as we were going into the station after the game, shots were fired from one end of the station. At the time, we didn't know that they were blanks being fired and I just dived for cover. An Italian stood there with a gun. I was only 18 or 19 and thought, What the hell's going on? It was frightening but a load of English lads soon realised they were only blanks he was firing, and they caught him just outside the station and gave him a real good hiding.

We now realised just how careful you had to be out there but later that day we all got chased near our hotel and, when the police came, they had us all spread-eagled against the wall. A lot of these pictures appeared in the *Sun* but, to be fair, some of the press blokes said we were the innocent party. But the police were having none of it and, while the Italian lads got away with it, a lot of English lads got locked up but were later released without being charged.

That's when I learned another lesson: don't trust the press, as the next day all the headlines were calling us thugs and louts with no mention of the Italians and police attacking us.

That same year saw major violence break out during the Home International game against Wales. These games were regarded as nothing more than a pain in the arse by many professionals! After a long hard season, most players wanted to piss off on their holidays and enjoy a well-earned break, but, instead, many were forced to go through the motions and play out a needless tournament with the only fixture of any importance being England v Scotland. That was the English and Scottish point of view anyway; the Welsh and Northern Ireland players, however, were more than up for a chance to lock horns with the English superstars, some of whom seemed to wear the three lions on their shirts with less pride than the fans in the crowd who had the badge proudly tattooed on various parts of their body.

One game which will go down as one of the most spineless performances ever witnessed by England's loyal following was on 17 May 1980 when Ron Greenwood took his side to play Wales at Wrexham's Racecourse ground and were trounced 4–1.

Events off the field proved every bit as chaotic as the England performance on it, as in-house fighting between the fans from both countries left the authorities wondering if the games should be allowed to continue. Although it was a couple of years before the curtain was eventually pulled down on the Home International Championships, this day saw the worst outbreaks of violence ever witnessed in the Welsh town.

PETE, CHESTER:
It was a dream game for us lot at Chester, the fact that we are just a few miles away from the Welsh border makes us even more patriotic than most and rivalry between us and the sheep-shaggers has always been intense.

We got there early and the pubs were full of England fans but we soon got fed up of the piss-strength Wrexham lager and we took a stroll towards the ground. The place was bedlam. On one side of the road by the car-sales place were about 100 lads all in these bright-coloured striped polo shirts and on the other were similar numbers of lads dressed almost identically. In between were about half-a-dozen coppers trying to keep them apart. The ones on the right were chanting 'Munich 58', while the ones on the left were huddled together and you could see it was ready to go off. We sussed that they were Scousers and Mancs, and the Mancs were all United while the Scousers were a mix of Everton and Liverpool.

It was time to fuck off as the mood was nasty but, before we could get past them, the lot went and there were bodies flying in both directions into each other. Fuck knows how they knew who was who, they all looked the same, no colours on, and it was organised chaos for a minute until the initial fight was repelled by the police and both lots were separated.

We got pushed towards the Scousers and they were a horrible lot. The police were trying to get them in the ground but they were all huddled together, saying they were going to some pub which the police probably knew never existed. Across the road, the Mancs were being held back and I swear it looked like there was a mirror image in the road as everyone was dressed identical. We couldn't get our heads around what was happening but now, years on, I realise it was our first introduction to the football Casual!

Foolishly, the police forced the Mancs up the road and left the Scousers to their own devices; in seconds, they were jumping over the turnstiles and into the Kop, which was half-full of the Welsh. Outside was not the place to be so we followed them, but, as soon as we were tagging along, it was a case of 'Fuck off yer wools'. They had that swagger and attitude about them which caused the whole country to hate them in the 80s and rightly so.

They made their way into the middle of the Kop and scattered the few Welsh who were gathering and singing some daft song about feeding them their pissy lager till they wanted no more! We kept our distance at first but soon got picked out by a mob of Wrexham who saw us as easy pickings rather than the striped-shirt Scallys who had just taken their end in seconds. There must have been three coppers in the whole end at this time and we were legged towards the Scousers who were now in full song with amusing lyrics about woollies and three-star jumpers!

Minutes later, a mass brawl broke out as a mob of lads swarmed from the back of the terraces into the Scousers; it was the Mancs and once again it was every man for themselves as this colourful collection of polo-shirted youths with funny haircuts waded into each other across the terracing. The Paddock to the right of us was full of England supporters and so was the end behind the other goal and they were trying to climb over to join in, not knowing that it was a Manc/Scouse thing not a Wales/England battle. The police had now formed two lines between the fans, a Manc/Scouse/ Welsh divide. All we needed now was a bus full of Jocks and we'd have the full house!

It had to calm down eventually and, as the game wore on, the charges slowed down and the three mobs seemed resigned to the fact that it would all be sorted at half-time. Only the brave ventured for a piss or tried to get the women to reopen the looted tea bar, the rest stayed put – safety in numbers if you like.

The second half came and went. Larry Lloyd was playing and his and the team's performance was one to forget; Wales thrashed us 4–1 and after every goal there were outbreaks of fighting all over the ground, the only ones not bothered were the mixed-up Scousers who were supporting nobody.

After the game, we filed out and tried to make a break for it. It was no place to be unless you were firmed up and we tried to make the bus station and get out of the place. But by now the home country's support were at it and were fighting all comers. The sound of sirens filled the air, shops were pulling down shutters and off-licences were closing before being looted as it was still not opening time. Those against all-day opening should have been about that day, when literally thousands of hooligans wandered the streets with Watney Party 7s and bottles of Brown Ale waiting for five o'clock to arrive.

We ended up getting a couple of taxis and got back into Chester just as the pubs opened. We hadn't even ordered our first pint when the window came in and outside stood 50-odd bloodied and battered stripe-shirted thugs after a fight with anyone happy to oblige. We never found out if they were Mancs or Scousers, as the fire door was booted open and we were off again in search of a safe haven – if such a thing existed that day. Long into the night, there were fights breaking out all over town, so God knows what Wrexham was like.

It is a day I look back at now as the maddest of my life and I still wonder how nobody was killed.

I remember the headline in one local paper that Monday read 'NEVER AGAIN'. I didn't bother to read if it was the police on about staging a match between Wales and England there again or if it was Ron Greenwood on about Larry Lloyd's international career!

The hooligan bandwagon was gaining momentum and, at a game in Basle on 30 May 1981, it rolled into town and the passengers got off and took no prisoners, as they set about local fans inside and outside the stadium. Normally, the scenes would receive the usual one-sided bad press set aside for hooligan incidents but at this game coverage was more damning than usual, as an England thug was pictured stabbing a Swiss fan in the back during one terrace skirmish and the headline was effective if predictable and read: 'A STAB IN THE BACK FOR ENGLAND'.

The reputation of England's away following hit an all-time low and the picture of the England fan, his face filled with hate, stabbing a Swiss supporter who was being held down by other English yobs was an image which shocked the nation. It was one of the shameful scenes, which also included scores of England fans brandishing sticks and poles that TV news channels took delight in transmitting worldwide.

It was another game Phil attended.

PHIL, LEEDS UNITED:
Basle '81 was when three English lads got badly beaten up by local Italians, proper caved in and they were in a right state. It happened two nights before the game and word got round for everybody to meet the following night outside Basle Station. A few of the main blokes seemed to know where the Italian area of the city was and we marched up to a bar where

they all went. Outside, all the motorbikes were lined up and somebody pushed this one motorbike and it was like a domino effect – the whole lot went.

The windows and bar doors opened, and they came out with their bats and sticks but there were so many English there it was absolutely frightening and the locals were run back in. My brother was with us and at the time he was a real hard bastard. He done one outside the bar, dropped him and left him in the gutter on the floor to get pummelled. Someone done a jeweller's, and the lad who robbed that cut his entire arm putting it through the window grabbing gold. In minutes, the police were everywhere and the night turned into a mini riot.

At the game, it was the same, basically a riot; there was fighting all over the ground and the tear gas got fired into the crowd again, after more trouble, more rioting – I could go on and on because the whole trip was a just one long riot!

The scenes, which were viewed by millions, prompted one Labour MP to call for anybody convicted of football violence abroad to have their passports taken from them, while Ted Croker said his initial reaction was that there must be a way to stop England fans travelling abroad. It would have been wise for him to liaise with the MP, as without a passport most people do find it difficult to leave the country!

On their return home, many fans shrugged off the 'shame' allegations and complained that gangs of Swiss hooligans known as the Swiss Youth Movement were actually responsible for most of the trouble.

Daily Mirror sports editor Frank McGee said that England were becoming 'derided and detested' and joked after the 2–1 defeat: 'Nobody is scared of us now, well, not on the bloody pitch!'

The FA and the authorities did not share McGee's humour, however, and they had good reason to be in a sombre mood about the fans' behaviour. Despite the defeat in Basle, England qualified for the World Cup Finals in Spain and that would see the biggest exodus of young males from the country since World War II. Many were worried that the kind of following England were assembling would have those followers believe that they were heading to the sunny shores of Bilbao and Madrid to cause World War III!

CHAPTER THREE

VIVA ESPAÑA
SPAIN '82

When Gerd Muller crashed the ball past a hapless Peter Bonetti on 14 June 1970 ending England's reign as World Champions, few could have guessed it would be 12 years before they would once again grace the most prestigious tournament in international football. And, after a disappointing qualifying campaign when Ron Greenwood's men only just managed to stumble through the group consisting of Hungary, Norway, Romania and Switzerland, the nation's hopes were not exactly high as the team and fans set off to the finals. Oldham fan Carl Spiers was one of the thousands who gave up work, emptied their savings accounts, invested in a few pairs of shorts and set off for their first taste of World Cup football.

Viva España!

CARL, OLDHAM:
Three of us Oldham fans had pre-booked on the *Pride of Bilbao* ferry from Plymouth to Santander in Northern Spain. In those days, what little money you had was better off in your own pockets than in the hands of British Rail and we arrived in Plymouth on Sunday evening having hitchhiked down from Oldham that morning. We got our final lift from Hilton services in a removal van containing about 20 drunk, but friendly Bury lads. They had hired it for just a day and the

owner would have been pissed off when he had a call from the police on the Monday morning asking him to shift the van from the port entrance. With no interest in how the vehicle was ever getting back to Bury, the driver just stopped, turned the engine off, told us all to get out, locked the doors and joined the hundreds of England fans attempting to drink Plymouth dry.

I will always remember the night before we set off for Spain, as, to put it bluntly, I was on the bones of my arse. I had very little money coming in and, although the trip had been paid for, my spending funds were virtually nil. I was so skint the night before we were due to leave for Plymouth that I had to ask this girl I had been seeing to lend me some money. All she had to her name was £1.50 and she reluctantly gave me every penny of it, as I told her I would need it for the phone when I called home every day from Spain to see if she was OK. She walked back to her flat that morning after we said our goodbyes as she had even given me her bus fare!

Of course, I never phoned her once while I was away and it was the last time I ever saw her, which was a shame really, as she was a good sort and a lovely-looking girl as well. Football is football, though, so I left Oldham that Sunday morning with just her £1.50 and a few quid I had begged and borrowed. I'm not proud of this but it shows how determined I was and the fact I stayed for three and half weeks all told and had the time of my life proves I made the right choice. There were plenty of young girls in Oldham who I could pull in those days and only one World Cup so it was no contest really!

With no interest in wasting money on a cheap B&B, we dossed down in the bogs near the docks, and we awoke at 6.30am to find dozens of other England lads all kipping on the toilet floors, something the Stone Island-wearing Casuals today would frown upon! In those days, it was the norm, your money was for ale and prozzies, not designer fucking sunglasses and i-Pods!

We boarded the ferry at 8am, and off we went. There were over 2,000 lads on that ship and what seemed like the nation's press were there clicking their cameras, dozens and dozens of them flashing away, as some of the lads waved but most showed them snow-white arses. The next day's headline on the front page of the *Sun* read: 'THATCHER'S BOOT BOYS HEAD FOR SPAIN!'

Britain had been at war with Argentina for the past few weeks and most Spaniards supported the Argies in their attempt to take the Falkland Islands away from the British. We felt like we were soldiers going to war, only there were no birds flashing their tits at us as we set sail for Spain. One bloke by me said he had heard that the government was concerned that we could be a target for the Argentinean task force, which put a bit of a dampener on proceedings, but soon I was sure he was talking through his arse.

As that boat left Plymouth, it was an incredibly patriotic scene, which if I am honest made the hairs stand up on the back of my neck and even brought a lump to my throat. I climbed on to a barrier and looked down on the sight of 2,000 England fans on the deck, waving at the press. There were hundreds of banners and scarves draped over the side of the ship and it looked fucking magnificent. Then, as one, the whole deck burst into song, singing the best World Cup record ever recorded:

This time, more than any other time, this time,
We're gonna find a way, find a way to get it right, this time
We're all together ... WE ARE RON'S 22
Hear the roar of the red, white and blue!

The deck was rocking and I knew this boat was unsinkable, as, if 2,000 bouncing fans going mental couldn't sink it, no stray Argie missile had a fucking chance of doing so!

On board, it really started to warm up, the bars opened at midday and, by five o'clock, most of the lads were pissed up and the rival teams' chanting begin. At about 8.00pm, a West

Ham fan got on the microphone and announced that a member from each team should get up and give a chant or song for his home-town team (a very early version of karaoke) and there were plenty of would-be Tom Jones willing to belt out a chant. I joined the disorderly queue, and got my chance; I chose an anti-Bolton song, Bolton back then being Oldham's hated rivals. It was a drunken rather than brave choice, as there were only three of us from Oldham and over 80 Wanderers in the audience as I gave it my big anti-Bolton chant, in front of over 1,000 boozed-up England lads. I got serious daggers from the Bolton firm, but the rest of the lads gave me a rousing cheer, as I looked for my Oldham pals who had melted away downstairs to the casino the minute the Cockney compere had introduced me and asked what I was going to sing!

Eventually, a Bolton representative got up and gave it 'We hate the Cockneys!' With this, Chelsea, West Ham and Spurs attacked the Bolton mob, and it all kicked off badly. It took the stewards 10 minutes to break up the brawling. A few Northern lads helped the Bolton lads out but it was very dodgy and it killed the atmosphere for a while, but an hour later all the England fans were chanting away, apart from a few who were sporting split lips or sore heads. Another memory of that trip was the amount of England lads spewing up over the side of the boat, dozens and dozens of lads all hanging over the side throwing up. It was a really choppy trip through the Bay of Biscay, at the side of France, but many lifelong friendships were made on that boat.

After a sleepless night due to the noise and fact you needed to keep one eye open, focused on your belongings, we made it for breakfast at 6.30am, and were pleased to see the great Bobby Moore having some grub. Even the ex-players working for the media had to go second class in those days, which today would be laughed at by some pundits who in my eyes were not fit to wear the late Sir Bobby's soiled underpants never mind his fucking football boots. As the ferry pulled into Santander, there were a few scuffles with different teams' lads and it was a tense time as we disembarked under the watchful eye of those spiteful Spanish Police who were waiting for an excuse to dish out some local punishment.

The word on the boat was the usual information which is still passed on to travelling England masses today: 'Get to the nearest bar by the railway station.' Regardless where you are playing, it is the meeting place and Bilbao, which was about 20 miles away, where the first three games were being held was no different. So that's where we headed after a quick wash and change from regulation denim to badly fitting shorts which, regardless of the style or shade, could not hide the fact that our legs had not seen the light of day since being forced to join in at PE in school!

With very little money and the Bury removals van probably clamped in Plymouth, it was every man for himself and we split up and agreed to meet in Bilbao. I got lucky and got a lift with some West Ham fans; they were top lads and, when I told them I was skint, they even gave me 20 quid, not flash cunts like the Chelsea lot, just proper fellas.

When I arrived there an hour later, there were hundreds of England fans milling about, including about 30 from Oldham who had come through France on the train. It was still two days before the game and the place was bouncing, The one downer was that I had lost my Oldham mates but I met up with two Pompey loons, Billy and Jackie. We were pally for the next two days, robbing the bars and cafes, doing runners, etc, we kipped in shop doorways and anywhere else that was not covered in piss or strewn with rubbish and cockroaches – it was cheap and nasty but the air conditioning was free!

On the Wednesday, I met up with my mates outside the Athletico Bilbao stadium, they sorted me a ticket out and I watched us beat France 3–1, with Bryan Robson scoring the fastest World Cup goal ever. The segregation was non-existent as thousands of English had bought tickets from locals and were everywhere. French and England fans mingled and there was a bit of scuffling when France scored but the performance and the result kept the violence on hold.

Outside was a different ball game and there were some very serious clashes with rival England fans. Chelsea had a massive firm outside the stadium and they were attacking any Northerners, but, unfortunately, the Northern lads were not sticking together and it was getting very dodgy if you could not throw a Southern-sounding sentence together. As a newcomer to the England scene, I was disgusted by these attacks but heard later that it was the norm and that Chelsea and West Ham liked to do their own thing, even if it involved attacking our own fans.

For the second game, we all got the buses into Bilbao, and I met up with four more Oldham lads before the game. I didn't have a ticket so ended up snatching a handful off a Spanish tout outside the stadium, and duly handed them out to England fans without tickets, forgetting that I was skint and not realising they were valuable beer tokens! As we were playing Czechoslovakia, there was hardly any trouble, apart from a few English kicking off with each other. We won 2–0 and I decided to stay with my four English mates who had an apartment in Bilbao. After giving the tickets away, I was still skint but Willis, one of the lads, owed me a big favour as I had lied on oath to get him off a serious charge a few months earlier; he told me from now I would want for nothing, and I didn't.

Bilbao was a fantastic vibrant city and we were based five minutes from the notorious red-light district, a long bustling street snaking down a hill. Every few yards, ladies of the night plied their trade, and there were some beautiful fit young birds on show. I tapped Willis for the one mill (about a fiver) required – it was one mill for any one prozzie – and I took my time, parading up and down this long street for half a hour, weighing up the best bird. I finally plumped for this gorgeous toned-up fit-as-fuck Latino babe, 'Fucky fucky Eenglaisy?' she asked me.

I didn't need asking twice! She was small and petite and grabbed my hand, leading me down this back alley as the taxi drivers howled with laughter as we walked past. If they thought I was going to let this bird rip me off or rob me, they were wrong. She was getting it, she may have been on the game and had many men from all over the world but she was in for a treat, some pure Oldham cock was going to have her begging for more and I'd be the one laughing when I kept the one mill for a refreshing ale after the deed was done!

Forget the beer, all I wanted to do was shag this fit babe and she took me to this big old scruffy apartment block. The free-shag plan was gone when she made me give the lady on the door my one mill before dragging me up the stairs. She seemed as keen as me, as we went into this pitch-black room with a scruffy old smelly mattress on the floor. I thought for a moment it was a set-up, but had nothing of value that could be taken and, if they wanted my shorts, T-shirt and trainers, well, they were fucking welcome to them, but she pulled me towards her and we both tumbled on to the mattress and began necking.

I took off her sparkly boob tube and she wrenched down my shorts, and headed south, licking me all the way down my chest, lager-filled belly and thighs – it was heavenly. Then she sucked my cock for a few moments, but stopped and pushed my head south and into her crotch, and, as I parted her skin-tight satin shorts, the most horrendous sight possible to any heterosexual man greeted me in the form of two small but defiant bollocks! And that is what I screamed out. I jumped up, and began spitting out, my head was spinning. I know I should have kicked the fuck out of this tranny who was staring up at me gobsmacked with its bollocks still hanging out, but all I wanted to do was get the fuck out of there. I ran down the stairs of this stinking hovel and into the night. As I hurtled down the street, the Spanish taxi drivers roared even louder with their laughter. I should have given them a slap but just ran all the way back to our local bar.

I was gutted but had to tell the lads in the bar in the hope they would join me in tracking the sick thing down and giving it a hiding. Most of them could not understand my problem; they told me 90 per cent of the prozzies were trannies, and that they had all been with them. Some didn't even claim to be pissed when they were tricked, which was going to be my excuse for not sussing out I had been sucked by a prozzie with a funnel not a tunnel. Disgusted, I went for a walk to gather my thoughts.

I wandered around Bilbao feeling dirty, and then noticed some commotion outside a bar as loads of locals huddled around the TVs inside. Being nosy, I went to check out what was happening and was just in time to see Maggie Thatcher, our leader and hero, announcing to the world that Argentina had surrendered and Great Britain had won another war. Within moments, hundreds of England fans were on the streets and in the fountains of Bilbao celebrating. 'We won the war!' they chanted and the locals joined in with the wonderful celebrations taking place; the Basques hated the Spanish who backed the Argies and the bars were giving free beer to any England fans, it was a wonderful heart-warming night.

The following night, me and Willis went for a walkabout in the early hours of the morning, found a few quiet bars and got pissed on the local lager. As we were staggering about round the Bilbao city centre, we found ourselves outside the very impressive civic centre of Bilbao. Outside this fine building was a huge wooden mast some 40 feet high, and flying from it was the flag of the Basque region, which was exactly the same as a Union Jack only in green, red and white. We foolishly decided that we were going to nick their national flag, not thinking that the police all carried guns and there was much terrorist activity going on in this region with ETA – the Basque version of the IRA – and we were very much into bandit country. Nevertheless, there was nobody protecting this building and Willis, who was only slightly built, clambered up the big mast, and relieved Bilbao of its national flag. I of course kept watch – fortunately there were no gun-toting cops hanging about – and Willis was up and down within a couple of minutes complete with this huge Basque flag. We folded it up and fled into the night, walking the three miles or so to our apartment on the outskirts of the city. We were so chuffed with it but there was the question of who now owned it and we tossed up for the rights, and unfortunately for me Willis won. He managed to smuggle the flag out of the country and it remained on his bedroom wall for several years, but subsequently it got lost during a house move.

God knows what would have happened if we had been caught – was it treason? We could have been languishing in a Spanish jail for years but at the time it seemed like a good idea!

At the next game, I met my cousin Gary Walker outside the stadium. Gary was a big Man United fan, and he was with a firm of Burnley fans and Burnley Reds. He's a top lad, and he said I could stay at his place for a week, he had an apartment in a little holiday resort called Laredo, about 10 miles out of Bilbao. Not wanting to outstay my welcome with the lads who had so kindly put me up and kept me in ale for a week, and more importantly not wanting to bump into the filth who had tarnished my sexual memory for life, I took up the offer to stay with him for a few days while I got my head together When I got there, I was pleased to see 10 Oldham lads also staying in that resort; in fact, there were loads of England fans there and a few Northern Ireland lads, and, as they were non-sympathisers, we all got on great. As you would expect, the locals loved us, and a few of us trapped off with the local birds who were all fit as fuck and pure women! I ended up shagging this gorgeous blonde bird called Tamara, she could not speak a word of English but I made her laugh, and you know the score, lads, get a bird laughing and you are halfway to paradise, as the great Billy Fury sang. There were over 200 England lads in this little resort, and it was great seeing all the various teams' flags hanging from the hotel balconies. Oldham lads had a massive St George flag which they flew from a mast on a little island 100 yards out to sea; everyone could see it, it made me proud.

We went back to Bilbao the day before we returned home, and, apart from the transvestite incident, I only had one other bad experience in Bilbao and that was this night. My partner in crime Willis went for a stroll down the old town district of Bilbao where there was a carnival going on and it was really busy and bustling. We stopped, had a few drinks and milled around, when we noticed a swarthy-looking lad who looked like a Spaniard, wearing a Halifax Town Union Jack banner wrapped around his shoulders. We approached him to shake his hand thinking he was a fellow Brit, only for him to spit in our faces and pull out a knife. He was obviously an irate local so Willis threw a bottle at him, which hit him right in the face.

All of a sudden, there were dozens of these local youths coming at us and we had to flee through dark alleys and entrances, with these local loons in hot pursuit. We eventually got away but they were within 10 yards of us for most of the chase and the majority of the cunts had weapons of some kind. We found refuge in our bar and the English lads wanted to go and hunt them down but I advised them against it, as there were possibly many more hanging about and with a day to go didn't want to end up in hospital or jail.

All told, I had three and a half weeks in Spain, saw three World Cup matches, had a couple of birds (one fella!) and had a wonderful time. But, despite the things we all went for – the football, the drinking and the women – I will always remember the trip for the night that we won the war. As a patriot, it was one of the best nights of my life.

Shaun was another England fan who made the trip.

SHAUN, SHEFFIELD UNITED:

The summer of 1982 was brilliant: very hot, loads of fanny everywhere and England playing in the World Cup in Spain. The Blades had been promoted to the old Third Division at the first time of asking and had got there on average crowds of around 12,000, often taking at least half that amount away from home.

This was to become a 'golden era' in football-hooliganism circles and Spain '82 was for many going to be the icing on the cake. The new Casual era had begun; actually, it was already well established at club level and every football club had its own 'mob' or 'firm', as they now liked to call themselves. The lads at all the clubs were as concerned about how smart they looked as they were about any 'offs'; to be honest, the two went hand in glove. Ask any 40-something 'lad' what was the best period for fashion and violence and I bet 95 per cent will say the early 1980s. Fuckin' mad times!

One of the lads mentioned that he'd seen an advert in a local paper for cheap travel and accommodation for the first phase of the competition with a company called Transalpine which was an offshoot of another firm called Sportsworld Travel. Turns out that they were offering 'deals for rail/camping tours from £249.50'. This was it, we've cracked it here, we're gonna do them froggy bastards good style. The Blades were on the march!

Most lads would hitchhike, go on the ferry, fly, hire cars and rob the shops on the way to pay their way, anything just to get there. No silly fuckin' banning orders or border checkpoints or any of that bollocks; just pack a bag and off you went!

For the opening game in Bilbao, the atmosphere was unbelievable. Then, as now, you can spot the English in a football crowd anywhere, simply because they always look smarter than all those greasy foreign cunts. There we all were in our smart Slazenger tops, cricket hats, Fred Perry shorts and Adidas trainers. We looked fuckin' amazing with our wedge haircuts, with a lot of the lads wearing 'Bulldog Bobby' T-shirts as well. The Basque town of Bilbao had never seen anything like this. We were here for a bottle and a battle – we weren't to be disappointed.

The stadium was ultra modern compared to the shit-holes we were used to back home; they actually had flushing toilets instead of mud huts to piss in and the stairways leading into the ground were concrete and not wood. It was like landing on another planet! The end that we entered was two-tiered and we were on the lower standing section directly behind the goal. Altogether a mob of about 400–500 English positioned themselves here and you could sense the uneasy atmosphere. We were obviously in the French end of the ground and it would only take a minor incident to start the expected violence. Supporters from many clubs were there from all over England: Peterborough, Lincoln, Hull City, Chelsea, Bolton, Millwall were all well represented with some solid little firms from Kings Lynn, Doncaster and Exeter, places you hardly ever hear about nowadays.

Most of the French lot had them fucking irritating air horns, you know the type that you can hear from a million miles away, and they were blaring out non-stop. Everyone was getting more and more pissed off with them as the match got under way but, with just 27 seconds on the clock, the horns were muffled when Bryan Robson, complete with trendy permed hair, headed in from, I think, Paul Mariner's cross. It was straight in front of the ranks of English Casuals and caused total mayhem. We all went ballistic, dozens of us surging forward like they used to on the Kop at Anfield, as we celebrated, 80 degrees, drunk and England 1–0 up after less than a minute – top that fucker!

Coins then began raining down on us from the seats above – typical cowardly French bastards. An Exeter fan, a big cunt with a Lacoste top on, threw a smoke canister into the nearest seats in the upper tier and then it all went mad for just a couple of minutes. Turns out you could buy these smoke bombs from any of the local shops; apparently, they were quite commonly used in the local bullfighting shows in the old part of town and anyone could buy them. The police soon moved in and started whacking anybody who was in the vicinity. Of course, by now the French do what they do best and started to back off; gaps were opening up on the terraces, 1970s style, and you could see the panic and confusion spreading amongst them. I thought, Fuckin' hell, this is brilliant, but at the same time you had to be wary of getting a clump off one of the Spanish cops and it was pretty scary. Anybody who says they've not been frightened while involved in any football violence is a fuckin' lying bastard; it's just that you get an adrenalin rush at the time and try and keep it together. I saw a few lads being carted off, but from what everyone was saying most were just ejected from the ground and not many locked up. If that happened in this day and age, the authorities would want to ban you for life.

The rest of the game passed off largely without major incident and afterwards we all trooped off towards the main town square area. A lot of the Northern teams stuck together; we mingled with groups from Leeds, which was previously unheard of, lads from Hull, Darlington, Middlesbrough, who were a very handy bunch, and a few Scousers who true to the name they are given were all professional thieves and conmen. We did this because word was spreading that a large Chelsea gang were attacking any non-Cockneys.

You hear a lot of this going on while abroad watching England, but I personally never saw anything like that happening. I must admit, though, that there was a strong 'us and them' attitude at the time, possibly due to the fact that the far right had allegedly infiltrated firms from Millwall, Chelsea and West Ham during the late 70s and early 80s to manipulate them and use football as cover for their own dodgy purposes. Watching Sheffield United at that time were a number of black lads and they were all game as fuck so we didn't want anything to do with any of these racist cunts who were spreading their poison amongst the Cockney teams.

By and large, the World Cup of 1982 was superb. Some of the lads had been to Italy in 1980 for the European Championships and spoke of how good that was for the battles in Turin, etc, but Spain '82 had been a memorable time for me; all the Blades stuck together as usual and gave as good as they got. England had exported their own unique brand of soccer violence complete with 'designer dress sense' and wedge haircuts into Europe and millions had watched it on TV. The Blades had been there as well and I was one of 'em.

I've still got my match ticket and the Pringle polo shirt I wore for the France game, just never got round to chucking it out; 38in chest – I'm more than that round me fuckin' waist now!

Legendary West Ham fan Bill Gardner was another who made the trip to the group stages but as a tour rep rather than an out-and-out England fan. While it is nice to get paid to watch your country abroad, there are aspects to the job which can make you wonder if it is worth all the hassle, as Bill recalled in his bestselling autobiography:

BILL GARDNER, WEST HAM:
England isn't really my scene. I like to be around people I can trust and I'm afraid that some of the Northern fellas I met at England games do too many beers for me and I've never had the same feeling for England as I have for West Ham. I was asked by Mike Ross of Ross Travel to take a coach load of England fans to the World Cup in Spain in '82. The coach left Knightsbridge and we travelled over to stay in a village in Northern Spain called Zuruats. We travelled 24 hours and only stopped twice to go to the toilet on the way. It was a horrible journey but then we arrived at this really nice little village with a big wide beach, and we stayed in this really nice hotel.

With the worst part of the trip over, everybody was now looking forward to it, most thought we had good chances of doing well and I remember some of the Chelsea lads had their heads painted red and white and were seasoned England followers. For the first few days, we played football on the beach and everything was all right, and then things turned for the worst, as they do! I got food poisoning and was in bed when I heard this noise and shouting going on outside so went to see what was going on. One of the England lads had his flag over the balcony and the locals were bricking the hotel and shouting abuse. I was out on a balcony area and was trying to calm the situation down because I was obviously the courier but was getting nowhere. Within minutes, they started bunging things at me and for self-preservation I started bunging things back. I was running out of things to bung so I asked the people on the lower balcony floor, two Tottenham fans, who had some frozen cans of lager to throw them up to me. There was quite a mob of them down below us by now and I saw that the main antagonists of the group were sticking their heads out and popping them back after throwing things up, so I threw a couple of cans one after another very quickly and the first one missed but as this lad stuck his head out I copped him with the second one and they carted him away, spark out.

The owner of the hotel was a nice fella and he couldn't understand the way the English behaved. I explained to him that this is the way many English lads enjoy themselves but they are a much quieter race than us, and he just couldn't really understand it. There was a lot of patio furniture thrown over the balcony during the bit of action we had with them, so he said to me will you come and help me sort it out and get it in, and as I was the rep I went down there. Before we got started, a hostile gathering are pointing fingers at me saying, 'That's the one, he's the one.'

I said, 'No, no, they've made a mistake.'

He said, 'They're saying it's you.'

And I had to talk my way out of that one. I didn't want to upset him because he was a nice fella. But we managed to pick up a few sticks that were left and take them back in. Funnily enough, the games of football on the beach ended after that day!

It got worse one night after one of the lads went out and paid some old brass for sex but didn't get it. He came back into the hotel and said to me, 'I've paid this old brass and she ain't come across – what can you do to help us?'

Now I don't think Ross Travel were paying me to sort these kinds of problems out but regardless I've gone into this club four-handed and these brasses were there, all sitting on the bottom floor in the corner.

As we got in there, there were two blokes in charge and we'd heard earlier that they were pretty upset, because they were Argentinean nationals living in the village. They seemed to be the main boys about town, which didn't help the ongoing issue of the lad not getting his money's worth from the brasses, who to make matters worse worked for these fellas! Regardless, as you do, I went up to these blokes and said, 'Look the fella's paid his money, she ain't come across with the goods, what are you going to do?'

He says to me, 'You'd better have a look around.'

And I looked around and they were all standing there with lumps of wood and all kinds of tools and I thought to myself, Blimey, we're in deep shit. So I said to the boys, 'We're going to have to go for the door.'

Anyway, we run up the stairs to get out the place, because we were literally surrounded; there was no chance of making the front door so we pile up the stairs. One lad got whacked and had to jump on my back, and we just jumped through the shutters to get out because it was quicker than the door. I got a nick on my ankle from what I can only presume was an iron bar, and it slowed me down a bit but it didn't break and we made our way back into the hotel just as a big mob of them came screaming round the corner after us.

We were standing in the hotel and the bloke had locked the doors when this Argie comes up the front steps and I thought he was just going to start mouthing off at the door, but he comes straight through the glass door. Unbelievable, he must have been high on something. Whatever, he's come through the door and we notice he's armed with a gun. I'm stood there thinking, Is this bloke for real or on a bluff, when he suddenly opens fire and shoots the fucking lights out, next second boom the fucking telly has gone and he's just missed me from five yards. I thought to myself, I'd better do something here before someone gets killed. So I grabbed a metal barstool and cracked him with it, but I whacked him a bit hard because it was stuck into him. He was walking around screaming with this barstool sticking out of him. All it needed was a midget or something to jump on his shoulder and you'd have a circus act. Anyway, he went back out the door a bit quicker than he came in and they carted him away.

He was history but the others kept trying to get in, and a couple of our people in there got hurt by the flying glass and bottles; everyone was in shock and then the police rolled up. There were two lots of police in Spain – the brown shirts and the blue shirts, one lot are the council and the other lot are a bit nearer the mark. They soon cleared the street and then came in and asked what was going on. I explained I was a courier and that some geezer had shot a few rounds at us and they sorted it for us to get to the hospital because a few of the boys were hurt. We had to give our names at the hospital and the next morning the police came back to the hotel and nicked everyone that had been to the hospital, including myself. So we were banged up in the cell, six or seven of us, and they kept us there for a day or so. It was another job I was not paid to do, but I said, 'We want to see the British Ambassador about this.'

Anyway, after a day, the Ambassador came up and we explained to him what had gone on and he said because of

the Falklands conflict they didn't want to make a big thing of
this. He said it would look bad if it came out that guns had
been used and added, 'If you keep quiet, I'll get you out, but
don't say anything to the press.'

We all decided to do that because obviously we didn't want
to be in there, so they let us out in time for the games.

I'd only done one more trip for Mike Ross, that was when
we played Norway the year before; it was the game when we
were beaten and the Norwegian commentator made that
famous outburst about Winston Churchill, Margaret
Thatcher. That was easy money and was a breeze compared
to Spain; on that trip, I had seen enough to know that there
were far easier and safer ways of making a few pounds and I
never bothered being a courier again!

Moving on from the group stages, England were drawn to play
Germany and hosts Spain in Madrid. It was a strange group
system used in the '82 World Cup and eventually England were
eliminated at the second stage, having not lost a game or even
conceded a goal. Off the field, things were just as bad, as
thousands of supporters had gone home after the first three
games, leaving what was left of the battle-weary troops to fly the
flag on the country's behalf. Many found the locals in Madrid
much less accommodating than those who had welcomed them
to the resorts, and the Spanish capital was a dangerous place.
Gone were the two-faced businessmen who were happy to put on
a false smile in return for increased takings and they were
replaced by violent street gangs backed up by a sadistic police
force who also showed the English no hospitality whatsoever.

The *Mirror* highlighted the problems facing the supporters
under the headline: 'KNIFED BY THE NAZIS'. 'England's World Cup
fans have become targets of the murderous neo-fascist
organisation La Fuera Neuva. Extreme members who are pro-
Argentinean sought out English fans after the match against West
Germany. One victim 18-year-old Mark Buckley from Derby, who
was wearing a Union Jack draped around his shoulders, was

stabbed in the heart to the shouts of "Malvinas", "Gibraltar is Spanish" and "Death to the British".

It was reported that Mark's heart actually stopped beating for three minutes before doctors at Madrid's central La Pas Hospital managed to save his life. Other England fans were also stabbed and beaten by Spanish thugs wearing ..r badges which stood for a Spanish equivalent of the UK's National Front called 'New Force'.

England fans complained that the Spanish Police had not called for ambulances at first, despite the seriousness of their injuries. One of them, Gary Smith aged 25 of Manchester, was stabbed in the hand, slashed across his shoulders and had six stitches in his head; another, Robert Wilson, 21, of Southport, had an 8in gash in his stomach and 14 stitches in his back; and another, David Moore, 21, of Surrey, was also stabbed and slashed.

The attitude of the police, as well as the street gangs, was a major worry for those who had descended on Madrid, as by now money was running out and many of the English lads who were left out there were taking chances. Mike from Stockport was one who hoped to stay for the duration, but he never quite made it.

MIKE, STOCKPORT:
By the time we made Madrid, we were skint; it had been a great few weeks on the coast but we had overindulged and by now were down to our last few quid. A bed was the only thing we wanted to spend money on, anything else we hoped to rob. Madrid was not like Benidorm, it was not even like Bilbao where they tolerated the tourists – they hated us in Madrid and, after just a couple of hours there, we knew it was going to be a shit place to stay.

Every bar and hotel wanted money up front; on the coast, you could set up a tab, drink for a few hours and walk off, but in Madrid it was pay now or have nothing. We had to go shoplifting to survive, just to eat, and that was not easy as we were dirty and smelly, sunburned to fuck and didn't blend in very well with the locals. We ended up getting a hotel, for about £5 a night, the room had four beds and there were nine of us in it; the old girl knew but was not bothered, she was one of the few decent people we met there.

On the day of the match against Germany, there were groups arriving from the campsite that had been systematically attacked and ambushed from day one. Lads had been stabbed, and it was strange as the Germans had even joined up with the English to fight the locals and we were told that about 30 had been nicked, including a good few Germans, during the fighting.

As the day wore on, the day-trippers came in and swelled our numbers. Thousands had gone home to their work and families and only the brave, jobless or stupid had joined a few rich Southerners for the duration. This new breed were either cocks who had too much money or were plain daft, as the trips cost hundreds and they were clearly being ripped off.

We were talking to one married couple from Swindon who had paid over a grand for two games and they were staying in a hotel an hour away, sharing with another two blokes they had never met before. They were each charged a £20 transfer fee to the ground and you could get a fucking bus anywhere for less than a couple of quid. Others had paid through the nose for packages and found themselves staying in rundown hostels that were dusted, whitewashed and called hotels while the World Cup was on.

The party mood began, the drinking and singing was in full flow as lots of the new arrivals bought us drinks in return for keepsakes we had pilfered from the first games and many were just happy to buy us beer and listen to the stories of the weeks up North. There was no problem with the Germans but the Spanish had started to show and the usual antics of driving past on the mopeds and jeeps singing about Argentina was back on. We were all outside a bar and were getting a bit noisy singing the usual nonsense about Gibraltar and the Falklands being ours, even though no one gave a shit about the places if they were honest, when a load of police arrived and they were backed up by a couple of dozen on horseback. In seconds, they had charged into us and the police on foot piled into the scattered crowd and lashed out at anyone who was daft enough to stand still. There were plenty who were, and many innocent English men and women were battered senseless by both the council police and their more violent army counterparts.

We managed to get in the bar and it was not a case of 'come on, fight back', everyone knew what was coming and cowered in the far corner. Seconds later, in they came and once again they knocked fuck out of anyone who was in striking distance. I have never seen anything like it to this day and I have been most places with England. They were the animals that the press seem to label us as so often.

A few were arrested, and the rest of us made our way to the ground. All through the holiday, we had been leaving our passports in the safety boxes at the hotels and it was no problem, but here they were stopping lads and, if they had no ID, were nicking them. It was pure over-the-top policing and I believe it was done to make those of us who were bumming around think twice about staying any longer.

For once, the British press were outraged and, the following day, the *Daily Mirror* even called for the Spanish government to take action against their own police authorities: 'SPANISH COPS WERE THUGS!'

Mirror man John Jackson reported, 'Spanish cops were trying to goad English fans to fight them, shouting in broken English: "Come on, we will show you how tough we are."

'The heavily armed police complete with riot shields, tear gas, helmets and big sticks tried in vain to entice the English fans who ignored them and settled into a bar outside the stadium. A few moments later, the Spanish cops stormed the bar for no reason and began attacking everybody in the bar including many women and children, it was a sickening sight as they crashed down their big sticks on innocent people's heads.

'Many Spanish people were appalled at such behaviour and the mayor of Madrid promised a probe into what happened. Assistant mayor Jose Barritueve said, "I am ashamed as a Spaniard and as the person responsible for the Municipal Police Force here in Madrid by the disgusting behaviour of some of our members.'"

MIKE, STOCKPORT:

The game was very poor and we drew 0–0 and needed to beat Spain to make the semi-finals. That night it was no go in Madrid, as the majority of England fans drove out to their no-star hostels, leaving those of us with no money and little spirit left in us to fend for ourselves. It was nearly a week till the next game and that was one of the things that did it for me; we had no money left to pay the old girl in the hotel, no money for food and if you were caught sleeping rough you were nicked for vagrancy.

One of the main reasons for giving up having come so far, though, was the attitude of the players and the FA. It was bad enough that the bastards could barely manage to give you a wave after the match, but we bumped into a few of them outside their plush hotel the day after the Germany game and asked if there was any chance of some complimentary tickets that would get us into the game for nothing, giving us a reason to stay there or even to sell which would keep us in food and drink for the next few days while we tried to stay on board. We never even got a no from the bastards, not even a shake of the head; they brushed past us as if we were tramps asking them for money for cheap cider.

Thinking back we certainly looked like tramps, and we most probably smelled like them, but we were not after money to feed a drink problem, we were after a ticket to watch the twats play for our great country, having given up our jobs and spent our life savings just to be part of it. We were wasting our breath and, less than an hour later, I collected what few bits of clothing I had left and made my way to the station and got ready for a three-day journey home with less than a fiver to my name.

Viva fucking España!

CHAPTER FOUR
DEJA VU
GREECE '82

We all have our own views on the most dangerous place to visit for a football match, both abroad and at home! Some will say Millwall, some Cardiff; some think Holland and others Germany – it's all down to individual experiences, as even the smaller towns and lesser-known countries are capable of turning you over, especially if you take liberties and don't show them the respect they can demand.

Turkey will always be regarded as a bad place to visit for obvious reasons, but for England games alone one place has been singled out by many as the worst place they have ever visited: Greece!

Mention Greece to many fans and they will talk about the last-gasp Beckham free-kick at Old Trafford which saw us qualify for the World Cup Finals in Japan or, more often or not, the holiday resorts of Corfu, Crete, Rhodes and the many other places frequented by thousands of tourists every year. Very few will think of the place as a hooligans' nightmare ... unless they have been there!

Lewisham of West Ham and Lee Spence from Oldham visited Greece on international duty in 1982 and 1989; it may as well have been the same day, as, apart from the finer details, both tales are the same and it really is a case of deja vu!

LEWISHAM, WEST HAM:
Over the years, I have been to some dodgy gaffs at matches but there is no question that the worst place I ever went to was Greece when we played there about '82 in a European qualifier. It was in the days when going by plane was too expensive for the average working man so I decided to go on the train using the dirt-cheap Inter-Rail. What a fucking journey and half that was. I left on Thursday night from Victoria, on my own but hoping to meet a few others to break the journey up, and I ended up getting to Athens Sunday dinnertime without seeing another soul who was going to the game. It was a long two and half days' travelling on the train so I was absolutely slaughtered by the time I got to Athens and booked myself into a hotel that night and crashed out.

On the Monday, I decided to go for a little walkabout, tourist stuff, up to see the Acropolis and all that, as I'm still on my own and still ain't seen anyone resembling a football fan, when, all of the sudden, I've come down from the Acropolis and walked past this little taverna and who should be sat outside – none other than Hickey, Terry Last and about 20 Chelsea who I recognised from various parts of London, I thought, Oh fucking hell, what a result, someone at last to have a drink with, to talk to and have a laugh with. We moved on and found a little Irish bar down in the centre of Athens and we were having a good old booze-up, no problems with who we supported, so we decided to all meet up again on the Tuesday for the Under-21 game that was being held near by.

We met up in the Irish bar again, before heading down to Pireas which is a little port where the game was to be played at Olympiakos's old ground. As soon as we got down there, I thought, Fucking hell, it looks a bit rough down here! There were loads of mobs of Greeks walking about, hollering and hooting, looking for English. None of us had colours on but they could tell we were English straight away, because, let's face it, we're not the best at blending in abroad, and there were not many of us with tans in fucking July and August, never mind November! As we scuttled past, they were all trying to stare us out and it was a really hostile atmosphere.

We made it into the ground and there couldn't have been as many as 100 of us in there. Hickey took control and marched us all to the top of the terrace, with the thinking being that, if they come at us, they would have to come up the steps, which is never easy. He was right, but it also meant we had nowhere to run if it came on top, which, sure enough, is what happened. The Greeks left it until the last minute before entering the ground and straight away came surging on to the terraces, loads of them, and in less than a minute, from the area being empty apart from our little mob, we were surrounded by fucking hundreds of the bastards. There was no segregation, as nobody was expecting us to even be there because it was only an Under-21 game, and I'm sorry to even say this, but we ended up all getting chased on to the pitch after having to jump over a dry moat to get away!

I will always remember that geezer that was in charge of the FA, Ted Croker, coming across the pitch and ushering us around to the main stand where all the officials were sitting and we were sort of sectioned off from all the Greeks and out of what was a very real situation. They kept us all in at the end of the game for about an hour or so then put us on buses back to Pireas, then left us there. Hickey took charge again and said that, when we get the train, we must all pack one carriage out, which was a choice call because we got four stops down the line and we were back at the station at the fucking ground which was full of Greeks. It's all gone off as the Greeks on the platform tried to get into the carriage, the windows were going through and it was a scary situation but we held them off, and done quite well considering the onslaught we faced. Had Hickey not have made that call, we would have been butchered at that station and, like him or not, you had to give the lad credit for his thinking in tight situations. So we survived and most of us then went back to that same Irish bar we'd been drinking in for the past couple of days and agreed that we had to stay tight at the main game. The general feeling was, if that is what an Under-21 game was like with just a few thousand in attendance, what the fuck was the main event going to throw at us? To be honest, half those fans that were part of the 100-odd English in that ground gave me the impression that they didn't fancy going up to Salonika, based on what they had seen in the ground at Pireas.

I was right on that call, as the next day at the meeting place I was on my Jack Jones as Hickey had hired a coach to go up there and on the train there may have been a couple of other England supporters, but if there were they were keeping a low one, as I never saw anyone who remotely looked like a fan, never mind someone who would be prepared to have a go if it came on top like the day before. I got into Salonika and bumped into a couple of West Ham geezers and we was having a drink by the station when it started to get a bit naughty again, a bit like it was in Athens with the Greeks mobbing up, spitting at us and all getting a bit hostile.

We moved on down to the ground; there couldn't have been more than 20 of us and there was a big sign up telling all the England fans to go to gate 15 or whatever it was. So we went in there and I couldn't believe it, here was a 40,000-plus-capacity stadium with a small block just for us but all they had us sectioned off from the Greeks with was a tiny bit of red fucking tape. We all looked at each other and realised that, if things turned nasty, there was no way that a ground full of thousands of baying Greeks would be held back by this little bit of tape!

With the day before fresh in our minds, we stood right at the front and prayed that lightning never struck twice, but in minutes all sorts of crap was getting thrown at us and fucking piss-bags and stones were raining down on us. Before the inevitable happened, the Old Bill came round and they opened this gate and took us all on the pitch, just like they did the day before, and led us around the pitch and put us in a stand near where the squad players were all sitting. The rest of the game went in a flash and we were kept in after the game had finished for an hour before being put on police buses back to the central station. There was no protests and just as well for we would have got annihilated because, as soon as we drove off, we were attacked from all angles and the Greeks were throwing bins at the buses and going crazy because they had lost.

Another thing I will always remember about that game was that, when we were in the stands, you could see out to the hills and I noticed a group of people outside up on a hill. I thought, I bet that's Hickey's coach; some say it was and claimed they didn't have the bottle to come in the ground. I have never asked them if it was, but I never saw his lot at the game and maybe it was one of his tactical moves which he keeps quiet about!

Seven years later, England played Greece again; it was a low-key friendly international and few made the trip – those that did were lucky enough to live to tell the tale! Among them was Oldham-born Lee Spence who had acquired a taste for football violence while following his hometown club Oldham Athletic. Over the years, he became a well-known face in hooligan circles and was a regular traveller with the national side. He remembers Greece as one of the worst trips he ever made.

LEE SPENCE, OLDHAM:
One of the worst places I have ever been to for being on top was Greece. Four of us booked on a British Airways schedule flight from Heathrow to Athens, which was a first for us, as we always went on the cheapest flights available. For some reason, we splashed out on this one and I expected there to be loads on the flight but only one more lad turned up – Shaun G from Cheltenham who is a right game fucker – so our firm was now five-handed!

It was a strange flight because old habits die hard and we were told by the stewardess to stop stealing from the drinks trolley as everything was free anyway! We got there on the Saturday, booked into a hotel late on and never ventured out that night, so come the Sunday morning we were right up for a good day and strolled into the city, despite warnings that it was not a good idea, as there was a local derby that day between Panathinaikos and AEK Athens. The hooligan problem was said to be bad in Greece at the time and in the weeks prior to the England game the FA had advised fans not to travel as their safety could not be guaranteed, which probably had the effect of putting a few wankers off but made plenty of hooligans who were not going to go in the first place book themselves a flight.

The authorities in Greece were that concerned that there would be serious trouble that they moved the game from an evening match to an afternoon kick-off hoping that most of the locals would choose work instead of terrorising the English!

We headed to Omonia Square which was supposed to be a big attraction like Trafalgar Square in London, full of bars and whatever, and it took us ages to get there. We must have walked about three fucking miles before we found it. We sat off in a bar near some escalators and had a beer, the only English in the whole square, and soon we were getting a few stares and the odd comment thrown our way. Out of nowhere, we heard a bit of a commotion coming up some escalators and a massive mob appeared dressed in green and white so we sussed that they were Panathinaikos probably looking for AEK's mob. We were right about who they were but they were looking for *us*, and in seconds a roar went up and, as they charged across the road, we literally had to run for our lives. We managed to jump into a taxi, locked the doors and shouted to the bloke behind the wheel, 'Drive, just fucking drive!' He got our drift and sped off; we passed him a card with the hotel address on and about 10 seconds later he stopped. We were telling him to keep fucking driving, as you could still see a few of this mob in the distance, but he pointed to our hotel – just across the road.

We had been walking around in circles for an hour and Omonia Square was only a five-minute stroll from the fucking hotel's front door. We jumped out, ran into the hotel and decided that we would fuck off to a nearby resort rather than put up with that shit all week.

Later that day, we headed off for the coast to some resort and bumped into a load of the Pompey lads and a few from Wigan, including Suddy who is one of their well-known faces. Everyone was sound with us and it was one of those places where you had to stick together and forget your differences at home, so we holed up in a bar called The Ship Inn. After a couple of hours, a few Greeks turned up and Suddy sparked one of them, and minutes later they came back firm-handed and attacked the bar. We grabbed what we could and piled out and had them on the back foot straight away. I don't think they thought for one minute that we would come out and we ended up chasing them and I thought we were well on top.

It then started to go horribly wrong as they regrouped, got more numbers and steamed back into us. We had no option but to get off and we were all split up; the Pompey lads knew where they were going and made into a hotel but me and John from Blackpool were chased on to the beach and had to run for our dear lives! Another lad, Albie, flagged a taxi down but the driver stopped, jumped out and started wading into him; it was one mad on-top place!

The next day, we told anyone who wanted to know that we were to get together and travel to the game in a fleet of taxis and then meet back at the Ship after the game to have a pop at this Greek mob who had terrorised us. We got a tidy firm together of about 50 to 60; lads from Carlisle, Brighton, Chelsea and Shrewsbury all joined us and it was a good firm of young and older lads that set off for Athens. We told the drivers to follow each other but as soon as they were off it was like the Grand Prix, some bombed off ahead and others went different ways. I'm sure the cunts driving knew what they were doing as, by the time we got to the ground, we were back to our usual-suspects firm, trying to blend in with thousands of Greeks.

We got dropped off and from the outside it was like Wembley; it was a massive stadium and there were thousands of these Greeks, all wearing bomber jackets staring at us. We kept our heads down and tried to find an entrance or even a sign in English and then we bumped into Pooley from Rochdale and Darryl from Shrewsbury who showed us the pay gate for our end. Usually, we would have a mooch about and look for a bit of mischief but this was not the place for stupid heroics and we went straight in. People reading this will be thinking that we were shit-houses but, unless you have been there, you will not understand how moody the place was. There was no police escort and, if you did ask a copper or one of the army blokes for directions or help, they would just snarl at you, as the reputation English hooligans had was obviously a bad one and they were not interested in us or our safety – live by the sword, die by the sword mentality, now fuck off!

Thank you very much!

In our section, there were about 300 England fans but more than half of those were lads who would have a go. The ground must have held 70–80,000 but the crowd was less than 10,000 and you had about 2,000 either side of us wanting to kill us! As soon as the game started, they were off, charging the riot police, slinging seats at us and playing up badly. The police in the ground, to be fair, saved us and in the second half we did a few phoney charges across the seats just to get the Greeks going. After about three charges, you could see the police getting fed up with us, so someone said, 'We'd better pack this in before they fucking move and let us get at them!'

We decided to get the tube to Omonia Square and try and

restore a bit of pride but after the game it was unbelievable. They told us we were getting kept in for an hour and the Greeks went mad; in the end, the police had to take us on to the pitch and form a guard around us, as the rest of them tried to clear the locals out of the stadium. It took them about an hour and a half before they could even start to escort us from the ground and the idea of the tube to Omonia was ditched and we all agreed to get taxis back to the resort and meet up at the Ship Inn.

We had about 70-odd in the Ship, so upped and went looking for it, which seemed a good idea at the time but in the end it went wild. I have been in a few ding-dongs over the years but Greece was wild. We got tooled up – lads had wood and gas – and we set off and soon steamed into a small mob who turned out to be English! I gave one Chelsea lad a crack around the head before we realised who they were, but it was all a case of shake hands, sorry, right, let's move on together, and we piled into a bar where the Carlisle lads immediately kicked it off. This time, it was Greeks and they put up a major fight. I had a plank of wood for putting the windows of the bar in but we couldn't get into there, as they were fighting like fuck to keep us out and then we had to get off, as someone said the police were on their way.

We set off for a bar called the Sussex and had to go through a big park, and we knew the Greeks would be in there and as soon as we entered it they came at us. It was dark as fuck but we stood and then went into them with lumps of wood, and they backed off time and time again, it was a great show by the English firm and we should have carried it on and stuck tight but the fuckers kept coming back time and time again.

Some of the older lads seemed to lose the stomach for the fight and quite a few drifted off leaving the Carlisle lads to initially keep it together; they stood out that night and were as game as any firm I have ever seen. One of them, a lad called Sparrow, went after a few and was ambushed and badly beaten and mugged.

Eventually, they became too strong for us, as quite simply they would not give up. There was no police there and we had to run, in fact, we had to run for our lives as they were wild by now, as they had taken a few casualties in the early stages. We made it to the Sussex bar and literally had to barricade ourselves inside with tables and whatever else we could grab to stop them getting in. The riot police turned up, blocked the street off and took us all back to our hotels where we were told we had to get our stuff and leave straight away for the airport, as they were struggling to contain the Greek mobs who were after us. Basically, our attack on the bar had upset the whole community and nobody complained about going to the airport – it was three in the morning and the whole fucking town was on the streets looking for the English!

Later that year, Swansea played in Athens and they went to the same town and came unstuck; no doubt, our antics had hurt the local community and I remember a few of the Welsh lads were locked up after they were attacked in the Ship Inn.

We made it home without major injury and without being nicked, but looking back at it now it is a miracle how nobody was killed. Greece was without a doubt the worst country I ever watched England play in.

By the time England next visited Greece for a World Cup qualifier in June 2001, the hardcore hooligan base had been smashed by the National Criminal Intelligence Service (NCIS) and the introduction of the dreaded Football Banning Orders (FBOs). The Barmy Army brigade had taken over with their drums and Great Escape ditties; but how these fans would have fared in '82 and '89 is quite a frightening thought.

CHAPTER FIVE

THE WAR ZONE
LUXEMBOURG '83

Bobby Robson had enjoyed a great start to his reign as England manager, losing just one of his first 12 games in charge, a worthless friendly against West Germany. Things were looking good and a result against Denmark at Wembley would have cemented a place at the European Championship Finals the following summer in France. But it was a disastrous night for England and they were beaten 1–0, leaving automatic qualification in the hands of the Danes, regardless of the result in England's final match in Luxembourg on 16 November 1983.

There are many games talked about by lads who have been watching England for three decades but one that always crops up is this game; quite simply, England invaded Europe that week and rampaged and destroyed anything and anybody that got in their way.

On the day of the match, the game itself was insignificant, as literally hundreds of hooligans rioted through the city, looting shops, overturning cars and at one stage even chasing the Luxembourg Army.

Kiddy is a 42-year-old Evertonian and it was the one and only time he ever watched England.

KIDDY, EVERTON:

For a couple of years, we had been going abroad on the cheap Inter-Rails and Transalpino tickets and simply took whatever we wanted from most towns we stopped off at. There was little or no security, customs was slack and rather than graft in work to make decent money it was a lot easier to graft abroad. Football rivalries never came into it with me, I was doing it for the money and the laughs, so over the years I made good friends with a few Mancs and lads from other clubs who were on the same game. It was only the Cockneys who were not easy to get on with, they believed they had the divine rights to everything and were best given a wide berth if you wanted to earn dough and come home with it all. They were happy to let you work all week and then liberate you of your swag on the way home. It was not as if you could tell anyone, was it?!

As a rule, we never used the football as an excuse, as we always did OK without the hundreds who could fuck it all up with their pissed-up antics but on this occasion thought that as it was a place we had never ventured to we would go along for the ride. I went on most of the grafts with Alex, a United fan, and we got a train down to London after fucking off Saturday's games, as Everton were home to Forest and United were away to Leicester. They were nothing games, so as usual we met on the way to London, leaving our domestic troubles for when we played each other at Goodison or Old Trafford.

The Transalpino ticket for a week saw you get change out of £50 and we got into London and caught the train from Liverpool Street to the ferry. It was on top from the first minute and every carriage was full of lads, all with the same idea: get over there on the piss or in our case the rob. It was a case of scarf up, head down and try and get a seat out of the way. It was probably full of West Ham or Chelsea but none of us bothered to ask. We were in the minority, as most of the United lads would have gone to their game and very few Everton or Liverpool went with England, so it would be full of Londoners who had watched their games and then set off for Europe straight after. One lad from Manchester who worked for British Rail was going via Amsterdam and was the only person we knew on that train. In those days, the Scousers were number one on the hit list of most, including the Mancs, so I was fucked; United were second on the list so it was a case of shut the fuck up and keep out of the way.

I think it was Harwich to wherever and, as usual, it was a case of get on the ferry, straight to the bandits and shackle every fucking one of them with the tie-wrap plastic strip which was the most important tool of our trade. We had the bandits boxed off and used to do shifts on them. It was simple but a top earner, you got your little piece of plastic wire and would rattle up 99 credits as fast as you could, while the other lads kept lookout. It was risky and you had to be fast but also careful as if you hit 100 it took you back to 0 and you had to start again. It was like having a wank and getting overexcited and shooting your load too quick, bang bang bang, 96, 97, 98, 99 ... oh fuck, back to 0, soft cunt, start again! We would then split up, leaving one lad playing the machine for nothing while we set credits up on another. It may take an hour at the most but with 100 credits you nearly always cracked the jackpot at least once on the crossing. Once the jackpot was hit, we would fuck off to the bar and an hour later the machine would be full again, as there were so many people on the ship wanting to play them on the level. The soft cunts were lining our pockets because, if they did win, they were usually empty, as the wire had been the only thing going in the coin slot!

On a good crossing, we would get three jackpots on each machine and they ranged from £20 to £50, so we could pull in £400 a crossing with ease. One Chelsea lad clocked us and I will always remember him saying, 'I like your style.' I knew he was after a touch and right on cue he added, 'Give us a bit of that.' He was fucked off but it was on top, as we had no option but to walk around with duty-free bags full of coins while he followed us. There was a big firm of Chelsea in one of the bars, all speeding their heads off; they will probably claim it was Charlie but in those days it was all speed and smoke. There were no major problems on the boat apart from these Chelsea taking the piss out of what few United were on there. There was only a few Mancs on board and they had to grin and bear it, as these gibbering Chelsea lot ripped them to bits verbally. I remember one of the braver Mancs who was pissed up saying to Alex, 'Wait till our firm get out there, we will do these Cockney cunts.' I also remember being glad that no fucker heard him, only us!

I was the only Evertonian on the boat on the way out, but on the way home I saw one of the younger lads, Spike, and he said he had got the ferry earlier and it had come on top with some Cockney Reds; the famous black fella had given him a slap and told him to fuck off to another country, so he went to Germany instead and didn't even bother with the game.

We got to Belgium and went straight into Ostend and straight on the rob, we had no interest in anything else; it was a case of get into the shops and clear up with anything we could steal. It was no good us trying to tag along with a firm, as we were not welcome, so we had to do our own thing. There was not much in Ostend, so we moved on to Bruges where we met a load of Hull lads who were on a minibus. After a journey with the London lot, it was good to meet a mob you could have a drink with and we went on the piss with them, as Bruges was played out by then and was a bit on top. There were also a couple of hundred England fans in town so we needed more space as we had not come over there to sing daft songs, smash windows and turn cars over. Loads of England had gone straight through to Luxembourg, which we thought was mad; what the fuck they were going to do over there for four days, God knows, but they battered it, in fairness, our mistake was ever setting foot into the place. We dossed in Bruges and then the next day moved on to a smaller town called Allst. It was a great little town, bang on, and we took the place to the cleaners. We had that much stuff we could not carry it all and were having to nick bags to put it in. We robbed these long designer padded leathers that were boss, fucking dead smart, we looked like the mafia in them. We travelled right across Belgium, loads of daft little towns, stopping a night here and a night there and robbing the place blind in the day.

We wanted in and out of Luxembourg on the day of the match so we were on the other side of the border the day before the match and we got a hotel there as our base and just popped over to Luxembourg to sound the place out When we got there, it was absolute chaos, total fucking bedlam. It was minus one, and as we got off the train the station was full of lads putting stuff in lockers and everyone had brand-new Ellesse and Fila bubble coats on, which, for the benefit of the younger lot, were priceless items in the early 80s; it was top gear, unlike today when even the fucking catalogue sells it!

We went in a bar and there was a load of United in there who told us that it was hard to get a drink as the Southerners had been smashing the bars up for two days. In one corner was a load of West Ham and a truce must have been called but it was weird all of them sitting on either side of the bar. We ordered a beer but never even had half of it when a young Manc jumped over the bar and banged the till – drink over, bar shut, fuck off out of here, cheers!

It was now getting daft, there were mobs of English playing up badly and I saw a normal bloke with his kids walking past and these total cunts were booting him up the arse shouting 'Come on'. These things were going on all over; it was not just isolated incidents it was worst-case scenario hooliganism, bang out of order, mainly down to ale but still not nice.

With no chance of a hotel and gangs walking around trying to have it with respectable people, we found a bar open but it was full on with the Cockney Reds. It was freezing outside and they were all trying to get us to sell them our leathers, all this 'Let's try it on first, mate' bollocks. Yeah, course you can – fuck off, let's get back to Belgium.

We got back to Belgium but by now the little town we had left in peace was overrun with England, everywhere you looked it was the same – smashed-up bars, windows going in, lads having tills off, mayhem! We scored some dope and I robbed a bottle of brandy and settled down in a small bar away from the lunatics. We met a couple of local girls and after drinking the best part of a litre of brandy ended up doing a bag snatch off one of them, which was daft but seemed a good idea at the time. I got chased all the way to the station so I jumped on this train leaving for Luxembourg which was full of England fans. The local police were already on the train and I ran straight into them with these screaming locals who had chased me, blurting out that I had some bird's bag. I got lifted and noticed that the carriage was full of lads and I was shouting to them to help me and they were all going, 'Fuck the Scouse bastard.' So that was it, I was nicked, the train was 100 per cent full of wankers. I was taken back to the bar and the girl was given her bag back, with a load of 'I'm very sorry, drunk too much, will never touch brandy again … honest!' It made no difference and I was locked up. The girl got everything back and I had drunk almost of a litre of brandy so I thought it was a bit harsh. What the fuck do they expect you to do after a litre of brandy?

The cells were a mare, there were a load of pissed-up Leeds fans in with me and every cell had about 10 lads crammed into them. The Leeds lot were pure cunts and they gave me total grief, they were pissing all over the place and for a few hours it was your worst fucking nightmare; one option – mouth shut, head down and hope that it was just a bad dream. Things took a turn for the better when all of a sudden a bloke opened the cell and everyone started to pile out. I thought we were getting released but one of these Leeds loons had lifted the keys on the way in and just opened all the cells; it was like the fucking Benny Hill show with us all running around after this fella as he rattled the keys and tried to open a big door which would have completed our escape. After a few goes, he found the right key and out we piled into a room full of riot police who quickly put their cups of tea down, drew their batons and ushered us back into our cells. The failed escape had a desired effect on them, though, as four hours later, they let us go with no charges, which was a right result. An old timer on the desk said to one of the Leeds lads that they were too much trouble to keep overnight and, as long as they left the town for Luxembourg, there would be no charges!

We all got the next train into Luxembourg and I was still that pissed that I took all my bags out of the lockers and took them with me which was a fucking daft thing to do and it was all down to the brandy. I dumped them at the station and the local police put on loads of free buses to the ground for us but the journey got the better of me and I made a drunken decision to get off halfway there and walk like a daft cunt in the freezing cold. The bus was full of England and they were doing my head in so it was another idea that seemed right at the time. I walked for ages and bumped into a firm of about 25 West Ham led by Taffy who were coming away from the ground. I soon sobered up and put my head down but, straight away, they were over asking if I was with United; they saw the mess I was in and give me a walk over, so fair play to them. One of them told me they had already had it with United in the ground and were heading back to town away from the police attention they had generated at the match – unfinished business, said Taffy in his usual psycho manner.

I got in the ground with no ticket and was in the wrong end but there were plenty of Mancs in there, keeping well away from the Cockneys in the other end. You could see the England lot doing a massive conga on the opposite side and the mood seemed good-natured but all the Mancs were giving it 'We're gonna do West Ham after the game'. I was not in the slightest bit interested, as someone else had said West Ham had robbed an ironmonger's of axes and massive blades and had told United they were getting it in town after the game.

Long before the final whistle, we did one and found a small café bar open. We should have kept a low one but Alex had leather off from by the bar, which ended up having a wallet in it as well so we had to clear off and set off back to town when basically we got lost. In the distance, we could see a big bridge we knew we had crossed before the game so we set off towards it when we clocked about a 150-strong mob coming towards us. We had no idea who they were and we were fucked. There was nowhere to run so we climbed on a ladder on the side of the bridge, which was mad really, as we were pissed and if we fell we were dead. You don't think of it at the time and, if we stayed put, we thought, we would be dead anyway, so at the time we thought we had nothing to lose!

They never saw us and we watched as they marched past when suddenly a mob came behind them in vans who turned out to be the Luxembourg Army. It was an unbelievable sight as they piled out and started making a load of noise, about 50 of them, all with their batons drawn and full riot gear on. The mob simply stopped, turned around and, bang, one massive shout of 'Chelsea' went up and they just piled straight into the army, no bouncing about, no 'let's keep it tight', just 'bang', straight into the fucking army who turned around and ran like fuck back to their vans! We followed the Chelsea lot back to town and it's like a war zone – windows gone in, cars on fire, fucking Cockneys walking around with mink coats on – nobody could do anything about it; the army had been legged so who was gonna stop it?

We collected our bags from the station and by now loads had seen enough and were jumping on the endless line of trains which were leaving. The police were low key; they had to be and were trying to get everyone out of the city to regain some sort of law and order to the streets. We thought, Fuck that, as the trains were full of these loons, so we started wandering about looking for a hotel when a van full of cops pulled us. We were put on a bus and I swear the back of it was full of Head bags, you could not see out of the back window. We were cuffed on this bus with loads of lads on and taken to the local jail where they told us they were confiscating all our bags, even the stuff we had bought back home, old jeans, socks, even fucking dirty washing, everything!

They went through it all and put anything decent into a separate pile of confiscated clobber. There was two coppers trying these fucking three-quarter padded leathers we had had on all day, and we were gutted as we had managed to keep them on our backs when the Cockneys and Mancs were trying to get them, and now the police had taxed them. I was bawling that our granddads had liberated their country and that they would be working for the Nazis if it wasn't for us. I could see them strip-searching Alex and they were all laughing because his feet were dirty and then shouting the other coppers in to come and smell them! They were all taking the piss that England hadn't qualified, but they were wasting their time on us and I told them to go and tell someone who gave a fuck, all I wanted was my gear back.

They locked us up, about 20 of us all squashed in a cell, and kept us overnight. They were pulling us out and interviewing us, asking where we had been and where we had robbed, as if you were just going to say, 'Well, officer, we had this from Belgium, oh, this was from that shop in the main street of your wrecked city, oh, and by the way, all this money is from the bandits on the boat!'

We lost all the gear but as we hadn't committed an act of violence we were released with no charges as the cells were full, literally overflowing with England fans. We had no money so we went to the Embassy and tried to complain that they had nicked all the clobber we nicked! Alex pressed the intercom and they wouldn't even let us in, four days' worth of robbed gear, for fuck's sake, and the women was on the other line crying, just sobbing, 'Please go home, you have wrecked our city!'

Back on the train there were plenty of new faces, apparently, we had missed a huge off at the station between Man United and the Cockneys, which was supposed to be bad. There were lads on the train who had the right idea and who had formed raiding parties, catching the trains into Germany, running into sports shops and snatching hundreds of pounds' worth of gear, it was a mental trip.

Eventually, we got back to Ostend with no bags, a few quid and our passports. We had nothing else to our name and it was a case of start again, so first bar we get in we have a bag off and pass it on to this young Manc Alex knew. He goes into the bogs and we waited and waited and then realise he has had *us* off – the complete trip consisted of the robbers getting robbed! We caught him later and gave him a pull; he was only a young kid called Chris and the older lot were going, 'Leave him alone.' I said who the fuck did he think he was? The Artful Dodger having Bill Sykes and Fagan off? So we took the dough off him and told them to keep their noses out.

We knew which ferries had the best bandits on, so let a couple go before getting on one that suited our needs. I fell asleep in the bar by the port and they couldn't find me, so I ended up running and having to jump off the side of the harbour on to the big door that the cars drive on because the passenger bit was closed with everyone on. The ferry bloke was going, 'You're fucking mad, you could have died.' As it was, the duty-free bottles I had lifted were the only casualties, so I was back to having fuck all again but my passport.

Homeward bound!

At the end of the day, we got home with a few quid, no clothes and it was the one and only time I ever went to watch England. It was a long six nights and I preferred to go in small gangs after that. I thought going under the blanket of England's finest would be a good decoy to fill our boots – it backfired. I was shocked that there were massive mobs from the likes of Hull and Burnley and clubs I'd never heard of, but I was quite simply not prepared for the scale of violence and lawlessness that I saw on that trip. It wasn't for me, each to their own. The day before and the day of the game were the maddest 48 hours of my life. You seriously had to be there to witness it.

Even today another lad who was with us laughs and always says, 'Everything was going great until you robbed that bottle of brandy!'

Steve, from Charlton, was also on this trip, even though he never made it to Luxembourg.

STEVE, CHARLTON:
Many of us going to this game viewed it as our last because quite a few of the boys were courting or in long-term relationships and, after fighting our way around Europe, it was wearing a bit thin. After good rows in Norway and Spain in which a few of us were deported, we decided Luxembourg would be a nice little boozy away game and we met in a pub to make our way to Dover. It was a good little firm, about 15-handed and mainly made up of Charlton and West Ham, plus a couple of Chelsea and Millwall.

Although most of us knew one another, some of the West Ham boys didn't like the Chelsea and Millwall boys and vice versa. So it was quite surprising that we made it to Ostend without any aggro! I remember thinking, if we made it off the ferry without trouble, we would gel, but the peace couldn't last and in a bar in Ostend one of the Chelsea boys stuck it on one of the locals, and quick as flash Mickey, a West Ham fan, whacked the Chelsea geezer, saying he was a liberty taker.

We headed for Brussels as Ostend was boring and we wanted to crank it up. A few of the bar owners warned us about the Brussels Police but it was a case of beers in brains out, and we boarded a train and a few hours later we were in Brussels, where we booked into a cheap hotel and hit the bars in the red-light area.

A few of the pimps and dealers tried to give the big one but we fucked them off, as we knew the Old Bill were always hanging about but after a few more beers a couple of the boys went to visit some brasses while the rest of us stayed in the bar. As we left, we all met up and set off back to the hotel. It was then that two pimps, built like brick shit-houses, came over and said someone had stolen money from a brass. This time they were saying they were going to do us unless we came up with the money and, although we all knew where it was heading, we tried to fanny our way out of it, but the more we talked the worse it got, with the added problem of the Old Bill sat near by watching.

We walked up the road and some of the boys went back to the hotel, leaving eight of us to find another bar. By 4.30 in the morning, we were mangled and as the last of us headed back to the hotel a Porsche pulled up and threw a couple of bottles at us. It was the two pimps from earlier and they drove off as soon as we returned fire with the bottles but only drove to the end of the road before spinning around. We noticed a skip full of bricks and metal at the end of the road and decided to do them if they came back. The Porsche was revving up so we loaded up and waited for them to either drive at us or fuck off. We didn't realise that it was a dead end and they had to drive past us, but, as they flew past, a brick hit the windscreen and the car hit the kerb and crashed. The two gorillas scrambled out and we let them have it; they were trying to crawl away but they had said and done too much all night and there was no mercy shown as we left them in the gutter. As we walked up the street, we were surrounded by vans full of armed police, batoned to the floor, handcuffed and taken to the police station.

We decided to deny everything, as it had worked in Norway where we were deported without being charged, but it didn't work here, as two hours later the rest of the lads were brought in from the hotel after being dragged from their beds at gunpoint.

Some were later released but the rest of us, including three of the boys who weren't involved with us, were taken to court. After court, we thought it was back to Ostend and deportation, instead we were taken to some Brussels nut-house prison. Three of us were put on the psychiatric wing because they said we had done the most damage to the pimps. We were there for six weeks and then released and told to come back for a trial. 'Some fucking chance!' We were given six months and a 10,000 francs fine in our absence.

The rest of the boys made it to Luxembourg where there was a lot of looting and violence and German troops were drafted on to the streets of Luxembourg to help out the hapless local OB who had lost control.

In those days, it was just another England away game.

No surrender!

The scale of violence throughout the trip shocked many and at times bordered on the unbelievable, yet the *Daily Mail* reported a very similar story to the ones told by the lads who made the trip. Leading with the headline '100 IN JAIL, AS FANS HEAD HOME' it went on to report, '1,500 English hooligans went on a rampage of destruction last night in Luxembourg, over 100 shop windows were smashed and six cars damaged; a man and his wife were trapped in their overturned car with petrol spilling on them.

'Earlier in the day, six England fans walked into a gents' outfitters in the centre of Luxembourg and threatened to destroy the shop if the owner didn't fit them out with suits; the owner complied.

'Another man who was delivering wine to a town-centre bar had his whole stock taken from him, dozens of crates of wine stolen from him by English thugs.'

Other papers reported that 50 England fans had been arrested in Ostend after coming off the ferry and fighting in the streets, while, in the Belgian town of Arlon, gendarmes were called after

20 England fans attacked the station master. A gendarme told a reporter, 'The English fans came off a train a few hours ago and began drinking heavily, chanting and singing songs, but they missed their train and began chasing it up the railway tracks; the station master tried to intervene and was attacked, and sustained injuries to his face.'

Luxembourg bar owner Anni de Nardo was also angered by the English invasion, during which his Moulin Rouge bar suffered £3,000 worth of damage, and he said, 'I wish I could go to England now with a machine gun, I would shoot the English people. Why do they come here and do this?'

Sports Minister Neil McFarlane was a little less controversial and he rather weakly protested that: 'I did warn the English fans not to get sucked into the violence!'

Unfortunately, but not surprisingly, Mr McFarlane's warning had fallen on deaf ears, and there were calls in the Luxembourg Parliament to ban any British sports team from ever returning to Luxembourg. A total of 500 civil police, 300 steel-helmeted police and half of the country's 700-strong army were mobilised, while weapons found on arrested English fans included axes, chains and tear-gas canisters.

Labour MP Peter Tatchell was a little more passionate and controversially was quoted as saying, 'Enough is enough, I would personally like to birch these swines myself, and tan their backsides! It makes you feel ashamed to be English.'

Reedy, a West Ham fan, was another who made the trip and, although he expected to be visiting Europe for about a week, he ended up staying a lot longer – and it was not by choice!

REEDY, WEST HAM:
At the time, I had just come out of a spell in the detention centre and got roped in to a trip to Luxembourg with another West Ham lad Glen. We got there five days early and went all over Switzerland and Germany and just fucking robbed every town we visited. In a few days, we had done a jeweller's. I had Armani jackets and leathers and bags full of clothes that we

just kept putting in the lockers, building it up. We got in Luxembourg a few days later and West Ham's firm had arrived by now, and to be truthful I just wanted to go home. I'd had enough of it, I'd been out there for five days and needed a break from it all. Once we met the lads, though, I decided to stay and within an hour I was back out thieving.

I nicked a camera but got clocked and was chased out the shop by the owner; he wouldn't give up and I ran for ages with this geezer chasing me. I knew our lads were in a Wimpy bar and I got near there but I was knackered and just couldn't get across the road because there was traffic everywhere and I have just collapsed through fatigue. So the geezer grabs my bag and takes the camera out while I'm on the floor trying to get my breath, but the West Ham in the Wimpy come out and think I have taken a slap from the geezer so they pile across and up him!

So I'm free again and am back on it and we had a go at another jeweller's. There were a few in there and, when the shop people were serving, I slid the glass on the window and put my hand in but I dropped a pile of gold. Glen's took over and got his hand in and grabbed a load of chains and put them in his pocket. Nobody in the shop clocked us but some fucking do-gooder outside has seen what we were up to and shouted some army or police over, so as we have come out of the shop there's Old Bill there. So, as we step outside, they pull us and tell us to empty our pockets, so Glen has tried hard to peel his pockets out without this big bundle of gold appearing as if he was Paul fucking Daniels but he was not even a poor man's Tommy Cooper, as he goes and pulls every one of them out. So I've had it on my toes and they've pulled out guns going, 'Halt, halt.' 'Course I'll halt! So I speed off ducking and diving through the crowd expecting to be shot in the back but nothing, they never even chased me and I'm away for the second time in an hour!

I found a pub that had a bar upstairs on the first floor and there were Villa, Portsmouth and a few other Northerners boozing up there as well as West Ham. Out of nothing, West Ham started performing as per usual and just started upping all the Northerners and they start going out the windows. The whole place just went fucking mad and soon we know the Old Bill's been called. So all the West Ham mob had it on their toes, running all round the streets, blind leading the blind, as nobody knew where we were going. We got into this bar and it is absolutely jam-packed with Leeds and we've got in there thinking they would be decent cover, the last thing on our mind was to start performing because the Old Bill had chased us all round the streets and it was getting a bit on top. Before we had a drink, a Leeds geezer's barged my mate Micky and got a bit clever with his attitude, and Mick was thinking, Let it go, because we need to keep a low one from the Old Bill, but I've looked at him and said, 'Don't suffer that.' I quickly pulled a tin of gas out and just sprayed it in the Leeds geezer's face, so the keeping a low one has gone west and it's erupted again. We've come outside and I just remember some Northern skinhead looking at us funny and I have gone up to him and said, 'You all right, mate?' as I put my hand round him, at the same time knocking him out with my left hand, then another pal come along and opened his scalp up with a Stanley knife and it's time for toes again.

I ended up in a shoe shop with Loughton and a couple of the lads, and we were in there trying shoes on, when the Old Bill come in, drag us outside and put us up against the wall. I've managed to slip out of it and I just remember one of the Old Bill putting his hand in Loughton's jacket and pulling an axe out! That was it for me – three lucky ones was enough and I was running out of lives, so I met up with the lads and decided to go to the game. But that was another bad call, as it was just fight after fight with the Northerners. I was fighting so much I've either fractured or sprained my right hand which was my best hand, and I couldn't fight properly, which was a bad thing, as when we were in the ground with a few other Under-Fives it went off with the Mancs and we were just running into each other for the full 90 minutes. I'm there with one hand, fighting the whole fucking 90 minutes just left-handed!

We came out of the ground and there was about 100 Mancs there – City and United were even sticking together as they had been having a rough time of things. There was me and just one more West Ham, a lad called Roddy, walking down the road. They had this kid, little Eddie, who was like their mascot, the equivalent of Jela at West Ham and the twat was bouncing in front of their mob, going, 'Come on, West Ham!' Come on West Ham what? There was only fucking two of us and, although it was bang on, there was no way we were running but just keeping a nice distance on our toes knowing he's got 100 of them behind him. Because we didn't run, we got away with it and they didn't come into us, despite the mascot egging the older ones on. We were lucky, though, as they could easily have battered us with the numbers they had. We got into the station and a few minutes later Chelsea's mob come along and they had good numbers and, a minute after they went into the station, all the Mancs came running out of the exit, it was fucking brilliant. Chelsea ran them everywhere.

By now, there were all sorts of police squads pulling in anyone who looked like they may have been up to no good; the place was wrecked, the OB had been chased and by now the army were having a go at reclaiming the city. I knew I had had a good run – I'd got out of three nickings, done a hotel, done the jeweller's, done loads of clothes and finally done the money out of the hotel we stayed in after the game. Good runs don't last forever, so the idea was to get out of there early in the morning. Plenty of West Ham had been deported but come back again to get their clobber and by now everyone was going home but the Old Bill were patrolling the station and I was in two minds whether to grab my clothes and try and get through them or wait another day. As I sat there wondering what to do, the police

left the station for a couple of minutes so I grabbed my bags
and went to get a train to anywhere – it didn't matter where,
I just had to get out of Luxembourg. That was when my luck
ran out, as I was trying to look like Johnny tourist with six
bags and a busted arm when, out of nowhere, the Old Bill
came back in and nicked me.

So all the lads have gone home and I'm the only West Ham
left. I got banged up in prison, just 18 years of age, with
about six Mancs, a black geezer, Mike, who was City, a few
Salford, a few Man United who were from Wigan and
Cannock, a Cockney Red, a Burnley skinhead and a couple
of Chelsea geezers from Brighton. The press were taking
pictures at the prison and we were in all the papers as the
ones who shamed England.

We were on remand so they let us out every day and we
used to play football with the foreigners – or locals,
depending on which way you looked at it! One day, we were
playing football and the foreigners have turned on us at the
end of exercise. They've kicked the ball at the Man United
geezer and it's hit him right in the chest and he fell on his
arse. Well, these Mancs have just stood there and none of
them have said a word. I said, 'Don't fucking suffer that,' and
picked the ball up and kicked it right in the foreigner's
bollocks. We then had to walk up the stairs all mixed together
and I could see this cunt shuffling up the stairs towards me so
I just thought, I'm not having it, and I turned round and
kicked the geezer in the face and I'm fighting with him on the
stairs before it was sorted out and I was thrown into my cell.
Afterwards, our lot were coming in the cell telling me this
geezer was in there for murder, then his lot were coming in
going, 'English' and doing the cutthroat sign so I lashed out
at one of them and all the Mancs kept saying, 'Leave it out,
West Ham, you're mad, leave it out.'

Things calmed down and we got into a bit of a routine in
there, you could buy two beers a week and we used to save
them up and then get pissed on a certain night. In between

the monthly drink binge, we used to smoke fucking peanuts to try and get high, we just wanted a buzz and even tried smoking banana skins!

I had my off days and one night I picked the bench up that was in the cell and tried to break us out. Another time I upset them – their hero was the German bird Nena, who used to sing '99 Red Balloons', and they've got a big poster of her on the wall in one of their cells; anyway, this foreigner has come up to have his daily wank over fucking balloon bird and I've gone to him, 'Come here, see her,' and I cut the poster to bits. I went, 'Me, cut it to bits,' just winding him up and he was like growling ready to go, so I told this Chelsea geezer to smash his bed to bits. He had to sleep on a bed where his mattress was completely gone through the bottom so they moved us away from them as we were causing them too much grief.

I got on with most of the English, apart from this nutty Burnley skinhead, so one day when he had a visit I went into the tuck shop and used his name, spent all his money.

So I'm lying in my cell with a big pile of food, fucking drinks and fags on my bed. And he's come in and gone, 'Give it here, it's mine, you bastard.'

And all the Mancs have started to back him up and were moaning, 'Go on, give it him, West Ham.'

I picked up a knife and told them to back off and they did – they thought I was nuts, they were all geezers, all bigger and older than me, and they let me get away with it. So I called Burnley in and gave him a pack of Treats but kept all other stuff. I look at it now and I think, Fucking hell, how did I get away with all that? At the time, it was just normal to me but with hindsight I know I was lucky not to get done over or sectioned!

One thing that stood out for me in that prison was that half the time the screws guarded you and at other times it was the army and they were the ones who took no messing. I kicked off with someone when they were on duty and they ran up the stairs to get me. One of the Mancs give me his coat to put over my head and I'm in the cell trying to hide when they burst in and suss me out. I'm trying to hold on to the radiator but they've bounced me by my hair all down the stairs and all over the cobblestones. They dragged me into the governor's office and they told me that from then on I couldn't use the same exercise yard as the normal prisoners, I had to go in a private one with all the lifers as I was too violent and vile.

We were awaiting trial with the recommendation that we all got a year, but in the end I truly and honestly believe that I caused that much havoc and so much disruption that, before the trial, we got a pardon from the King, who just wanted us out. We were more aggravation than it was worth. So, just before Christmas, when we had done nearly two months, they told us all we would be released if we agreed to pay a fine.

This well-known pop band somehow got roped in on a campaign to get us freed as one of them was connected to someone who was locked up with us and they claimed they paid the fines to get us out which was bollocks. I had a video camera at home which I had robbed and one of them gave us £250 for it which they put with the money to get us out of there. For the publicity, one of them came over and paid the money for our release; she's sitting there with the press and they've let me out of one entrance and she's sitting outside another one, so I've gone to the station and she's not there. I've come out, the train's just about to leave and there is nobody else there. I had to bunk the train and the ferry all the way home because I didn't have a penny to my name.

When I got back, they were all over us again, they appeared in London as quick as they had fucking disappeared in Luxembourg, and I got a call about going on the telly with them. The Cockney Red didn't want to go on it so I went on there with a Chelsea geezer and these popstars are saying how it was a disgrace and we were good lads, but the night before I had been in a fight and I'm standing there next to one of them with a fucking big black eye!

CHAPTER SIX
GRAFTERS
FRANCE '84, PART 1

For many years, Premiership managers have moaned about the 'pointless friendlies' that interrupt the smooth running of their clubs. Today, they are deemed worthless, as wholesale half-time changes have become the norm and even many top-class players are known to pull out of the games with 'mystery injuries'!

But it was not always like that, and there was a time when it still meant something to pull on the England shirt and to represent your country, and, in fact, many players on the fringes of the international scene have used such games to force themselves into the reckoning when the serious tournaments kick off.

The fans have never felt the same way as today's overpaid and overrated 'superstars'. Going away with England has always been the highlight of the season for many, while, for others, it has been a way of making a few quid while on a jolly. And for a dedicated few, it has been the best way of obtaining serious money, as a city full of drunken boisterous football fans can act as the perfect foil for gangs of thieves and robbers out for easy pickings in places where security is not as tight as it is back home.

Colin Blaney is a 50-year-old Man United fan, and for three decades has been in and out of jail in many countries, and has 'earned' hundreds of thousands of pounds stealing everything and anything that wasn't nailed down while touring foreign cities.

The authorities call such people thieves; Colin and the people he worked alongside simply looked upon themselves as 'grafters', which was the title of Colin's book.

COLIN, MAN UNITED:

One game we did was in '84, when England played France in Paris. Think we got beat 2–0, although why I say 'we' fuck knows, as like most of the lads at United I never gave a flying one for the national side. We had been at the grafting lark for a few years, and any game involving England or United in Europe saw small firms of the lads on board as the pickings were easy and the money that could be earned was far more than some of the cocks draped in their flags would earn in a year. We called ourselves the 'Wide Awake Firm'.

Most people have the Mickeys down as the main thieves; let them have the tag, but I can swear our firm from Manchester were the original grafters and we were the main firm at it for over 20 years. The Scouse lads had some top thieves and blaggers but mainly concentrated on the sports shops and were happy to look the bee's knees and earn ale money and a few nights out in the Grafton. We were into the jacks [Jack and Jills = tills] and the tom shops; we were after serious money, although there were times when we had to take what was on offer, which in those days was plenty!

We always went on the Hull to Rotterdam ferry using blag student cards. A single trip over was £17 and included two meals which gave you a top buffet breakfast and a dinner of the best steak and chips. In between meals, we would hit the duty-free shop with the word 'duty' deleted, and, 400 Regal, a couple of bottles of Bells for the old man and a bottle of squirt for the lady later, the trip was paid for and we were in profit before we had got into Dutch waters!

Every trip had the same start, off to the Dam, score some weed, then off to wherever, and a new adventure would unfold. This time it was Paris, picked purely as England's following would be in their thousands and that made our job so much easier. We left all the fighting and scallying to the 'bulldogs' as we called them and there were plenty off their leashes in Paris. This game was on all the news and scenes of battling in the ground was beamed back to ITN and Moira Stewart to have a moan about; what they never witnessed were the riots all over the city miles away from the stadium. Surprisingly, Derby and the usual suspects West Ham were the main firms there, and the Cockneys were really running any Man U out of town, just like they did in Luxembourg a few years before.

When we got into Paris, we soon sussed out that the other firms at that time were miles behind us on the robbing front. The first high street we scanned around for a kop was full of England's wannabe thugs trying to turn into thieves, and they were running out of shops with crates of cheap ale worth buttons and clobber that you wouldn't wear unless you were going to a fancy fucking dress.

They were the perfect foils and, while security and the local police were chasing after them, us well-dressed oust Landers, as we were called, were clocking for tills and casing the place for small safes. After a quick snatch of the day's takings, we slipped into taxis away from the mob and deposited the cash back at the hotel. By this time, we'd been at it seven years and in our eyes we were untouchable. We were well dressed, polite and had plenty of cash, so hotel staff wouldn't blink an eyelid when we wandered in and out all day. They were more concerned with the hooligans trying to sneak the contents of the minibar and a few towels and soaps on rope bearing the hotel crest out in Head bags, rather than worrying about us They probably blamed the hooligans and not us the following day when they realised that there was £200 missing from the bar till!

Sometimes, we took the game in, other times we never bothered, depending on how we had got on; a good graft was not worth losing because the local police tarred you with the same brush as the thugs, and many a time we would be on the ferry before Emlyn Hughes had tossed up to see who would kick off. Paris had not been great, the locals were far more clued up than the Swiss and Belgians so it was a case of going to the game and seeing what came up on the way home.

In the stadium, the bulldogs were all together on the bottom tier but above was a mix of England and French, and mingled in were a load of Algerians. At half-time, the fights had just started up above and now at the middle section where we all came together for drinks and bread rolls, etc, it went nasty for us. The main lot of East Enders bashed around the locals and then turned on us. It was pointless but they had this North–South thing in their heads and most of our lot all got either ran out or run down. It was no better after and we met up at the main station in a bit of a state to say the least. The truth was Man U in those days were never the keenest with England, although it is fair to point out that Man City have always had more of a hardcore base on the international scene. Even combined, which we never liked doing, the Manchester firm was on a hiding to nothing, so it was no surprise when we all put the White Flag up and fucked off sharpish into Belgium.

The following day in Antwerp, lots of England with monster heads were all getting their last piss-up in the red-light area while we got offside for a mooch. We had divided the jack money up and the lads were very relaxed, as we all had a nice few bob and when in this mood you don't really have to push it, and it's amazing that these are the times when a wedge comes crashing your way.

As we were having a wander around the back streets, we clocked a small family-run tom shop, which was owned by a Jew. Two of us got the bloke talking, while my brother slipped in the back and went upstairs. He was outside in minutes and we knew he had had a touch, as he never even gave us the nod. Back at the hotel, he lobbed a small cashbox on to the bed and we cracked it open with a small jemmy bar. The contents dropped out and we noticed nothing special, a few bits and bobs in mixed money, few American Express dollars, etc, what we didn't realise at the time was that the biggest kop we'd ever had was now in our laps. A small envelope contained three Ice Russian diamonds which were in a special plastic mould complete with a chip that could be slipped into a PC and the cut of the diamond would come on to the screen. There was also a sheet with all the info and receipts from 10 years before, stating this fella had paid over £10,000 each, so they were worth far more now. It turned out these diamonds were not for rings, etc, but for cutting and we knew 100 per cent that we had hit the jackpot as, even at 10 grand a throw, in 1984 that would buy us a decent semi out of town each.

We decided to stay another night and let the bulldogs return home under police guard, so moved away from the hot spot and booked into a jolly hotel and stashed the tom. We hit the red-light area where surprisingly many of the England mob were still in full bulldog mode. We tried to swerve them and hit a bikers' bar with the England lot next door, so we could smoke a few joints then get a Chinese and get a good kip dreaming of our wealth and starting on the property ladder. In reality, we knew whatever we got for the gems would be blown in weeks on ale and drugs, but we were dreamers and reality only ever kicked in when we were skint and back on the ferry to Holland with the blag student cards.

As we were leaving, our kid sat on one of the locals' Harley Davidsons and was laughing saying he's gonna blow his fortune on one and bike all over Europe grafting. In seconds, it kicked off, apparently, sitting on their bikes is like shagging their birds and they came out all swinging bars and bats. I hate to think what we would have got if the England mob had not been next door and the battle went on for a good five minutes with us having to drag our kid out from under a car after he'd been KO'd. We got him in a taxi up to the hospital where we all needed patching up. After about half an hour, we had just got out the main doors, when a dibble van pulls up full of bikers and locals all in urgent need of help. We swerved them and got back to the hotel. We were that paranoid we buried the diamonds in the bottom of a plant in the hotel corridor and the next morning dug up our treasure. We were over the moon once homeward bound via Dover, which was the best in those days for us to pass through and was never really on top.

Back home in Manchester, we touted the gems via a few old contacts but they were out of the local fences' league. One bloke gave us a few ton deposit and told us to enjoy ourselves while he sorted out a well-known firm called the Quality Street gang to come and view the things, which we were now desperate to unload, as every fucker in town had heard about them. We were walking around like we were top dogs dressed in all the best gear and we all had Tissot or Longines watches, and gold Dupoint lighters. What we never realised was that, overnight, from being a gang of sneak thieves, we had set ourselves up for an almighty fall and, sure enough, the next day it came.

These blokes from the Quality Street met us and we gave them one gem. Off they went and left us in a pub with a few of their mates. It was freeman's all day and we were treated like the main men we thought we were; they took us to pubs and we met more blokes in long cashmere coats who normally didn't give us the time of day. These were the real deal and the respect they had from everyone was awesome. In one pub, we were told they needed the three stones and the paperwork to gauge the price they were going to pay us. We argued that one was all we were handing over but the pub was now full of their men and we reluctantly handed over the three, thinking it was the last we would see of them. The mood never changed and they passed them around, and our heads were spinning trying to clock who still had the fucking things, but the main man assured us that we would be well looked after until a price was agreed.

After a while, another bloke came in and we were told he

Three Lions

Paul Ince

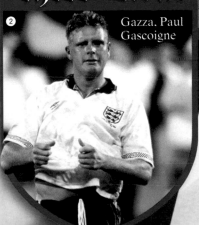

Three Lions

Gazza, Paul Gascoigne

Three Lions

Terry Butcher

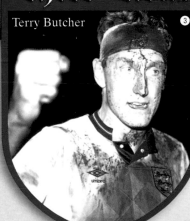

Scotland's football fans The Tartan Army didn't celebrate their team's victory over England at Wembley – they mutilated it!

Above: "Deutschland Hooligan, Deutschland Hooligan!" the Germans with flare guns and gas wanted to know in and around Dusseldorf station during Euro '88.

Below: Down the road we see a mob of Dutch front up the English prior to the game between the two countries. Be afraid – as this firm contains orange barmies wearing Viking helmets, plus all their troublemakers sporting mullet hairstyles.

Mad dogs and Englishmen.

In the eyes of many the rivalry between Ireland and England was intense but friendly:a myth blown out of the water after the Dublin riot shame that caused the game to be abandoned after just 27 minutes.

(14)

Above: Riot police clear Trafalgar Square when events turn ugly after England lost a penalty shootout with Germany in the Semi-Finals of Euro '96.

Below: Police break up fighting soccer fans gathered in Trafalgar Square after England defeated Scotland 2-0 at Wembley stadium during Euro '96.

(15)

England fans clash with the Italian riot police at the Olympic stadium in Rome during the '97 World Cup Qualifiers.

'It was an Italian firm, pure Italian: all greasy hair, Lacoste and no bottle!'

was the top man. He called us over and shook our hands, telling us that the diamonds were the finest he had ever seen. I was thinking, Ten grand each, go on, you cunt, tell us how much and let's get the fuck out of here. He then looked at us and said in a low tone that we had brought it on top for ourselves by thinking we were the main men; at the end of the day we were a gang of rough-arse Mancs from Collyhurst and we still had a lot to learn. He then told us that this day was our most important lesson and I began to think that the dark reality was that things were going amiss. In my mind, I was getting desperate, I thought, Ten grand between us will do, mate, just get fucking on with it, but still hoping for at least twice that. Then he told us that we were getting nishman's for the haul. Not one fucking penny! He told us to keep our heads down and whenever we got anything else he would give us a fair price, but on this day our wages was paid with advice, and that was that. If we thought we were the business, we had a lot to learn. I had tears in my eyes, and with that the place emptied and we sat there with not a penny in our pockets to get the fucking bus home.

The Wide Awake Firm had been caught napping and it was lesson learned.

Believe it or not, a few weeks later, we got some Rolex watches from some gaff and the Quality Street found out. We were gutted and expected the same outcome, but the bloke was true to his word and gave us more than a fair price for them. We dealt with them for years and, thinking of it now, they probably did us a favour teaching us a lesson, as we were too big on the scene too soon and that kind of money in our pockets would have probably seen us press the self-destruct button. Lesson leaned or not, it was still a long walk home that night.

Still easy come easy go!

CHAPTER SEVEN

WE'RE WEST HAM NOT ENGLAND
FRANCE '84, PART 2

Trips to Europe watching England were just an excuse for many lads like Colin Blaney to go in search of 'wages'. For years, Liverpudlians had been calling Switzerland the 'Big Scouse Warehouse', and most clubs had lads who went away with England purely 'on the rob'. Many more went for the football and the drink and a hardcore went just for the violence. Right from the very early days when England fans began travelling abroad, there has always been in-house fighting but there is one name that crops up time and time again as major instigators in the problems caused between people who are from the same country and speak the same language … West Ham!

The trip to France in '84 saw some of the worst in-house fighting ever witnessed at an England game and, true to form, West Ham were in the thick of it.

Will is a Man City fan who lives near Stockport and who has followed City, County and England home and away since the 70s. After years of trouble between rival English supporters, which many believe began in Luxembourg in 1983, he is now on reasonable terms with the West Ham fans who have been on the scene as long as he has and the Stockport County lads he used to go abroad with. But that was not always the case!

WILL, MAN CITY:

I was working at Hatfield when the France game came along and as such arranged to meet the lads in Shakes Bar outside Victoria Station. It was a Persil vouchers trip for the boys, that wonderful era when everyone was travelling for free, thanks to the washing-powder company.

I was already in the pub when the lads arrived about 15-strong. There were some West Ham already drinking in there, and they decided they didn't like everyone turning up mob-handed so Taffy and his mate decided they should have a word with a couple of our lads. Unfortunately, his not-so-polite request to leave ended up with him and his sidekick getting a slap from a couple of the Stockport lads. There were a few little kick-offs all over the pub, which ended when one of our lads whacked a couple with a coat stand. The numbers were about even, and West Ham left the pub and we stayed put and had another drink before catching the train.

Later West Ham claimed that this little off was Chelsea and, of course, the might of the ICF had seen them off – sorry, but Taff must have been on the drugs, Chelsea were not in there, it was Stockport and they did the 'doing'!

We got on the train and nothing much was happening, although when we got on the boat it was clear that was not to be the case. Our first purchase from the duty-free was a bottle of Blue Nun each and it wasn't for the shite wine; the feeling was that the bottle might be of more use, especially when word got to us via Chelsea that West Ham had been canvassing the Southerners with one of the comments being: 'You're not going to let them Northern cunts come here and get away with taking liberties, are you?'

So they had just done Chelsea and were now asking them to help them do the Northerners – work that one out!

At this time, I started to feel sorry for a couple of Blackburn who had attached themselves to us, as on the boat were over 100 Chelsea, 80-odd West Ham and approximately 30 other London fans, who were not about to team up with 20 Northerners, 75 per cent of which were Stockport fucking County!

Halfway across the channel, it went off good style; West Ham and Chelsea decided they didn't want to be mates any more and bottles, stools, glasses and basically anything not too tightly screwed down got involved. Just as quick as it kicked off, it quietened down again, as the law and the captain appeared and there was no further incidents, which suited the Stockport and Blackburn alliance just fine!

When we arrived in France, the inter-England rivalry subsided as the lads found a load of brand-new cars waiting for export with the keys in! How fucking stupid can you get? Lads would rob the bandits, the duty-free, the cabins and the ship's cat if they could have caught it, and then they leave a load of brand-new motors open with the keys in?

Cue dodgems, with the sea and each other as the main obstacles. There were quite a few casualties, mainly cars which were driven to the end of the quayside and pushed into the sea.

Taffy's little gang couldn't – or wouldn't – forget the Shakes incident, and words and threats were extended all the way to Paris but somehow we managed to keep apart for the whole time in Paris with a couple of minor exceptions. I ended up booting one of them down the terraces and another County lad threw Taffy's hat on to the tube line after the game as a direct challenge, which the infamous one backed away from. In the ground there was fighting throughout the game and West Ham were the main culprits; there were French and local immigrants fighting with the English and then there was West Ham fighting with anyone who crossed their paths.

There were lighter moments, though, and one of the funniest things I ever saw was when the local Gestapo gassed our metro train and the Chelsea boys pulled on the swimming goggles and piled into them, train fare free, ale expensive, the look on the local police faces – priceless!

The day after the game, I managed to snag myself a cheapo flight back which would let me get a couple of days' work in.

I gave my train ticket to one of our younger lads who had managed to get from Stockport to Paris with less than a pound to his name and, as was the case in those days, he actually got back with more than he went with. He told me that on the train home the lads managed to liberate a few cases of vintage wine and also by mistake opened one container that was full of live eels which were released for the rest of the passengers to play with!

Another lad on the trip had been nicked at York a few weeks earlier and got away with the old false name and address gag, but he managed to get stabbed in Paris by one of the West Ham lot and his picture made the papers. His five minutes of fame backfired as the copper from York recognised him and turned up to meet him off the ferry!

A final word on the West Ham attitude to England games: while they were never at every game, when they did show, which was usually at close overland games, they were always mob-handed and always had this attitude of 'We are West Ham not England'.

Most of us thought, If that was their attitude, why fucking bother going?

Most England at the time just ignored them and let them get on with it as we had enough problems at away games from the locals and police without worrying what they were up to as well.

I've always subscribed to the theory that club differences are best put behind you on England duty, as you never knew when you might have needed each other; it was a theory that West Ham did not agree with and, because of that, you were always watching your backs when word got around that they were about!

Reedy was one of the West Ham lads who didn't share Will's theory. He was at the game in France and his story backs up the Northerners' claims that West Ham were indeed a law unto themselves!

REEDY, WEST HAM:

We used to get the Inter-Rail cards where you can travel all over Europe for buttons, so me and Glen have gone grafting all over and bagged loads of clobber. We made it into Paris the night before and we've joined up with Lee who was Chelsea, Jason H, another Chelsea geezer, and Keith, who was Arsenal. They were lads we used to have it with but we're going round Paris in the middle of the night, just young lads, and we're thinking were safer together as England. We were trying to cream all the hotels, do the safes and that and they were good lads. But then, of course, the day of the game comes and they was a bit wary of meeting the other West Ham, so we have gone, 'No, no, you'll be all right,' which was a bit optimistic but worth a try.

Anyway, we meet up with some of the older West Ham lads and all the others and the look on our guests' faces was: 'Fuck! It's on top!'

One of them just grabbed Keith round the head and says, 'You're all right, but know where you are and who you're with!'

I did plenty of boxing as a lad – one time I went in the ring with those fucking Thais abroad and did OK – so we're going round the ground and I'm knocking geezers out. Any Northerners I could lump, and I'm still 18 here, and the Chelsea geezers are counting them. They're going, 'Fucking hell, Reedy, that's another one.' I remember doing a geezer from Leicester and they said, 'That's nine on the spin!'

We needed tickets so we go up to this French geezer who thought he was a bit of a Spiv and I went, 'Have you got tickets?' So he's got his tickets out and I've gone bang! He's gone flop, one punch and out, and I've grabbed his tickets and got us all in the ground.

In the ground, it was just kicking off everywhere and I remember picking up a barrier and running at this little firm, who were Turkish and French or whatever. Now, as West Ham do, I've ended up right at the front and gone into the

French mob but ended up going through them and out the other side! They are still fighting with England and I'm at the back of their fucking mob and the problem is these lot have all pulled out blades so England can't get into them and are having a bit of a stand-off. You've got England here, the French there, and I'm behind the enemy lines and I've got to get back through there and past the blades. Anyway, I just run through them and I got back amongst our own, but I honestly thought I was going to be stabbed to death.

On the train on the way home, I've got all my clobber that I've collected through the thieving and I've crept round the buffet and done the till full on, away with all the money. Problem was I have got all this clobber and a load of money and the French are screaming, looking for the person who's robbed the till. Before they collared me, I managed to pass it to Paul from Barking but, as we got off at Calais, they took all my clobber off me and, after doing so well, I went home with nothing but sore hands from knocking Northerners out!

People used to complain that we were always upsetting everyone on these trips but at the end of the day we didn't give a fuck.

We were West Ham not England!

CHAPTER EIGHT

I SAID I'D BE BACK!
NORTHERN IRELAND '85

The political problems in Belfast have for many years caused a divide between the British and Irish people and, while it has rarely affected the football clashes between the two countries, as the Northern Irish supporters are predominately pro-British, it's unlikely that the streets of Belfast would welcome a gang of English hooligans with open arms!

Since the Troubles began, England have played many times in Belfast and on only one occasion in over 50 years, when the terrorist threat was deemed a major security risk to the visiting players, has the fixture been switched to Goodison Park.

Before the World Cup qualifier in February 1985, though, very few lads had ventured to Northern Ireland, as quite simply it was regarded as unsafe for the British troops in body armour and carrying guns, let alone hundreds of scarf-wearing football supporters wandering around Belfast drunk. English people in general were targets of the IRA at home; those that ventured into Belfast were looked upon as very brave or more often plain stupid!

In 1985, things changed and Mark Chester – 'Jasper' – was one of a select few who decided that the place was worth a visit. Whereas many of the other hooligans on the trip had never been to Belfast before and were unsure what to expect, Jasper was in no doubt it would be a dangerous journey.

A year earlier, he had completed a tour of Belfast with the British Army, and, when the draw was made for the World Cup, he was determined to make the game, as, unlike the rest of the lads out there, he had unfinished business to attend to.

Mark is the bestselling author of *Naughty*, and in December 2005 released his second book, *Sex, Drugs and Football Thugs*. Respected all over the country by fellow hooligans and fans alike, this is Mark's story of his Northern Ireland experience.

MARK, STOKE:

Once we had stopped and gone to ground, my sweat-soaked combats turned cold and were uncomfortable to wear. Glad of the breather, I was also very much aware that I had now gone from being a moving target to a sitting one! I lost my balance briefly and for a second fell clumsily backwards into the garden, the weight of my weapon and ammunition taking me over. I knew almost instinctively from my training not to stand back up immediately, so I regained my composure and moved professionally back into my knelt prone position just inside the ageing rotting-wood gateposts.

Bomber, our section commander, looked over from his position across the street and hand-signalled me to see if I was all right and ready to carry on. I was and, regardless of how much the pain in both my knees was killing me, and beyond the thought of wanting to be back home with the lads down the match, I signalled Bomber back. Prepare to move then, came the next instruction, and all four of us darted from our cover running in a zig-zagging movement, before breaking back into our normal pace street patrol several yards later.

I was completely enchanted by Mr Mellor, my history teacher at school. He didn't lead me to believe but taught me to understand that, to be a man in our country, you had to serve it first. He went and did it, as most men of his age did, but then again I now know that their generation were one of the last greats in our prolific history, and what they achieved for us through sacrifice and guts was, as it stands today, unappreciated and seemingly easily forgotten. As, no doubt, my own time serving in Northern Ireland will be too!

Thanks for everything, lads, we will just all turn liberal now and give it all away at the negotiating table. Oh, and by the way, stick around because, if it all goes wrong, we may have to call on you and your brave friends – those that are left that is – again!

And do you know what? The craziest thing is that those men *would* be there again and always will be. To put it bluntly, politicians live in their world and we live in ours. They get trigger happy with speeches, while Average Joe is the one that is on the end of the incoming slaughter! That will never change and it is for that reason alone that I find myself patrolling the streets of Crossmaglen, South Armagh, for Queen and Country on a crisp spring morning in 1984. And, not reluctantly either, I was proud to be there!

We went to ground again, only this time there was a real problem. One of the section had picked up a distinct tone in the earpiece of his Fast Chimp. The series of fast-moving bleeps he was hearing alerted us to the fact that somewhere in the near vicinity there was a concealed explosive about to be detonated. We moved no further, as Bomber alerted the other two sections in the nearby terraced streets of our situation.

As the gunner of our section, I was placed at the rear, and went to ground again in the gateway of a small heavily overgrown garden. My senses were pinned with excitement, my mind racing as I set up the two legs of my LMG machine gun, then settled calmly down behind the sights and prepared my breathing. I so much wanted a proper contact. One with a full-on gun battle that lasted for minutes instead of the usual sniper shit that we had been dogged with since the beginning of our tour. Over the last three months, I had been verbally abused, physically punched, kicked and spat on, shot at twice while in helicopters and even fucking mortared early one Sunday morning after I had queued up for two hours to use the phone to ring my friend Turney back home to see if Stoke had had it off with Arsenal the previous day. I just about heard my mate tell me that about 60 Gooners had come into the town centre and got run badly when the phone went dead. How inconsiderate was that!

Combine all that with the fact that, as I was preparing to go into combat that morning, I was carrying a green booklet inside my jacket pocket with the Rules of Engagement that categorically stated that I should only return fire once we had been fired upon and then only if we had sustained a direct hit and I could positively identify the perpetrator of the attack! Well, thanks a fuckin' lot for those set of rules then, I might as well just stand up and say 'Yooohooo, we are over here!' and see what happens!

And that is exactly where all the frustration came from. Not just for me but for all of us. We were there taking a load of shit and not being able to give it back. Our hands were tied by the very people that sent us there in the first place!

BOOOOM!!! A car bomb explodes hundreds of yards away up the street sending its bonnet 30-odd feet in the air. No spectacular flame display like in the movies but just a large hollow thud and plenty of smoke and screaming from shocked passers-by. No carnage, no fatalities, no sign of the perpetrators either, just a direct message from them saying that you're in a place where you are not wanted, soldier, now leave.

When we did eventually leave, the Grenadier Guards relieved us, the 1st Staffordshire Regiment, of our duties. I remembered back to the first day of our own arrival in Ulster. How, when we got off the Chinooks inside camp and ran in line across the small helipad to take up our positions, I couldn't help noticing the smiles and relief on the faces of those Royal Green Jackets as they ran passed us to board that chopper out of there. Today, our expressions were the same as theirs had been. We were all happy to be going home, most to see their families and loved ones, me to get down the match to be with mine. Happy to be going home but frustrated to hell that we hadn't had the chance to give some of the shit back. One day, I swore to myself, I'm coming back here, and that time I was going to punch some fucker's head in! Guaranteed!

Nine months on. I'm now a civilian forging out a new existence with a dishonourable discharge from the army weighing heavy on me. They (the army) had taught me to stand broad and upright like a true Englishman should. They had put a gun in my hand and made me deadly with it. They also showed me how to repress certain emotions, and how to react in a split second. How to remain courteous and respectful at all times. Be loyal and honest and, most importantly, they taught me how to fight with no fear of the consequences. Charming, then, that my crime in their eyes was to be a football hooligan, who remembered to use all of the above attributes but chose to use them elsewhere.

Elsewhere to me was following Stoke City Football Club, the new battlefields were the terraces and streets that surrounded any of the grounds in any of the cities and towns in which Stoke City played.

The new regiment! The Naughty Forty!

The rest is history!

I spied Richie from some distance away. He walked at pace, politely avoiding other pedestrians and occasionally managing a smile to the odd pensioner as he should. It was not a match day in Stoke, yet Rich had that purpose about him that led me to believe that, whatever it was he was up to that morning, it had a football connotation to it. I chuckled and darted into the doorway of a bookies before he could spy me and deny me my element of surprise. Too late! Football lads don't usually miss another football figure being shady ahead, no matter how busy the street is.

He smiled, and we shook hands. The greeting was short and swift, typical hoolie style, a nod and a wink and a quick scan of the street each way to make sure we were sweet before we broke into conversation.

'Seen the World Cup qualifiers, Jasp?'

I now realised that the four shopping bags that he was carrying containing a dozen boxes of Persil washing-up powder was for a specific reason. Persil were doing a rail-voucher offer. The more vouchers you collected, the more free rail travel you could get. And that included across Europe as well.

'No, I haven't seen them yet! Who have we got? Where are you going on the train?'

Beaming, Rich replied, 'Finland, mate! Me, Podge, Hoss and a few of the others are going to rob Scandinavia blind!'

'Nice one, get me a couple of nice trackies then, Rich! Who else have we got in the group?'

'Erm … Turkey and … oh yeah, Northern Ireland!'

My jaw dropped in sheer delight! 'You're fucking joking me! What, home and away?'

'Yes, mate, home and away! Windsor Park in Belfast on 26 February 1985. You going?'

The evil glint in my eyes answered Richie's question for me! I took a carrier bag and the two of us boarded a bus to Trent Vale to see if we could muster a few numbers up for either of the trips. In my mind, particularly the one to Belfast!

I mulled it over in my mind as I stirred my bowl of pea and ham soup continuously. Who, out of the lads I knew from down the match, would want to come with me to a bomb-blasted city, where an element of the local population hated our guts and detested everything we stood for? I sympathised to a certain extent with a few of the concerns raised at the next home game. But I certainly did not share them!

Twelve of us had decided to make the trip in the end. Four would travel by car, six would catch the midnight flyer from Crewe to Stranraer and the other two would catch the first train the very next morning. Not a massive crew by any standards but not bad for our fledgling firm of the early to mid-80s, taking into consideration we were all aged between 17 and 20 at the time!

We met in a dodgy backstreet boozer in Crewe and drank

heavily before we made our way on to a ghostly quiet deserted platform just before midnight. The film *The Warriors* flashed briefly across my mind as we spied two other solitary crews of young men stood at either ends of the platform. We arrived in the middle of the two groups and stood confident, exchanging silent glances with each other. Were they friends or were they foe? In the hooligan world, there is a thin line, if any, between the two!

I spoke briefly with Wilson and Eddie. We discussed discreetly who we thought they might be, and acknowledged that if they were unfriendly they would surely have both kicked off with one another before our arrival. Maybe they were the same as us and only wanted to have it with the Irish and stick together with the English. The looks on their faces told me that they were now thinking the same as us. Without a word, all three groups closed in and introductions were initiated. Almost immediately, a strange little alliance based mainly on the fact that we were Northerners was formed. Six Stoke, four Birmingham Zulus led by a tall white lad called Simon and four Bolton whose spokesman was a mixed-race fella called Vaughn. In the brief discussion we shared before the sound of a moving train could be heard approaching the platform, we all expressed our concern about what Cockney firms might be on the train and, most importantly, what the outcome of our appearance might be!

The engine lights appeared as the slow winding train continued on towards us. There was a nervous edge to us all, but that is what makes this life so exciting; most of us thought about taking a couple of steps back and having a look at the situation. But none did. We were getting on regardless. How can you possibly deny your own body such an extreme rush of adrenalin and excitement at a moment like this and then live with yourself the next day? It doesn't bear thinking about!

Total fear was the next emotion to have an ice-cold grip on my body! In the space of 60 seconds, I had been hit by them all. Up and down, in and out, round and round, your mind spins! And all of a sudden you are hoping that your startled and bemused shocked-like state is not as obvious to the 20 or so evil and nasty-looking faces that are crowded behind the yellow-tinted window of the carriage that has just passed by you.

'Fuck!! Who the hell are that lot!!?'

None of us could take our eyes off the window, as the carriage's occupants all stood up aggressively and gestured to us to come in and join them!

'Oh shit!! It's West fucking Ham! It's the ICF!'

I can't remember who it was that came out with that remark, but I do remember the feeling it gave me. Yes, we were all expecting there to be some Cockneys on the train, and yes it made us edgy, but for me it was a real thrill being terrorised by West Ham above all of the other London mobs! With a real fresh wind of excitement, I was the first of our group to board the now stationary train – albeit several carriages further down the train, if I'm honest!

We found our spot and filled the tables closest to the lavatory with our bottles of Blue Nun wine and cans of Harp lager and sat down. After a minute or so, the train began to creak and slowly pull away, resigning us to our fate. Or West Ham's fate, whichever way you want to look at it!

Several minutes later, two youths of similar age to us appeared and timidly approached our party. We were becoming like a set of mercenaries banding together in a common cause. We asked where they were from and they said Cheltenham and asked if they could join us, as they were worried about what they had seen after the train had left Rugby.

'Why, what happened, mate?' Wilson asked, as he handed each of the new arrivals a can of lager.

They told us how a couple of Tottenham fans much older than us, probably in their mid- to late thirties, had been targeted by several members of the ICF. Once the two of them had dropped back off to sleep after scanning the platform at Rugby Station, as most people do while travelling on a train, the ICF had crept into their carriage, the one that the two Cheltenham fans had just boarded, and rather casually doused the legs of both men in lighter fuel. The Tottenham fans were then lit and West Ham left the carriage and let them burn! It was something and nothing really, as both victims awoke and put each other out before it became life threatening. All the same, nobody felt like having a quick kip after hearing that story.

Their account of proceedings might well sound a bit far-fetched but I can assure you such was the feeling of ice-cold tension on that train we all believed them, and an hour or so later I saw for myself that what they'd told us was true!

I leaned over the table in front of me and whispered into Eddie's ear, 'We're going to have to keep it fucking tight on here, mate! This could turn well nasty!'

Eddie took a slug of cheap Scotch whiskey from the bottle and grimaced back at me. 'If it comes, Jasp, we'll just have to get straight into them or we will get caned!'

If anyone can remember back to those heady days of the 80s following England, there was no Transport Police keeping an eye on things then. You were on your own, and looking back that was what made it so good!

I sat in deep thought and reviewed the situation unfolding around me. Nine months on from leaving the army and Ulster itself, I find myself heading back there – to a place where most levelheaded people would avoid at all costs. But I was glad to be going back, as I personally had some unfinished business to attend to there. Just like the first time I went, on 14 February 1984, Valentines Day, I was scared again, and enjoying that feeling again also. But this time I wasn't scared of the terrorists and what they might do to us, as I had already been through that. No, I was more scared of the 20 or so West Ham United fans sat only a 100 yards or so away from me, who at any given moment might walk through our carriage door and turn that midnight sleeper into the Nightmare Express! As for the rest of the lads I was travelling with, well, for the moment at least, they were just on the ICF thing. They had never encountered bombs and terrorists before, but I was sure as hell certain that, if we did all survive this train journey, it wouldn't be long before they did!

Preston came and went, Penrith approached, and still there had been no sign of any of the Cockneys. And then someone tempted fate by mentioning the fact that they had not bothered to approach us! On cue, the door to our carriage slid slowly open and he stepped casually inside.

He stood as bold as brass, scanning the carriage and its silent occupants at his leisure. He was alone but may as well have been surrounded by hundreds more, such was the weight he carried with his aura of an East End hooligan with a countrywide reputation. He looked down to our table and at Wilson in particular, who was in the seat closest to him. The silence was excruciating for us all and it seemed an eternity before he opened the dialogue. In a slow methodical movement, he reached forward towards Wilson and ran his finger around the leather collar of his brand-new purple Pooh jacket bought especially for the trip.

'That's a nice jacket! Give it usss!' He carried on the 's' sound at the end of his word almost like a snake hissing before a strike – adding more drama to an already moody situation.

Wilson, as young as he was, was by no means a mug either and I sat opposite him with my stomach forcing its way up my windpipe, as I watched my best friend's glaring eyes following the sweep of the Cockney's intrusive finger. Coat inspection over, Wilson remained seated but looked the man directly in his eyes, before saying in a gutsy manner, 'Take it!!'

He held his stare for what seemed another eternity before the man spoke again, addressing us all and not Wilson in particular. 'Where are you boys from then?' He had covertly dismissed Wilson's defiant challenge as either good humour or bottle, only he knew which!

But now the unfolding situation had awoken Eddie who raised his face from the pile of vomit he had fallen asleep in. Eddie was harsh and direct with his comment! 'We're fucking Stoke City! Why, who are you?'

Personally, my guts started to churn with a sudden bolt of fear combined with an aggressive excitement at the challenge in Eddie's manner. This situation could now go either way and we all knew it. But the Cockney remained ice cold in his demeanour, regardless of how he interpreted our mood. 'Stoke, eh!' His eyes gave a slight movement as if remembering by-gone days. 'You boys are all right! You stick with West Ham over there and you'll be OK!!'

With that, he was gone. Maybe to fetch his boys to come and give us a slap? Or possibly to remark on a game little crew he had found three carriages down, who might be of some use if it went off with the Irish? Who knows! But he left us without another word and that was that. Quite literally!

'Jesus Christ, that was Taff Eldridge!' came an excited remark from within the group.

Nobody disbelieved who the man was. Like none of us disbelieved the Cheltenham lads' story about the Tottenham supporters being set on fire.

When we did eventually arrive at the ferry terminal in Stranraer early that next morning, on leaving the train I noticed a large contingent of Scottish police officers at the end of the platform awaiting what looked like to be our unwanted arrival. As I walked with the others slowly towards them, I saw something else. Two rather smelly and charred-looking Tottenham Hotspur fans with newspapers placed under their arms stepping out of a carriage and casually going about their business of following the national team, seemingly unmoved that only hours before they had been set alight while sleeping. Set on fire not because of the country they came from, but because of the North London football club that they followed. But that is football, and that was what following football in the 80s could be like at times. So, do you stay at home and watch the highlights later that night on television? Or crack on and get on with it for club and country! I know which I'd prefer to be doing!

In a couple of hours' time, we would all be pitting our wits against each other once again. This time within the confines of a sea ferry. Looking back, I can see the slight concerns of the other 80 or so England fans, as they queued up nervously to be body searched alongside a not overly arrogant but well confident tight mob of the ICF. I remember thinking to myself as I saw them together in their pack, Thank fuck we have had our grilling on the train, because, for those that had not, the ferry must have seemed like they had woken up in a nightmare onboard a sinking ship! Let's face it, there was no hiding. No hiding at all!

Without any further incidents – well, none that we saw or heard of anyway – we passed through the passenger terminal at Larne and made our way, unaccompanied by police, by rail again into Belfast city centre.

West Ham continued to be like a magnet with their pull over the rest of the English, and most that came from the same fraternity trailed along with them, albeit from a comfortable distance. Us, in spite of Taffy's kind invite, decided that we would do our own thing and rob a few clothes shops. You know, pick up a bit of knitwear for when the temperatures dropped later that night! After several hours of non-stop walking and searching, we decided that, apart from the Benetton shop which had already been robbed blind, there was little else worth taking a risk over. So we headed to the bars and started to drink heavily in preparation for whatever conflict might come our way. By midday, it was quite clear to one and all that the England following for this fixture was going to be minimal. At a guess, it was just short of 500, and mostly hooligans!

For most of the afternoon, we stayed closely together, Stoke, Birmingham, Bolton and the two kids from Cheltenham as well. It felt safer to have the numbers and few ventured off alone! Now it had sunk in where we all were, and all the *Panoramas, World in Actions* and news bulletins screened from the province that we had all seen as children now had a taste and a smell to them too! The realisation of living amongst fear and intimidation had kicked right in – the haunting sounds of continual sirens, too many sirens near and far, and the nervous glances at the sound of anything untoward that at home we would take for granted. A slamming door, a car back firing, a drunk farting loudly at the bar all brought a response from those that surrounded us. In all honesty, it was a little unnerving for some of our party and, as the afternoon continued and the Belfast sky grew darker, the tension about us intensified. For whatever reasons, our new companions drifted away until there was just the six of us Stoke left together alone. That's OK, who needs passengers anyway? After we have sunk these pints, we will head over towards Windsor Park and suss out the score with the match tickets. Pass us the skins first, I will knock us one up!

We were happy in our own company once again, even though several comments were passed around the table, while we all sat and watched Eddie in a drunken oblivion, as to how hard it must be to be a serving soldier over here, and how when you mentioned the word 'soldier' the pub took to a four-second silence, before returning to just being wary!

It was time to leave the city centre bars and head to the ground in search of match tickets which none of us had. But first we had to find some new underpants for Eddie who had fallen asleep in a cubicle after filling himself full of diarrhoea. Wilson and I entered on our final robbing spree and returned 20 minutes or so later with the biggest pair of Woolsey Y-fronts imaginable, and the only thing worth robbing all day. We helped our friend clean himself up and dressed him again. Well, you've got to look after your mates, haven't you!

With that done, we left the pub and as a farewell gesture Eddie's shit-soiled undies were flung over the bar towards a man who had not stopped staring at us since the moment we had walked in the place. The weighty underpants were dodged quite neatly really but still found a proper resting place. Right on top of the Irish whiskey bottle that held centre stage on an extensive row of optics.

'Have one on us, you Mick bastards!' Wilson chirped with a sneer, as we left the pub and headed off for some more uncertainty. Normally, I would not have found that kind of behaviour too amusing, even though I have been fascinated by poo parcels from an early age myself. But today I cared little as to who was abused or upset. That was what I had come back for. And remember I still hadn't punched anybody yet!

We moved quickly in unison as a team. Our cocky casual hoolie strut (a trademark of anyone from our culture) keeping us different from the rest. Just how we liked it!

We passed by the Europa hotel for possibly the fourth or fifth time that day, and noticed a small gathering of other hooligans leaving Robinsons, a pub opposite. We slowed with caution but continued to cross over the road, as mischievous temptation always gets the better of a careful mind. We wanted to know who they were, where they were from, had they been fighting yet that day and were they about to go and do so! Oh, yes, and did they have any spare tickets for the game?

Botch, a member of our group, immediately pointed out, 'These are Chelsea!' Familiar with one or two of them, mainly because of his right-wing tendencies, he raised his hand as a gesture. It was accepted and shaken firmly.

Within minutes, we were listening to their story of how they had travelled over on Hickey's coach and that members of their group had travelled along the Falls Road in taxis looking for a punch-up. This story coincided with what Wilson and I had seen when we were out getting the Y-fronts for Eddie shortly before. Four maybe five taxis had pulled up along the pavement we were walking along. When the occupants got out and saw us, one man started to laugh and speak to me and Wilson, telling us where they had been and that it was that rough even the kids were firing at them with air rifles from the rooftops. The man who was speaking to us was quite thin and had an unconventional haircut for a hooligan. What I remember about him the most was his huge smile and charisma.

I looked at Wilson as the Chelsea fans outside Robinsons continued with their tales and said, 'That was Hickey before, mate!' I sounded chuffed that I could say I had met him!

'I know, Jasp! They are all over here, aren't they!'

We walked on together away from the Chelsea heads. In my mind, particularly, I was wondering if the Chelsea firm had bumped into West Ham yet, and what would happen if they did.

Time was moving on and the six of us decided we had better head off towards Windsor Park, a good half-hour stroll away. It was pre-mobile phone days, and, after not bumping into Richie, Woody, Brasso or any of the other Stoke lads who had travelled separately to us, we anticipated they would be hanging around the ground eagerly waiting for us to make a show.

We walked along together, looking for any sign of some trouble that fortune might throw our way, as well as sharing exciting stories of well-known people we had met and madcap things we had witnessed along the way! After a mile or so, we hooked up with four Geordies. The Newcastle United fans were all at least five or six years older than us. They were not particularly Casual in their dress sense either, but, all the same, they were there for the same simple reason as ourselves. They told us that earlier on they had been drinking with the same West Ham lads we had encountered on the train. By all accounts, they had all got on together and the Geordies were full of nothing but praise for them. A good job then really, because a half a mile or so along that road we chanced upon them again as they left another drinking den.

Acknowledgements were thrown about and almost as natural as a spring lamb being born in a dew-filled field we were amalgamated as one. Fifteen West Ham, four Geordies and six Stoke. That was the England crew that crossed the railway bridge directly behind the stadium and got stuck into the first major row of the day! It was now 6.30pm, pitch black and sinister. The hundreds of mural-painted buildings and bombed-out homes merged into the blackness creating shadows that haunted your thoughts!

Together, we crossed the bridge with confidence! We looked solid and showed no fear at the immediate sight of a packed-out public house just to our right. It lay in the shadow of the ground's floodlights, under the burning glare from high above.

Outside the pub were several hundred Ulstermen, many carrying the Cross of St George with the red hand emblazoned through the middle of it. To our left were several parked-up land rovers and a dozen or so of the RUC who brandished long sticks and carried sub-machine guns. They acknowledged our appearance but made little attempt to turn us back! If at any time any of us were fooled into thinking that those men congregated across the road outside that pub would welcome the arrival of 20 or so Englishmen, we were hopelessly mistaken! Almost immediately, a demonic roar thundered into the night and we were attacked full on. We were heavily outnumbered physically and stunned psychologically by the sheer weight of the hatred they carried for us! It seemed all we could do was stave them off, as all and sundry charged towards us. My split-second glance over to my left to weigh up the police situation showed no response from them whatsoever. It seemed that for now the RUC were more than happy to let battle commence. Which I thought was rather generous of them when you consider how far we had all travelled to do so!

'STAAAND!!!' went up the roar from the ICF, as we filled the width of the road, our arms outstretched. Now on a personal note I was disappointed that we were not facing a charging mob of Catholics, but there was little time for sentiment or change of heart! Death and hatred were in the faces of the front rank of their Orange army, as they set about imposing that very sentence on us! In the 10 or so seconds before the first blows were traded, I was surprised at how Casual some of our attackers looked, several wearing those leather and suede patchwork jackets that had a rounded neck with leather crisscross ties similar to what Robin of Sherwood wore. We had obviously missed the shop that sold them on our robbing spree that morning!

BANG!

The two mobs clashed head on in a flurry of punches and kicks. We moved slightly backwards as we staved off the attack, but found a tighter formation as the bridge gave us some security from any would-be side-on attackers.

'FACKIN STAAND!!'

West Ham were holding it together with their ingrained confidence. But in all honesty it was the Geordies who were right in the middle of the fighting. Blue lights suddenly appeared to our left. The RUC had decided we had all had enough fun and were about to disperse the two feuding mobs.

Knowing it was almost coming to an end, and taking into consideration that for most of the 30-second attack we had been slightly on the back foot, the ICF gave it one last massive effort and three of them in particular led us all in a charge right into the depths of their still attacking mob.

This was it! This was my chance to fill a little bit of that hole in my guts that I had carried for months and still do to this day. Chin tucked in, I chose my target only feet away and launched a solid kick into the man's bollocks, dropping him on the spot. A blow cracked me across the shoulder; I winced but still moved forward looking for another quick shot before I got back on my toes and away from arrest! The noise grew even louder as men roared on the battlefield. Got him! He was already reeling to the side from a blow off one of the Cockneys, so I just finished him off with a sly peach of a hook!

'GET IN THERE! I SAID I'D BE BACK, YOU CUNTS!'

Gritted teeth forced my saliva to froth out of the corner of my snarling mouth! I was at the top of my buzz and loving every fucking second of it! We all were! Outnumbered and away from home, England were having it off, and more than holding their own as usual!

Seconds later, the noise level was still the same but the fighting had broken down into scuffles, as the Irish tried to break the police cordon we were now surrounded by. I grabbed Wilson and we hugged each other hard before shaking hands with the Geordies and likewise with the ICF! All together as one, we were moved on through another cordon and left to make our own way around the ground. Freedom again within minutes of battling. Left to go and do it all again. Those were the days, eh!

The fight on the bridge had been a stand-off at the end of the day. Neither side could say that they did the other. Although, when you take into consideration that the English were heavily outnumbered and made no attempt to disappear back from where they'd come from once the hostilities had begun, I think it is safe to say we got the result on merit if nothing else!

Twenty-seven thousand and five hundred people crammed into Windsor Park on that cold night. We were told not to travel without tickets. It had been bandied about in the press for weeks that we would face fortress-like conditions, and it would be much simpler to stay at home. Funny that, because I got into the ground by hurdling a turnstile, as did Wilson. Eddie got in under a fence and was thrown out almost immediately for being drunk and disorderly. Ten minutes later, he was back inside and stood with us behind the goal of the away end we had been placed in. We were gathered in after the game, which we had won 1–0 courtesy of a Mark Hately goal. Pretty much all of the 400 or so people had gained entry by one ticketless means or another. Bribery was mentioned a couple of times too!

Nevertheless, even though England had nicked the result on the pitch, we still had to try and get home in one piece and the RUC had a struggle on their hands trying to stop the locals from killing us!

The Irish kept up a continual bombardment of house bricks and bottles as we were walked slowly along. But you get bricked everywhere you go anyway, so that did not bother us one bit. The car bomb a street or so away did raise a few eyebrows though, but mostly brought chuckles!

Most of the English wanted to head back to the port of Larne, some had to hang around for Hickey's coach, and the four Geordies were more than happy to try and resume old acquaintances with the mob that attacked us on the bridge. But little was going to happen – not with the RUC being in the mood they were in. No-nonsense tactics worked that night, and, even though we were continually ambushed and attacked, we never got one opportunity to retaliate in any way!

Chuffed with the fact that I had returned to Northern Ireland and had managed to get a bit of revenge off my chest at last, as I dodged another house brick, I thought to myself, Let's just get back home safe to Stoke. Home nice and safe and tell all the lads about our little adventure across the Irish sea.

Anyway, I thought, you never know, England may well draw Eire in a competition one day and play them in Dublin. With a wry smile on my face, I turned up my collar against the cold and promised myself once again. England v Ireland in Dublin!

Now that is another fixture I would not be missing!

CHAPTER NINE

THE BACK OF BEYOND
FROM ALBANIA TO SLOVAKIA

When England kick off against Trinidad and Tobago at the 2006 World Cup Finals in Germany they will be the 80th side we have played at full international level. From Albania to Slovakia, the A–Z of opponents reads like a world atlas, and at all of these places visited for the past 30 years England have been well represented by a loyal and hardcore support, many of whom have followed them around the world and back.

There have been problems off the field on many of these trips but even some of the so-called undesirables are also loyal supporters, and the press and authorities should remember this when they slate the country's followers at the first sign of trouble.

Danny from Hull missed only a handful of games over a 10-year period when England were as poor on the field as they were good off it, and he was one of the hardcore fans despised by the likes of the FA's Ted Croker, simply because they did their own thing and refused to be part of the official tours Croker and his cronies organised!

DANNY, HULL CITY:
Being a Hull fan meant you were brought up with affection for our national side. We always had one of the largest followings with England, because, like a lot of the smaller

clubs, we never played in Europe, so holidays and savings were available for England away trips. In the late 70s and early 80s, Hull City were in decline and our only escape was away with England. My first trip away was to Denmark in 1982 and it was crazy. I remember keeping the papers for months after and reading the headlines over and over again.

There were 26 England fans arrested after fighting in the ground and what could only be called a riot after; it was a great night for a young lad to make his debut at an England game. I will always remember the trouble in the ground after they equalised and people were trying to get the game abandoned.

It is funny the kind of things you remember, and I always laugh when I recall that obese MP Cyril Smith saying we should all be birched and stoned – the birching was taking things a bit far and everyone was already stoned. You would think he would be more concerned about losing a bit of weight and giving his heart a chance, but he typified the Liberals and plenty of other publicity-seeking politicians at the time.

I learned a lot that night, the main thing being that, although the Danes had some big lads, the facts were that, when it went off, they had no bottle!

After that night, I was hooked and, even though I was a £30-a-week apprentice, I tried not to miss many games. The next one came around too soon and I couldn't afford the trip to Greece but listened in awe at the next game as the Chelsea lads told us all about the serious problems they had out there. Chelsea were the largest contingent of England fans at nearly all the England games in those days and I made some great friends from London. Unlike West Ham, they made you feel welcome, and they were a great set of lads.

I was in Luxembourg when the place was taken apart by what was, in my opinion, the best ever collective mob of England, and also in Hungary, which was probably one of the scariest trips at the time but, looking back now, I would regard it as one of the best.

The best year of my life was in 1986 – I was earning good money abroad and went to England games in Egypt, Israel, Russia and Canada before making my way to the Mexico World Cup via the USA. I flew to San Francisco in the May so I could go up to Canada for the game in Vancouver. England won 1 0 and I spent about a week up there before travelling down to Mexico on a Greyhound bus route via all the usual tourist spots like Vegas, Phoenix, etc. I bumped into a couple of West Ham fans and a Colchester lad I knew from previous England games while in Dallas. Then it was down to Monterrey and I spent about a month there and it was fantastic, even though it was one of the most humid places I have ever been to.

I saw all three games there against Portugal, Morocco and Poland, and the local Mexicans were brilliant with the English. I don't think there was any trouble there, even though we had a couple of thousand fans out there. They were great people, great women and a great place to go on the lash. We even arranged friendly football matches with some of the locals that their local newspapers and radio covered, although, funnily enough, our press lads didn't show any interest in the proceedings!

While I was there, I met up with a couple of other Hull City mates and, along with some Southampton and Chelsea lads, we went down to Acapulco for a week. We booked a hotel on the beachfront, flights from Monterrey, via Mexico City to Acapulco and it cost us $104, which at the time was 60 quid! After that, I spent just under a fortnight in Mexico City for the Paraguay and Argentina games, After that game, I saw the first and only trouble during my time there when a few carloads of Argies drove past a bar we were in singing and playing up, not realising that there was traffic lights which were on red, forcing them to stop and take a bit of a shoeing.

A few of us went to the coast and stayed in a place called Zihuatanejo for a week as we didn't want to hang around for the final and we spent a couple of more weeks up in

Monterrey before going around the United States for a month, as we had plenty of money left due to the cheapness that was Mexico!

Over the years, I have met plenty of the players and they were usually OK. I met Bobby Charlton in Mexico and Peter Shilton and Gary Lineker in Egypt. Shilton had a great rapport with the fans and was one of the most respected. The press were always sniffing around and I always did my best to avoid them after the infamous 'throw this brick through the Argentinean Embassy window so I can take a picture for cash' offer to an England fan in 1982.

In general, I found most places were decent, Albania was probably an exception to the rule, but, if you can survive places like Ayresome Park, your Turkey, Greece and Polands are a breeze!

Danny mentioned Hungary as a best and worst experience; another fan who made that trip was Lewisham from West Ham.

LEWISHAM, WEST HAM:
This was a game I'd always remember as a scary one; we were in some great big stadium that only had about 20,000 people in but less than a thousand were England fans with about maybe 200 of that being mob. Right at the end of the game, the Old Bill had kept us in for about half-hour and, when we came out, we lost all the idiots and had a nice little firm which was being led by Hickey. We went into this station and it reminded me of Earls Court – you had the double platforms with bridges at both ends – and as we'd gone on down the stairs, on the other side of this platform was all this firm of Hungarians. All of a sudden, Hickey has gone, 'Get yourself together here, boys, it's gonna happen here!'

He was a master at that kind of thing and he was spot on, as all the Hungarians had began running down the platform towards the bridge at the end of the platform, with us doing the same thing in their direction, resulting in both firms meeting at the top where it's gone right off! All the Hungarians were like greasers and they all had chains and it's gone right off; we got stuck into them and ended up getting the better of them before we got back on to a train when the Old Bill turned up.

Hickey ordered everyone to stay tight, knowing that it would be on top at every station we pulled into and it was another good call as there were mobs of them on every platform and the old train windows were going through. Eventually, we pulled into Budapest main central station and that battle lasted for ages and a few of us, if we are honest about it, will say that we were not too disappointed when the police got it under control and rounded us up!

Later on in the evening, we had gone up to the Hilton hotel because that was where all the players were staying and we always liked to pop in and say hello, as you do, but we got talking to a *Daily Mirror* reporter who told us that, when we were fighting at the station, there was 1,500 Russian troops on manoeuvres being transported back to Russia by train, and, apparently, the fighting and the rioting was that bad that the local government were considering calling the troops back to sort us out! You can easy look back and think it was nothing much but, at the time, after a day on the beers, this went down like a lead balloon and it quietened us down a bit!

At games like that, where not many people used to go and everyone knew everyone, there was no club fighting, and it was in Hungary where Hickey formed the England Away Firm, the EAF, very simple and not very original but from then on we called ourselves the EAF, as it was a quality little firm of all the regulars that went everywhere!

Games to the Eastern Bloc increased when the boundaries were opened and many of the smaller states were liberated and gained the right to compete at international level. Many of these places were dangerous, though, and the police and locals had little or no respect for the English fans' reputation. One such place was

Slovakia, and both Mick, a West Ham fan from Portsmouth, and Stretch, from Bristol City, had frightening experiences over in Bratislava, before, during and after the game.

MICK, WEST HAM:

We flew out of Luton on the morning of the match on a well-organised trip and landed at Bratislava in the pouring rain. We had coaches waiting to take us to the hotels, and after checking in headed to the town centre and toured the bars that were packed with England fans. The mood was good and as the beer flowed the songs started ringing out, and the only problem was the weather as it was still pouring with rain. The lads that had arrived the day before told us it had been raining non-stop since they had arrived on the Friday morning, and we started wondering if the game would even be on.

As kick-off time grew nearer, we were told the game was going ahead and we started to make our way to the ground. It was a cold and wet walk but there was no problems from the well-behaved England fans but as we walked along you could see these large groups of Slovak Police dressed like robocops, and their faces were hidden by balaclavas so all you could see was their eyes.

That day, England had Ashley Cole, Heskey, Ferdinand and Dyer playing, all black players, and, as we know following from football abroad, some of the host country fans are very racist, and on this occasion the home fans started to throw coins towards the pitch and at England's black players and started singing and gesturing what you could tell was racist nonsense. Then the coins started to come towards the England fans and I remember looking towards the fence, as two England fans started to rattle it, and that was all the robocops needed as they came through the flimsy fencing and, with batons drawn, started to lash out at anyone in their way. Our first reactions were to help the women and kids out of the way, while trying not to get a clubbing ourselves.

England went on to win 2–1 and we left the ground after the customary lock-in while the ground emptied, and descended on the area just outside the ground where we were met with large groups of our friendly local police with drawn batons and covered faces. After a chorus or two of 'God Save the Queen', we moved on towards the centre hoping to have a pleasant late-evening drink but that wasn't to be, as the bars were all closed. We managed to get a drink at a hotel some England fans were staying at and the night passed with no problems. As our flight wasn't till Sunday evening, we passed the day away sightseeing around the bars that had been forced to close the night before.

The first bar we went into had the highlights of the previous evening's entertainment highlights and headlines of England's violent fans; it was a joke and everyone knew it, all that happened was that the police battered innocent people and treated us like shit. We get used to it but I will never understand why we do, nobody else is treated as poorly as the English are and, although the fans used to be a major security risk, it is time the police treated us for what we are now instead of living in the past.

STRETCH, BRISTOL CITY:

We had flown in from Heathrow to Vienna and had got to Bratislava on a coach that one of the lads had booked in advance to pick us up from the airport. We had 10 spare seats on it so a couple of the boys went back into the airport to flog the spare seats so we could get a bit of our money back. As luck had it, they flogged the seats to a few Chelsea lads who jumped onboard without knowing we were all together. Chelsea had the 'We're here, lads' attitude, typical Chelsea, until they realised the whole coach was another mob then they went a bit quiet! They even thought they were travelling on the cheap but in truth they had paid double what we had paid, and that night, when we were drinking in this bar which was called something like the Kelt Bar, every other round was 'Cheers to Chelsea' because basically they had paid for us to go on the piss for about four hours in Bratislava! The poor Chelsea lads couldn't understand whenever someone ordered another pint they would turn round and raise a glass with a 'Cheers, Chelsea'.

Later on in the evening, with the weather absolutely pissing down, someone said things were looking a bit lively and we went to have a look round and moved on to another bar. We were in there when a mob of kiddies came around the corner, sort of locals, skinheads and some beefy-looking guys that were all tooled up. All of them had a baseball bat or a cosh and they sort of gestured towards us to keep walking. They moved like a real tight unit and looked like they could do some serious damage but we decided to follow them, and next thing you know you could hear like fire-crackers which turned out to be shooting.

It was this little firm who obviously had an agenda, and it turned out that the bloke who ran the bar we had been in earlier had tried to close it but nobody was moving, so he had made a call and all the local bouncers had turned out and, when they saw the mob we had, they even fired a few shots into the bar to let everyone know they were for real!

When we got back down there, a kid was on the ground who had been shot and there was total mayhem, and it soon got worse when the Old Bill arrived on the scene. We legged it straight into a load of them and they got a bit jumpy and trigger-happy; they started shouting at us and, when we stood our ground, they just fired tear gas at us. Lads had been on the lager for a day and some kiddies started to pick up the tear-gas canisters without realising how hot they were. You could only get them about two foot off the ground before you'd have to let go of them so what they started doing was the old rugby drop-kick with them and were booting them back over the police lines. Before long it was getting out of hand and we made a decision that, if there were real bullets and tear gas that we were up against, then it was time to get back to the hotel!

When abroad, the general feeling is that, if you can stay clear of the local thugs, bouncers and the police, then usually you will also stay out of trouble, but that is not the case in some countries and Darren from Mansfield will vouch for that after watching England play in Moldova!

DARREN, MANSFIELD:

In 1998, 10 of us flew to Bucharest with the plan of catching a train from there on to Chisinau. Once in Bucharest, we decided to go on the piss and, after a few beers, we ended up meeting this Russian geezer who had got talking to one of the lads. He kept asking us if we had money for Moldova and, even though we kept telling him we were all right, he insisted on taking us to some bar. When we walked in, he got the locals to move from their seats and they looked scared to death by the presence of this bloke and did what he told them. He then got the barman to bring us drinks which nobody seemed to be paying for and it was weird really because he would only talk to one of our boys and he spoke to us through him. He kept telling our mate that we should buy Moldovan money from him because we'd get a better deal. We thought he was going to try and rip us off, so we let him have his say but mainly ignored the cunt. He kept buying the beers, so we just enjoyed the hospitality He was just like a villain out of a James Bond movic, all brash and very confident.

When we left the bar, our lad told us he was part of the Russian mafia and we all thought it was a wind-up but the bloke had arranged with our lad to meet him to sort out our cash for our trip the next day. Curiosity got the better of some of us, so we decided to meet the Russian at Bucharest Station where he then told our lad to walk along a certain platform where we would meet a guy who would tell us were to go next. On the station, this other geezer approached us and told us where to go; we decided not to take up the offer but he said everything was OK; some of us held back as we became aware of a few sets of eyes on us. There were no Romanian Police about, so we knew it was getting fucking dodgy. We strolled along the platform and came across this bloke dressed in shorts with a rucksack on, he had all his hair swept back and looked like some wide-boy from Miami.

One lad was told to follow him to the end of the platform to a disused building; the first lad went, then reappeared minutes later and sent the next one of us in. Once inside the building, the bloke opened up his rucksack which was packed solid with thick wads of money of every denomination you could think of. Most of us just changed a small amount of dosh because we all thought it was dodgy money; also, every one of us had thought about doing the twat over but you just knew he wasn't alone and we wouldn't get away with it. He gave us an excellent deal like the Russian said and it turned out that the money was also kosher.

We eventually caught our train and the lad who had spoken to the Russian got a call from the main man asking us to meet him back in Bucharest on our way home, as he had a job for us which involved some collecting and delivering to London. Obviously, we didn't see him again, but he kept ringing our mate up when he was back home promising to make him a very rich man! He wanted him to fly back to Bucharest and to bring large amounts of sterling with him, then to return to England with guns for his 'friends' in the UK. Fuck that, we were football lads not arms dealers!

In 1986, Danny went to a game in America on his way to the World Cup Finals in Mexico, and, at the time, football – or soccer, as they prefer to call it – was not very popular. Eight years later, the USA were due to stage their first ever finals tournament and, the year before, England visited for a summer friendly tour which gave the police a chance to try out their security measures. They convinced Lee Spence that, if England did manage to qualify for the finals, that it would be one country he would avoid causing trouble in!

LEE, OLDHAM:
For the games in the USA, we flew to New York, 15 Oldham
and a couple of Blackpool, and just did a tourist thing and
travelled all over the States before the first game which was
in Boston. We got there and it was pissing down as we
pulled into the train station, which had two huge
platforms, one of which was full of police with rifles and
cowboy hats on. There was hardly any fucker there and we
were looking at each other, going, fucking hell, this looks
moody. It was all a show, they wanted us to be scared of
them and go home and tell the lads that, if we did qualify
the following year, it was not a place to fuck about in. One
big lump from Manchester, a City fan, did something daft
like drop litter or stand on a crack in the pavement, really
serious shit whatever it was, and they just beat him up.
They were hammering the poor bloke with their rifles, they
ripped his clothes off and the pitiful fucker was standing
there in the rain, covered in blood, with his bollocks swinging
in the wind. He got it because he was the biggest in the crowd
and the message was clear: 'Don't fuck about with us!' They
locked him up, and he lost us and he lost his luggage, but I'll
give the bloke credit, he was undeterred, as he turned up at
the next game in Washington in a camper van!

We went to Georgetown in Washington and were in a bar
when this bloke came up to us asking if we were the famous
English soccer fans and we all went 'Yeah, mate', thinking he
wanted to chat shite to us and buy us beer, but instead he
went on to tell us that the fucking FBI had been in his bar
looking for us. He said, 'You guys look OK, though, why are
the FBI looking for you guys?' He was bewildered that the FBI
were after us.

It turned out they had pictures of known hooligans and
were trying to find us and grill us about our plans for next
year. It was madness! We hadn't even qualified yet and they
were spending top money trailing us across America! There
were a couple of hundred England there in total and not

many were firm, what a waste of fucking time and money that was.

We went into a club after the game and I remember the track 'Naughty by Nature' was on, and I thought, That's about right. The place was wall to wall black and we were the only white people in there and it looked like we were going to get lynched. A massive surge began and we were ready to leg it out when we realised there were two gangs of girls fighting on the dance floor. Loads of police turned up, the club emptied and off we went; it was a well dodgy sketch and I don't think I have been to a more on-top place, but the mad thing was that, in Washington when England played there, there were about 10 murders a day and there were the police and FBI roaming the streets looking for fucking soccer fans!

CHAPTER TEN

SOMBREROS AND SNOW
SPAIN '87

By 1987, the ban handed out to domestic clubs after the Heysel disaster was hitting hard and a steady flow of England's finest footballers jumped ship and either headed abroad to play their football or joined the gravy train stationed at Ibrox. The lack of European football at club level also meant that the fans had to concentrate on England if they wanted to take their football fight club abroad.

One trip that appealed to many was a friendly in Spain on 18 February 1987. Regardless of the time of the year you go to Spain, the vast majority believe you will need shorts and sun cream and Gary Clarke was one of those who made the trip with exactly that attitude. 'Boatsy', as he is also known, is the author of *Inside The Forest Executive Crew* and this is the story of the first of his many jaunts abroad with England.

GARY, NOTTINGHAM FOREST:

I'd been itching to go away with England for a couple of years and was always listening to Scarrott and a few of the other lads after they came back from various trips with all the stories of causing bedlam across Europe. It seemed every time you'd meet a lad from a different firm one of the first questions was: 'Have you been away with England?'

The fact was I hadn't, even though I'd been threatening to go for ages. Something would always come up, usual football things like curfews, money (or the lack of it!) and court appearances. After one match, Forest and England legend Mr Paul Scarrott was out with us, telling anyone within a mile who would care to listen to him that some of Chelsea's finest were organising a coach to Madrid for the friendly against Spain and he managed to talk eight of us from Nottingham into making the trip.

We got the National Express down to London that Sunday afternoon, with Paul taking his famous mobile off-licence on board, and met up with the Chelsea boys that night. I was introduced to the lad that organised the executive coach, Chris Henderson, and he was a bang-on lad who made us feel welcome. Chelsea had some right loons on that bus, so I was sure we were gonna have some fun. It was not all Cockneys on board, with a few Darlo and Villa lads joining us there too. So, off we went, leaving behind a miserable night in London, all thinking it was bound to be warmer in España, me, minus a coat and Giles of Chelsea in shorts and a sombrero! Chris was charging just £50 return to Madrid, which was a fair price as the coach was quality. The Northern lads claimed upstairs, with Chelsea taking the lower deck, the North–South divide was already in operation as we pulled away from London!

First stop was Gay Paris and we pulled up and parked next to the Eiffel Tower. Off we went in various groups in different directions to sample what nightlife Paris had to offer. Us Nottingham lads mainly stayed together but Scarrott wandered off to entertain the Chelsea lads with Gez in tow. We got back to the coach around midnight with everyone coming back with different stories; some had been fighting, a couple had been nicked, including my mate Gez, who did a bit of damage to a pool table by all accounts. So, with Paris glad to see the back of us, next stop was Spain (minus Gez).

It had been nearly two days without a shower or bath now,

most were wearing the same clothes and the less hygienic on board the same socks and underpants, as we entered the Spanish border. We got one or two funny looks from the local plod and had decided to head for Burgos, a one-horse Northern town where the Under-21s were playing on the Tuesday night. We set up camp there for the night and what a night it turned out to be!

We decided to knock the game on the head so we all headed for the local disco which we managed to nearly fill, but the locals didn't take too kindly to being invaded by some of England's finest and it was amazing that it only took around an hour for it to totally go up. It went pear-shaped when Giles was messing around with a crossbow that had been ripped from one of the walls. When he started aiming it towards the bar staff, all hell broke loose and the local police were soon on the scene with their usual anti-hooligan ploy of gassing the bar, regardless of who is in it, and clumping everyone as they pile out, regardless of who they are! As we made our way back to the coach, which was doubling up as our hotel, Old Bill sirens filled the cold night air and I realised that maybe I should have brought a coat!

We all woke the next morning with the coach windows all misted up and a right commotion going on outside. I rubbed the windows to see the coach surrounded by Old Bill and soon they ordered everybody off to be identified by around half a dozen Spanish blokes with injuries, including one who had been stabbed in the arm. We were lined up against the coach with the irate locals walking down the line, pointing people out. They arrested around five of the lads, including two of my mates from Clifton who ended up spending two weeks in a Spanish shit-hole prison, with their families eventually paying fines to get them home.

Although Gary thought the local justice system seemed a bit harsh, given the fact that a man had been stabbed, it was remarkable that the Spanish authorities even let the coach continue its journey across Spain. With no English club problems to report on abroad, the press were quick to pick up on any trouble involving England fans and the *Daily Mirror* led with 'FIVE MONTHS AFTER SOCCER'S LAST SHAME – HERE WE GO AGAIN' and 'ENGLAND THUGS ON RAMPAGE WITH CROSSBOW'.

'England's drunken soccer louts were at it again yesterday as they rampaged through Europe leaving a trail of shame!

'Last night, 18 fans were behind bars in Spain after a ticket collector was almost thrown off an express train travelling at 90mph, beer bottles and cans were hurled at passengers and a disco was smashed up. Crossbows and coshes were seized. The appalling scenes have dismayed football chiefs and any hopes of an early return to European club matches have surely been dashed.

'Violence broke out as English supporters travelled to Madrid for last night's friendly with Spain, and also in Burgos where the Under-21s were playing, where a coach load of England fans was stopped and police seized a crossbow, three catapults, two clubs, knives and fire-crackers. Later, five fans were arrested after thugs wrecked cars and smashed up a disco.'

While the 'rampage with a crossbow' headline about was a little over the top, the facts were there for all to see and the game was still a day away!

GARY, NOTTINGHAM FOREST:

Next stop the Spanish capital, minus three Forest out of eight! We arrived in Madrid around noon and parked right outside the decaying Bernabeau, which was still an impressive sight to a young Forest boy on his first England away trip. It was freezing, as we walked up the road in search of excitement and San Miguel. We holed up in a small boozer around 45-strong and for the whole afternoon we stayed close together as there was talk that a couple of Pompey lads had been stabbed.

Everything was fairly uneventful until we were in the ground, where we were stuck in the middle tier with the Spaniards above us pissing on to our terrace below. We tried to make a charge up the steps, but were baton charged back and my memory of the game is that I was freezing my bollocks off and it was pissing down with rain.

After the game, you knew it was gonna be dodgy with all the stories going round about stabbings. There was only around 500 England fans there, as those were the days when no one really went, and all the snotty-nosed twats nowadays who think they're proper England fans were probably still in school.

Everyone said stay tight and stick together as the Old Bill let us out at the same time as the El Gringos. We had to turn left under a subway for the coach and it wasn't very well lit up but you could make out a big mob in front of us, and, within a minute, the bricks rained down on us. Rather than back off, we just went forward and a few slaps were dished out and the Gringos were off, scattered in all directions before the Old Bill finally got it together and put us back on the coach and escorted us out of the city.

As we headed North, the weather was getting worse, as most of us drifted to sleep, including myself, and soon I was well away. Two days of drinking and playing up had taken its toll, but without warning I was awoken from a deep sleep and was thrust forward, smashing my head on the seat in front of me. I could hear the windows going in and thought we'd been ambushed on the motorway by the farmers who were up in arms with British lorry drivers at the time over some daft dispute or other. I was way off the mark blaming the farmers, as it turned out we'd driven straight into the back of a lorry that had jack-knifed on the motorway in the blizzard.

It was a scary few minutes, we were in pitch darkness and someone came running up the stairs screaming that someone downstairs was dead. In true Corporal Jones fashion, someone else was shouting 'don't panic' but everyone was, as we had to get off the fucking bus, as there was the danger of traffic coming into the back of us. Some daft bastards were jumping out of the windows straight on to the motorway and there were still cars shooting past in the lanes that were not blocked; it was amazing nobody got killed after the smash let alone in it. Some people were trapped downstairs, including the driver who broke both his legs and had to be cut out. One of the Chelsea kids, Andy, who was only about 18 and a really nice lad also had to be cut free and was in a coma for months. He was flown home by one national newspaper trying to score brownie points to increase ratings. It took over an hour for the emergency services to arrive and we were all taken to the local hospital in a state of shock, in a town called, you've guessed it, Burgos. I was one of the lucky ones with only a few cuts and bruises. So most of us were released after a couple of hours and taken to a hotel in the town to recover for the night.

The press were at first naturally sympathetic to the victims of the horrific crash, but the following day, as the full horror of the crash Gary had been involved in made national news, some papers added a hooligan slant to it: 'SOCCER COACH CRASH BOY FIGHTS FOR HIS LIFE. TERROR IN SNOWSTORM AS ENGLAND FANS RETURN HOME'.

'A teenage England fan was fighting for his life last night after a coach carrying England supporters crashed in a blizzard. The crash happened in Burgos in Northern Spain where 48 hours earlier six armed fans from the same coach had been arrested after rampaging through the town's streets.

'The badly hurt teenager, Andrew Rutledge, 19 years old, from West Hampstead, London, is still in a coma with serious head injuries; also in hospital is coach driver Arthur Broad aged 46 of Oakengates, Shropshire, who has both legs broken. Mr Rutledge and Mr Broad were trapped in the wreckage for over an hour.

'Another fan David King, aged 19 from Tunbridge Wells, was kept in hospital overnight with a broken jaw and a further 18 passengers were released after treatment for less serious injuries. The crash came 150 miles from Madrid where the fans had earlier seen England defeat Spain 4–2.

'The coach which was a double-decker hit a lorry which had jack-knifed across the snowbound motorway, before ploughing into two other stationary lorries. Police described the weather conditions as appalling. People on the coach, however, hit out at the length of time it took police to arrive on the scene.

'Co-driver Roger Sugden, aged 43, said, "We managed to stop some passing vehicles but most just sped straight past us." Passenger Mark Smith said, "It took the police an hour and a half to arrive, people were running about screaming and shouting, and others were moaning and groaning in pain in the snow, it was terrible."'

GARY, NOTTINGHAM FOREST:

After we'd cleaned up, we all made phone calls back to England at the hotel's expense, as everyone wanted to let relatives know we were OK as by now the crash was hitting the headlines around the world. Before long, though, we noticed a local mob gathering outside the hotel and they wanted blood for the battle at the disco the night before. We had a police guard on the hotel door and, before long, all the press were there and one paper offered to pay all the hotel expenses in return for an exclusive interview with us all. In between all this, not to miss out on an opportunity, we had Scarrott running round the posh hotel seeing what daft ornaments he could thieve. By the next day, we had run up a massive hotel bill on drinks, food and phone calls back to Blighty but had given no story, and, as another paper said they would pay for our train fare back to the British Embassy in Madrid for a story, we agreed and told them a few tales about the horror crash we had survived.

We had no money to pay the hotel bill and a British Consul bloke turned up but refused to pay the bill so the good-willed Spanish Police let us go and locked him up! I think the *Sun* sorted it, or someone did because we were back on the train to Madrid with a lot of angry locals behind us. Once back in Madrid, the Embassy wouldn't let us in and didn't want to know until one of the Chelsea lads, Salford, made out he was delivering something and managed to get past the door. Once in, we refused to leave. With a bit of negotiating, out came the bacon sarnies and they eventually laid on another coach for the lads that wanted to travel home that way or let us arrange flights home over the phone. I took the latter choice – fuck travelling on a coach through Europe again.

When I arrived back at Heathrow, I bought one newspaper and was disgusted to read in their comments column that we were all a bunch of hooligans that should have been left to die in the snow. My mum and dad have never bought that paper since, bless them! *Central News* and our local paper wanted the names of the Nottingham lads locked up and there were reporters and television crews knocking on our doors for the story. With being off work on the sick, I declined to give my story and left it to Scarrott to give every interview going in return for ale and more notoriety! It was not a bad England debut away, and, if anybody gives a shit, England won 4–2 with Lineker getting all the goals.

As well as the coach crash, the press were reporting that there had been more problems involving England fans and that one group of fans (described as 'Rowdies'), which included a 21-year-old girl, had reportedly wrecked a train carriage, while travelling through Southern France. It was alleged that, as the train got under way, beer bottles and cans were hurled at passengers and some of the English thugs were challenging the passengers to fight. A ticket collector claimed that, when he tried to calm things down, he was grabbed and threatened with being thrown off the 90mph express train. Police in the Spanish town of Tolosa then lined the platform as the express train pulled in and hauled off the so-called troublemakers, who according to the police, once again began fighting.

A spokesman said, 'They just looked like ordinary lads but behave like animals, since sobering up they showed no indication of being sorry. They even requested a television to watch the match in their cells, a request that was turned down by the Spanish Police.'

Those arrested had a different story to tell and amazingly one of the anti-English fan papers ran a story about their plight under the headline: 'WE WERE FRAMED SAY FREED BRITS'.

'Eight British soccer fans were held in a Spanish jail for 40 hours on trumped-up charges, claimed a pretty blonde England supporter, Anita Goddard, aged 21 from Rochdale in Lancashire, who said they were treated as scapegoats because of the reputation of British hooligans abroad.

'The eight were dragged off a train at Tolosa as they were heading for Madrid for England's match versus Spain. Anita said, "I was terrified as I had done absolutely nowt wrong, and I hadn't even had a drink!"

'A ticket collector claimed England fans tried to push him of the train which was travelling at 90mph but Londoner David Robinson aged 22 said, "He must have a wonderful imagination!"

'The eight were finally released yesterday after being kept in cells smeared with filth and the only food offered was maggoty bread. Four other England fans were still being held until their £250 bail was paid for each of them.'

The papers were full of such stories and once again it was suggested that England fans had shamed the nation and prevented club sides getting back into Europe with their bad behaviour. In reality, only a handful were charged and once again it seemed that our press were trying very hard to sensationalise even the smallest of incidents just to sell papers. There was a small line in one paper about three England fans who had been stabbed outside the ground when they were attacked by a mob of 50 Spaniards – if that had been the other way around, what would the reaction of the media have been?

Five years later, England returned to Spain and, while the chances of scoring four away from home had gone thanks to the appointment of Graham Taylor, some things had not changed and, during the match played in Santander, 300 England fans were attacked on the terracing by the Spanish Police. They clubbed people mercilessly and indiscriminately, and even a female FA representative was struck by overzealous local police, who were well trained in indiscriminately lashing out at anything not Spanish that moved.

Many of the victims expected national outrage and a furore in the morning papers as they arrived home the next day at what they had had to endure, but there was nothing. Not one paper gave the incident an inch of column space. Many of the fans who were attacked complained to the FA and the Press Complaints Authority that, if they had turned over a bar or battered some Spaniard senseless, there'd have been countless reports and photos depicting the shocking events; not surprisingly, the complaints fell upon deaf ears.

That was the way things were after Heysel; English hooliganism was big news, and tales of good behaviour didn't make headlines, but bad behaviour did; and, no matter how small the incident was, it was always deemed big enough to make the tabloids. It was that kind of media approach during the 80s that made the press the enemy and, even today, the vast majority of them are despised at England away games!

CHAPTER ELEVEN

THE ANTI-CLIMAX CHAMPIONSHIPS
EURO '88

After a comprehensive qualifying campaign that saw England drop just one point in six games, the team left for Germany with high hopes of winning the competition. Off the field, the authorities braced themselves for an English invasion and prayed the fans would behave, as FIFA had threatened to expel England from the competition if the fans misbehaved. At the time, I was on a football-related affray charge but, as the banning orders of today were not in force, I tried my luck at joining the thousands of lads who were set to face a tough tournament off the pitch, as both German and Dutch hooligans were making noises that they were ready to challenge England for the number-one slot in the hooligan league.

Many of England's finest turned out for the supposed battle of Düsseldorf prior to the game against Holland. At the time, the Dutch were quite a force domestically and most thought England would have their work cut out off the pitch at this game. It turned out to be the biggest non-event ever. Train after train arrived bringing thousands of Dutch fans across the border and there was not a firm of 20 amongst them. They were pitiful, and it was just as well, as the mob of England outside the Swordfish pub near the station was massive and a match for anyone.

The lads from Mansfield went and came home with the same view as my good self, that the Dutch bottled it!

DARREN, MANSFIELD:

One of our first trips abroad was the Euro '88 Championships in Germany. Around 10 lads travelled out and we based ourselves in Cologne and then travelled to the games the night before. Most evenings during the tournament ended with the English brawling with the German Old Bill, who often just stood back while we drank in and around the main train station area, which was always the thing to do at the time.

One night, all the lads were part of a huge mob of England waiting for the Germans to return from their game against Denmark in Gelsenkirchen, as earlier that day a mob of 100 or so Germans had approached the main station and were about to be attacked by the English. Before it kicked off, one German told us to wait until a specific time that evening for their return when there would be no police about. They wanted to go to their game first and have a row later without the police attention, which was a fair call, and our lads, aware of the police presence, agreed.

There were some rows about it; some said they should have got stuck in when they had the chance and others said there was no way they would turn up, but, surprisingly, they did and bang on time. We should have known how efficient the cunts are and they came in big numbers. A few English lads scouting the station got legged, but we were waiting and, as they poured out of the station and steamed towards us, the bars emptied and it was game on.

At first, they had us backing off, the cunts were throwing flick and lock knifes at us, but the thing was, as soon as they chucked them, their bottle went. Some lads were picking them up and 'returning' them to their owners. The Old Bill in full riot gear didn't have the numbers to deal with it and we piled into the Germans that tried to stand but the poor cunts were getting hammered. A couple of Germans got a leg and a wing through nearby shop windows and they were in disarray; they started to split up and we legged a mob up a side street, but some older leather-clad meatheads came back into our group of 50 or so from another side street and they were far gamer and we had a good toe-to-toe with them before our numbers overwhelmed them.

The riot police had obviously called for back-up and our little group containing a few Leeds lads didn't budge when they ran at us; they stopped about 20 yards from us and we launched anything we could find into them. Behind us, other English came to help us and a nearby bar had all its furniture brought out on to the street and hurled at the Old Bill. They didn't know how to deal with us. More and more sirens signalled the arrival of van loads more and we were eventually forced back on to the main road where all the English were regrouping. We had a stand-off before the English ran at the Old Bill and they tried to drive their police vans at us but we just went round them. This continued for a while, and the Old Bill just seemed content at keeping their distance and us contained in the area. As for the Germans, they had long gone and the evening slowly melted away. This was the norm every evening, sometimes a mob of Germans would turn up, get done, then leave the Old Bill to get the brunt of our fun.

Cologne was a good place to stop and it turned out to be one of the few places where there was actually any action. We went to Düsseldorf for the Dutch game with high hopes of more of the same but it was unbelievable, they simply didn't want to know – orange this and orange that and not a lad in sight, it was the biggest anti-climax ever at an England game.

Bonzo from West Ham was another fan who went over there thinking it would be a good trip on and off the pitch and was another who returned disappointed, albeit later than most who went over.

BONZO, WEST HAM:

Expectations were high that summer for football fans from England as their team had a decent chance to win a trophy for the first time since 1966 and the lads that liked a little more from their days out had the game with the newcomers of the English disease to confront on foreign soil again – Holland. So much was being said about what they were going to do to the English in Düsseldorf that we started to believe that at last they would put up a decent fight against the world's most notorious football hooligans and that they could make a major name for themselves. What a load of bollocks!

We flew to Frankfurt, hired a Volkswagen Golf and drove into the centre where we had arranged to meet some mates at Dr Muller's, and we enjoyed the bright lights of Frankfurt's city centre so much we stayed for two nights. Early Sunday morning, we then drove down to Stuttgart for the first game that England were involved in, which was against Ireland and a game we'd expected to win comfortably, only to get beat 1–0, which was not the start we wanted and a few Paddies got a slap as we left for taking the piss. Pissed off, about a dozen of us walked into Stuttgart's city centre and came close to kicking off with a mob of about 15–20 Millwall on the way. A night out in Stuttgart with loads of pissed-up Paddies is not what you want when you have been beat, and the centre was full of green and white as the Irish celebrated their win and again a few of them took a clump for celebrating too close to us in a bar, but they were not our main target and our thoughts soon turned to Düsseldorf and our meeting with the Dutch.

For some reason, we decided to drive to Düsseldorf on the morning of the game on Wednesday and that was a mistake, as Tuesday night was very lively by all accounts. As we arrived early, we were met by small groups of English who kept telling us about the previous night's events and how it kicked off for hours with the Germans, as the Dutch were again nowhere to be seen. We plotted up in the train station which had large sets of escalators going up into the main drag and before long groups of Germans were picking off small groups of English. With that in mind, we mobbed up in one big firm and before long it was mayhem, as it seemed like it was off everywhere. The Germans also had large numbers but they were easily clocked by their terrible dress sense and their uniform of colourful jumpers and jeans that finished six inches above their white socks and basketball boots.

We joined a group of Pompey who I knew well and a group of about 15 of us slipped off and headed down some side streets to try and get behind the square where the Germans were and we pulled it off big time as this little group of Pompey were as game as fuck as they steamed into the Germans with no thoughts of the small numbers we had. It was a major result as Germans hit the floor all over the gaff, but we then found ourselves in the middle of the square surrounded by Germans and it looked like we were in trouble until this small group of close mates steamed in again and again and backed off the locals before we were surrounded by the Old Bill and marched back to the train station, where the rest of the English who had witnessed the small mob of us bashing the Germans bought us more beer than we could drink!

There were more skirmishes all around this part of Düsseldorf as groups slipped off and took it to the German hordes, but the major disappointment was that the Dutch were nowhere to be seen until we got to the ground which was full of Dutch all kitted out in their orange garb and there were a few fights as at last we bumped into what few boys they had.

A couple of us had tickets in the wrong end and made our way there and found another 100 or so in the upper tier, but all the Dutch around us were dressed like Christmas trees so we knew that there would be no trouble, even though we were basically taking the piss in their end. We got hammered on the pitch and were out of the tournament, so for a grand finale we mobbed up at the back of the stand and steamed into the Dutch as they came out and loads of us took whacks from the German Old Bill's sticks.

That night was lively, as most of the English knew they were heading home and, despite very large numbers of police, there were brawls outside most bars and around the train station until the early hours. We eventually left for the drive back to Koblenz and the day had taken its toll, so we stopped in a lay-by for a kip. In the lay-by was a car with an England flag hung up inside it and we parked up close by and all fell asleep. I was awoken by a large bang and we all jumped out of the car to see the British-plated car with a scaffold pole through the windscreen and four fellas running off towards a car parked up on the side of the road. We gave chase but they were gone and the couple who were from Brighton were shocked but very lucky, as it just missed their heads; we were also lucky as we had a German car with German plates, which may have been the reason we were not attacked, although it may have been the stench of five pairs of stinking feet which put them off attacking us!

The next morning, a load of the lads decided to leave Germany early and head for Yugoslavia but I foolishly stayed for the last game in Frankfurt, which we lost again. I then headed for Munich and caught the train down to Kardelijevo going through Sarajevo and Mostar on the way, which was the drabbest part of the world I had ever seen at that time of my life, before landing on the Adriatic coast and enjoying the summer of '88 far more than I enjoyed watching Euro '88!

There was some trouble with the Dutch, but it was caused by the English who'd holed up in Amsterdam and not the invisible Dutch hooligans who had threatened so much yet ended up a laughing stock. Gary from Oldham recalls his first away trip with England.

GARY, OLDHAM:

Oldham has always had a decent following for England games and I gave up the usual two weeks in Spain to join the 80-odd lads who were going to Germany. Twenty-four of us flew into Amsterdam four days before we were due in Germany, as we had worried about the German cops turning a few of the lads back as they had all been in trouble with the courts at home. Hundreds had the same idea and it kicked off all over the gaff, English v the Dutch, v Immigrants, v Pimps and most annoyingly v themselves.

We had only just booked into a shitty hotel when the sound of police sirens filled the air and there were mobs chasing each other through the narrow streets and alleyways. We could not make out who was who at first, so we got ourselves into a bar to watch the proceedings. We soon sussed out it was, in fact, West Ham on the attack and a small mob of Stoke came into our bar and told us that the Cockneys were once again attacking the smaller Northern firms, which I couldn't get my head around, as we surely had enough on our plates with the Germans, Dutch and the German riot cops?

We arrived in Düsseldorf two days before the game, there were dozens of German riot cops with snarling Doberman dogs waiting for us on the platform and we all settled in some bar called the Effeneeger Bar, which we joked was an NF boozer!

I was young at the time and not bothered about all the talk of German thugs mobbing up to do us or the threat of the Dutch mob, as that is what we were there for, but I will admit that I was a bit twitchy when a few lads told us there was a gang of German thugs with handlebar taches snatching young England fans and taking them down alleyways and buggering them senseless! Fuck me, I thought, I'm sticking close to the mob from now on, there would be no fucking walkabouts for me!

That night, a mob of Germans kicked off on us and they had the numbers, and at one stage it was a bit risky as they were bombarding us with all sorts. I thought briefly of running but then remembered the serious risk of being snatched by those big bent Germans and getting pleasured by them mob-handed so stood my ground preferring a sore head to a sore arsehole!

When we were making our way back to our hotel, we were ambushed by a mob of 30 German skins so we all dived into this little pokey bar and grabbed anything we could get our hands on. Our main lad Tommy Mac grabbed a big piece of stained glass and the first German through the door copped for it right over his swede. Down he went, blood gushing out of his head, as Tommy then steamed outside with us lot behind him. The other Germans ran off leaving their mate knocked out with his head oozing blood in a right old state, crumpled up on the deck. The cops soon arrived and cornered us in this alleyway, and the bar owner came out and grassed on Tommy who was duly arrested and sent down for six months just a few days later.

We went to the game but were glad to fuck off back to Amsterdam where, after a few days in the coffee bars getting stoned and pissed up, the lads decided to tell me that the German gay-rapist tale was a wind-up, which was a relief as I was having trouble sleeping thinking about it!

The European Championships had been shite for us and on the way home we were vowing never to watch England again, knowing full well we would all be back in Italy just two years later!

CHAPTER TWELVE
THE TIDE TURNS
SCOTLAND '89

Following the destruction of Wembley in 1977, many vowed that the Scottish invaders would never be allowed to take such liberties again. It was not going to be an overnight job, though, as for years Scottish fans had been travelling South for both domestic and international games and faced very little resistance, as sheer weight of numbers and their drunken bravado meant there were few who felt confident enough to oppose them.

Villa Park, St James' Park and even Old Trafford had been overrun long before Wembley was targeted and the assembly of a firm strong enough to prevent it happening again would take years to build. As these years passed, revenge was sweet and by 1989 England's hooligan element had finally gained a reputation which meant that never again would the Jocks be allowed, or indeed feel brave enough, to take them on in the manner in which they did in 1977.

Since 1872, when the countries first met at Hamilton Crescent in Glasgow in front of a crowd of just 4,000, the fixture was a major one in the football calendar and the two sides had met over 100 times by the time the crossbars came down 105 years later. It is a sign of how troublesome the fixture became off the field that, in 1989, the friendlies were scrapped altogether and, since 1977, only 15 games in total have taken place, which includes the three European Championship clashes, which could not be avoided.

One year after the shameful scenes at Wembley, very few Englishmen made the trip North for the return game and, although thousands of Scottish fans once again descended on Wembley in 1979 and saw their heroes soundly beaten 3–1, there were far more England supporters in the sell-out crowd, although once again in 1980 they were guilty of a no-show at Hampden Park.

It was in 1981 when Scotland won 1–0 thanks to a John Robertson penalty that the first sign of an organised rearguard was formed by the English, and West Ham's Terry was one of the few who attempted to repel the Tartan invasion.

TERRY, WEST HAM:

It was for this game that England were meant to have a proper meet and give it the Jocks, as leaflets had been printed and every man and his dog was supposed to show. As it was all the Jocks were waiting for us when we made our way to the ground but there were no English there, just West Ham and that mob consisted of just 10 of us!

One of the lads, Brett, had bought a few silver pac-a-macs and, as it started raining, he had dished them out and we were walking up Wembley Way in these daft fucking see-through plastic throwover macs surrounded by Jocks! The Jocks have got straight on to us and have said to Brett, 'Where's your leaflets?' We've acted daft and they start all this 'What's happened to do the Jocks or fucking bash the Jocks?' We were giving them the blank one, then this geezer showed me a screwed-up leaflet which had something on it like 'All England meet and do the Jocks'. We were fucked now so we started fighting with this firm, and one geezer pulled a blade out on Brett, so I've jobbed him and Brett's jobbed another. We've upped a few Jocks and were proper fighting with loads of them and in minutes were getting fucked, but at least we were there and having a go. With it being a bit of a no-show from the Chelsea lot who had printed the leaflets, we were in two minds whether to go in but Brett said, 'Well, we're here and we're West Ham, so let's fucking go in.'

It was not one of his best ideas and soon we were inside the stadium having a nightmare. Our section was full of the Jocks and they were all fucking drunk, and we were all split up, as the few Chelsea who eventually showed had fucked off leaving us with a few Northerners making our firm about 35-strong.

At half-time, we went downstairs together and a big firm of Jocks came up to us and we thought, Fuck it and it's gone off. We were only kids but we were game kids and had a go until another mob came bouncing down and joined in. We thought our time was up, but they were Rangers and they steamed into the mob we were fighting with who may have been Celtic or Hibs, fuck knows, but they just went and steamed into the Jocks we were having it with and left us alone – it was a right touch!

In Wembley Stadium at that time, you were able to walk all the way round, so we've gone, thank you, and slipped off as they were fighting; we just said to the steward, open up that fucking door and fucked off sharpish!

It was not exactly a result of any kind but at least England had stood and fought with the Scottish fans in the ground, something they never did in 1977. Now it was time to take it to them in Glasgow, but once again, after much hype, few made the trip and West Ham were once again left to pick up the pieces, as Reedy explains.

REEDY, WEST HAM:
It was another poor show by England; for weeks before, word was that we would all go firm-handed and stick together and forget our club differences, but once again a few of the so-called main players were blowing hot air out of their arses. I can remember one of our lads telling us that they were in one pub and some England fans had been collared and the lot had gone pear-shaped and the boozer got smashed up badly by the locals who took offence that English geezers had dared show in a pub on their manor.

In the end, two Under-Fives were trapped in the corner with a bar full of Jocks round them shouting, 'You English bastards', when our lad and Lorrie Pearman shouted back, 'Fuck off, we ain't England, we're West Ham!'

The Jocks stopped the onslaught and one came over and said, 'You're brave, mate, shake my hand,' but Lorrie Pearman just fucked him off and pushed his hand out the way!

That summed West Ham up for me, we always went to England matches in those days and all the other England lot used to go, 'Oh fuck, West Ham's here,' and give us a wide berth, the mentality of them was there was England and there was West Ham England!

It was on 1 June 1983 that the tide actually started to turn and Steve Cowens, a Sheffield United supporter who wrote the bestselling book on their firm, was part of the English support who had finally had enough of the liberty-taking Scots and who fought back!

STEVE, SHEFFIELD UNITED:

Like most English youngsters at the time, I used to hate watching the Jocks take over Wembley every time that England played Scotland. I'd sit there thinking, Where's all the England fans, as the TV cameras panned around the ground showing masses of tartan and ginger. In 1975, I watched *World of Sport* as Trevor Brooking and Kevin Keegan tore the Scots apart in a 5–1 win that hardly any English actually watched in the flesh. As an 11-year-old, I couldn't understand how our national stadium could be taken over so easily and why the English never turned out for this fixture, after all the Englishman's home is supposed to be his castle. That frustration as a youngster erupted into a punch on the settee's arm, as two years later thousands of sweaties swarmed on to our hallowed turf and wrecked the joint after beating us 2–1.

I remember thinking that one day I'd go and defend

England's home, even if no one else could be arsed. So, with that thought in mind, in June 1983, I put my England shirt on under my Munsingwear jumper and set off along with two Sheffield United boys in my Morris Marina: our destination Wembley, our opponents Scotland. I'd been to the dentist the previous day as I'd got an abscess under a tooth and I was in agony. My face was swelled up to John Merrick-sized proportions but I put this to one side as I went to defend England from the invading hordes that came down from chilly Jocko land.

When we arrived, it was a real eye-opener as the Jocks were everywhere. We'd been told by an English lad that a big firm of Chelsea were at Euston and an even bigger firm of West Ham were at Leicester Square. Sound, I thought, as we headed off to find an English firm that us three 19-year-olds could tag along with. We saw Chelsea on a tube interchange, they looked 200-strong but we missed them as they were boarding on the other side of the platform. My mate Doyley insisted we headed back to Wembley, as he figured that was where Chelsea were heading and didn't want to miss any action with the Tartan Army. Once we got back to Wembley, I took my jumper off and walked out of the tube station and into the sunshine. What greeted me was hundreds of Scots singing 'Spot the loony, spot the loony', all pointing at me as they sang. I gave them the one-fingered salute, as by now I was itching to get some action.

'Where the fuck are the English? This is wank. The Jocks are taking the piss and there's no cunt hear to stop it,' I grumbled as we walked up Wembley Way.

To be fair to the kilt wearers, they could have mullered us but they preferred to take the piss. One pissed-up Jock asked for a photo with me, as he said I was the first Englishman he'd seen in his three visits to London and quite a few Scots even asked me if I was all right, thinking I'd been battered because of my swollen face!

We then heard the unmistakable sound of a firm's roar

prior to battle and a quick glance back down Wembley Way saw hundreds of Scottish supporters scattering all over the place as a large group of English had come out of the tube and without further ado had called it on. It was too far away for us to help our countrymen but by the look of it they were doing OK without three skinny teenagers. We waited as a good 300-strong firm marched up towards Wembley with sporadic fighting breaking out as they walked towards the famous twin towers.

'This must be the Chelsea firm,' I mumbled to Doyley as they approached but was wrong, as they were mainly West Ham with other firms' lads mixed in. We tagged along and at the top of Wembley Way thousands of Scots were charged at by the English firm and there wasn't much resistance! The Scots I'd met beforehand didn't seem aggressive; they just took the piss a bit, so when hundreds of English hooligans started chasing them about I didn't class it as a result, as far as I was concerned they were like shirt-wearing supporters not hooligans, but these same people had for years been terrorising London and it was time where enough was enough and England had to start to defend its manor. The OB charged around not really knowing which way to turn, there would have been arrests galore if it had been now but at that time they were happy to get between the two sets of warring factions and keep the peace.

I was pleased to see loads of the English lads entering the same part of the ground as us, the tunnel end. Inside, the Jocks were everywhere and it took the English a good part of the first half to get a big enough mob together to get stuck in. England scored and I was pleased to see that there was more English in the ground than I first thought. It kicked off to my right and this was the big Chelsea firm who swatted the Jocks down the terracing without much problem. Then the English around us waded in and it became a free-for-all. Punches were exchanged and the English were going down the terracing and the Scots were overpowered. 'England,

England', rang out loudly and I remember the feeling was immense. We'd put up a fight and this day was the final time that the Jocks just took over Wembley without a fight. I felt proud that we'd been a part of England's fight-back and to make it even better we won the game 2–0!

On the way home, my car tyre blew out in the third lane on the motorway and a lorry nearly hit us, as I careered across to the hard shoulder. I didn't have a car jack so had to drive around three miles to the nearest service station where a van full of Scots manually lifted my car and changed the tyre. I felt a little guilty because every Scotsman I'd met that day had been friendly even when taking the piss, but England had regained control of Wembley and the only question that needed asking was how the Scots had taken over in the first place!

Wembley was reclaimed and, although the national news reported on the shocking scenes which saw the jovial fun-loving Tartan Army come under attack from mindless English hooligans, many of the capital's population refused to condemn the violence and very few tears were shed for those injured during the fighting. The problem now was that England had to travel North, as another no-show would be an embarrassment to those involved in the battle at Wembley. There was a full year to organise it and for once the English did not disappoint, as one Hull fan wrote in *City Psychos* by Shaun Tordoff, although it was not exactly what he was hoping for!

GARRY, HULL CITY:

My first real scary moment following England was at Hampden Park in 1985. I remember Richard Gough scoring for them in a 1–0 win. We'd travelled up on a coach from Hull (50 of us) and we joined up with the rest of the England party just outside Glasgow and came in under escort. Inside the ground, I took stock of our numbers and was totally dismayed when I realised we only numbered around 200 fans. Can you imagine that, 200 amongst 72,000 hostile Jocks. We were stood at the bottom of Section M and about 30 minutes into the game it went off. The Scots surged down, hitting out at any England fans in their path, and we were pressed up against the fence; it was all we could do to fight them off. We punched, pushed, pulled and kicked ourselves into exhaustion and my full body ached, yet they still came down at us. This pummelling lasted until just after the half-time whistle when the police finally arrived on the scene (nearly 20 minutes after the trouble began) and they made a wedge between both sets of supporters, then opened a gate on to the pitch which we proceeded to tumble through. We were then told the police were taking us to a secure section, so off we set passing hordes of screaming, spitting Jocks (to them, we were the half-time entertainment). The police led us through this section, where they opened a gate at the back and booted us out with 'Fuck off, you English scum' ringing in our ears.

At first I was seething, but with hindsight the police did us a favour.

Other English fans claim to have fared better that day, especially in a few of the street battles that took place before and after the game but, once again, the numbers game heavily favoured the Scots. But numbers were rising in the England ranks, and the next time they travelled to Hampden they had been joined by hundreds more including Lee Spence, who was only 17 at the time.

Most lads fondly remember their first England away and it was defiantly one Lee would not forget in a hurry!

LEE, OLDHAM:
Scotland '87 was my first England trip and, like so many after, it ended up with me getting nicked! We set off to Glasgow in a mob of about 50 Oldham from Manchester Victoria and were joined by a good firm of United, as a lot of the older lads knew each other. There were lads from all over on the train

and I will always remember pulling into Carlisle and being very impressed by the firm they had with them. I was in awe of it all, it was new to me and the buzz and the banter as we got nearer Scotland had me hooked.

We got into Glasgow and were met by loads more English lads and hundreds upon hundreds marched out the station, but even when I was with such a huge mob my luck was down as I still managed to bump into a West Brom lad who the week before I had been booting in the head; he was on my case so I kept out of his way for the short time I was there!

I will always remember one of the lads pointing out Forest and England legend Paul Scarrott with his World War II helmet on and thinking, I'll have some of this. All the talk of Scotland being moody to me seemed nonsense, we were there firm-handed and were taking the piss, and every minute someone was pointing out main lads from all the firms. As a 17-year-old lad, I thought it was the business. I was impressionable and it all made me realise that this is what I wanted to be a part of!

There was no chance of a drink as there were too many of us in one firm, so we wandered off in our little mob and did a bit of fucking about before two blokes walked over to us and grabbed me and a mate and pulled walkie-talkies out of their coats and called for assistance. We were baffled and they just kept saying, 'Shut it,' and that we were nicked. A van pulled up and we were slung in it and we were indeed nicked and our day was over!

It was 100 per cent a stitch-up, neither of us had done fuck all apart from maybe act a bit cocky within a mob of about 50 lads. We were locked up in a police station and the day got worse when these Bolton fans were slung in with us and proceeded to tell us they had been nicked for fighting with ... Oldham! They were much older than us, so once again it was a case of heads down. The fucking nightmare had begun!

We were kept overnight and on the Sunday taken to the court cells to appear on the Tuesday, as the following day was a Bank Holiday Monday. In court, we were given the charge sheets and it made grim reading, attacking plain-clothes officers, resisting arrest and a load of other nonsense. It finally dawned on us that we were in the shit and I and thought, Aye up, I may be here for a few more days! I was right – we were all refused bail and were sent to Barlinnie Prison.

Barlinnie has a terrible reputation; it was built on farmland at Riddrie in 1880 as a response to the overcrowding that existed in the prison system in Scotland. It was designed to hold 1,000 male prisoners, who were required to perform hard labour and submit to strict discipline but who had access to education facilities and a library.

The external appearance of Barlinnie has changed little since it was built, although there has been internal upgrading, and the regime is less harsh. From 1973 until 1994, the world-famous Special Unit placed emphasis on rehabilitation, the best-known success story being that of reformed Glasgow gangster Jimmy Boyle.

In recent years, Barlinnie has suffered from persistent overcrowding and a depressing reputation. Between 1996 and 1998, eight inmates committed suicide. An official report in 1997 described the jail as a 'national disgrace', although a subsequent report acknowledged that some improvements had been made.

When Spence was arrested and sent there, the improvements had not yet been made, and the prison would have been a frightening experience for a hardened criminal, let alone a teenager who was under arrest for the first time of his life.

LEE, OLDHAM:

About 200 England were nicked and we were all taken to Barlinnie in a convoy of vans and buses; when we got in there, we were greeted by a main face from West Brom who was a proper hard bastard standing there with a fresh black eye. They had picked the biggest one of us out and let him get a smack just to let us know what to expect – all psychological bollocks but, as a 17-year-old kid, let me tell you, their mind games were working!

That day was the worst of my life at the time; we were locked up in the reception area, which was Victorian age, and all of us were sat on a big old wooden bench and given a bowl of stew or something similar – it was seriously like what you saw in fucking *Oliver Twist*. We were taken into the main jail and I was thinking, What the fuck is all this about? All night, the screws were coming to the spyholes and shouting, 'Yer gonna get cut in here, yer English bastards.'

Worst day and longest night of my life, no doubt about that!

I thought things were getting better the next day when 10 of us were told that, as we were juveniles, we were getting shipped out to Airdrie. There was a couple from Oldham, a Geordie, a couple from Lancaster and a few others who were all made up at first … until we got there. It was like the scene from *Scum* – when we came through the gates, every single person had a donkey jacket on and was marching about with the screws in tow bollocking and booting anyone who was out of line or not keeping up. We all looked at each other and you could see the fear in everyone's faces, and it does not bother me one bit to say I was fucking shitting myself and anyone else in that van who says different is lying.

They paired us off and were going to put us on separate wings but, as we were waiting to get showered, a load of Jocks steamed into us; they were fucking naked, straight out of the showers and into us. It was like: 'Fucking hell, we're gonna get killed here if we split up,' so we made a stand and said we were going nowhere unless we were kept together.

The main screw came in and asked if we wanted to see the governor and 10 voices blurted out: 'YES!'

We were marched up to the governor's office and had to stand to attention, while this cunt, who was like Mr McKay in *Porridge*, walked past us spitting that we were weak, and this place would make us stronger, and that us seeing the governor was a sign of our weakness.

The main man came in and looked us up and down, called us a sorry bunch and took us all to this huge window in his office. The view outside looked right across the recreation yard and there were literally hundreds of donkey jackets, milling about, playing football, huddled in corners smoking and generally looking sorry for themselves. He turned to us and for as long as I live I will never forget what he said: 'Are you men or mice?'

He then went on to say something like, 'If you're men, you will go on the wings and mix in with the lads, you will be allowed to play football, pool, table tennis and watch a little TV. If you are mice, you will be locked up for 24 hours a day and have no privileges.'

Then he repeated himself and said, 'So are you men or mice?'

We looked at each other for about two seconds and I said, 'Well, you lot can act fucking hard but while I'm in here I'm a mouse!'

Then, as one, the rest all shouted, 'MICE!'

Mr McKay was pissed off, as I am sure he had marked our cards with the Scottish kids and then he had to get his fellow bastards to empty a complete wing and rehouse a load of angry Jocks to make way for us!

The following day, we met our brief and he told us to expect at least three months in there before we went to trial, but out of the blue on the Thursday morning they came in and told us to get our stuff as we were up that day and in an hour we were on our way to court, where, apart from an unlucky few, we were all bailed.

There were Jocks waiting outside the court and one of Carlisle's top faces was stabbed and very nearly died, which caused a lot of bad feeling, which resulted in an ambush on the Jocks the following year at a service station where a load were stabbed and a few Carlisle lads including Doddy were jailed.

Going home on the train was like the united colours of Benetton, there were lads from every firm on board who had been nicked, and it was like a big party, a good Stella trip!

Months later, we went back up and all the charges had been reduced and I got a £150 fine, which was still harsh for what I had done, which was fuck all.

The night in Barlinnie and the short sharp shock that was borstal should have put me off for life but if anything the fear and the excitement made me want more, and from that game on I missed very few trips with England until I was eventually banned.

As Lee said, the stabbing of the Carlisle supporter outside the courts in Glasgow led to an attack by Carlisle hooligans the following year at Killington Lake service station. It was a bloodbath, as eight Scots and one Carlisle lad were either stabbed or slashed and as serial hooligan Paul Dodd, who claimed to be England's number-one hooligan was involved, the subsequent trial received massive media attention. It resulted in nine English supporters receiving just under 20 years' imprisonment.

At Wembley, the Scots finally met their match and it was the game where England hunted down and attacked the travelling support all day long. It was not all one way, though, as within the Tartan Army were a new up-and-coming firm of Casuals who didn't care for the national side – in fact, many preferred England to their home country – they were there for the violence only.

Fat Pat is a well-known Chelsea fan and was part of the English firm that fought with both the Tartan Army and their Casuals that day long after the game had ended in an attempt to prevent what had become a twice-yearly piss-take by the Scottish hordes.

FAT PAT, CHELSEA:

The last big one at Wembley when they were given thousands of tickets was '88 and there was absolute murder and the fighting on the terraces led the FA to rightly scrap friendlies with them in London. There were about 200 arrests on the day and from early that morning until long after the game we had it with them. The meet was at The Three Kings in West Kensington and about 400 English answered the call, with top turnouts from Chelsea, West Ham, Stockport, Forest and a lot more Northern outfits. We headed off towards Trafalgar Square and all got off at the Embankment and gathered outside the bottom of Villiers Street.

We got our lot together, there was about 70 of us left, all the ones that knew each other including a good few from QPR who had Gregor with them – like him or not, he's a game lad and knows the score so off we went to The Admiral Nelson on the corner by Charing Cross Station. Once we had regrouped, we walked through the back streets, towards the Swiss Centre and, as we got to the top by the clock, we looked to our right and there was a firm walking up by the Hippodrome.

We thought, It can't be the Jocks because they're fucking Casuals, but as they were coming across the square we noticed a few kilts in amongst them so we spread out and walked towards them and called it on. They went for it straight away and were game as fuck chanting 'CCS, CCS,' meaning we had bumped into the Hibs mob. One geezer pulled out a big blade and he went to stab Gregor but the blade went straight through the side of his jacket and I squirted the knife man with a Jif lemon bottle full of ammonia. As I'm jiffing away, another one's booted me in the shin and it felt like he had broke my leg so I've fucking hobbled away trying to stay on my feet, and as I looked back I couldn't see our lot any more as the Hibs mob had backed our lot up the street. I'm limping around in the street, gutted by now, as it was going badly wrong, but from nowhere our lads gave it one last go and I saw the Hibs lot going backwards before getting completely run the whole length of the square. It was a great sight and as the lads were walking back they were all clapping each other which was funny as fuck and took my mind off this fucking lump which was growing by the minute on my shin.

We walked back down towards Yates and the Jocks tried to come back at us, chucking bottles, glasses and bins at us, so one Chelsea lad who is actually from up North picked up a Westminster bin and held it up like a shield before running down the road towards them. There was fucking bottles and everything bouncing off this bin and we're all behind him running down the road and we scattered them again which was when the Old Bill came in and started to split everyone up.

We all got off and agreed a meet at Edgware Road but, as me and a mate are walking along, I said, 'Fuck it, shall we go to Wembley?' We soon bumped into Gregor and another well game QPR fella, Smiffy, who all agreed to go and see what's happening at the ground. As we were heading for the tube, my mate has tapped me and said, 'Who's that cunt there?'

So I looked and noticed this fella walking parallel in the road to us. I had seen him earlier, as I remembered this red jumper he was wearing, I had another look and noticed this daft blond feather cut and he was smiling at me. I turned to the lads and said, 'Fuck me, that's one of them Hibs cunts,' and as I looked back noticed about 30 of them creeping up behind us. Now I can't fucking run at the best of times but my shin was in bits and two of our lads have gone past me like racehorses, so I flew through the doors of the Trocadero! In seconds, all 17 stone of me hit the deck as I was rugby tackled by two security guards. I'm going, 'They're after me, fucking let me go,' and looked around expecting to see this Hibs lot ready to cut me and there was nobody there. They didn't even follow me into the Trocadero so I've had to give it the old 'Oh shit, I'm sorry mate, my mistake, thought I was getting chased' bollocks.

We made the ground and managed to get in and there was pure uproar in the ground, with fighting constantly on the terraces. The Old Bill had a line down the middle of one end and there was England on one side and the Jocks on the other side and it was just going off all game and I could not tell you the score of the match if I tried.

After the game, the meet was on top of Wembley Way and

we got out and about 500 English were already assembled and it was mainly Northerners. To this day, I don't know who they were, every accent was there – Mancs, Scouse, Geordie, Yorkshire, West Country, fucking South Coast – everyone was there and, if you looked round, you could see that this lot were not going anywhere, you could just see it. There was a lot of broken noses and bloody noses, it was a proper Popeye crew!

As we stood at the top of Wembley Way the Jocks have come pouring down the hill. You couldn't see the back of their firm, it was like an army of ants swarming towards us and as well as the usual kilts there were plenty of Casuals in with them. And it's just gone, bang, like a scrum. The Old Bill were trying to get in and pull people apart and it turned into one of the Gaelic football fights in Australia and they were literally dragging people away from each other; people were rolling around on the floor – it wasn't like a football fight at all.

The Old Bill managed to get a wedge in and they pushed the Jocks back up and us down Wembley Way, so we jumped over the wall into the car park and ran parallel to the road leading down towards the station. Fuck me, as I looked up to see if any had made the move, all I could see was hundreds of them coming down with no Old Bill. We came out the car park and it was all their Casuals at the front who may have been Aberdeen as they were not the Hibs firm we had clashed with earlier and as we shaped up we've gone steaming through them and they started to run back. The sheer weight of numbers coming down made them stall up, there was nowhere for them to run; they were sandwiched between us and their lot so they had no option but to fight and there must have been at least 2,000 Jocks and about 500 English crammed on to the road fighting.

Every now and then, the fight would break up, and a mad Jock would come in and do a solo, do a flying kick, and none of them would follow him. The Casuals were more disciplined but the daft Jocks were fucking mad and time after time you would see a Jock flying in, miss and land on the floor, followed by bits of tartan being thrown up in the air or a sporran being thrown back at them. It was proper crackers, geezers in Partick Thistle shirts and kilts would run in shouting, 'You fucking Sassenach bastards!' and it would be, boom, boom, boom, next!

At one stage, a big gap opened up and I got pushed right to the front and some Jock's stuck his fingers right into my eye, and that was me gone. Gregor grabbed me and alongside us a Jock has done some English geezer with a plank of wood on the side of the head. They made one big last steam to get us on the back foot but we held the line even though the sheer weight of numbers they had was wearing us down and they were starting to get the better a bit.

In the end, the Old Bill managed to come through and they pushed us away from them. Regardless what the bullshit merchants say, had they given it another minute or two, I think on sheer fatigue they would have got in and done us. But I'll tell you something now, to this day, to anybody who was there, I would like to tell them one thing, they were fucking superb and they should be proud of themselves because how we held that that day was unbelievable. The thing is I didn't know who most of them were, there was no leader, there was no top boy, there was no one person and it was mostly Northerners, but whoever they all were they did England proud and from that day on Scotland have never come back mob-handed and took the piss like they used to, and never will!

The trouble at Wembley set things up nicely for the return game 12 months later. Every year, the stakes were getting higher and it was time for England to finally turn up en masse in Glasgow and take it to the Jocks. Once again, they didn't disappoint and this was the game where the tide finally turned!

It was a game that saw the Shrewsbury lads come out in force and a chance for the lads from Hull to get even after the torrid time they had endured on their previous visit:

BRENDAN, SHREWSBURY:
I started going to England games in 1989 when I was just 16. I went to Hampden Park after being invited along by the older lads from Shrewsbury. We caught a train to Glasgow and I always remember it was the eleven o'clock from Crewe and it cost £13! It was my first England game and, although young, I was really buzzing and well up for it.

There was only four of us on the overnight train but we were meeting another 20 Shrewsbury when we got there who had travelled up on a coach with Rochdale and some West Brom. I'd heard so much in previous years about Scotland and England, fighting with Hibs and Hearts and all the Aberdeen Casuals. Over the years, England had been taking more and more up to Glasgow and this was the one where it was rumoured that we would have a big enough firm on board to cause a riot. We got into Glasgow at about five in the morning, all you could see was just lads everywhere, there's mobs of 20s and 30s all over the station, lads from every club. More importantly there was no in-house nonsense, it was a case of everyone wanting to get stuck into the Jocks not each other.

We waited around all morning at the station and realised that all the England mobs were gradually dwindling so we went wandering to find out where everyone was going, we bumped into a load of lads who were already pissed and it turned out hundreds had gone drinking in the pubs used by the market lads that opened at half-six in the morning!

Eventually, we marched to the ground, hundreds and hundreds of lads trying to get at the locals and at times the police were struggling to control the size of the mob. Loads of small mobs were breaking out and all around you could hear roars as it went off. None of us had tickets and then somebody told us they were selling them in a hot dog stand at Hampden Park for £5 each. It was crazy because for weeks they had been saying don't travel, nobody will get in, and here they were selling fucking tickets from a hot dog stand!

There was just pure lads everywhere and the police did well to keep us all apart outside and inside the ground. We were kept in for ages after the game and escorted back to the trains and we finally left Glasgow at about seven o'clock. All the Inter-City trains were jam-packed with lads and, although there was not the violence I had expected, it was the game where everyone said England had finally taken the piss in Glasgow.

Ten years later, after an unconvincing campaign which saw Sweden win the group by nine points, a goalless draw in Poland gave England a chance of qualifying for the 2000 European Championships in Holland and Belgium via the play-offs. The draw was made and Scotland were paired with England in a game the press dubbed 'The Battle of Britain'. It was an old term often used for games against the other home nations but, to many of the lads who followed both nations, it meant exactly that. From the minute the draw was made, battle plans were drawn up and it was a game which captured the imagination of many – for all the wrong reasons!

The biggest security operation in the history of the game was put in place and it worked, as a huge police presence was maintained in Glasgow throughout the day, stamping out potential incidents before they could escalate.

More than 250 Transport Police from England were sworn in under Scottish law to travel with English supporters taking trains across the border, and in a parallel move 111 English hooligans were identified by the NCIS and served with orders requiring them to report to their local police stations in England just before kick-off.

Despite claims that the police operation was a huge success, there were still well over 200 arrests, and, according to the lads that went, had Scotland shown any kind of interest, that number would have doubled.

NICK, NOTTINGHAM FOREST:

This was my first trip to Scotland with England and to be honest I left rather disappointed, not with England but with the piss-poor turnout from the Jocks. We landed in Glasgow around 7.30 and headed for a bar called Eastender's in Barrowlands, but before we had made the doors half a dozen Jocks flew out of some other rundown boozer and rained punches on us and, although they were not doing any damage, it still surprised the fuck out of us, as the streets were deserted apart from the odd paper boy and milk float.

It was a great start to the day and these lads seemed up for it as we traded blows when most people were still in bed, but out the corner of my eye I saw some blokes running over with a camcorder and, as it was too early for *Beadle's About*, we guessed they were police. It was a decent call and it made matters worse that one of them was the Forest spotter who seemed quite happy to see us. It looked like we were going to be nicked before we had even had a pint or some cornflakes, but the Old Bill just told us to get into the pub with the rest of the lads.

We got into a bar near the city centre and the day was going flat; we had been wandering about for an hour with not a sniff of the famous Hibs or Aberdeen Casuals.

We then walked into the centre with a large mob that was growing rapidly and there was not a Jock firm in sight. Shoppers and workers stood by, looking through the windows with a real fear in their eyes. A few slaps were dished out to mouthy Jocks brave enough to come anywhere near, but they were just passionate Scots who thought we were taking the piss, they were right and their football lads should have been backing them up, as it was an embarrassment for them. I was only a small kid when

Scotland smashed Wembley up, but there were older blokes than me in the mob, laughing that it had taken over 20 years to put it right but now the ghost of '77 had finally been laid to rest.

In my eyes, that was nonsense, walking around the city centre was not good enough, but without any opposition it was the best we could do. Then, out of nowhere, they finally appeared, and what a firm – 200 Casuals all panning out across the road who looked well up for it. These lads looked the business, unlike the sorry bunch who had been scurrying about all morning, who in the main were just Glasgow street rats. We started to walk slowly towards them when our mob burst into a run and the other mob never budged an inch and we got within yards of them before they all started to bounce about shouting, 'Stand ... England!' It was then that both mobs realised that they were English! We joined up and carried on the walk, but to be honest I felt like twatting them anyway just for spoiling the moment. The two mobs combined were an awesome force but it meant that no Jocks would come near, so a few club firms split off and Forest did see some action when they had it with a mob of Aberdeen or Dundee – they were not around long enough to find out!

At the ground, the OB looked unsure what to do with us when this mean-looking fucker on a horse came forward and shouted, 'Everyone with tickets come forward.'

Not one fucker stepped forward so he blurted, 'Get these bastards into town!'

The walk back was more of a stroll, on every corner there were mobs and they were all English, the city had been taken and, apart from a few barmy Jocks who came in on suicide missions, the baton-happy police and their mates on horseback who charged into us every half a mile, all we saw was Jocks with scarves covering their faces looking at us in embarrassment.

I knew that when we were all split up by the police they

would come out of the woodwork and, sure enough, little pockets of them took to picking off any groups of our lads who were daft enough to stray away from the few places we were allowed to drink in. Where the fuck were you, Scotland? You had the chance to get back some credit after your shit showing at Euro '96 but all you did was make your rep worse!

GILLY, WOLVES:
This is the big one for everyone! Scotland v England – who could have imagined it, the Auld Enemy playing in a play-off for a place in the European Championships in Belgium and Holland. Along with every other loon in the country, I thought, I've got to do this one!

For obvious reasons, we arranged to stop over in Hamilton before the game and we had a good firm of lads and ended up getting taxis to meet some Plymouth mates who were staying in East Kilbride. About 20 of us got taxis which drove through the famous Gorbals. Fuck me! I've been to the Bronx in New York and that shit-hole beats the Bronx! I'll always remember driving past this pub at some traffic lights – it was a green building, so I take it it was a Celtic pub in a Catholic area. Some silly bastard shouted out of the taxi something about England and 'Fuck off you Fenian cunts', which was not the brightest call as we were in traffic, and I thought, Fuck me, we are dead here! The pub emptied and glasses and bottles came our way, as the driver swerved the queue and drove off laughing as he was a Rangers fan.

In East Kilbride, we had a good night, no hassle at all, but when we got back to Hamilton 12 of our lot had been nicked after it had kicked off in the town centre and a quick call to the local police station confirmed that, as is the norm in Scotland, you are here all weekend until getting taken to court on the Monday.

The following morning, we caught the local train to

Glasgow Central where there was lads everywhere. We went into the Wetherspoons where Birmingham had already given it to Villa, fuck knows why. I thought it was England v Scotland this day, but that's Blues for you, say no more.

We were going round all the city-centre pubs and to tell you the truth we saw very few of these so-called Scottish Casuals that everyone was talking about. We were in one pub when a mob marched past and we looked at it in awe – no question about it, there must have been 1,000 lads on the march to Hampden Park. We joined up with them and it got bigger by the minute, too big, as no mob was going to come at this lot, we were untouchable. There were small outbreaks of violence and I hate to say it as they are my biggest rivals but I saw a firm of West Brom fighting with Hibs and small numbers of West Brom more than held their own.

We must have walked three miles and had seen very little when out of the blue some lads came out of this boozer saying, 'Come on, we're Aberdeen.'

I laughed my bollocks off, and questioned their sanity, but soon the local police intervened and it went off with them instead.

All day was the same, small mobs of Jocks trying to save face and heavy-handed Old Bill lumping the English hoping to get a reaction, and plenty obliged. Eventually, we were frogmarched back to the station as nobody had tickets and there was a few minor squabbles with a handful of Scots who stood their ground. They were a minority, though, and all I saw all day was the English taking the piss. There was more fighting between ourselves, which in this day and age seems to be acceptable, which is a shame.

Gilly's sentiments about the in-house fighting are backed up by Fran, a Man United fan, who admits that United's firm that day had very little interest in the Scots, as they wanted to take on any English firm who wanted to know.

FRAN, MAN UNITED:

That was the game when we really showed the rest of them that we were the best at the time. From the minute we got on the train until we got off at Preston late that night, no firm came near us. The so-called main players on the England scene, your Chelseas and West Hams were nowhere to be seen and the Birmingham lot and the Spurs firm were both phoned, as they were supposed to be firm-handed and neither wanted to know.

We took the piss that day, England had hundreds out but we went as United and, to be honest, apart from the numbers game, England were nothing special, if they had been, surely someone would have come to us, as they all knew who and where we were.

As for the Scots, well, they should give it up after that day, they basically let mobs of plastic hooligans in the regulation badged-up jumpers take the piss all day!

On the way home, we had a call from Preston who told us to get off there, as they were ready to have a go. I'll give them credit because when we got there they had a go, and they were the only ones who did that all day.

During the day, police made 230 arrests and 170 people appeared in court in Glasgow the following Monday in connection with trouble before and after the match. Police admitted that the biggest security operation ever mounted for a British sporting event had been severely tested after the final whistle when fans clashed in Glasgow city centre and outside the Hampden Park ground following England's 2–0 win.

It had taken 22 years to finally erase the memory of the game at Wembley in 1977, and four days after what was looked upon as humiliation in their own city the Scottish mob were given the chance to regain some respectability at the return game – most agree they blew it!

NICK, NOTTINGHAM FOREST:

After such a pitiful showing, everyone said that the Scots would turn up for the second leg at Wembley the following Wednesday and like so many others I believed all the hype and turned out for them. All I can say is they will have to live on past showings and, even though most of today's Scottish boys were not around in '77, they need to make the most of it as that is all they have to cling on to!

CHAPTER THIRTEEN

HOOLIGANS FIGHT!
ITALIA '90

By the time Italia '90 came around, Bobby Robson had assembled himself quite a tidy squad of footballers. Since losing three games on the bounce in the 1988 European Championships, Robson's side went on a 17-game unbeaten run which was only ended by a 2–1 home defeat in a warm-up game against Uruguay days before the squad left for Italy. Agreed, the run contained many draws and many of the games were against less well-known opponents, but it was still a decent record and gave the nation hope that England might have a chance of doing well in the tournament.

Robson had been in charge for eight years before the 1990 World Cup and was ready to step down immediately after it. While he was treated disgracefully by the press – a well-known paper even gave 'Robson Out' badges before one game – he had the respect of the players. New talent like Platt and Paul Gascoigne were bloodied with the old guard of Shilton and Lineker to give us all hope that this could be our year.

Off the field, England's first World Cup tournament in Europe since the new wave of hooligans had emerged was worrying the authorities. With the massive problems that the thugs had caused in Germany two years earlier, as well as the memory of the Heysel disaster, still etched in their minds, a massive security operation was mounted to prevent known troublemakers getting into Italy.

They failed miserably!

There was even a claim that the hooligan issue had been the reason behind England's group games being staged away from mainland Italy on the island of Sardinia. If this was the case, it was an intelligent move, as things could have been a lot worse if the firm England assembled on the island had been let loose on the likes of Milan, Turin or Naples. As it was, the draw had not been kind to the authorities and in the same group with England were Holland who had their own massive hooligan problem in their domestic leagues, with Dutch gangs being accused of copying the English thugs in the hope of emulating their notoriety in the hooligan world.

It seemed that Sardinia was to be the neutral venue for the battle between the hooligan sorcerers and apprentices, while there was also the added problem of thousands of Irish fans being on the island as well. Hopes were not high that the group games would pass off peacefully!

So, with our Cup song 'World In Motion' climbing the charts, England's hooligan army departed for Italy, many of whom were not even sure where Sardinia was, as they got ready for one thing only – the Dutch.

Darren from Mansfield was far from impressed with his time in Sardinia.

DARREN, MANSFIELD:

It was a bit boring in Sardinia, the local police just gave everyone a hard time and it pissed off most of the 30 Mansfield lads out there. A lot of them ran out of money and went home after the first round. There had been bits of bother with rival English but everything had been blown out of proportion by our press back home, as it always does. A few of us got caught up in the tear-gas episode before the Holland game and we were all forced to sit down on the forecourt of a petrol station with loads of others while the rest of the English just gave the Carabinieri the run around. It was a good laugh, we're all sat there while everyone else is just throwing everything they can get their hands on at the Carabinieri. The Dutch completely bottled it and the only bother was with a few Irish in bars and the local police, and there were plenty of stories going round that some English had been taking truncheons off the Carabinieri and battering them with them. Another story concerned an English lad taking a gun which had rubber bullets off its owner, which had the local cops on their toes. There must have been 2,000 English involved that day, and some of ours ended up near a wedding that got ruined when the rioters ploughed through the wedding party as they were all getting photographed, which was a shame. But who in their right mind would get married in a town the day we played Holland?

Italia '90 was one of the first trips that saw a large turnout of lads from Shrewsbury. Neil and Brendan were just teenagers when they made the journey to Sardinia.

BRENDAN, SHREWSBURY:
One of our first trips abroad was to Sardinia, there was about 25 to 30 Shrewsbury there in the end but we played it safe and all went in little gangs to keep out of the way of the police. We went in a group of six but only three of us came back as planned, as the rest of them got deported after doing about two weeks in prison. We went around Europe on the way to Italy, left a week early as the police had raided my house, Paris, Barcelona, on the Inter-City and we got to Sardinia five days before the Ireland game. That's where I met Spence from Oldham, he came off the train and as soon as he saw us he asked us where we were from. We got on and that was the start of our friendship with Oldham and Newcastle. It wasn't all handshakes, though; on the way out there, we were sailing from Marseille to Sardinia and a few Forest lads started on us and it kicked off and the disco was shut down which fucked the journey up a bit.

It was a one-off that, as, in those days, we never used to

argue against each other that much; we were looked at as a
small firm from a stupid village and nobody bothered us, we
would meet Chelsea, West Ham, Tottenham, Newcastle and
get on fine.

Once in Sardinia, we just hit the drink from the first night
and bummed around; we would spend all day chilling and
then at night get pissed up on cheap Italian lager. It was just
a real good crack, it was warm and you would kip anywhere
just to save the cash for beer, as you do when you're young.
We ended up mobbing up with a load of Leeds lads and they
were game as fuck. Neil was 19 and I was with my older
brother who was 17! They were both nicked after it kicked
off in a nightclub so I ended up sleeping in some Italian's
house. It was a mad situation – I was only 16, lost on some
fucking Italian island, wandering around pissed when this
lad noticed my English bulldog tattoo and said, 'Are you
English hooligan?'

'Why?'

'You can stay at my house.'

'Yeah, OK, I'm a hooligan!'

So he put me up for the night, it was going well until I took
my shoes off and, they were stinking their kitchen out, so his
parents soon got rid of me in the morning.

When the lads got nicked, I was left on my own with just my
rucksack but I met some West Ham who were good to me,
sorted me tickets for the games and kept an eye on me. I
remember we had met a couple on the boat who were going on
holiday to Sardinia, nothing to do with the football, a weird
couple of Goths from Bristol. On the day we played Holland,
we were all mobbing up at the station, hundreds of us, every
firm was there; it was the biggest mob I'd ever seen. From
nowhere, these Goths come up to me and said, 'Hi, how's the
holiday, Brendan? What time does the procession start?'

They thought we were waiting to start a fucking procession
to the ground! I just had to tell them we were mobbing up for
a row with the Dutch and they soon pissed off!

So we all mobbed up for this procession, as she called it, and then set off for the ground. Soon we saw a load of Dutch standing there, all singing, and, although they were not what we were looking for, we still scattered them, then literally it was just mayhem for about two hours solid. We were fucking with the riot police, it was going off mental; they threw tear gas at us in the end and I will always remember this big Man City beer monster just picking the tear-gas thing up and throwing it back at the Old Bill. One of the police blokes got stuck in the middle of England's firm and got absolutely obliterated. It just went mad, there were cars getting rolled over, a proper riot, it was an unbelievable two hours.

When it kicked off, we got chased through all these gardens and they were firing tear gas into us. I was knackered and saw this Italian woman looking out of her bedroom window; she must have felt sorry for me for she said, 'Come on in!'

She opened the door and a load more piled in to get away from the police and the tear gas, everyone just barged into this old girl's house! She was spot on and kept us inside while everyone was getting battered outside. This BBC TV crew came in the house and she told them to stop filming things. Eventually, the woman and her husband drove us to the ground for the England v Holland game, they actually give us a lift to the ground!

NEIL, SHREWSBURY:
We were actually let out in time for the riot, it was crazy! We had been locked up and I had kicked off because one of the lads was only young. I ran out of the cell and got him, and said to them that he was my brother so they put us into this cell together and said we were flying home that night. In the end, they just kept us for a few hours, give us loads of shit, smacked us round the head and let us go to cause rampage.

Every night after the game, the locals would be out waiting for us. They would turn up in little mobs, dressed in those fucking denim coats and they all come up to you waving chains and showing you their blades. It was a dangerous place if you were caught on your own so we soon cottoned on and stuck together. One night there was about 40 England and about 80 of them, and I was only 17 and had no fear so got into them with a belt I used to have tied around my sleeping bag, England were into them in seconds and they all done it on their toes, even though they were all tooled up. It was an Italian firm over there, though, not the immigrants like on the mainland or in France, pure Italian, all greasy hair, Lacoste and no bottle!

Apart from a wrecked wedding, a few fights with the Irish and the small matter of the Carabinieri getting put on their toes, the group stages were hailed a success. Even the team made it to the next stages, albeit after an unconvincing three games, when, although Robson's men were unbeaten, only a Mark Wright goal against minnows Egypt saw us progress.

The failure of the Dutch to show up, having decided to announce that they did not follow the national team and only represented their individual club sides, made it difficult for the hundreds of press holed up in Sardinia to earn their wages, so even the smallest of incidents made good reading for the thousands back home who were led to believe weeks earlier that World War III was about to start!

The papers reported that 20 England fans were arrested after an ugly battle with riot police in Sardinia's main town of Cagliari, after the mob had earlier stormed a bar packed out with Irish fans and began chanting 'No surrender to the IRA'. Many fans claimed that the Carabinieri were using over-the-top policing methods; however, when told that Italian Police had attacked innocent England fans with rifle butts, Sports Minister Colin Moynihan, a former Oxford Blue boxing champ, said in a statement, 'They got what they deserved and I fully agree with the stance that the Italian Police are taking; we are grateful for their swift, tough and decisive action.'

FIFA Chief Sepp Blatter joined Mr Moynihan in praising the

tough tactics used by Italian Police and commented, 'They are doing an amazing job.'

That may indeed have been the case on the night 22 England fans were arrested to save them from a massacre when they were surrounded by a mob of over 400 armed locals in the Northern town of Olbia in Sardinia. A senior police officer said, 'They would have been seriously injured or even killed and we arrived just in time to save them from being lynched.'

Elsewhere, other England fans had problems; the tournament was over for 26-year-old Chelsea fan Steve Clayton who was shot in the back, legs and head by pellets after a local mob stormed a café bar packed out with England fans who would not pay for a pizza, and another two England fans were shot and one stabbed on the island of Corsica. Back home, 40 England fans battered a policeman in Bedford, just outside London, after celebrating England's victory over Egypt, while the national papers took great delight in reporting that public enemy number one, Paul Scarrott, the notorious England hooligan, had been jailed until after the World Cup by Nottingham magistrates.

Next stop was Bologna where England played Belgium; en route, Rimini was the favoured destination and, not surprisingly, it was wrecked!

DARREN, MANSFIELD:

Only six of us went on to round two. The next game in Bologna had been designated an alcohol-free area so word spread amongst the English to go to Rimini, the famous holiday resort on the Adriatic Sea. When we finally arrived, we heard that the locals were already baiting the English and as usual things started to get going. Some Londoners were attacked early one evening and sporadic bits of bother occurred with lads chasing larger groups of Italians. Small groups of English were mobbing up in bars near a square just off the main seafront, but as usual the Carabinieri were letting the cowardly locals do anything to get a reaction from us. A mob of Leeds who'd been doing the tills in bars and some other Northerners kicked off an incident which saw the locals petrol bomb us, but it didn't stop us running them once the flames were put out and the smoke cleared. The Italian riot police showed no mercy, though, and were very heavy-handed and were happy to nick everyone and anyone who they took a dislike to. We sought refuge in a bar but they were happy to tear gas it and batter everyone who came out for fresh air.

The worst night was the eve of our game, there were hundreds of English drinking in the bars and Italy had won their game and, as is the case over there, they all come on to the streets in their cars and on those mopeds, beeping their horns and waving flags. It was bound to go at some stage and before long a bottle was thrown either way, the police were right on to it and it turned nasty with the tear gas and batons coming out. Loads were arrested and deported, including blokes who were totally innocent.

The following day, we went to the game and it was a massive police overkill, no bars were open and the tickets were on sale in a field with queues stretching back for about four hours. It was a disgrace but that's how we were treated. We won the game with a last-minute goal and were off to Naples to play Cameroon in the quarters but loads of lads were spent up and had to go home. It did kick off in the ground with the Belgians in this big neutral section which was rare over there, but apart from that little off the Belgians were nowhere to be seen.

The riots in Rimini were captured by the world's press and were the worst scenes of violence to be broadcast during the tournament, even though lads who were involved in Sardinia say they were actually far worse and the media missed much of the action. In Rimini, they were able to witness some of the sickening police brutality which many innocent fans were subjected to, although once again it was not reported that way.

One tabloid reported that police tear gassed English thugs in the

Italian resort of Rimini, and that six fans were badly injured, as English and Italians clashed in a bar. Manchester man Derek Burns, aged 34, claimed that police stormed another bar containing over 100 England fans and began indiscriminately hitting anybody in their way, which was the initial cause of over 400 English fans rampaging through the resort later. Eventually, 246 England fans were herded on to a plane and deported back to England after the riots in Rimini, and many claimed to be innocent victims of police brutality. Many were not even allowed to collect their belongings, money or passports from their hotels before flying home. The group deported from Rimini took the number of English deported since Italia '90 had kicked off to over 300.

But, if Rimini was bad, Naples was threatening to be far worse, and the day before the Cameroon match one headline read: 'YOBS FACE DEATH IN THE MAFIA CITY OF NAPLES'.

Italian hooligans, known as Ultras, said in a statement, 'It is a matter of honour and we intend to avenge the death of the Italians killed at Heysel.'

Nicky Stevenson from Nottingham was at this game.

NICK, NOTTINGHAM FOREST:
This was my first time abroad with England and it was mental from day one. It is quite disturbing how much happens in a few days following England, it is one incident after another. I had heard loads of tales of how mad it was but thought some were a bit far-fetched. I was wrong! And this was a mad introduction to following our national side.

I flew to Rome with another Forest lad 'Mush', and we then got the night train down to Naples for the Cameroon game and somehow we managed to get tickets for it. I could not believe it in the ground, the tense atmosphere, uneasy truces between lads you would usually be fighting with – it was eerie. In those days, out of 2,000 fans, 1,500 would be lads who were up for it. Today, we have 10,000 fucking face-painted shirters that follow England and a couple of hundred lads, while all the lads who fought when it mattered are on bans. These cunts with their brass bands and foam hands frown at the few who still go, but the only reason they get away with acting like panto pillocks is that the reputation we gave England makes it safe for the helmets to go in the first place.

It was a cracking game and, after looking like we were going out at one stage, we got a couple of pens that the big-eared one who shamelessly makes a twat of himself in the crisp adverts dispatched and it was 'let's all have a disco' and the semis here we come!

England were now just one game away from the final and the authorities were now preparing themselves for the worst-case scenario, an Italy v England final! The mayor of Turin even claimed that the country would face a war if England made it to the final against the host nation, while around Turin graffiti on walls contained death threats to the English hooligans. It was a far cry from the treatment the Tartan Army had been given during the qualifiers in the same city; the Turin authorities had been so impressed with the behaviour of the Scottish fans they had lifted the alcohol ban that had been imposed on match days for them. Not surprisingly, the ban was back in force by the time the English arrived!

While the original hardcore following in Sardinia had long gone home, hundreds more were now flying out to replace them. Trevor Tanner from Spurs, John, a QPR fan, and Nick were all there to see the biggest game England had played since the World Cup Final in 1966.

TREVOR, SPURS:
I started on the England scene in 1990 when we went out to the World Cup. There were not a lot of Tottenham going with England then but we had started to take liberties with Chelsea about that time, and we all know they have a massive England following so we needed to have enough about us to go out there as a proper firm, which we did. I went out with a pal of mine and we got a flight from Gatwick, last-minute

sort of fucking thing, those last-minute tickets you could buy at the airport if you were not choosy who you flew with; it only cost £85 or something like that and we slipped out to Italy unnoticed and spent about a day travelling to Turin.

We were just outside Turin, on our way through, when we stopped at this little bar sort of thing. We were drinking, having a bit of food, nice and peaceful, then when we came outside a couple of bods came by on scooters and one jumped off and pulled a blade out. I just went straight into him and picked up a bit of wood and what have you and fucked him off. It was an eye-opener, though, we were minding our own business and in a split second you could get stabbed up. I never got in the game but we still had a little go at the Germans after the game, as we were all gutted that we were out but the Germans were just not in our league when it came to it. So after this little trip I've got the real taste for it. Italia '90 was sweet.

JOHN, QPR:

Italy was a good trip because we came down from Milan, there was probably about 12 of us because a mate of mine had won 10 grand on the horses and paid for us all to go out. He literally rung me up the night before we went out: 'Here, let's all go to the World Cup!'

That was how I went there, one day sitting at home thinking I was watching it in the pub, next day, I was out there.

Anyway, we get to Turin and I can remember thinking we were in trouble; it was like when you get to Manchester and you're coming out the station and they're all out there and they're waiting for you, it was like that at Turin, hundreds of Italians and I'm thinking, Oh my God, why did this fucking bet come in!

There weren't many of us as we got off the train. The police surrounded us and walked us on to the main concourse but, as we got out the station, there was a tremendous roar, and there was a few bottles slung and things getting smashed all around us. It was looking very much on top when just as we got to the doors a big roar went up and a load more England came out. There was still only a small firm of us but it sounded probably ten-fold because we were still echoing in the station. That was all it needed and the Italians were off, boom, gone, nowhere to be seen!

We got dumped at the ground and were there too early, no England fans were there at all and I can remember me and my little lot were standing there looking at hundreds of the old sausage-munchers with the blond hair, big taches, scarves round their wrists, a lot of black, red and orange or whatever it is all around. So the Italians had gone but now I'm thinking, Fucking hell, we're in trouble here, this is not good.

Anyway, we're just standing there like sitting ducks and, although the Germans were not really firm lads, they are all getting a bit leery and start moving in closer and closer and they're getting more and more around us, ready to start something, one bad word or one punch would have set it off, it was like a time bomb and we were waiting for it to go bang. But in the distance I could hear this little hum, I had no idea what it was but it was getting louder and louder and, just for a few moments, it took my mind off what was happening. I thought, What's that, there's some noise in the background. I heard more and more noise, it got louder and louder and louder and, as it got louder, I'll never ever forget the sight of scores of these shitty little buses with the big windows with all the England flags hanging out, and the buses were bouncing, literally bouncing up the road towards us. These buses were coming along the road near the ground, fucking bouncing, full of England fans singing and, within seconds, I looked around and there was not a German to be seen, like magic they had disappeared. It was unbelievable, one of those sketches that make the hairs on the back of the neck stand up.

It wasn't to be on the pitch and we lost on pens. I was heartbroken, I'm not ashamed to admit that I actually sat in the stands crying at the end. I was sat next to Garth Crooks and we were hugging each other at the end because we were so upset. My mate bought me a ticket off a tout and it was an Argentinean FA free ticket and that's why I was sitting next to Garth Crooks. I was right up there with all the England knobs with a ticket that some bent bastard in the Argie FA had sold, crying with Garth Crooks. I was made up at the time that I had met him but now, after seeing him on the telly, it makes me cringe that I was hugging the soft bastard as, the way he is on telly, is an embarrassment. That was it, World Cup over, but I will take the sight of those buses coming up that hill with me to my grave.

Thanks to a bent Argentinean FA official, John saw the game. Nicky Stevenson was not so lucky and he missed England's biggest game for 24 years, but it was not through the lack of trying!

NICK, NOTTINGHAM FOREST:

On the night before and on the day of the match, it was going off everywhere. Any German or Italian who looked remotely like a lad got it, England were on the march and mullered anyone who had a crack at them. There were English casualties, mostly victims of sly stab wounds at the hands of the Italians. This pisses me off, not the fact that lads are cut, but the fact that everyone was in uproar when yet another casualty ran into the bar, having been slashed or cut by the moped mobs. Dirty Italian bastards – yes; stupid English cunts – yes, also! You know the territory, and yet every time the national team or an English club play over there some soft bastards go wandering off and end up crying when they get cut. Wake up, have you not heard of Heysel? For fuck's sake, it's going to be dangerous, leave your drum kit and foam hands in the fucking hotel and stick tight to the lads, safety in numbers and common sense, and unfortunately many novices today don't have it!

Money was running out, so I planned to go to the ground and rob a couple of tickets from touts, whether they were

Italian, German or English, in that order; if there were none about, then some soft bastard was losing their prized possession, no room for sentiment when a place in the World Cup Final is beckoning! A pair would be nice, one for getting in and one to resell for beer money which seemed a good idea at the time.

On a bus up to the ground, I met a young Chelsea lad called Jason (not Marriner) who as well as being on the same bus as me was in the same boat as me cash-wise and was up for some ticket collecting, and as soon as we got by the ground we spotted our targets.

A middle-aged German couple were trying to offload some briefs and we asked them for a look; he thought he was clever and told us we look with our eyes not our hands and put them behind his back. He was not as clever as he thought and my new Chelsea mate snatched them in a split second. The problem was he was not as clever as Benny from *Crossroads* and, instead of running, he just stood there waving them in the face of this irate German who was getting madder, as Jason shouted, 'Fuck you, you German cunts.' All sorts of people noticed the commotion and the German was going berserk, so I cracked him, hoping it would shut him up; his wife went hysterical and this was becoming a nightmare with people running to their assistance. By now, there were German lads by us and this bird was pointing at us and screaming at them to stop us. So, as you do, instead of giving the tickets back and making it out to be a huge language breakdown we steamed into them and it went off big time. I was bouncing around trying to whack anyone who came within a yard of me and was soon on the deck after an Italian copper battered me over the head with his baton. He was shouting in Italian at me, I presume it was words to the effect of 'you're nicked' and I was soon cuffed. A Spurs fan was taking photos of it all for some daft reason and he and Benny – sorry, Jason – were all bundled into a van with me and we sped off to the local nick.

The Yid was taken away – he may have been undercover OB for all we knew, as we never saw him again – but me and Jason were locked up for a couple of hours before being taken into another cell where there was just one copper sitting in the middle of the room with a truncheon in one hand and a cup of coffee in the other. Here we go, all sorts go through your head, you've seen *Midnight Express* and that baton looked like it was either going over my head, across my back or pray to Jesus not up my fucking arsehole! Jason was white; I had picked the wrong partner in crime here and the colour was draining from his face by the second. Fucking Bonny and Clyde were an odd couple but me and Jason were the Laurel and Hardy of the ticket-tout snatch squad and were about to be dealt with accordingly, and there was no judge and jury to make it a fair hearing.

We stood against the wall for ages and this twat just kept grinning and slapping the baton against his chair; the cunt knew what he was doing and Jason had lost it and was by now shaking like some cunt with Parkinson's disease. I was thinking to myself, Come on, you cunt, give us a few slaps, have a wank and be done with it, just get it over and fucking done with.

After what seemed like two hours but was probably 20 minutes, the door opened and a guard walked in with two huge German boneheads in tow who were handcuffed to each other. They were the business, full-blown skins, Docs, braces, mid-twenties and looked like they could have a right go. I was 17, Jason 16 and we were out of our league if they were going to leave these twats in the same cell as us. Jason by now had turned into a gibbering wreck and my only hope was if they kept the two of them cuffed to each other and gave me a few free hits; in reality, I knew it was not going to happen and I was right as the flat-cap twat clacked his truncheon on the chair and his sweaty oppo was told to undo the cuffs.

The boss man moved his stool to the far corner and casually stepped back with a stupid smile on his face. I fucking knew what was coming next, luckily my shaking

Chelsea mate didn't or I am sure the smell of shit would have made its way through his jeans. I started to psyche myself up the minute they had been brought into the cell and then the time came and the flat cap shouted, 'English hooligans stand! German hooligans stand!'

Then he blurted, 'Hooligans fight!'

I looked at Jason and, before he started crying, I thought, Fuck it, and windmilled into the German bastards.

I woke up in another cell and thought it may have been a terrible dream but saw blood everywhere and then realised that my head had been used as a football. The bastards had gone to town on me and it hurt, but I got up, realised there was no major damage done and thought, If this is what it's like following England, then fucking great, this is for me. Jason had fared a bit better and they had just given him a few digs and he looked a lot happier than the last time I looked at him.

We were cleaned up and we thought we were going to be out to watch the match but they locked us up and took us to the airport the next morning. In the departure lounge, we sat there with fuck-all money and a five-hour wait when the German boneheads walked in. Give them credit, they were OK and even left us the rest of their lira when their flight was called. Wankers!

I heard nothing more about it for three years when I got a letter saying that I had the chance to appear in court and defend myself – fuck knows what they had been doing for three years! Whatever, I wasn't going back and got another letter a few months later saying I was banned from Italy for life – big fucking deal!

What a first trip, I was hooked!

England went on to play Italy in the play-off for third place and the game was turned into a carnival with a party atmosphere. Throughout Italia '90, England fans had been shot, stabbed, imprisoned and deported – had the third-place play-off been the final, Italia '90 would probably have seen deaths.

CHAPTER FOURTEEN

FOR THE LOVE OF THE IRISH!
ENGLAND V EIRE '90/'91

England returned home from Italia '90 with their heads held high! They had come so close to making the World Cup Final, so hopes of a reasonable European Championship campaign were met with great optimism. Off the pitch, the fans' behaviour in Italy had been reasonable, a few riots here and there and the usual deportations and arrests made national news, but overall Italia '90 could have been a lot worse.

Domestically, football violence was in decline, the rave scene was in full swing and the memory of Hillsborough was enough to put many off for life. Those who were left to keep the hooligan flag flying were hardcore, though, a more organised, more sinister and more violent breed of hooligan.

In late 1990 and early 1991, England played two European Championship qualifiers against the Republic of Ireland. Previous meetings at Euro '88 and at Italia '90 had seen minor disorder between the two nations, which was mainly down to drunkenness and a poor showing by England on the field. This bad feeling was growing like a cancer and there was a simmering hatred towards the Irish from the hardcore hooligans who labelled all their followers under the same banner – IRA sympathisers!

Among this hardcore were many of the younger lads who had missed the boat hooligan-wise and they were keen to get it floating again. One of this new breed was Lee Spence from Oldham and he took great delight in being a leading figure in the new England firm. Lee was a main player in bringing together various firms in an attempt to form a national mob and eliminate the in-house fighting which had plagued the national scene since fans started following England abroad.

LEE, OLDHAM:

Ever since I was jailed in Scotland in 1987, I became hooked on the England scene. With following one of the smaller clubs, there was little or no chance of going abroad to watch football and England gave many people like me the opportunity to do so. We had a ball! Many of the older lads are forever telling us we were 10 years too late – what the fuck were we supposed to do, travel to Turin in 1980 when we were still in nappies?

By the time I was 20, football violence was dying, everyone was into pills and very few still bothered going to the game looking for trouble but I was different. You could do both and I was determined to make sure Oldham were well represented in the hooligan world, both at home and away with my club and at England games.

After a few trips with England, I had met plenty of lads the same as me, the same age, into the same things, and, yes, we were all disappointed that things were not as violent as they used to be, but we were keen to keep the English disease alive.

Things were changing, abroad, European mobs were keen to have a go and we had to curb all the in-house rivalries which had always gone on, as, if we were not as one, we were in danger of losing the reputation which lads from the 70s had fought to build.

The likes of Oldham, Newcastle, Shrewsbury and Stockport started to mob up together and this made us a formidable force, soon even the main Cockney mobs realised that we were decent and within a year most of us all got on. There were exceptions; Millwall were always going to be Millwall, and West Ham were always doing their own thing, but their numbers were dwindling so they either had to put up or shut up on most trips.

Ireland in '91 was a game where, had we not stuck together, we would have had serious problems as it came very much on top! It was a midweek-afternoon kick-off as the Irish never had floodlights and it also coincided with the day some political prisoner was being extradited from Ireland to England. How the fuck they let it go ahead under those circumstances is a mystery and anyone in the know will agree that this game saw more actual violence than the game that was abandoned four years later.

It was the first away game after Italia '90 and all the main faces who had been over there met up in Dublin. United had a good mob, Oldham had 30-odd, there was a tidy firm of Luton – combine all the usual suspects and it made for an unspectacular but close-knit firm. We didn't know it at the time but we would have needed the Paras, the Marines and the fucking SAS had we wanted to take the piss that day!

Initially, it was pretty much low key, we had a few drinks around the usual haunts but there were no lads in Dublin who wanted to know and most of the other Irish were happy to put up with us, as they are used to all the tourism shit they get over there. We were walking up towards the ground when from nowhere a minibus drove past with a tricolour in the back window and, as we thought it was full of Eire, some clever fucker threw a bottle at it. That was it, they slammed on and we noticed that on the side it had Belfast Van Hire or something and every fucker on it looked well up for a fight. We got ready and expected them to pile off but they stopped, turned around and then drove straight at us, up the kerb, proper trying to run us down. It was a scary moment, the driver was not fucking about, he was 100 per cent trying to mow us down! We ended up getting some bricks and bits and he drove off rather than risk the van getting smashed up but deep down I knew they would be back.

None of our mob had tickets so we got off into a pub and minutes later we saw this crazy mob of Paddies coming down the road towards the pub we were in, armed with wheel jacks and spanners, fucking iron bars and what have you. We all got outside ready to have a go but the Garda got between them and forced them back up the road, before telling us that they were known to the police and that they had nothing to do with the football but were here for the march against the extradition, which made us realise we'd thrown a bottle at the wrong minibus. That set it off and they must have passed the word around to watch out for the English, as what we came up against later that day was unbelievable.

We watched the match in a pub and had a tidy firm of about 80 who set off back to town after the game, but as we crossed the bridge on to O'Connell Street we bumped right into the march and in seconds we clashed with them. We were mainly young lads and thought it was great at first, the Irish were game as fuck and no one was moving; it was probably some of the best street fighting I had seen at the time. We were doing well, really holding our own but then the whole march turned on us and every Irish person in the street got involved. Thinking back now, we were mental calling it on, as there would have been some serious people involved in that march, hundreds were there from Belfast, but at the time it was the thing to do and we just about got out of it alive!

It went badly wrong when the Garda joined in and they were letting them rout us, their street was deafening with the chant of 'Kill a Brit' and the Garda were just wading into us and splitting us up into little mobs, and after not very long it was a case of every man for himself and once again we had to run for our lives!

Lads were chased on to housing estates, into shops, others were trying to flag taxis down, it was a mad scene, about 80 lads getting run by Dublin's fair city! People always exaggerate numbers but I'll swear it was not hundreds, it was fucking thousands of them after us, and all I could think of was those army lads who were caught in Belfast after getting trapped and who were murdered. I could not get it out of my head that if these cunts catch me I could die here. I do honestly believe, if they had caught us, someone would have been killed. It had fuck all to do with football, it was a political attack on British people by the Irish, but to be honest it was all our fault!

Somehow, we all made it back to the ferry and I don't think anyone was seriously injured but that night we got off sharpish, it was no time for heroes, it was a case of get the fuck out of the place.

Dublin that day was mental and we did well to get home!

We didn't have to wait long to have a go at squaring things up, as a few months later we played them at Wembley. By now, we had a good firm of lads from all over the place and, apart from a few outcasts like the Villa lot who wanted to do their own thing, we would meet up and get on great. That day we all arranged to meet in The Hog in the Pound early doors and it went pear-shaped for me before I had even had a few pints!

On the Saturday, we had played Blackburn and I was talking to a few of the lads from various firms about how we had turned up in Bolton after the match and chased them all over their own town when crack! I took a lump around the head from Bordell or Bowdell, whatever his name is, who I had not noticed sitting next to us.

He's a main face at Bolton and looks a bit like Klinsmann and he had taken the hump that I was slating his firm, and straight away that fucked it up as everyone dived in and there was a load of pushing and shoving and it split us up into two camps, which was exactly what we were trying to avoid. Eventually, we agreed it could wait and it calmed down, so we got the tube to Kilburn, and I went into the Black Lion and noticed a few Brighton lads who were Irish sitting there with a load of Paddies.

Before I had a chance to get them outside, the lot went. In

minutes, the place was totalled, there was a load of building work going on outside and there were bricks and all sorts coming through the windows which was a bit daft as there was a few of us in there. Next minute, something hit me full in the face and later one of the lads said it was a chunky pint pot and it opened my head up. I couldn't see a thing and was grateful to the big Arsenal bloke who managed to get me outside and across to Rumbelow's where the staff helped clean me up. I was in the back of this shop with a tea towel around my head and outside all you could hear was the sound of sirens and alarms and the shattering of windows going in.

When I came outside to see if I could get a taxi to the hospital for a few stitches, a bin flew through the air from a pub with a broken windows. There were still small groups at it but the clever ones were long gone. There were loads of shoppers and locals in the street and looking out of the windows, wondering what the fuck was going on, 100 per cent bemused!

It was an amazing sight, there was smoke coming out of one pub and it was later confirmed that Chelsea were up to their old tricks with the flare guns. Glass was smashing as it fell out of broken window frames and there were casualties in pub doorways wondering what the fuck had happened; it was the perfect ambush and I was gutted that I had missed it. On the plus side, no police came for a good few minutes, and after people were saying that they had let it run because of their hatred of the people who drink in those pubs.

I actually went up to the ground later and went into the game, as I was that fucked with this head injury. I met a few of the Oldham lads and they told me that the Irish were game and loads had a go; early doors they were getting caned but with the help of the doormen at one stage it got a bit tasty.

Apparently, the place went crazy, every pub on that road was getting attacked and they were pulling shutters down as England were getting near them. The Irish were having a go, getting fucked but having a go, doormen were pulling hammers and coshes out of their coats and one lad had a hole in his head after taking a smack with something.

In the ground it was evil and I saw loads of Paddies with tickets in the England end getting slapped, and for once the English got on to the fact that these lovable cheery Irish fans were happy to sit in the pubs in Kilburn all week, slating the English and throwing their change in the collection tins for 'The Cause'!

Those two games saw extreme violence, yet didn't get massive media attention, and in the eyes of many the rivalry between the two nations was intense but friendly. Less than four years later, that myth was blown out of the water, but that's another story!

CHAPTER FIFTEEN

THEY WANTED TO FIGHT US OR EACH OTHER
POLAND '91, '93, '97, '99

There cannot be another nation who have been paired with England in World Cup and European Championship groups as many times as Poland have. Since the fateful World Cup campaign in 1973 – when the goalkeeper dubbed 'The Clown' prevented England qualifying for the finals in Argentina, a game which also was the beginning of the end for Sir Alf Ramsey – to 2006's final group game in the same tournament, England and Poland have clashed 15 times competitively. During this time, the countries have met in five of the last six World Cup campaigns and in two of the last four European Championship-qualifying stages.

In 1989, when the sides drew 0–0 in Katowice, the Poles didn't have a reputation as a hooligan nation but many England fans came home having been victims of violent assaults. So, by the time England visited again in November 1991, for a European Championship qualifier, they were well prepared to face this new challenge to their status as number-one nation in the hooligan world.

Jason Marriner is a well-known and respected Chelsea fan; he was jailed as part of an undercover television documentary operation, which furthered the career of investigative reporter Donal MacIntyre. Jason is a free man today and has published his own book, *It's a Funny Old Game*, recalling his life as one of the most notorious hooligans in the country:

JASON, CHELSEA:
Poznan, Poland, 1991
In 1991, I decided to go to the Poland game in Poznan. There were quite a lot of Chelsea going, because, unlike today, we were not good enough to play in Europe, there was no Champions League, we were skint and, more to the point, crap, so Poznan it was! Chelsea have always been big on the England scene, we were probably the best-represented firm on the circuit and loved to make a proper trip out of it – none of this in and out, we liked to shake it all about a bit while we were there!

Chelsea liked a bit of sightseeing; loads of England fans get a flight directly to the place we are playing at, book a hotel near the station and then sit in the hotel bar or pub nearest the station for the duration of the trip. What's all that about? I half expect to see them playing dominos and asking the barman to put fucking *Coronation Street* on the telly!

When we went, we would always try and go via another country and have a night out there, and this was the case for the game in Poland, where we decided to go via Berlin. I hired a car and drove over with just three of us in a seven-seater, just in case we couldn't get anywhere to kip – nice motor with a bit of room which, if push came to shove, turned into our accommodation as well. Our first destination was Berlin, where we arranged to meet up with TC, Fat Pat and a few of the other Chelsea herberts. But what I will always remember was that we went to Checkpoint Charlie when we were over there, and one of the lads in the car, Trev, a Man City fan, said to me, 'Fuck me, is that Johnny Cash over there?'

I looked across and said, 'Do you know what, I think it is.'

So I've gone walking across there and said, 'All right, Johnny, how are you, mate?

I was half-expecting him to look at me daft, wondering what the fuck I was on about, but he turned around and replied, 'Yeah, man, not too bad.'

I was well happy by now, the geezer was a fucking legend! So I asked him if it was OK to have a picture with him and he was spot on. We had a photo and Johnny said, 'How did you recognise me?'

I was on a roll now and laughed. 'Well, you know what, Johnny, it's fucking minus something silly out here, and there ain't a lot of penny-in-the-banks walking about with open black shirts on with big medallions, so it was quite a giveaway!'

That was the highlight of the trip and we carried on and did all the tours, we even bought a bit of the Berlin Wall, because that had just been knocked down a few months earlier, and, of course, we all bought one of those daft Russian hats with all the fur round it just to let everyone know we were tourists!

Apart from Johnny Cash, the Berlin Wall, Checkpoint Charlie and the Brandenburg Gates, we just went on the drink, and, after a day, a lot of the English were slowly but surely coming into Berlin. A few hours later, it started to warm up and the Old Bill were all round us and it was obvious that a few of the football hooligan intelligence spotters were about; and, because there were certain people and certain faces who were very well known, it meant that from now on we would be shadowed by the Old Bill.

We holed up in between two bars and then some lads have gone and had one of the armoury shops off, and before long we were all tooled up with a bit of tear gas and that – it's just as easy to get that gear over there as it is to get a fucking Mars bar out of the sweet shop here. The mood began to change as the beer took its toll and this firm of Old Bill knew we were on our way to Poland, but didn't know we were not going that night and, before long, they tried to move us on, and of course it's all kicked off. People started steaming into the Old Bill, the tear gas goes off, the fucking bars get smashed up, and, once again, we gave the papers something to write about.

Usual eventful night on tour with England!

We slept in the car that night and started making our way to Poland the next day, where we met up with a minibus from Manchester who we followed, as the driver was Trev's pal who was a long-distance lorry driver and knew the roads well, which was double handy. So we got to Poznan a day early, booked into a top-notch hotel and went into their exclusive restaurant; four of us sat down and ordered the same, best bit of steak, chips, salad, bread and butter, a few drinks and it was nice and civilised and set us up well for the day of sight seeing and cheap lager. We were ready to go and this geezer brought us the bill and it was as long as a fucking milk round with a million and one noughts on the end of it, but the truth of it was it came to something like a fiver each, and that was with the vodkas and beer, I'll never forget it. I kept the bill but the police nicked it when they raided me a few years later and I was gutted because it looked like I was a millionaire!

That day I expected more from the Poles but we had seen no sign of them. People kept saying, they will come just give them time but all night it was one false alarm after the other and no one would turn up. We spent the night chopping and changing different bars, meeting different people, and after a full on day on the drink I ended up going to bed at some daft hour.

I could not have been asleep for long when, bang! There was a knock on my door, and outside everyone was shouting, 'They're here, they're here.'

I said, 'Who's fucking here?'

One of the lads burst into my room and shouted, 'The Polish! Seriously, they are fucking here!'

I've looked at my watch and replied, 'Don't be fucking ridiculous, its half-past eight in the morning!'

It turned out that there were about 25 of the lads

downstairs sitting round the table, some drinking who had been there all night and some who had been to have breakfast, when a huge mob of Poles had come bouncing in and ambushed them!

I've looked out the window and there was a mob of about 150 outside the hotel and I thought to myself, What time do they set their alarms? It's fucking half-past eight in the morning!

By now, it was like a comedy sketch; everyone's knocking on everyone's door, everyone's getting back into their trousers, running down the corridor putting their clothes on. People with feet in the same leg falling over, jumpers on inside out and back to front shouting all sorts of bollocks!

We ran down the stairs mobbed up and they were all outside, loads of scruffy skinheads in their tight denim jeans, mad trainers and really loud tracksuit tops; as far as I'm concerned, they must have had a few quid because they spent fuck all on clothes! Despite their poor dress sense, they have called it on but it didn't take long for us to finish it and we have turned it right round and have done exceptionally well. We really did get our act together which, to be truthful with you, at half-past eight in the morning when most people have been on the piss till fucking three or four o'clock was a major result. As soon as we ran at them, they didn't want to know, they were happy bullying 25–30 lads sitting down with their egg on toast drinking vodka and orange, but when we got amongst them they knew that we were the guvnors and soon it was back to bed. I woke up a couple of hours later and thought it had been a dream, it was like, 'Was that for fucking real?' It was half-past eight in the morning and there were about a hundred grown men running about in our vests, chasing scruffy Poles about before you have had your fucking cornflakes or bacon and egg!

Later that day, we met the others and just sat round drinking all day waiting for the game to kick off, as there was absolutely fuck all there to do apart from drink. As you do, a few of us went for a walkabout and we actually bumped into a mob of Poles by a crossing over a dual carriageway that took you down to a train station. The Polish were on the train station and we piled down the stairs towards them, knowing it's easier to fight downwards than it is to fight going upwards. I'll give them credit, though, they came up to us and we are just standing there kicking them down and giving it to them. It was about even numbers, there was about 30 of each of us and like I said the Poles wanted it as much as we did.

We ended up back at the main bar and, about an hour and a half before the game, we all left together, a top firm of about 300–400 on the march. It was a fair old walk and we had the Old Bill keeping tabs on us but it was not a tight escort at first and the Poles had a few opportunities to come at us from the side streets but they didn't want it badly enough. We kept surging towards them every time we saw little mobs on the corner of the streets but they back-pedalled straight away. As we got near the ground, the police got their act together and, although our mob was a fucking good mob and there was a very big mob of them, there was a line of Old Bill three-deep, all with riot shields, the helmets and the truncheons and the tear gas all ready, just blocking either party off. Just before we got to the ground, we went past a tram load of them and there was about 40 Polish in each carriage, singing and giving us the big 'un; it was unlucky for them, as they stopped right next to the cream of our firm and, as soon as the doors opened, we ran up to the tram and pulled them out.

We gassed them and really gave it to them. It was at this game that a load of us Chelsea lads bought swimming goggles to protect us from the CS gas and we had a mad photo taken which would have gone down well in fucking family album.

Inside the ground, the Poles seemed content with knocking fuck out of each other; we stood there for most of the game watching them battle non-stop. After the game, we were well wrapped up by the Old Bill. It was a moody place but I was more than confident in our firm, in those days, it was all the right people following England; unlike today, when someone puts a Stone Island jumper on and thinks he can have a row, you had to fight at these places. That day it was a case of England having too many – 80 per cent of the support was hooligans and no firm would have got near us that day.

Katowice, Poland, 1993

Two years later, I went again and there was more trouble than the first game, as we were in a much smaller mob. There were a stronghold of Chelsea out and we decided to do our own thing and peel away from the main firm and try and get in with the Poles in the ground. We had a few small altercations on the way but managed to make it right up to the ground, when one of our spotters just stumbled across us and radioed through to say we were on our way. We'd marched to the ground and we'd marched to represent our country. The Poles knew what we were there for, we knew what we were there for, and the police knew what we were there for; it was a proper football mob and we nearly pulled it off.

As soon as we got in the ground, we tried to ambush them. They lit a torch flame and we've tried to attack them but the Old Bill intervened very early and got it sorted. It was a pity that the Old Bill got on to it early, as all the barmies were in the ground putting their flags up and obviously, when we walked in and went over to the fence, we stood out like a boil on your arse. We walked straight to the fence as near as possible to them but that call from the spotter meant that we were sussed and the Polish Police kept a lid on it just in time; had that spotter not have been so lucky – it was not intelligence, it was pure luck – we would have been in amongst them and that would have been some battle.

As soon as we got in there, we made a beeline for them, there was no point in standing in the fucking middle behind the goal when the Polish are there. We've gone in there then we've charged towards them and took them by surprise a little bit.

But, to be fair to the Old Bill, they were on the ball and they stopped it before anything really happened. The Polish Police had their hands full again, though, as it all started between themselves; the Poles were mad, they wanted to fight us or each other, they were happy as long as they were fighting!

They still had a load of mugs giving us verbals over the fence and throwing all the hand signs at us and screaming and shouting nonsense, but what was the point? I kept telling these people, 'Shout all you fucking want, there's no point in talking to me like that, mate, I can't understand what you're saying. I'm not fluent in Polish!'

Chorzow, Poland, 1997
I went to Poland again in '97 with Andy Frain aka Nightmare; we flew straight in for a couple of days as, to be truthful, after two trips there, I knew what the place was about, you've only got one thing to do over there if you can handle it and that's drink. We found a bar that all the English had holed up in and I bumped into Lee Spence from Oldham who I'd been nicked with in Amsterdam when England played Holland.

We ended up cracking on with him and his pals, drinking all night and expecting trouble but it was as if the Poles only came out to play on the match day, as we had no problems at all that night.

We had had enough of drinking; I didn't want too much of a hangover the next day for the football so we ended up getting hold of a cab driver when we found out Auschwitz was only an hour away by cab. I'm not being funny, but if you're in France you go to the fucking Eiffel Tower, it's an important bit of history, so we decided to go to the biggest tourist attraction around. The cab driver had obviously done it a million and one times before and he even came in with us to show us around and it was a massive eye-opener. It was an eerie place, very quiet, you could hear a pin drop, you wouldn't hear any birds tweeting, it was soulless and I learned a lot that day.

There was two concentration camps actually, the main one and another named Birkenau, where they used to keep the prisoners until they thought they were ready for work, then they would take them to Auschwitz. As you walked through the gates, there were two posts with a big metal sign above it, in a horseshoe shape and written on it in Polish or German was something like 'Work brings freedom'. So they'd go in there, work their bollocks off, to wind up in the fucking gas shower. It was a ringer, it was a moody bluff. We got back and told people about it only being an hour away, and said they would be mad not to go and have a look at a proper bit of history.

A few years later, that trip came back to haunt us, as, when me and Andy got nicked for the TV documentary, it was used against us that we had been to Auschwitz. We were portrayed as sick people but the programme never mentioned the fucking coach loads of Germans that were there at the same time, and the thousands of tourists who go there every year. Two football hooligans go there and it is a sick thing for us to do, but all the other people in the world can go there as it is an historical landmark? I still find that confusing.

Sightseeing over, we just carried on and on the day of the match there were a few running battles, nothing spectacular, nothing to get too excited about when you've been involved with football violence for years. I think the police over there liked it because they were the same as the locals, they had fuck all to do, the highlight of their year would be when England were in town.

The Polish Old Bill made me chuckle at times, you would see them unshaven and in a bar having a quick half of lager and a woodbine while on duty. They are not interested in stopping you over there for having no tax disc, or for doing 36 in a 30mph-limit area, but they were interested in some football violence because just like myself they'd want to hit some cunt here because there's nothing else happening. We give them reason to hit us a few times and they did; we had no moan about that, they were OK. I look at it like this sometimes, if you've got 500 dogs in a cage, eventually one's going to fucking bark and one's going to bite, and that's what happens with human beings; we're all the same breed and eventually someone will want to punch someone else!

The Polish were about in mobs, but we all marched together to the ground and there were minor scraps here and there but it was nothing to write home about. Their papers were full of it, though, I suppose that's the only way to sell a newspaper over there. There were loads of photographs us and headlines saying something like 'THE ENGLISH ARE IN TOWN' and 'HOOLIGANS CAUSE MAYHEM', and I thought, Fucking hell, you ain't seen nothing, this is low key compared to a few years ago. It was the same old bollocks that our papers used to print, the same type of nonsense they leave out now because they don't want to upset the Home Office, because they want the likes of the Olympics over here and the Rugby World Cup at Twickenham; they need to generate more custom, more money, and bad press would fuck it all up, so they are under wraps to leave it out, allegedly!!

After the game was a non-event, we had lads but there was not the urgency that was there in previous visits to take it to them. Some say England bottled it, I disagree, we were just bored of Poland. How many times can you walk around trying to call it on, only to be stopped by the police and given a clump with a baton? It was always eventful and still to this day I rate the Poles. They're game, but them pulling a firm today is probably like us in the mid-80s, they're just that far behind in the times. One thing is for sure, they are the only firm I know to call it on when the lads are having fucking breakfast!

As Jason said, in Chorzow, he met Lee Spence, and he has a different view of England's firm on that trip.

LEE, OLDHAM:

It was a quality turnout from England and it needed to be after the previous problems we had over there. We all knew that Poland was one of the few places we would get a row at and not have to look hard for it. Loads of clubs had their firms out there, the likes of Wolves, Shrewsbury, Villa and Chelsea all had decent firms, not 10s and 15s but 40- to 50-handed.

On the day of the game it was on and then it was off, here they are, no they're not; it was like a pantomime at times and eventually, when they did turn up, loads never bothered, as they thought it was another false alarm. It was a disgrace, if I am honest, as a few lads came into a bar and said that the Poles were on their way and they had a serious firm with them; we all went outside and they were there, it was no false alarm but the problem was plenty of the lads thought it was and stayed put. Either West Ham or Villa decided not to come out and play, and some shithouse locked the doors of the bar so, when it came on top and their numbers overpowered us, the lads who stayed in the bar – and they know who they are – have a lot to answer for. If they had come out, or let us back in to get some tools, we would have faired a lot better than we did.

The police came and split us up and we were with the game lads from Carlisle in a bar and a few West Ham were in there with a couple of black lads. Villa came in with their usual NF bollocks so the Carlisle main face told them to shut the fuck up and it got nasty and Mr Villa took a dig from the Carlisle bloke. Again, everyone who was there knows who was who, so it's not for me to name them, it won't take Columbo to work it out!

It was at this game that we all met in the hotel bar and Villa came in and called it on with Newcastle; every firm in there knew the group of Geordies, they had been going for years, so Oldham, Shrewsbury, Carlisle and a few others all started getting up saying, 'We're with Newcastle!' At the game, Villa were paranoid, as they had pissed that many firms off they had run out of lives, and they left the game at half-time, the same time a small group of Carlisle had got off as well and they ended up on the same train as Villa going to Berlin.

At the next game in Italy, the Carlisle lads told us that there was seven of them in one carriage, fighting on and off for the whole journey with this mob of Villa; we are talking *hours* here, and they say it was the most mental journey of their lives, even though they were heavily outnumbered and did well.

What happens at the Italy game, Carlisle turn out a full mob and in the ground they end up right by Villa who were not so well represented, and for 90 minutes they were tortured by Carlisle. Outside in the coach park, everyone turned on Villa, they had pissed everyone off again and a few of their well-known ones won't have happy memories of what happened.

Back in Chorzow, we all agreed that, after the game, we would get into the centre, do a U-turn at the station and meet the Poles. This was the major disappointment for me, as, although we had a big police escort, it was easy to slip away and, in my opinion, England didn't fancy it that night; the escort was breakable but most of the lads were happy to stay tucked up inside it. About 25 of us got to the meeting place and, luckily for us, Poland never showed, as if they had done we would have been in trouble. That was a big, big disappointment and again the lads who didn't fancy it will know who they are.

Times were changing and the Polish hooligan force was growing, while many would argue that the English scene was in decline by the time they next visited for the 1999 European qualifier in Warsaw. The game was a drab goalless draw in front of just 17,000 fans but it will always be remembered for a huge battle that took place in a park in the city that afternoon. Many believe it was one of England's darkest days in the hooligan years; Darren from Mansfield is one of them.

DARREN, MANSFIELD:
Warsaw, Poland, 1999

Poland '99 saw the park incident. Some Mansfield had travelled out with a few Forest and that was another day when the Poles were led by that fucking German who shows up all over Europe wherever we play. He kept turning up outside our bars with a couple of Poles, telling us to go to the park near by. Everyone knew the Poles were tooled up and some lads were wanting to go straight over to them, even though not all England's firm were present. Shit happens and around 60 got excited and went off to this fucking park where the German mouthpiece had directed them to, leaving 100-plus behind who wanted to drink up and get the full firm together.

We lacked leadership to be truthful, there was nobody there who could take control and say to everyone, 'Yes, go' or 'No, stop', and it was our downfall. One Mansfield lad decided to go straight away with some Birmingham, some Huddersfield and a mix match of others. When they got to the park there was a mob of Poles about 200-strong and, even though the English charged, the Poles stood firm and being tooled up to fuck with axes, hatchets, knives, etc, steamed the English. Our lad got hammered and was knocked unconscious because he stood his ground when it came on top, a Birmingham and Sheffield United lad also got badly injured as the Poles went to town on them. The rest of the English eventually arrived and it was game on and we ended up running the Poles through the park after a bit of a ding-dong. Our mate had to go to hospital and the Notts police liaison officer who was on international duty helped him get a new passport because the Poles also robbed his as well as his wallet, phone and match ticket. His face was a right fucking mess and, long after, everyone was arguing about it. At the end of the day, our lads got done; would it have happened if they were more disciplined, we will never know. Most lads will agree that the Poles are very good at home, but would they show here two nights before, make themselves known and look for it or go to a pre-arranged one in a park? I doubt it. Until they do, they will be like the rest of the Europeans – second rate.

It is an interesting point about the Poles, as they did turn up for the return leg in the 2006 World Cup qualifier at Old Trafford and they did go looking for it. But there are now so many residing in England nobody knows if they were immigrants or lads who travelled over for the game.

CHAPTER SIXTEEN
THE BLAG ARMY
EURO '92

England set off to the 1992 European Championships under the managership of Graham Taylor. The nation's hopes were not high! Only a Gary Lineker goal which earned England a point in Poznan in the final qualifying game against Poland saw them through to the finals and the group record of three wins and three draws against mediocre opposition; and the fact that the side had scored just seven goals in six games meant that only the most optimistic of patriots believed Taylor's team were in with a chance of doing well.

The sceptics were right, it was a woeful tournament and England were eliminated after three games in which they won none and scored just one goal. Players like Keith Curle, Carlton Palmer and Andy Sinton hardly set the place alight, and during the 2–1 defeat at the hands of the host nation in Stockholm, joint all-time leading scorer Lineker was replaced by Taylor, much to the annoyance of the player and the England fans in the crowd and the bewilderment of the watching millions at home. It was a sad time for Lineker who never played for his country again. And it was another bad time for the English FA, as predictably the visiting fans they had pleaded with to behave took no notice whatsoever and rampaged for the duration of the time it took their heroes to get knocked out.

The violence in Stockholm came as no surprise to some, as for years the media had covered the exploits of the 'Black Army' who many believed were a hooligan mob that were based in the Swedish city. In truth, the mob was nothing more than an independent supporters club by the time England visited. In the 70s and early 80s, they were a force to be reckoned with but the firm who clashed with England that night were not the Black Army, they were a new breed of football thugs. A breed who were now evident in most countries, who were fed up of England fans arriving en masse in cities all over the world and taking liberties; a breed who were determined to put up a fight and a breed who over the years had become addicted to the 'English disease'.

A few years before Euro '92, England had played a friendly in Stockholm and that trip saw violence which surprised many who thought that places like Sweden were a soft touch:

PAUL, NOTTS COUNTY:

It was a low-budget trip after the World Cup and just a couple of us went by train and ferry, only arriving on the day of match, no digs booked, no match ticket – the type of fan that makes the FA cringe, twats that they are! We got in a bar and as usual Chelsea were holding court telling everyone that they were going to attack the Argentinean Embassy, which a few lads said they had done previously. We had a few beers and gave the Embassy attack a miss, the beer was expensive enough, so fuck knows what the fines out there were like!

Later, some young Chelsea lads said they had attacked the Embassy and claimed 30 England had smashed it up; a few older lads said it did happen but that the building was the wrong one – whichever one you believed, you had to admire their bulldog attitude! Whatever the building was, it brought the police into the equation and we were rounded up and taken to the ground via the tube, where we met head on a group of local skinheads. It was usually the case that one shout of England went up and they were off but, to give them credit, they were up for it and, but for one mental copper with a dog between us, it would have gone off good style. They kept on our tails, though, and at the ground there was a small kick-off by the home end and a few English were nicked.

The game was dire and we got beat 1–0, but 10 minutes before the end the gates were opened and a mob left early and walked to the home end; it was a bit stupid and not the usual faces you see but, give the lads credit, they held their own when the Swedes came out and we ended up getting back to the central station where the skinheads were trying without success to get into us all on the platform and down the escalators.

DAZ, PLYMOUTH:

It was the game when a few England in their end got jumped and their Union Jack was set alight, so, after, we went around there and kicked off. They were off but realised there was only about 40 of us and it was the first time I saw us get run ragged. We took them across a forecourt but then it was the back foot all the way to the station – no good lying, we were done. A well-known Chelsea lad was trying to hold us together but the firm was young and they were shocked that it had come on top. England v Sweden is not the game you expect to get a kicking at but these places are big cities and proof if you take liberties you can come second. That night, we came second outside the ground. Some Yorkshire lad was stabbed in the underground, and when that happens it brings the fight out in you and after that we did much better and in the few skirmishes at the station we had them on the run a couple of times.

So it seemed that the tide was turning and England were not as invincible as some thought. What was a cert, though, was that, when they next met, England would not take the Swedes so lightly. Unfortunately for the FA, the next time it happened was in the European Championships in the Scandinavian country when the problems were covered much more extensively by the world's press than they were on that night in 1986.

It was another tournament that Nicky Stevenson attended, and, despite England's poor showing, Taylor's tactics and Lineker's humiliation, he had a ball!

NICK, NOTTINGHAM FOREST:

Although I enjoyed Italia '90, I never watched England in between the World Cup and the European Championships in Sweden in 1992; it was all down to money and the fact I fucking had none! By the time this one came around, I was flush and the talk of a lads holiday in Spain or Greece was rubbished – Sweden, here we come! The fucking Black Army are getting it. I never knew who the fuck they were but a few of the older lads who had heard about them said they were game, so who was I to question their intelligence.

A good mob of Forest went over and I travelled with Sonny, Danny G, Malc Wright and Graham Algie on Inter-Rail passes, which took us to Copenhagen. We had decided to stay there rather than get ripped off in the Swedish cities with their inflated hotel and ale prices, although from what I heard they were already out of our price range before they were doubled at the start of the Championships.

Copenhagen was a dream, all day we robbed what we could and it was so easy it was laughable. It is no wonder the Scousers were at it in the 70s, and 15 years on many shops were none the wiser and we had the pick of all the main names like CP, Stone Island and Bonneville. We were filling our bags and in the end slinging the clothes we had come over in to make room for new stock. We had one aborted attempt at doing a smash and grab on a Tag Heuer watch shop but, unlike the clothes shops, they had been stung once too often, security measures had been introduced and the brick just bounced back at us from the reinforced glass we had expected to shatter.

It was in Copenhagen that we met Parmo and Butler from Mansfield with their firm, they are well respected on the

England scene and we got on well, and are still mates to this day and for a small club they have a decent firm to their credit. Before this trip, I could not get my head around all this mates with other firms shit but, once you meet lads away from home and have a beer and get on and see them watching your backs, it changes your attitude to the situation.

We crossed the river and went to Malmo for the French game but it had quietened down and the only trouble we saw was when we rolled a few very game Turks; the football was dire and it must have been the most boring team England had ever had and we headed for Stockholm needing a result against the host nation to progress. Well, that's what the lads were saying, personally, I didn't know the ins and out of the qualification process and to be bluntly honest didn't give a fuck as long as we bumped into the local firm or Black Army that everyone was harping on about.

As it was, we got there late and missed anything that may have gone on before the game so had a stroll around the ground to see if there was anyone who wanted a pop. There was a small mob of about a dozen that looked up for it but looked nothing like Swedes and they turned out to be Wigan. We got chatting and they were sound as well as being game as fuck. One of them was arguing with some Chinese who were running all the little stalls around the ground, and next minute he come over with a belter of a shiner shouting, 'Come on, these cunts want it!' How many times have you heard that, the thing is they probably *don't* want it and have no doubt been provoked into action, but to us that is a clear indication that they fancy a go, so without any hesitation we were into them.

It was a bad move, I swear they were robots and not human, we were raining blows on them and these Jackie Chan lookalikes were just laughing at us, they never budged an inch and soon started waving those little bars they have on chains above their heads. Now they did want it and were full of adrenalin while we were full of ale and knackered. The shout went up of 'run' and I thought it was a bad call, as there was only a few of them and I was sure if we backed off peacefully they would leave it at that without the shame of getting on our toes. I then looked around and saw about 40-odd riot police charging towards us and realised that the time to fuck off sharpish had indeed arrived!

It was the blind leading the blind as we split into two mobs, Danny shouted go one way, the Wigan lads shouted go the other way and like a twat I went with the Wiganers straight down a road which was a dead end. Forget what you have heard about the Swedish filth being very soft, they were straight into us. We all put our hands up and it made no difference, they battered us and we were bundled on to a bus and taken to the nick – second trip, second nicking, 100 per cent record intact!

We were all on separate seats with our own riot police officer assigned to each of us and, as luck had it, mine was a dead fit bird. What the fuck she was doing in the police force, God knows, but it was a waste, she should have been in fucking *Razzle*. It had all calmed down so, for a laugh, I squeezed her leg and looked into her blue eyes and joked that I knew she fancied me. Big mistake! She went crazy and hammered her truncheon straight into my bollocks. I was totalled, my eyes filled up and my pants were soon wet, and I thought that I had either pissed myself or the slut had split my knacker sack with the blow.

We got to the nick and we were split into groups of three, I was in with two Wigan lads who were falling out over who should look after the drugs they had. I had more pressing problems as I was dying for a piss so knew the dampness in my boxers was blood. I was banging the door pleading with them to let me have a piss and they made me wait an hour before I was allowed to have a go at passing piss.

It was pure agony, the blood from my bollocks had all dried in my Jap's eye and nothing would come out, so I had to get my thumbnails in and clear the passage, which, for the

Above: The English and Dutch fans fight running battles in the streets of Düsseldorf before the game – Euro '88.

Below: World Cup France '98 – The Marscille riot police form a barricade to stop the English and Tunisian fans from rampaging through the streets of Marseille without success.

Above: A Turkish fan is arrested after smashing up bars and hunting for English fans after their team's victory against Belgium in Euro 2000.

Below: English football fans pictured inside a Brussels police station after being arrested when violence erupted in the capital during Euro 2000.

Above: Euro 2000, English and German fans fight in the square in Charleroi.

Below. 'No surrender.'

Another England fan
banned and deported
in Portugal during
Euro 2004.

benefit of those of you who have never done it, fucking hurts!

Strangely, they let us all out soon after and me and Algie headed straight into town where it was going nuts. In minutes, we saw a couple of Swedes getting slung through shop windows and a couple of times the police were on the back foot, which is always nice to see regardless of what country you're in! We rightly guessed by the mood of the crowd that England had been eliminated!

We were scurrying about in small mobs trying to find the main England firm who were doing all the damage and turned a corner only to bump into a 300-strong mob of the Black Army who were being led by a bird. We had no option but to swerve it and get into McDonalds and, as we were stood at the counter, a lad approached us asking who we were and what was happening. As a young up-and-coming thug, I was star-struck when someone said it was Hickey from Chelsea. He knew Scarrott, Boatsey and a few other Forest lads and was sound with us; we left well happy that he rated us.

It turned out that the Swedes had bumped into a huge England firm led by our very own Sonny, Danny G and the Mansfield boys and, although our lads said they were game, England had gone through them, including the bird who took a kicking for her troubles. Sonny, Malc and Butler were all nicked and from our firm only Danny got away scot-free that night.

We got back home the next day, another England trip completed, another nicking. That's what it was like for me, fight, get nicked, fight, get nicked. I didn't give a fuck, you never seemed to get fined and I never gave a shit about missing the match. England were crap and the only reason we went was for the trouble, if the truth be known.

As is usually the case, the trouble caused by the English made round-the-globe news but once again it seemed that the world's media overlooked the fact that 'it takes two to tango'. The Swedes, according to many, did have a firm of sorts out during the tournament but many also thought they were simply out of their league. Brian from Blackpool was one of the lads who made the trip and was not impressed with the opposition England faced during the 10 days he was there.

BRIAN, BLACKPOOL:

The day of the matches and especially after the match when we were eliminated, England took liberties, and if anybody says any different they were obviously not there. The Swedes were just another two-bob firm who have never travelled but act hard at home when they play the numbers game. The numbers they have were only average but the quality was not even that and they were very poor. Some European mobs turn out for England and are far better than the Swedes, the Eastern Europeans being the only ones to really want it, in my opinion, but until any of them come to England they will never be rated by us, and that's not just the Swedes, it applies to all of them – and by all of them I mean the Jocks and Taffs as well!

Euro '92 was poor on and off the pitch. The Black Army, as has been said many times, were nothing more than a supporters club led by birds and backed up by spotty teenagers. They had mobs of skinheads who were like peacocks strutting around Stockholm but when push came to shove the girls were far gamer, how sad is that? A few of them ended up getting a slap as they tried to have a go, unlike the lads in the mob. Imagine being in their boozer after, the birds sitting there with black eyes, bollocking the lads for running!

I will always remember that straight after the game we bumped into about 30 lads and they called it on but as soon as they saw what we were about they ran; there was not a punch thrown. They ended up running into a load of lads who had not been in the game and they were ironed out; it was caught on TV and is on a documentary and it looks like a few innocents are getting done in, but those lads were calling it on and once again the film editors failed to show what really happened, just a few seconds of action which put us in bad light.

In Stockholm city centre, they tried but failed badly, though England did have one hell of a firm on show. Some cowards were driving past and squirting people in the face with ammonia and that was the night a shop window went in and everyone was walking about with new SI jackets on.

One lad recalled that his lasting memory of Sweden was pulling up on the outskirts of Stockholm on the morning of the game and seeing 200 model-like blondes doing aerobics to music – well, they would have probably put up more of a fight than the so-called Black Army did. And, as for them rattling on that they don't mob as an international firm as they fight each other, well that is a crock of shite! English firms have been fighting each other at England games since the 70s and never once did it stop England taking firms all over Europe.

The criticism of the Swedes came after one member of their albeit unrated firm posted on the internet that England were guilty of attacking non-firm members and general lawlessness throughout the tournament.

Regardless of how poorly the English rated the Swedes, there were still plenty who could not resist going, Trevor Tanner was one of them, and at the time was responsible for building one of the best mobs in England.

TREVOR, SPURS:

I was like a tiger straining at the leash in '92 and could not wait for the Euros to start. Unlike past trips when we had been away with England but not been organised, this time we'd made arrangements to go out there and have a little firm together. But as usual everything gets fucked up one way or another, through travel arrangements or what have you, and I ended up going out there with just a couple of mates, which was not such a bad thing as the Old Bill were starting to get to know me and I was starting to draw a lot of attention to myself through one thing and another.

We tried to get in this campsite and it was like a fucking hellhole, an absolute shit-hole, full of all the scum from everywhere, of every fucking team, Northern teams and fucking scummy London teams that I hate altogether, and it made me fucking sick and I thought I'm not staying in this shit-hole. But obviously you've got to stay somewhere and all the time I'm running round like a loose cannon trying to find my own little firm because they were coming over by car and plane and ferry and I was just running around trying to get hold of them. By now, it was getting close to kick-off and I've still got to find a ticket, never mind the fucking Spurs firm, because I wanted to go in after coming all that way.

So off I go, marching down towards the ground trying to get hold of a ticket and I bumped into a few bods that I know and a couple of Palace that I've been pals with for donkeys years. They were under this underpass when I saw this big old Swede, a fucking great big blond geezer, waving a load of fucking tickets around. And I thought, I'll have some of that, fuck it, I'm going in. So I jogged over and just grabbed hold of him. It was like a comedy sketch, I went to grab the tickets and he just grabbed me in his other hand and he wouldn't let go of the fucking tickets. So I've clumped him and he's fucking still holding on to the tickets and by now we're having a proper wrestle for these tickets when I notice the full squad of riot police standing above us on this little overpass. In the end, the tickets ripped in half because he wouldn't let go of them and it broke my heart. So I've had to run off and thought, Fuck it, I might as well go and have a beer.

After a few beers, I didn't give a fuck if I ain't got a ticket. It was getting near the kick-off so I decided to watch it in a bar but ended up going into this McDonalds on the flyover just as it started to proper kick off now with the English and the Swedes. It went big time and I saw a Swedish geezer laid out on the pavement and he was in a bad way, they were getting caned. So I've ended up in fucking McDonalds of all places watching the game. As soon as it started, there was tension in there, a few of their little skinhead bods came in and right away it kicked off and we give a couple of them a slap. There was only a handful of us in there and a couple of these little Black Army remnants of that little firm we'd had it with earlier came sniffing around the McDonalds with some doormen; they started getting involved, so they got a dig as well so the scene was sort of set.

Anyway, to cut a long story short, because of that absolute parasite Taylor, we lost again and we were out of the European Championships. We were fucking let down again by the same old shite that we're going to win everything, well, we never fucking do. And it's gone right off now, properly going off. It started off where I was in this McDonalds and it spilled out on to the forecourt, went down on to the flyover and there was a fairground and they'd got immigrant stallholders. I don't know if they were Turks or Iraqis or Greeks, or whatever they were, or fuck knows. And they started backing the Swedes up and started waving around dishes and fucking things. I can remember seeing a couple of them getting their stalls turned over and they were proper getting it. One was trying to get me with a bit of a bar and I picked up a bit of wood and clumped him round the head with it. We just rampaged really through the fucking place but you had to watch your back because you didn't know where it was coming from, it was really going off with the stallholders and everything else by this fairground. Because I don't think the Swedes to be truthful would have done it without these pikeys as they're not in our league. But these were obviously local bods that lived in Sweden and they had the fucking hump seeing England taking the piss and they fancied having a go, but they were getting proper done as well. A few of them were game, but they were getting done.

The next thing I remember is a van reversing through the

crowd. And I thought I was fucking gone, I thought it was like some Swedes or some of these stallholders had got hold of a van and they're just going to start ploughing into people. And your life sort of flashes before you and it's too late to even run or move, you can't move. And it just came reversing, hurtling towards me and stopped about – fucking I don't know – a foot in front of me. The van doors flew open like something out of *The Professionals* and these bods all masked up and balaclava'd up jumped out, grabbed hold of me, slung me in the fucking back with another geezer and then drove off about 80mph. Obviously you can imagine it – what the fuck is going on here?! And we'd obviously been nicked. It was a proper snatch squad, it was their naughty Old Bill, because their main Old Bill were complete wankers, they were just like kids, but these were like the robot naughty Old Bill we have over here.

They were 100 per cent sent in to get certain people out and we were on our way to fucking jail. Not just proper prison, they had a whole wing of a prison put by for the English because it had been going off for 48 hours by now and they'd had a kangaroo court set up and that and they were just nicking, boom, boom, boom. So I thought, Fucking hell, maybe they're just trying to shit the life out of us, scare us a little bit. But the Swedes outside the fucking court started attacking the Old Bill van like you see on the telly when some bad killer is taken into the Old Bailey and I was thinking, Fucking hell, what's going on here?

Once inside, we were stripped and all that carry on, hosed down and put in a fucking orange boiler suit and I can remember going in a lift and up into this area of the nick, and put up into a cell. It was one of the weirdest experiences I've had in my life because it had a big window right up in the roof which just shone light through when it was light and over there at that time of year it was light for about 18 hours a day and it really fucking threw you out because you didn't know whether it was day or night or whatever. It played havoc with your whole system. Then there was this fucking TV that would just come on every now and again and it would just show fucking *Poldark* – I'll never forget it because I used to watch it, it was a seafaring programme. And it used to be in subtitles and I'd be fucking sitting there trying to watch it with Swedish subtitles.

After a couple of days, I obviously started realising this is getting a bit serious. And then the geezer from the British Embassy come round and there was me and four other geezers left in the whole jail, which is where the famous England headline came from: 'ENGLAND'S FOULEST'. We were the last five in the whole country still not to be deported, still waiting to be put on trial for whatever they had locked us up for.

The first thing he said to me was: 'You're in a lot of trouble,' through the hatch. I didn't even know what the fuck I'd done. He wouldn't have any of it because, as anyone who travels with England should know, you're guilty until you can prove yourself innocent, it's not the other way around. If you're an England fan, you're guilty first, simple as that, in the eyes of the law in this country. It was proper frightening because you've got your own government really sanctioning the Swedes to do what the fuck they want with you. He then told me that the bloke I had seen get badly hurt on the flyover was fighting for his life, which ain't a good thing obviously. And the next think you know he tells me that it was all over the news at home and that they had film taken from a helicopter above us all and they had a geezer with long hair, which I had at the time, with a white hooded top or a white baseball cap on, which I was also fucking wearing, which is just my luck and the next thing he blurts out, he's wiping his hands of me and fucks off.

Eventually, I went to court after a few days and there was some geezer from Leeds, a little Scouse tealeaf and some other bloke up for small-time charges but they wanted me and this other geezer for doing the bloke in hospital who was still in a bad way Now I knew I didn't have anything to do with it but obviously, because I looked like the bloke on the film, I was getting the wrap for it. The British Embassy bod didn't even turn up in court and I had to have an American fucking tourist as an interpreter and for all I knew he could have said anything, but thank fuck he didn't and he did me proud.

They've got one of the oldest court systems in the world, the Swedes, and I was told if you get put on remand there you can be up there for months, even years, because it takes such a long time to process foreigners. It was literally on this judge's say-so whether I was going to get remanded or not and I am big enough to admit it shit the life out of me. It all boiled down to my baseball cap, I said I didn't have it on, and they said I did, or so the Yank told me. Because they couldn't prove it, I got bail, which was a fucking unbelievable relief. They released me there and then and I went upstairs and can remember hugging this little bird who was a copper. 'We're going to release you,' she smiled and I felt fucking great. I was taken back to the campsite and the Germans were crawling all over it by then. I got my passport from a locker and the Swede bird OB put me on the plane, I even got her number and she wrote to me a couple of weeks after, but there was no way I was going back out there, not in a million years. When I got off at the airport, it was a mare, I didn't think anyone knew apart from a few lads and my family but it had been all over the papers and that headline 'ENGLAND'S FOULEST' caused me no end of grief.

A couple of weeks later, I was at the Southampton away game and we were all firmed up in the boozer we used to meet in called The Cow Herds. I was standing outside having a beer and two geezers come out of a van driven by Tottenham Old Bill. I'm looking straight at them thinking, What's going on here, and recognise the fucking sky-blue uniforms, dark-blue trousers, it was two Swedish OB. Well, I tell you, you've never seen anyone fucking go through the woods behind the pub so quick in your life, because I was not hanging around to find out what was going on and I don't know to this day but after about two years I got a letter saying that I was exonerated of all the charges as they couldn't prove anything different and that was good enough for me.

Whereas Trevor Tanner was trying to build Spurs' reputation on the England scene, smaller clubs had already established themselves by the time the Championships kicked off. One of the most respected travelling firms at the time were the EBF from Shrewsbury and, true to form, they turned up in Sweden and were involved in most things that went on when trouble occurred. Neil Jones and Brendan were early gang members.

NEIL, SHREWSBURY:

Yet again we just got in our cars and shot over there and we got based in Malmo after dossing about, robbing everywhere, as you do when you go abroad watching England. We always looked dead smart when we were with England, it was that easy in these places to have what you wanted. Around this time, we were well in with the Geordies, so we all mobbed up and met the Geordies and got the campsite sorted, went on the drink, just had a good old holiday really. Bit of robbing in the day, few drinks then a good time at night on the piss and a bit of rampaging. We just got tanked up and all got together and had a bit of a rampage for the hell of it, they set the campsites up with beer tents and then someone shut the bar and we just tossed all the seats in the tent and all the coppers went a bit mad, as is the case when they got a bit frosty, it just went and the place was totalled. That night when it kicked off, all the Geordies done the jewellers, it went berserk in that square … all because they shut the bar!

BRENDAN, SHREWSBURY:

It went off badly after the Denmark game when an England lad got cut up by some Lebanese fella. England started getting tooled up then and we all ended up with Stanley knives that we stole from some local hardware shop. We did the business after that when we had it off with the immigrants. I will always remember a Fulham lad getting into them with a chair.

They had slashed some kid for no reason whatsoever, so we mobbed up and ended up chasing them but they all had massive knives on them, and when we got a bit isolated the tide turned and they started to steam us with them. We had no tools so it got right on top and the bastards were trying to slice us up. If you were at the front, you were probably going to get a cleaver in you. So everyone backed off. It was nothing to do with the Swedes, it was purely an immigrant incident and we learned fast that you had to fight fire with fire, so loads of England got tooled up – including Neil and as usual it ended in disaster for him!

NEIL, SHREWSBURY:
We went from Malmo up to Stockholm, and the coppers were going mental if you hadn't got a ticket; we were all sorted but everywhere you went they were searching you, asking to see your ticket for the match. We had been taking these purple acid tabs that the Wigan lads had, and I went up to the bar and they said it's fucking such-and-such for a pint. I said, 'Excuse me, love', jumped over the bar, just pulling optics off the wall and passing them to the lads, totally on my way out now full of acid; loads were on it and we were drinking away in Stockholm, having a right laugh. Before long these tabs started playing up with my head so I took a Stanley knife and pulled it on some fucking skinheads; it was the drugs telling me I needed to protect myself so I'm wandering around some street when the coppers got me and, bingo! I've got this fucking knife and I'm off my head so I'm nicked. It was nothing really but over there they made a big thing about it and I ended up in the fucking cells for days in solitary confinement, which I thought was a bit harsh!

I ended up in court, and from nowhere came these two lads who were involved in the same case as mine. I was a bit nervy with them as I didn't know who the fuck they were and then they spoke to the judge telling him I was going to fucking stab them, I couldn't believe it! I said my bit and told them that I wasn't going to stab anyone, I'd pulled my Stanley knife out because I'd been on the campsite and that's what I used the Stanley knife for, cutting ropes and bollocks, and it was broke, so I was just playing with it in the street trying to fix it on the way to the campsite. This judge asked to see it and thank fuck it fell to bits in his hand. I said, 'See, told you it was broke!'

He had a chat with the clerical bloke in the court and they told me that, as I'd been in jail for so long, I could go, which was nice of them!

BRENDAN, SHREWSBURY:

After the game, England went mental and smashed the place to bits but we got split up and it was probably one of the scariest moments I'd had watching England. All you could see was this fucking huge mob of the so-called Black Army and there's probably about 15–20 England in our mob at the most, as everyone must have gone the other way to the underground station. We were looking around at each other, a few Tottenham, some Wigan, some others I don't know who they were, who had come out the ground with us, not a tight firm at all, and we ended up walking down the road and I was thinking, Fucking hell, if we bump into the Black Army we're going to get hammered here. Before they saw us, the Old Bill started getting into us and we were ushered down a ramp into the tube and somehow made it back to the campsite in one piece. By the time we got there, the place was surrounded by riot police, no one was allowed in and no one was allowed out, so we climbed on the walls and watched all the England fans singing around what appeared to be this massive campfire. It looked a bit big and out of control and then a copper told us that it was the campsite on fire, a mob of Wigan lads had grabbed a load of wood and pulled tents down and set the fucking whole thing on fire! It was an amazing site, the whole place was alight with hundreds of drug-crazed, drunken lunatics dancing around it!

As expected, the press had a field day and the *Daily Mirror*'s front page read: 'DOZENS HELD IN BLOODY RAMPAGE AS SAD ENGLAND CRASH OUT!'

It went on to report that 'dozens of English soccer thugs were arrested after shop windows were smashed as 300 English louts went on the rampage. Despite being kept in the ground for an hour after the game, breakaway groups began scaling an 8ft fence and wading into celebrating Swedish fans.

'Fighting spilled into a nearby shopping mall where fans clashed and looted shops before the riot moved to the main street in Stockholm, some two miles away, hooligans smashed windows, looted more shops and hurled bicycles through windows. Many Swedes were attacked by English thugs carrying wooden staves and throwing stones, cars were overturned during the rampage.

'Bus loads of riot police were drafted in to quell the riot and combat the warring fans and the paper also reported that the Swedish mob followed England fans back to their campsite where more fights broke out well into the early hours of the morning before the riot police finally took control of the situation.'

So the European Championships had been a disaster for England, eliminated without winning a game and disgraced by rampaging thugs. It was also a sad time for Gary Lineker who announced his retirement from international football soon after.

Unfortunately for the FA and the police forces across Europe, the people responsible for the rioting in Malmo and Stockholm had no intention of following Lineker into retirement!

CHAPTER SEVENTEEN

WELCOME TO HELL
TURKEY '93

Since the English disease was exported abroad, their followers have suffered many casualties. More often than not, it has been due to cowardly attacks on small groups and individuals rather than a large firm coming unstuck and most lads will say that over the last 30 years only the Polish mob have been really interested in a proper toe-to-toe.

So-called firms in Holland, Germany and, once the tide turned, Scotland have all been brushed aside with relative ease and very few European mobs have been able to live with the kind of firms that the English have assembled.

No doubt there will be fans who have their own view of the most hostile or on-top place to visit, as every city in the world can be dangerous, but most will agree that any trip to Turkey would see violence on a level unprecedented anywhere else. In fact, the Turks would be more than happy to take on the English regardless of where they were playing, as they have large immigrant populations in many European cities. They also freely use weapons and that is why they have made the top of most English hooligans' hate list.

The deaths of the two Leeds United fans in Istanbul has been well documented, and was the spark that relit a fuse that had been smouldering away for many years. English fans visiting Turkey to watch football on both the club and the international scene have been subjected to hatred and violence which only seems to be getting worse.

The hatred has not appeared overnight, however, and, long before the Leeds lads were brutally murdered, local gangs made it very clear that they did not take kindly to English football fans roaming the streets and allegedly showing disrespect to the very passionate Turkish nationals.

Will, Lewisham, Darren, Phil and Mark have all been to watch England in Turkey and, apart from Lewisham who was with the EAF in '91, all have horror stories to tell!

WILL, MAN CITY:

I flew to Istanbul from Gatwick for the game in '84, with the usual dozen or so Stockport lads but we had not done our homework and had all opted to make a week of it. Istanbul was in the Middle Ages compared to the rest of Europe at the time, alcoholic beer was scarce and what was available was shite and, unlike today, the place you could be sure of getting a half-decent pint in, the Irish bars, did not exist. We found a hotel and to a man wished we could move on the day after, as once we had booked in and settled down we realised it was a shit-hole and, once night-time came, was situated in an area which was very dangerous.

Because it was so moody there, boredom sets in, you can't sit in the hotel bar for a week so it was inevitable that it would go off, and nearly every night it did! One day, we were minding our own business, wandering the streets, when about 100 locals steamed into us from some badly lit alley; to this day, we don't know who they were, probably Galatasaray or Besitkas, although it mattered not, as we were well outnumbered and we had to do a tactical retreat, which, as any of the old boys from those days will tell you, was very rare when away with England. One of our lads, still to this day, has a moan about losing his hat and claims we should have stood longer and, although we felt we did well to get away with no serious injuries and more importantly alive, he believes we did not do enough to save that precious fucking hat of his!

One night, I left the lads in a pub near the hotel while I went to pick up a mate of mine who followed Man City from the airport. Unfortunately, while I had been gone, the boys had discovered 'white beer' which was actually Raki and water, which is vile to drink but does the job nonetheless. So, we arrive back in the bar after I have told the lad that you have to keep a clear head out here, it's on top, be alert, don't drop your guard, etc, etc, and we walk into the bar to find everybody shit-faced, slumped over the tables and acting up.

Another night we noticed a bar which had about 200 blokes in it, all cheering, we sussed it out and they seemed OK and we thought it was a strip joint. We got our beers, nudged our way to the front and to find a television and a load of pervert Turks creaming themselves over the girls in an old *Benny Hill Show*!

The night before the game we got into another fight with some of the locals, again there were too many for us to cope with and we were chased into a posh hotel. One of the lads cleverly shut the main glass entrance doors behind us and we stayed in the lobby to see the first barrage of bricks and bottles hit the doors before we were off out the back and into a local bar to regroup.

On the day of the game, none of us had any tickets, the FA had told everybody not to travel so we decided to go to the Sheraton hotel, as that was where we had heard the players and more importantly the jumped-up bunch of wankers masquerading as the FA at the time were staying. Graham Kelly and Ted Croker appeared and announced that no tickets would be made available for us, as we shouldn't have been there because they had told us not to go!

This was the cue to kick me off into one of my finest speeches, which went something like: We'd got that far, so getting in the ground would be no challenge, with or without their help. If they wanted 200–300 lads all over the place in and around the ground, then so be it; then I warned them that we could not now be responsible for our actions!

Sure enough, the wankers shit themselves and sorted tickets within the hour.

The game was a formality and goals from Robson 3, Woodcock 2, Barnes 2 and Anderson gave us an 8–0 win, and I will always remember the noise from the locals being something else considering the hiding they took as a team. After the game, we all piled on to the street to find a reception committee waiting at the top of the hill, cue uphill charge until the cops stopped us, when the weirdest of things happened. The cops chased their fans off the top of the hill and down below us, then turned to us and invited us to give them a kicking, seemingly pissed off with the hassle the locals were causing them. We didn't need to be asked twice and, as they were all split up into little mobs, it was top fun and games and we finally got a bit of payback.

We retired back to the Sheraton bar to find the team were all fucking off home. Only Ray Wilkins who at the time was playing in Italy was staying over. Some of the lads sort of knew him from his time at United when he lived in the Bramhall area of Stockport, so he came over and sat down with us and even bought a round.

That was it for us. We flew home the next day after a final night on the white beer, it was not overly bad out there but certainly an eye-opener that, if you didn't have your wits about you, or if you wanted trouble you would find it with ease. We were probably one of the first mobs to go out there for the match and got back safely, unfortunately quite a few who have been since have not fared so well.

England were paired in the same group as Turkey in the European Championships qualifiers for the tournaments in 1988 and 1992, and the World Cup qualifiers for USA '94. Phil, a Leeds United supporter, visited Turkey for the first time for the game in Izmir in 1987.

PHIL, LEEDS UNITED:

This game was probably the only time I have feared for my life at a game. I'd gone for a week to Izmir and we had no problems at all before the game or the night before, as the Turks were absolutely fantastic when we were out drinking and mixing freely with them, but when it came to the day of football they just flipped their lids!

Even before the game, we were drinking around the place and it was still all right, but in the ground there was no more than about 250 English supporters and, although it was hostile, we were not prepared for the onslaught that came our way after the game which ended 0–0. We were kept in for half an hour after the match while the police cleared all the Turks away and, when we came out, the first two to three minutes were fantastic and we were walking down like we were strolling in the park. But a moment later everything changed and there were Turks everywhere. There were good lads in the group and England run into them and they were off, so we all dived on bus to go back into Izmir.

We got about half a mile up the road when the bus stopped, it couldn't go any further due to the amount of locals who were blocking the road; they were in front on the road, behind the bus in little mobs, all over the pavement, everywhere your eyes looked was just a sea of Turks. There were that many of them that you couldn't put numbers on them but there were hundreds, probably thousands of them and quite simply the driver stopped the bus and just took his keys out of the ignition and got off the fucking bus, leaving us absolutely surrounded by all these Turks!

Tottenham Tony went up the front of bus and tried to start it as he used to be a bus driver in the army but he couldn't do a thing, and in seconds that was it, the atmosphere changed. As I looked through my window, there was somebody running at the bus with a car exhaust in his hand and he put it straight through my window. By the time he'd done that, everybody lay on the floor, some lads at the back wanted to get off and have a go at them and some lunatic actually opened the emergency door but we managed to talk him out of jumping off into them.

The police showed up eventually but every window of the bus went through and by the time they arrived we were all curled under the seats as bottles, planks of wood, lumps of metal, bricks and just about everything else was flung into the coach at us. At one stage, personally I couldn't see any way out of this and had never been so scared at a football game. There was a lass with us and she just curled up in her seat, petrified, but it wasn't a girl thing, as there were lads who were just as frightened. After what seemed like eternity with the police all now properly on the scene, the Turks dispersed and with glass everywhere we got off and flagged a taxi back to our hotel.

Amazingly, nobody was seriously hurt, just a few scratches here and there and that was it. We had a few beers back at the hotel and were just saying to each other how none of us could believe what it was like and what we had experienced back there and basically we were in shock. Turkey had seemed like a nice place but all decided that we weren't going to go out at night and stopped in the bar. But the following day everything was back to normal again like nothing had ever happened with everyone making us feel welcome and they returned to being nice people.

Obviously when it comes to their football, they are as passionate as anybody and something inside them turns them into animals. That may have sounded harsh at the time, but years later ask any other Leeds United fan what their views are and they will agree.

Lewisham was by now a regular traveller with the national side and made the trip to Izmir in 1991.

LEWISHAM, WEST HAM:
I went with a few boys from Grimsby, London and Bristol; by this time, the EAF were very well known and more people

wanted to get involved in it. The only group that were not made welcome were the Mancs because all they ever wanted to do was fucking fight us. It was a decent trip because we had a week in Bodrum then took a four-hour coach journey to Izmir on the day of the game.

It started kicking off as soon as we got there and we found it a bit naughty with the Turks. There was only about 20 of us when we got off this coach and straight away we were fronted by locals; we were a bit outnumbered but we stood our ground which is usual enough to see them off – if you run over there, you are fucked, stand and front it and you are in with more than a good chance against them.

Later on in the day, more and more people started turning up and England were mobbing up in the bars and the Turks didn't want to know so much. That was one of the best England firms I had seen for a game that far away and we had a few more than the usual hardcore who went everywhere. England won the game 1–0 with a Dennis Wise goal and, as soon as we came out the ground, we tore straight into them. They had two mobs but were not organised, as they were waiting on both sides for us. We ran the first Turk mob one way and the Old Bill didn't have a clue, so we regrouped and came back and ran another mob the other way – same old story take it to them and they were all over the place.

It was going off all night with groups splitting off and having it with the locals but eventually everyone started sticking together because you had to in a place like that; today everyone knows how it can get naughty out there but at that time there were plenty who didn't and before long many had come unstuck. Later on in the evening when everything had fizzled out, we made to travel back to Izmir and from their back to Bodrum. We hit more trouble when we'd stopped in the early hours in some small town for something to eat and freshen up, when a few locals tried to take it on with us, we were only about 15-handed but we give it to 'em and that was that.

That was how Turkey was, it didn't matter where you were, if a football match was on and you were not supporting Turkey, you would find trouble as they are a nation of patriots – a bit like us really but the main difference is we can fight!

Darren went to the games in '91 and '93.

DARREN, MANSFIELD:
We went to the game in Turkey in '93, it was a qualifier for USA '94 World Cup and the trip got off to a bad start when one of our lads was nicked at Heathrow for using dodgy notes. Unbeknown to the other seven that travelled without him, Interpol monitored us all the way to Izmir. Some of us had been to Turkey a couple of years earlier and had been involved in major disturbances every night with the Turks who used to stand outside your hotel 24 hours a day and kick it off as soon as you left. It was like they were on fucking shifts. One occasion, we had a good battle on some wasteland, which saw one Mansfield lad get a slab of concrete smashed into his chest much to the merriment of the Turkish Police.

Later that same evening, we (two of us) were walking back to our hotel when we realised there was loads of Turks hanging about the vicinity of our hotel; some of them spotted us and came running at us, armed with sticks and clubs. We were too heavily outnumbered and got legged back up the road where we luckily bumped into 30 West Brom lads. The Turks stopped and moved off, like they always did when the numbers were even, and then the Albion boys walked with us to our hotel and the Turks just stayed their distance, due to the fact a couple of police vans were parked near by and probably because we had the same numbers as them.

Back to '93, we arrived there OK and, as soon as we left the airport, we jumped into two taxis to take us to our hotels, but didn't know that the police were following us to our destination and, as soon as we had paid the Turks in English money, we were swooped on. Three of the lads ended up in Turkish prison for four months while the rest of us ended up on 'hotel arrest' and had an armed guard for the entire duration of our stay before being finally allowed to leave to fly back home.

The three lads in the nick endured severe hardship, it was absolutely boiling and they had to share an 8ft by 8ft cell with 14 other inmates, which they said stunk fucking vile. One of the lads was a Marine and, after a few weeks, the Marines were alerted about their man being inside, so all his fellow soldiers started sending money in for him. His actual army bosses did not help or even recognise the situation and, true to form, the British Consulate did not want to know either. Foreigners in Turkish prisons had to buy their own food, so the money that was sent in was used to buy a small gas stove and packets of rice, as well as bits of donkey meat, which they cooked in their cell.

The only English-speaking person in the prison was an African who had murdered a few people in Turkey and he could speak broken Turkish, so he did the translating for the lads. Eventually, our local MP got the government involved but it still took four months before they were released.

I know it was daft of the lads to go back if they faced charges but four months in a hellhole was barbaric. Imagine the uproar if a holidaymaker was arrested in England and was treated like that, pointless argument really because we all know it would never happen, they would probably be given a few hundred quid and housing benefit!

Although the above stories make grim reading, Mark from Brighton endured a far worse trip to Turkey.

MARK, BRIGHTON:
On 14 October 1987, I ventured up to my first England match, a European Championship qualifier against Turkey

with a place in the tournament finals to be held in Germany in the summer of 1988 up for grabs. It was an easy 8–0 win in front of just 42,500 at Wembley Stadium, as in those days Turkey were the whipping boys of every group and finished bottom of this group below Northern Ireland. Little did I know the impact of watching us play Turkey would have on me!

In March 1993, I decided to travel to Turkey for the 1994 World Cup qualifier. I knew of the trouble that the England fans experienced in May 1991, but I had the bug for following England abroad after spending five weeks in Italy in 1990 for the World Cup and had attended the majority of away matches since.

I was disappointed when the match was confirmed in Izmir, an industrial city on the Aegean coast, but thought, What the fuck, let's go anyway! I booked up with a travel company called Travelex and we flew out to Izmir on the Monday. The following day we ventured to the Under-21 match and got an early taster of what to expect. About 200 of us were segregated off in the bottom corner of the stand, and soon became the target for the many Turks that turned up. They continually chanted 'Fuck you, England' and made gestures of slitting your throat. Next it was the coins and various small rocks being thrown and the riot police stood by and did nothing, until one of the 'generals' got a coin in the face. They then battered the Turks back and we were left in relative peace. That evening, we went out and about for a few beers, the place was full of dodgy backstreet places and rough-looking bars and, although we made a night of it, everyone was on edge as you expected to get set upon at any moment.

Match day came and we waited for our coach to pick us up from the hotel to take us to the ground. We had a few beers in the hotel bar, as the locals didn't exactly make us welcome, so we opted for safety in numbers and stayed close to the hotel. The coach didn't turn up when it was supposed to, so a few of us jumped into some cabs and left the rep of the company to wait for it and load our luggage, as we were heading to the airport straight from the game. We got to the ground and had to run the gauntlet of gestures and abuse as we made our way to the away section. Our coach finally turned up just after us, minus most of its windows as it was attacked on the way to the ground, plus we were now minus our bags which had been stolen when the coach was ambushed.

We felt safer once we were in the ground, there were about 500 in the official section and a few more England fans who paid on the day next to us. They were the first to be set upon, but the police pushed off the Turks near them. To our right the mob became bigger and more and more agitated. 'Fuck you, fuck you, fuck you England' was ringing round the ground. Almost unnoticed, the match kicked off and England were soon 2–0 up and at half-time the players were showered with coins as they left the pitch; Lee Dixon was hit by at least one coin before the Turkish fans then turned their venom back on us. Coins, rusty bolts, bricks and rocks hailed into our section, and the police did nothing apart from holding shields up to protect themselves, but did nothing whatsoever for us.

I was standing about halfway back in our section, when I turned to look back, and felt something smash into my face. I was later told it was a small corner chunk of a brick and the sharp edge had hit me directly in the eye. I was blinded on the spot, basically, my eyeball exploded on impact and there was blood everywhere. A US aid worker saw what happened and came to assist me, while the police just stood round not having a clue what to do. I was eventually taken down under the stadium and they asked the England team doctor to come and see me as there were no medical facilities at the ground. He couldn't do anything, so I was put in an ambulance (unequipped) and taken to a local university hospital. As soon as I got in, they took my credit card and then I was dumped on to a table next to a bloke who had been in a road accident. The doctor who saw me tried to treat me without wearing gloves; I protested and warned of Aids/infections, etc, but, according to this fuckwit, people in Turkey don't have Aids! To my relief, someone from the travel company had found out where I had been taken and turned up with the British Consulate. They got my credit card back and took over, including having me moved away from the blood-soaked emergency room I was in.

I couldn't be treated that day, as my face was too swollen so I had to wait 24 hours or more for the eye to stop bleeding. It was a night I will always remember vividly, a large room just for me with about a dozen empty beds. There was a violent thunderstorm during the night, and I remember lying in bed wondering if this was really happening to me. My eye was still bleeding, I was still in the same clothes covered in blood, in a place where nobody spoke English and the toilets were awash with God knows what, and to make matters worse there was no lighting as the storm had caused a power cut. I finally got a change of clothes from the British Consulate and some food and drink, as nothing was provided, as in Turkey relatives are expected to do most of the caring. I was eventually taken for surgery and the two surgeons who operated spoke perfect English and the treatment was as good as it could be (they were trained in Moorfields Eye Hospital in London). They stitched me back together and gave me the details of the operation and their opinion as to the extent of my injuries to hand over to Moorfields when I got back.

The travel company, the British Consulate and the FA sorted out a hotel and flights back to the UK with Swiss Air via Zurich about five days later, once it was considered safe for me to travel home. The problem was the effect the cabin pressure would have on my face and eyes due to the injury and the surgery. In the days leading up to my departure, I had to have injections every couple of hours to fight any infection; they allowed this to be carried out by the nurse at the Hilton hotel so I didn't have to go back to the hospital.

Once back home, Moorfields confirmed I had been blinded on impact and the treatment I received was top class and that, even if they had been there when I was hit, nothing could have been done. It took a while to adjust to being blind in one eye as you lose depth of vision so it's difficult to judge how close things are. I eventually returned to work four months later, my employer was very good to me and I remained on full pay despite only joining them six months prior to my accident. I had to live with the prospect of an adverse reaction in the other eye for about 18 months, which added to the stress.

In the end I got compensation from my travel insurance, which took nearly a year as they tried to wriggle out of paying and the Turks got a £6,000 fine and banned from playing at home for six months, which was pathetic as they didn't have a match for seven months! They never once admitted responsibility and we all know how other fans have suffered at the hands of Turkish supporters since, and the bad memories were all brought back when the two Leeds fans were murdered in Istanbul – compared to that I got off lightly.

I refused to let the Turkish incident beat me and I was back out following England in Norway June 1993 to see us lose 2–0 and eventually fail to qualify for the USA.

Some local Turks in Brighton were outraged at what happened to me and even paid for me to go to Istanbul on holiday (I managed to see Besitkas play a local Turkish league game) to show that I had not met the real Turkish people. I was interviewed on Turkish TV and appeared in several papers. They linked the incident to the behaviour of England fans in Heysel and generally blamed anyone but the real culprits for what happened.

I have seen England play Turkey since, at the 2–0 win at the Stadium of Light on April 2003. The atmosphere was the best home experience since beating Scotland in Euro '96. I found it a farce that England got fined more after that game for the two pitch invasions than the Turks did for the injuries caused to me. I didn't go over to Istanbul for the October return, I watched the game at our local in Brighton. I found it difficult to control my feelings at both these games and desperately wanted us to win on the pitch. Off it, did I want revenge on the Turkish fans? I'm not sure really, as it would probably be some innocent Turk like me to get the comeback. In my opinion, they should have been banned from the match at Sunderland, but in this politically correct world we couldn't be seen to be discriminating against the Turkish, could we!

CHAPTER EIGHTEEN

DID THEY NOT LIKE THAT!
HOLLAND '93

In a recent poll to find the greatest ever England side, the 1966 World Cup winners collected over 95 per cent of the vote with a few younger supporters bizarrely opting for the Italia '90 and Euro '96 teams. It was an easy choice, as the '66 side were head and shoulders above any team that has been assembled since.

If a poll was set up to find the greatest ever firm England had turned out, then the result would be a lot closer! Cagliari, in 1990, Scotland in 1999 and Dublin 1995 would all feature, but many people's money would be on the game in Rotterdam in 1993 when the England hooligan army was classed as the best firm to set sail from these shores since Nelson!

The importance of the game helped the cause, England under the management of Graham Taylor were struggling, a defeat and a draw against Norway and dropped points against both Poland and Holland meant that they needed to beat the Dutch in the penultimate group game in Rotterdam to stand any chance of qualifying for the finals in the USA the following summer.

Another important factor why such an army was assembled for the trip was that, at previous meetings, the Dutch were an embarrassment, both in Germany and Italy at major tournaments, and after so much hype they had not turned out a firm of any description. While the Dutch did show in small numbers at Wembley, if England were to dismiss them as pretenders to the crown of World's Best Hooligans, they needed to spank them on their own soil.

Mobs assembled from nearly every club in the country and a main Chelsea Headhunter was a major influence in putting any club differences on hold, the theory being that, if England were to do the Dutch, they would need to be as one. Domestically, the Dutch were rated; Feyenoord and Ajax had travelled to games in England and Scotland while the smaller club side Den Haag were regarded as the Millwall of Holland. Utrecht, PSV and other club sides had problems at their games, so the stage was set – if the Dutch would not come to England, England would go to them.

They did not disappoint!

Trent from Brighton, Gilly from Wolverhampton, Lee Spence and the Shrewsbury EBF were all part of the English invasion, and all agree that the firm out there was up there with the very best that had ever left home soil and invaded foreign lands!

TRENT, BRIGHTON:
This was one you could not miss. England needed to win to qualify for the finals in the States, throw in a bit of a holiday full of red-light delights, a few beers, smoke some weed, have a bit of a crack and splatter the Dutch – it was a game sent from heaven and we had a lovely time!

There was about 25–30 of us, we were all in the bar somewhere in Amsterdam when some fellas come in and said, 'It's kicking off in the red-light district.' Those were the days when you used to rely on rumours and stories, so we all fucked off, jumped in cabs and got back to the red-light district. Sure enough, it was chaos, everywhere you looked there were broken windows, the Old Bill were running around, England had landed and fans littered in their hundreds, as we drove back from the Dam Rack through to the red-light district.

We were standing there in awe of the scenes, we had left the place a few hours earlier and all was well, night falls and the lot has gone off. The Dutch were blameless initially; our old friends the Moroccans started playing up and that was the case for most of the night. Everyone who has ever been to the Dam will know what they are like over there, they are one major pain in the arse, slimy little knife merchants. They sell talc as coke and dog shit as dope, they are true scammers, yet always seem to find some silly bastards to give them money.

We got into some boozer that was still serving the English and in they came, a group of them, 'You buy Coke, Hash, Ecstasceeeeeeeeey' – they always seem to manage to draw that one out to maximum effect. You had to admire their front, but they had picked the wrong bar and everyone's gone absolutely fucking mental and started smashing these geezers. As they were running away, everyone's booting the fuck out of them and sticking planks of wood and anything else that was available over their heads. It was a laugh but this was going to be going on all weekend as they were in your faces so much. My worry was that the police would get the place under wraps before we had a chance to take it to our main targets the Dutch.

I shouldn't have worried, as minutes later from out of nowhere came a load of Dutch. There were people shaking in excitement, all the lads were shouting, 'Here we go, keep it tight, no fucker move,' all the little gee-ups you need to let you know everyone was up for it. It was brilliant; this was who we had come for, not a load of wretched drug dealers whose lives were worthless. The first mob of Dutch came running down the road and everyone's bolted towards them, expecting a major battle – it was like bonfire night when it pisses down with rain or the first time you take a bird's bra off and realise the bumps you have been tugging off about all week were tissues, in other words, a major disappointment. The Dutch just turned and fucking ran off up the road.

The police came in on horseback and soon formed a square block of England fans who were cornered into one little area and I was lucky that I had not followed my mate, as he was stuck in with the 200 England fans in this little square and that was it, everybody was collared for an early trip home, including two of my mates who'd only just got there about an hour earlier! One of them was sharing a room with us and, later on that night, we're sitting there laughing about what had been going on when six Old Bill in riot gear have turned up. 'We have come for Mr Smith's things,' said one of them, so we've thought, Well, it saves us having to carry the fucking bag home and at least we knew he could leave, as his passport was in the bag, so I went, 'Here you go,' and passed him the bag. They took his stuff and he was deported a couple of days later. In his luggage were a couple of bags of hash and they've shown him them and said they were taking them from him, no problem. But the sly bastards have only gone and put them back in, so, when he got to Gatwick and faced the British Police for questioning, they have searched his bag and nicked him for possession as well. So he had two hours in Amsterdam, a fucking nightmare trip and a drug conviction for good luck!

We went back out and it was just as bad and during the riots one small group of Old Bill were separated from their squad, cornered by a mob who were ready to lynch them, as they were the ones who had been giving it out with their truncheons earlier. Everyone started throwing stuff at them when two officers calmly pulled their guns out and started pointing them at people. It was like a fucking comic sketch, the lads at the front all dropped their weapons and put their hands in the air. It was getting serious, nobody was daft enough to stand there and think they were tough enough to fight police with guns, so we all lined up against the wall and one of them came up to me and put a gun to my head, shouting that he wanted my camera. 'No problem officer, you're welcome to it.' It was thrown on the floor and the film was pulled out, before he went over to the next fella who had no camera so was smashed in the face with the gun.

This went on for a bit and they were toying with us, as after a few minutes, a van pulled up and they jumped in and drove off. The walk back was just as bad, though, as the police were everywhere and just battered and chased us back to the hotel. They'd taken a bit of stick early on that night but by now were well on top of it and basically were letting us know that they were not to be messed with. We went back to the hotel and at 3am I went for a stroll thinking it had all calmed down but outside there was a mob of about 200 England just throwing bottles at the police who were charging at the mob, it was crazy, so I went straight back in and left them to it!

It was an eventful 24 hours and was well covered by the media, who for once seemed justified in their condemnation of the English invasion.

The *Daily Mirror* felt the behaviour of the fans in Amsterdam was worthy of the front-page headline which simply read, 'SHAME AGAIN!' and was backed up with 'ENGLAND YOBS GET THE BOOT'.

The report went on to say that, 48 hours before the match, over 5,000 English fans had arrived in Holland, and 30 yobs had already been deported after they wreaked havoc in the red-light district of Amsterdam. The paper also stated that Home Secretary Michael Howard had promised to ban convicted hooligans from the following year's World Cup, although the general feeling was that it would be Graham Taylor not Mr Howard who would be responsible for the USA not having to put up with loutish behaviour from the English!

The number of fans arrested and deported grew and later editions of the paper claimed that 160 had been held after going on the rampage in red-light district. It was also reported that six policemen were hurt, one after being thrown into a canal by English thugs, and two police dogs were seriously injured by broken glass.

It did not make happy reading for the authorities at home, given that a game which could see England eliminated from the World Cup was still 12 hours away!

TRENT, BRIGHTON:

The following morning everybody was up early and we made our way to Amsterdam central station. Queuing up for the train, you could see that all the passengers would be England lads, no one in an England shirt, it was pure firm. The Dutch were keeping a real low profile, as were the Moroccans, and it was a wise decision; the night before had been badly organised, today this firm was unmovable.

We ended up getting into Rotterdam Station and were split between a few bars. A few Old Bill in riot gear turned up but they were keeping a low profile. A bloke in a red coat, who turned out to be a main Chelsea face, was saying, 'Come on, we're going,' and that was that, everybody did, he was like the pied piper with a few hundred fucking mice behind him, marching through Rotterdam. It was one of those walks when the two most common shouts was: 'Here they are,' 'No they're not'. Everyone would bolt down the road and then stop as they realised the mob in front were either shoppers getting out of the way or more English joining the mob which was by now an army. Every time a tram went past, a bin or bottle would bounce of it, as lads got bored with walking. Then it went, a mob of Dutch, who we were later told were Den Haag, fronted the English fans up. They could not have known how many we had, as they were not that well represented, but for a minute it went off as they piled out of little side streets. The police got in the middle of it all and it was soon sorted and their ploy was to keep order so nobody was nicked.

If anything, the mob was too big, and we ended up splitting off and went for a beer, as more and more police were turning up. We went from bar to bar heading towards the ground and, in every bar we went into, lads were coming in saying it had been going off. There was no point going back into the city due to the police now rounding mobs up and arresting them. One lad came in shaking and told us that someone had thrown a bomb into the England mob and that another one of the lads had been shot; it was getting lively so we decided to get up to the ground and rejoin the main mob as we were in danger of becoming sitting ducks.

We got to the suburbs of Rotterdam and jumped on a tram and went for a few beers in a quiet bar where the locals were really friendly people. It was like that in Holland, one minute you were their guests, the next minute you were in danger of being killed, there was a fine line between good and bad in Holland. If you behaved and stuck to the local bars, you were made welcome; play up in the usual tourist haunts and you could come well unstuck!

We jumped the train that goes directly to the ground and, as soon as we got there, you could see the Old Bill making themselves really busy, just collaring people and grilling them and as we didn't have tickets we jumped over a fence and took the long way round to the stadium.

In the distance, you could hear the unmistakable roar of football violence it was probably a mile away but the air was full of the sounds that cannot be described. If you have been there, you don't need an explanation, there is no other sound like it in the world, and it makes the hairs stand up on the back of your neck. We didn't know where we were going so the roars were our guide and we ended up wandering across some wasteground which brought us on to the main road outside the ground just as the mayor of Rotterdam turned up.

He was stuck in traffic and I was a bit pissed and stoned so I tapped on his window and said, 'Hello, fella, any chance of some tickets?'

He looked at me in absolute disdain and disgust and went, 'No, no, no,' and urged his chauffeur to drive on; he proper fucked me off, but, given that he had the big gold chain and limousine, it was worth a try!

We got to the ground as the pre-match entertainment arrived in the form of the big band. So I tried to smuggle myself in as one of the band by walking in amongst them but they all had big hats and daft coats on and as I'm getting near I've thought, I'm fucking in here, when a security bloke dragged me out and I was fucked off for the second time in less than an hour.

So out of a 1,000-strong mob, I'm now on my jack, so I thought I'll find a boozer to watch the game in and walked right round the back of Feyenoord's ground, when I heard the roar again, only this time it was not a mile away, it was coming from a few hundred yards away. I turned around and saw a mob of 100-odd Dutch with umbrellas, bits of wood, charging past towards the forecourt where they had noticed a small mob of English who were stuck outside without tickets. They met the Dutch head on, I had a great view of it and it was the first time I've seen someone stabbed at a football match, as an England fan got stabbed in the shoulder while some Dutch bloke was slashed right down his arm. The Old Bill ran in, and briefly things calmed down, giving me a chance to join up with the mob. I recognised one lad and said, 'Where the fuck is everybody?'

He told me that, as soon as everybody turned up on the train, they were locking the train-station gates and, if you didn't have a ticket, you weren't coming out of the station. They kept hundreds of England fans in the train station and turned up with army trucks, loaded them all on and drove off to wherever. All that was left were the few people who'd climbed the fences and a few people who got there earlier.

Amongst our mob were a few Brighton, a few Cheltenham, some Wolves and some Shrewsbury, a couple of Stoke and many more who were from all over the country and who were doing England proud. Had we split up before the game, we would have either been arrested and deported or murdered. Much of it was bravado mixed with fear and, unless you have faced such odds, you will have no idea what feelings and emotions overcome you.

In moments like this, you need a leader and that day a

lunatic Geordie initially kept us together. During the attacks, he had been stabbed in the neck, stabbed in the leg and stabbed in the arm by either blades or sharpened umbrellas but he didn't give a shit! He was standing there wearing a pair of stonewash dungarees and was probably the worst-dressed man in the world, but he was standing there telling us all, 'I'm not fucking letting these cunts have me.'

Apart from his dress sense, you had to admire him, and we did and stood there with him, as every couple of minutes yet another little firm of Dutch would walk past and charge in, umbrellas flying, backed up with the occasional shot from a flare gun. Eventually, we became whipping boys, the game started and, while inside the packed stadium, 50,000 Dutch and 10,000 English booed each other's anthem, outside 50-odd battered and bloodied English lads were not looking too confident against hundreds of Dutch hooligans who had no interest in joining their countrymen in the ground. Before long, 50 became 40 and 40 became 30, as every couple of minutes someone else would go, 'Fuck this, I'm going!'

We gave it one last go and, as another firm charged into us, we've gone 'Fuck it' and steamed back into them. It's gone right off and we were really having it with them. The Old Bill have left us alone by this point and before we knew it a couple of England geezers had been stabbed to fuck and the Dutch backed off leaving them on the floor. We chased after them but they stopped and turned on us big time.

Call it what you want but there was nowhere near enough of us and we could not hold it together any longer against the whole of the fucking Dutch firm and we got legged.

We saw a cab and jumped in, telling the driver to take us to Rotterdam central station; some loon who used to go to all the Brighton games was asking us to come with him to get his fucking flag from wherever he had left it. He was an absolute nuisance and was shouting that he couldn't go without some fucking flag. I've gone, 'Fuck off, we're staying in this cab, mate,' and, although it may seem a bit out of order, we left him there. If he wanted to risk getting stabbed up by these Dutch loons over some daft flag that was his look-out.

We got into the centre of Rotterdam and asked the driver to drop us somewhere we could watch the football but he told us we were mad, as it was too dangerous, as there were people who wanted to kill English fans! We were like: 'Yeah, we fucking know that, look at the state of us but there must be somewhere we can have a drink in the peace and quiet!'

He drove us to a place called the Crystal Palace, which was funny, as everyone knows it is the arch-enemy of Brighton; it was like a Thai restaurant/bar so we have swerved it and went round the corner and ended up finding this little Dutch pub. We went in and watched the game and the Dutch were spot on, we didn't spend a penny in there all night, the locals bought us all our drinks. They were the Old Dutch walrus-type blokes, big grey moustaches, big bellies, all shaking our hands saying, 'You are our guests, you have not caused any trouble, have another beer!' Little did they know, we'd been beating the fuck out of each other less than an hour ago!

Once the game finished, we made our way back to the central station and were soon clocked by a small mob that chased us; we took a few slaps until the attackers realised we were English, the same as them! We all got back to Rotterdam Station and there were loads of England milling around. I asked the lads where they had come from, as none of them had been to the game and they were part of the hundred who broke out of the army camp! A few Dutch turned up expecting to wait for the English to get back from the game, instead they were met by these really, really riled-up English fans who have gone mental and chased them on to the rail tracks. They had picked on the wrong group, these lads had been locked up for hours before escaping and they really wanted to kill people.

I never did find out if the badly dressed Geordie lived to tell the tale or if our daft mate from Brighton ever got his flag back but, even though we'd lost and gone out of the World Cup, we had the best result that night as it took the cream of the Dutch firm over an hour to shift us and, if the players had shown that kind of spirit, we would have been booking to go to America instead of thousands of cunts dressed from head to toe in orange!

GILLY, WOLVES:
I had heard that anyone and everyone were going to this game so I decided, 'Let's try England away!' I had never bothered with England before, all my activity – as I will call it – was at Wolves games but the word was that this was one not to miss, so me and my pal, Gary Payton, flew from East Midlands Airport two days before the game and met up with some lads from Mansfield who we shared a poxy room with, as they were scarce and it was better than roaming the streets and cheaper than £40 an hour in the windows!

From the first time we went for a beer, the trip was crazy. Every hour of the trip was the same, littered with violence! Night one: meet in the Grasshopper, Dutch came up the road, 60 or 70 of the lads piled out of the bar, ran them up the road, OB come suited and booted and laid into the English! It was like the news on the radio, on the hour every hour, same thing for two days! And after the first hour I remember thinking to myself, Yes, this is for me!

For some reason, I have always enjoyed having a row with the OB more than the other mobs, and, apart from a few mobs of Dutch who had a go, the trip was mainly England v OB. In the Dam, the fighting got more and more intense and the water cannons came out and the OB were really heavy-handed. My mate was running about taking pictures of it all and, when he ran out of film, he went off to buy another. I sat in a café out of the way watching everything and was there for at least 45 minutes thinking, Where the fuck is Gaz? Finally, he comes in bashed up; the OB had got hold of him, while he was clicking away and quite simply caned him! We sat off in a bar watching these running battles all night and, when I went to bed in the early hours, I thought to myself, What the fuck is it going to be like tomorrow?

I got up early as we had to meet the rest of the other lads from Wolves and I was buzzing my nuts off. We met up, sorted some digs out and set off for Rotterdam; we were with some older lads from Chelsea, QPR and Sheffield, who all looked up for it and we boarded the early train, 200-strong, all smart and looking good, ready for war.

I was surprised in Rotterdam that the OB just let us walk through the station. I thought, Fuck me, this is mad! We got to the main square where there were bars and a large group of English were already drinking there, 200-plus, which, combined with what we had brought, made a good firm, far too good for a group of Dutch lads who appeared throwing stones and shouting. There was one almighty roar and the English came out the bars and just ran at them. The OB had no control, but suddenly all you could hear was a loud bang and a cloud of smoke filled the air. The Dutch had chucked a nail bomb in the form of a tennis ball at the lads and still nobody backed off. That was it, that was the start of the day England took Holland, if a bomb was not going to put this mob off, nothing would.

About 250 English went on a walkabout and soon we bumped into a mob four times the size of ours; for a few seconds, I thought, Here we go, this will be touch and go, when lads at the front started shaking hands with each other, England were now 1,200-handed and the mob was growing by the minute. I had never ever in my life seen so many lads and was in my element. I got talking to a lad from Germany, Ronald from Cologne. I was new to all this and was amazed to know that loads of lads from other countries followed England away just for the row. Something triggered the lads off and the riot began, and I mean a riot, about 1,500 lads rowing with the Dutch and the police, who eventually got it under control and put everyone in a square in the city centre.

Coach after coach, bus after bus came to the square and lads were forced on to them and were taken away, some said they were going to the ground and loads thought it was a set-up, which it was with most being nicked and lots more being locked in a cage near the ground. There was about 100 lads left and they ran out of coaches and buses and that was it, we were left to go free and, within minutes, we had bumped into another group of Dutch lads and it all started again.

Without the numbers, it was a lot livelier; luckily, we had good lads with us, in particular, a lad from Pompey who had a proper firm out there. During one charge from the Dutch, I stood there egging everyone on when this lad from Pompey laughed and pulled a machete out of his mac. It was huge! I just looked at him and shouted. 'Fucking hell, go on, my son!'

Towards kick-off time, we got the train to the station where I saw the cage with hundreds of lads in who were helpless and had to watch as we came under attack from the locals who started to get brave because our numbers were only a fraction of what they had seen earlier. It was going mental as the lads in the cage were running at the cage and at the Old Bill, trying to knock the fence down. The Dutch were tooled up and I saw an English lad get stabbed but the bloke that did it was tripped up and got kicked to fuck by some Plymouth lads who caught him. For 30 minutes, there were running battles all over the concourse. Police horses were injured, lads were stabbed, both English and Dutch, and I thought, This is mad as fuck but what a buzz!

I got talking to some lads from London and, because we never had any tickets, we decided to head back to the station and, on the way, a police riot van pulled up with seven Dutch police officers and two English spotters in it. They all jumped out and dragged a lad in the van. I didn't know at the time but it was TC, a main head in the Chelsea ranks.

When we got to Rotterdam Station, there he was, covered in blood; the OB had given him a right kicking. He said the English spotters had pointed him out and they had all had their 10 bob on him, as they had him down as a main organiser of the firm that day. I don't know if he was but I do know that Churchill and Hitler would have been proud of the army we had in Holland that day!

Trent and Gilly had made it to the ground but not managed to see the match; Lee Spence managed neither and was one of the hundreds who were locked up in the army camp before the game.

LEE, OLDHAM:
Like so many others, we predictably went to Amsterdam before this game and the night before was the first time I ever saw the police try and close the red-light district down. It was mental, and all the rubbish about England being as one went out of the window in the early hours, as the likes of Forest, Derby, Shrewsbury and Mansfield tried to kick shit out of each other.

On the day of the game, we all met in the Grasshopper. TC had a massive firm with him and put a lid on the in-house mither and in turn put together one of the best England mobs of all time with everyone being made welcome apart from Tottenham. We got to Rotterdam and, within 10 minutes, bumped into Feyenoord's mob and there was no messing about, no fucking daft noises and bouncing up and down, we went straight into them but were soon sent back when they threw a fucking nail bomb into us. The smoke cleared and there was a QPR lad with his trainer completely blown off, so we carried on regardless and went straight through them, bombs or not!

It was a few hours of running street battles, we would stop off at a street café and have a beer, then off we go again, hours of playing cat and mouse, with us, the police and the Dutch all participating!

Inevitably, the police got a grip of a few hundred of us and sectioned us off and, before we could do anything about it, a load of buses pulled up and we were put on them. They were saying we were going to the game but we were taken straight to some fucking army camp in the middle of nowhere and dumped in the yard. Quite a few managed to swerve the buses and made it to the ground and had murder with the Dutch who claimed a bit of a result on the forecourt, but there was about 800 of us under arrest and, had we got up there, a Dutch result would have been impossible.

Back in this camp, they let us all off the buses to walk about and we soon decided to escape; it was not planned and was not pretty. Basically, a few hundred of us ran to the fence and just smashed our way through it; there were hundreds of us rocking it back and forth and in the end it gave way and we were out.

The problem was we didn't have a clue where the fuck we were and we just headed towards the city lights, which at the time didn't seem that far away, but it was misleading because we were walking for ages through muddy fields; it was pitch dark and we were traipsing over fucking streams and hedges, it was an absolute ball ache of a walk. Every so often, the police helicopter would come above and we were splitting up and losing people.

Lads were laughing and saying it was like the great escape, but it wasn't funny; we were now in fives and sixes and ended up on some moody estate on the outskirts of Rotterdam. Luckily, we caught a tram and we must have looked like a load of tramps getting on, covered in mud and shite – it's as funny as fuck thinking of it now but at the time it was a mare!

We got into town and the police were everywhere, they really had got their act together and they had it boxed off. We were gutted when we heard about what we had missed at the ground, but just glad we had not been flown home from that fucking camp like so many of the others. People will always remember the game for Taylor's comment: 'Do I not like that'; well, I'll tell you what, he would have liked that fucking walk a lot less!

Despite the drastic measures taken by the police, thousands still made the game, among them one of the Shrewsbury lads.

EBF:
We took a great firm out to Holland but, by the Tuesday, half of the lads had been deported after two nights of continual rioting in Amsterdam. As soon as we got to Rotterdam, it was absolute mayhem, as the Dutch for once attacked us, with distress flares and tear gas. I remember one lad with his coat on fire and another who nearly had his head blown off by a stray Dutch flare! The police had this mission of splitting us all up and it played into the Dutch hands, as, if we were left as one, they wouldn't come near us. Once we were in smaller numbers, they got brave and we were in one bar when they came in and we were coming unstuck until a load of Boro turned up and bailed us out. I heard the same thing happened with another group of lads who would have been taken apart if it weren't for the Leicester Baby Squad's intervention. They were a firm who were always well represented at the time and I had a lot of time for them as they were as game as anyone on tour.

Inside the ground was like the 70s and mid-80s, seats were ripped out and thrown at the Dutch during the second half, as all sorts rained down on us. The toilets downstairs were flattened and blocks of concrete and advertising boards ended up going into the police who were a bit heavy-handed in the ground and seemed to let the Dutch take the piss a bit. We thought that outside after the game would be mental but we were kept in for ages and, when we bounced out, the concourse was empty and we were slung on to trains that were either going to Amsterdam or the Hook of Holland. Plenty had to get off at the Dam and get back in to Rotterdam, as they were staying there! The police must have been sick to death of us and, after the game, there was no middle ground, we were pushed, battered and treated badly. I had no complaints, not many could moan, as, out of the

7,000 English support out there, I'd say 5,000 was pure lads. I was there for five days and when I got home the quietness of it all was strange, as the whole time I was in Holland all I had heard was the sound of breaking glass and police sirens.

English fans' behaviour had once again shamed the nation and many MPs were of the same opinion that it was fortunate Taylor's side had failed to qualify for the finals in America as it prevented our greatest allies having to put up with what was now the majority of our travelling support.

The press called it 'The battle of Rotterdam' and the final figures released stated that over 1,000 England fans had been arrested and more than 430 thugs deported out of the country on specially chartered flights. One paper mentioned that an England fan had been shot by a Dutchman in a revenge attack, while others had received minor injuries when Dutch fans hurled homemade bombs in tennis balls at England hooligans during street fighting.

While the US organisers breathed a sigh of relief at England's failure to make the finals, their Dutch counterparts were left to clean up the mess. The mayor of Rotterdam, who had refused to help Trent out with a ticket, was not best pleased with the damage caused to his city and the Feyenoord stadium, claiming that it was the biggest clean-up operation since the Germans invaded the city during World War II!

CHAPTER NINETEEN

NO SURRENDER
DUBLIN '95

When England defeated San Marino in Bologna on 17 November 1993, few could have guessed that it would be another 15 months before the national side played another away game. First the failure to qualify for the World Cup in the USA and then the aborted attempt to play Germany on Hitler's birthday were the main reasons that the travelling masses were kept at home. Many believed that another reason was the FA's reluctance to jeopardise the European Championships, which were being held in England in 1996, knowing that any serious outbreaks of violence might see UEFA implement a ban on England competing in the very tournament they were hosting.

If this was the case, whoever arranged the game in Dublin on 15 February 1995 had a lot to answer for!

It was one of the darkest days in the history of our national game as England's hooligan army rampaged inside and outside the stadium and caused the game to be abandoned after just 27 minutes.

Many people were blamed for the riot, the National Front, Combat 18 and, of course, hooligans from most clubs in the UK; but, when the dust had settled and the full facts came to light, there were quite a few people and organisations who needed to take a long hard look at themselves, as, if one ounce of common sense had been used during the planning of the game, the infamous 'Dublin Riot' could have so easily been avoided.

In the aftermath of the riot, a serious breakdown in communications between the British Police, including the NCIS and the football-hooligan units and the Irish Garda came to light, and, for this alone, so-called intelligence officers' heads should have rolled!

It was reported in the national press that English Police warned their Irish counterparts that troublemakers were on their way an amazing *30 hours* before they landed! Now, call me a clever cunt, but most people with half a brain could have predicted that troublemakers would be there in their droves five minutes after the fixture was announced. With no games away for 15 months and no World Cup the previous summer, they decide to play Ireland away, a game that will no doubt interest the Loyalist contingent in England, as well as every Tom, Dick and Harry who fancies a cost-very-little jolly. Then they 'predict there may be trouble'! Do me a favour!

In a nutshell, it was one police cock-up after another, and the British Police tried very hard to apportion most of the blame to the Irish Garda with one Manchester Police spokesman claiming that they had offered their assistance in policing the game but the Garda 'did not want to know'.

It was also reported that there were 20 flights from Manchester to Dublin over the two days prior to the match and thugs fooled police by using these flights and not the supporters' travel clubs, which would have made them easily identifiable!

Are they for real? Those people deemed 'undesirable' would never have been allowed to join the official face-painted army who piss everyone off with their drums and stupid songs, so how else, apart from the ferry and scheduled flights, were the thugs going to get there?

The Garda and Irish airport officials were equally pathetic with their excuses about how hundreds of known thugs had been allowed to attend the game, but the comment from one spokesman won the gold medal for talking bollocks when he was quoted as saying: 'Without the need to show their passports, they slipped through unrecognised!'

Manchester police intelligence, determined not to be outdone, were quoted in the *Sun* with this classic: 'It is our job to provide intelligence to the Garda, which we did, they chose to ignore it! We informed them that there was an arranged battle in Dublin between Oldham and Leeds hooligans and that England fans would riot as soon as the national anthems were played. Although the information we supplied regarding Leeds and Oldham was incorrect, we were not too far out with the time of the riot!' (Even though the flashpoint came when David Kelly put the Irish 1–0 up in the 22nd minute!)

Believe it or not, these people do get paid a very good salary to supply such intelligence!

Then there was the question of segregation and ticketing and the blame for this was passed across the Irish Sea like a hot potato. Mr Connolly, general secretary of the Football Association of Ireland, argued, 'We distributed tickets to the FA for their travel club! I have no idea if the original purchasers were here tonight.'

The English FA responded by insisting that they had only sold tickets to official club members and that they had returned 1,100 tickets the week before the game to the Irish FA.

What both FAs declined to mention was that these tickets were put on general sale in Dublin, and touts from both countries snapped them up with many then ending up in the hands of English louts.

Had the English FA kept or sold them to fans on their database or had the Irish FA left that section of the ground empty, this chapter in the book would be a very short one. But they did not and what resulted was a classic English performance ... off the pitch! Despite the cock-ups by the police and FAs from both countries, a riot can't happen without up-for-it males and, on that trip across the Irish Sea, England had plenty who were more than happy to join in the fun.

NICK, NOTTINGHAM FOREST:

After Euro '92 I was banned and had a prison sentence hanging over me for trouble at a Forest game. The three-year ban was like an age, it's not just the football you're missing that pisses you off but the drinking with the lads and then all the nonsense of signing on every Saturday and when England are abroad; it gets you down in the end and I was glad when it was over.

Was it a deterrent? Was it fuck! All I was waiting for was to get back with the lads and go again. When the ban was up, I didn't look at it like it was an opportunity to watch football again, I looked at it as an opportunity to fight for Queen and Country again and the first game after my ban was perfect for it. The Republic of Ireland v England, a match made in heaven!

I flew out with one of the lads from Birmingham Airport and was amazed how lax it was. I expected to get turned back but nothing, and we were on the pop at midday. We wanted to stay one night and one night only, fuck all this 'let's have a few days out there and a nose about' – get there, do the business and then get the fuck out of the stinking hole. That applies to most of the places we go, sightseeing is for Yanks and Japs, not the English; we go for the drink and to fight, yes, it may sound like a load of macho bullshit but you ask any lads who went a few years back what they went for and the honest ones will tell you the same. A few destinations may throw a prostitute into the top three answers but football and fucking sightseeing will not feature in most lads' top three!

While many more lads flew out, the majority took the cheap and easy option and got the Holyhead to Dun Laoghaire ferry. The journey was not plain sailing and, before the ferry had even set sail, there were serious outbreaks of fighting between English fans.

Paddy (he's English by the way!) from Huddersfield was

hoping to make it to the game but was involved in a brawl, described as 'drunken madness' by the media, who went on to report that 42 Huddersfield fans had been sent home from Holyhead before they even got on the boat. They had been involved in brawls with other hooligans on the train to Holyhead and at the terminal, which gave the Transport Police and the captain of the ship, the *Hibernia*, no option but to refuse them an option of joining the ship for the crossing.

PADDY, HUDDERSFIELD:
We were changing trains and got on to a carriage full of Stoke lads who seemed amazed that being born in England, holding the same passport as them but being of a different colour did not instantly disqualify you from following England. 'Who brought the spooks?' being one of the lame remarks to come our way. On hearing this, one of the Town lads put both his index fingers behind a Stoke lad's eyeballs and gouged them, leaving him screaming in agony.

Fighting erupted in the carriage, and it is not the easiest thing in the world to fight in such a confined space, so a lot of lads were taking blows from all angles – not all necessarily aimed at them. At times, it was a struggle to move, let alone throw a decent punch. The Transport Police were more or less already on the scene, so, after the clash, it was quickly decided that we were the aggressors and a carriage was cleared for us at the front of the train.

There was no doubt in my mind that it was going to go again as soon as we reached Holyhead. As the train pulled into the port, we knew that we would possibly have to front a train full of lads. There was a fair bit of conversation along the lines of 'just do it' and 'don't fucking move'. The police line wasn't the most co-ordinated, and, as two of their lads came round the corner giving it the old arms-outstretched gesture, we just literally waltzed through the police line and went into them. The ones that were coming behind them had nowhere to go so it was chaos at one point. The police, after being so lax, went into 'if it moves, hit it' mode and they backed us off to the point where we started from.

That was really the end of it. To add insult to injury the captain of the ferry refused to take us. It was a long journey back to Town that night.

Stoke's view is somewhat different; Cossack is a founder member of the Naughty Forty, Stoke's notorious hooligan firm.

COSSACK, STOKE:

I'll agree it was a stalemate at the ferry terminal but Huddersfield were given an option of getting the next ferry and sorting out our slight disagreement in Dublin. They decided to leave it and go home, what does that tell you?

The lads who flew had no such problems.

NICK, NOTTINGHAM FOREST:

In Dublin, we got straight on the piss and I was slaughtered; we met the Mansfield lads and a few Forest, and we were a decent-size firm if anyone fancied a go but, unlike many England games, there was little in-house trouble, as everyone wanted to smash the Irish. I got everyone out of the pub and told them it was time for action. We headed for the ground and I feel no shame as a Loyalist saying that anyone was regarded as fair game en route. That may sound like we were bullies but this was personal and most lads know the score. The bad thing is loads of fans don't and think that the Paddies are a lovely bunch of people, the same way they think the Tartan Army are just a boisterous bunch of piss-heads. Like fuck they are! The Irish are the same as the Jocks, fucking bigots, and that night they got all they deserved.

People forget that they wave those flags and sing those

rebel songs and I wouldn't be surprised if most of them had a drink when the news of pub bombings came through; at least the Northern Irish Catholics admit to fighting their corner and admit they are IRA sympathisers, the Southern lot sit on the fence and fund the cunts, which is the coward's way in my eyes.

So anyway they were getting it!

We started the march up to the ground and the atmosphere and the mood changed in minutes, even though there was a chill in the air and things were warming up fast. Basically the walk turned into punching practice, as anything Irish that was in our way got it – flag sellers, blokes in suits, people waiting by bus stops. OK, we were no better than the Tartan Army, but we never gave a fuck.

How we never got nicked, fuck knows, but we made it to the ground before the Garda swamped us and then it was every man for himself, as the scramble to get into the ground began. A few stupid touts who came offering tickets were battered and it was a no-go area for anyone other than English lads, as the mood was mental. Make no mistake, it was not all one way, and there were little pockets of Irish who were prepared to have a go; they had taken the hump that so-called fans had been clouted – no problem, bring it on. Outside, though, when the main firm had gone in, it was a bit dangerous, and the Garda were trying to clear the place of us, and anyone daft enough to get caught trying to jump in was either nicked or took a hiding. I laughed when I read Paul Dodd's book *England's Number One*, no surprise he was one of those nicked.

I went back to town to watch the game on the telly and was well pissed off when I saw the riot in the ground; they happen once a lifetime and, if you miss them, you don't often get a second chance! The people in the bars were disgusted and more so when we were cheering and decided to head back up as we knew it was going to be mental after the game.

Nick and many more ticketless fans had missed what will go down in history as some of the most disgraceful scenes ever witnessed at an England game. Mike from Stockport was one of those who saw first-hand what went on.

MIKE, STOCKPORT:

I'd been to loads of games away but this was the maddest, it was a disaster waiting to happen, who in their right mind would sanction such a game?

At the time, there were ongoing Anglo-Irish talks in Ulster and, although there was talk of it all being the work of organised fascists, a typical slant some of the media always played on, it was 100 per cent good old football hooliganism! Yes, England had lads with strong pro-Loyalist sentiments – plenty of them followed County – and, yes, the game was played at a time when some nationalist hooligans believed that the whole peace process favoured the Republicans, but to claim it was orchestrated by the right wing is a load of bollocks.

From the minute we got there, it was madness. At the ferry we were met by hundreds of riot police who proceeded to let us all go on the beer! This was great but, before long, the booze took its toll and, once a few locals had finished work and started drifting about, there were running battles around O'Connell Street and that big road before the game. Everybody was playing up and a Shrewsbury lad was making a video of it all; thinking of it now, we were mad. It was all on film and, to be truthful, some of the stuff going on was out of order and could've got lads some jail if the Irish had the sense to take the film from the EBF kid.

We got to the ground and it was a free-for-all getting in; lots of lads didn't have tickets and were just jumping over the turnstiles, touts were getting belted, and the appalling stewarding and policing played a big part of what went on in the ground. The lads had been put above the Irish in a crap stand with wooden seats that were easily ripped out. Below, it seemed to be a mix of English and Irish and, when the anthems started, all you could hear was 'No surrender to the IRA' and them singing 'You'll never beat the Irish'. The atmosphere was poisonous, and bits were getting dropped on the lot below but who they hit was anyone's guess, and it was a bit out of order, as there were families down there as well as our own fans.

When they scored, the lot went up and it was carnage; fans spilled on to the pitch and I think we then had a goal disallowed and, within a minute or two, the game stopped and the players were taken off. I'll never forget David Platt coming towards the rioting fans and gesturing for every one of them to calm down; his pleas were ignored, as hundreds told him to fuck off. All you could hear was 'No surrender to the IRA'. It was unbelievable.

Down below, there were English lads getting booted by Paddies, and I remember seeing Jack Charlton in the papers the next day pictured grabbing an Irish fan by the throat for throwing a bottle into the English crowd. Fair play to him, but he still got loads of stick, as the English chanted 'Judas, Judas' at him for managing the Republic!

The ground emptied and we were kept in for ages; there were a few charges at the police and they were taking no shit by now and loads of lads took a hiding from them. When they let us out, many fans were put on buses and taken straight to the ferry port, regardless if they had belongings in hotels, etc. We went into town and it was dangerous if you were not with the main firm, for the English were getting picked off in city by mobs of Irish. We got into one bar and were locked in for 'our own safety'. Every Irishman that night was out for English blood and the pub we were in was attacked by locals. Even B&Bs, guesthouses and the hostels were not letting lads in to get their gear and loads were put up in a police station because they didn't want them roaming the streets.

NICK, NOTTINGHAM FOREST:

As soon as I got out of the bar, the sound of sirens were deafening and there were police cars flying in every direction. We walked into the main road and saw about 150 English, and across the road a bigger mob of Paddies all calling it on. I jumped over the barrier and shouted to the lads to join me but was that pissed I hadn't noticed about 50 Garda in riot gear spread across the road keeping the English back. Whack! I was on my arse and a couple of Garda waded into me and dragged me into a shop doorway and told me I was arrested. They were spouting rubbish about Combat 18 and saying I was fucked and that they knew I was a leader. I had no interest in all that political crap, I was a proud member of England's hooligan army not C18, the BNP or fucking CND.

They bundled me into a van and off we went; the driver shouted something like 'You're not going to enjoy this little ride,' and I realised that, as they were all putting their gloves on, the ride may not be to the nick. This was my third England trip and third nicking, so it was nothing new to me, but, like it had been personal for us before this, now it seemed personal to them, and, as the minutes ticked away, I began to prepare myself for the inevitable hiding that was coming my way. After about 10 minutes, it came – Whack! My nose was gone. Bang! I have an eye shut, blood was pouring into my mouth and my throat was retching, as I tried to swallow blood and get my breath back at the same time. They were holding me up in the back seat, and then another crack to the side of the head, then a stamp on my guts as I tried to break free and cover myself up.

The ale I had drank started to come back up the passage it had gone down a few hours before and they still carried on – slap, crack, boot! Until one said, 'Right, he's had enough.' I still thought I was getting nicked, so tried to tell them I was lost earlier and was just looking for my digs and I managed to pull out a leaflet with the guesthouse address on. The boss man driving said, 'Pass it here,' and he read it and said, 'We'll take him there, he's took his hiding.'

I was chuffed and thought that was that, but then this women copper said in a menacing voice, 'Let me have a go first.' I thought it was a wind-up but she climbed over the seats into the back and got me around the throat and spat her words into my face: 'You fucking English make me sick.' The feeling was mutual, darling! And she then waded into me with girly punches, which would have been nothing if they were not landing on my already busted nose and bruised eyes.

She had her wicked way with me, probably creamed her regulation knickers and then climbed back into the front as if nothing had happened. Minutes later, the van stopped and I thought, Here we go again, the driver wants a go, but they opened the door and slung me out across the road from my digs. I was in a right fucking state as I rolled on the pavement and could hardly walk.

A few lads came over, turned out they were Shrewsbury, normally we are not the best of mates but they were spot on and took me into their hotel and cleaned me up. They were top lads and bought me a Chinese takeaway and a few beers. There were stories doing the rounds that there were mobs of Irish attacking our lads on the way back to the digs and a few went off to see if it was true. I had had more than enough and stayed put.

The EBF's name cropped up every time this game was mentioned and the filming of the trouble was supposedly done by lads from the firm. Brian and Neil Jones admit they were filming the violence.

NEIL, SHREWSBURY:
I had a camcorder with me out there and got some mad film of loads of various incidents. I basically recorded the fucking lot going off! When we got back to Shrewsbury Station on the Thursday or Friday, the entire Shrewsbury Police Force were waiting for us. There must have been thousands of pounds

wasted, as every copper in the land was waiting for us. I had the camcorder and some copper said, 'I'm going to have that in the morning, Jones.' True to form, they fucking raided my house the next morning. Anyway, they took it down to London to the hooligan branch, the Chelsea copper thing and weeks later sent it back and had put on it in marker pen 'EBF tape'!

BRIAN, SHREWSBURY:

It was a great turnout from our lads, there must have been 60 at least and then more came over. We met up in a pub in Shrewsbury and got the train to Anglesey and got the ferry over to Dublin, which was the day before the game. On the crossing, we bumped into a few lads, Bristol City and Wigan were just a couple I remember, and they were like 'Who the fuck are this lot?' It was a laugh because everybody thinks we're mugs because we're from a stupid little town called Shrewsbury, a village firm, but with those numbers and all being lads we were the business. We were mates with Oldham and Newcastle and knew if we all met up we'd have the biggest firm out there as they were both 40-odd-strong. A few Bristol City got lippy and we knew some of their lads and warned them to shut the fuck up, as there would only be one winner. When we got to Dublin the night before the game, we had it with a mob of Tottenham. One of the lads from Shrewsbury did a bit of drugs or whatever and was dealing when a few lads walked past, about a dozen boys, and they started on him. Their top man said, 'Who the fuck are you? We're the fucking Yids.' Our lads went into them and absolutely fucking demolished these Tottenham boys. They were well, well pissed off getting done by little old Shrewsbury. and I was getting threats for a good few years after that. Weeks after, thinking about it, to be fair, we did have the best firm there, not just in numbers, I mean the quality of the boys that were there, it was all good lads, only a few young kids there, it was all our generation.

The press had a field day and MPs, ex-players and the usual sociologists were all only too eager to offer their opinions, while both managers seemed oblivious to the fact that many innocent Irish people had been hurt.

Jack Charlton commented, 'The thugs should be ashamed, they were bombing their own people.'

Rival boss Terry Venables said, 'I have not got words strong enough to describe how I feel, I'm appalled.' But he then upset the injured Irish casualties in true Tel fashion by being quoted as saying: 'Luckily none of the players got hurt!'

Irish Police informed the press that they were alarmed that many hooligans were wearing NF insignia and singing 'No surrender to the IRA', while many Brits were equally alarmed by the picture in most papers showing an English fan being kicked in the head by an Irish steward, while a member of the Garda is standing back laughing!

Sports Minister Iain Sproat did not wish to comment on the riot, but Tory MP Terry Dicks did not sit on the fence and blurted, 'The Irish Police should have gone in and cracked a few heads, it's the only language these idiots understand.'

The *Mail* went on to report that the England fans had been kept in for two hours after the game but battled with riot police, 100 had escaped and made their way to O'Connell Street where more than 40 were arrested in street clashes.

Earlier that day, it claimed that in the Dublin terminal England fans clashed with each other and locals and 500 police were put on alert, while two English appeared in court on the day of the match after a barman received a 12in stab wound.

As usual, the *Sun* was quick to call for drastic action and its editorial led with the headline: 'KICK THESE THUGS INTO JAIL'. It went on to blast, 'The disgusting scum who haunt England must be rooted out and stamped on! The FA must ask themselves what kind of example they have set by their own pathetically weak treatment of men like Cantona.'

So that is who's to blame! A Frenchman who was nowhere near the game that night!

The *Today* newspaper was more direct in apportioning the blame and looked towards MPs and the peace process rather than King Eric when condoning the thugs. 'DUBLIN SHAME' read their headline. 'It was appalling that the pond life who purport to follow England should riot in Ireland of all places, and at such a politically sensitive time simply defies belief!'

Labour MP Tony Banks was not happy and said in the same paper, 'They are sticking two fingers up to everybody, the game, MPs, the players and the clubs!'

The leader of Fianna Fail, the Irish opposition party at the time, even accused the FA of having NF supporters with them in the VIP area. 'It is unbelievable that some of the officials from the FA were identifying some of these people as National Front people. They knew them!'

The far right were widely condemned as the culprits in the riot, and Irish Chief of Police Fergus O'Shaughnessy commented, 'We have no doubt whatsoever that the whole terrible episode was pre-planned by the National Front, we had been on the lookout for these boot boys all day!'

Fergus had obviously not moved with the times, and was always likely to fail if he believed that England's hooligan army would be marching around his fair city sporting shaved heads and bovver boots!

Chelsea chairman Ken Bates was more direct in his approach to the troublemakers and blasted, 'I will track every single one of those bastards caught rioting in Dublin and, if they are in anyway connected to Chelsea, I will expose the vile scum!'

Nick laughs at the allegations and the press reaction.

NICK, NOTTINGHAM FOREST:

As I said C18 and the NF had nothing to do with it, and all that talk of us getting banned from the World Cup and even not allowing us to stage the European Championships was nonsense, and everyone was glad it never happened.

Dublin was not a football thing, it was personal!

CHAPTER TWENTY

IT'S COMING HOME!
EURO '96

In 1996, England staged its first major football tournament since winning the World Cup in 1966. It was a major achievement by the government and Football Association to win the right to stage Euro '96 in England, given that the hooligan problem that existed in the country was always going to go against the bid.

There were fears that any trouble would harm a further bid to host the 2006 World Cup Finals and the authorities and police staged a huge operation to ensure that the festival of football passed off peacefully. Against all the odds, they pulled it off and, despite attempts by hooligans from all over the country to join forces and prove that they were still the world's number-one hooligan firm, it was a lack of credible opposition rather than the police operation that kept things under control.

LEE SPENCE, OLDHAM:
There was so much hype before Euro '96 that Germany, Holland, Scotland and even the Czechs were coming that the hooligan underworld was in a frenzy! For months before, there were meetings going on all over the country between every major firm and most club rivalries were put on ice, as many of the main faces agreed that we needed to be as one to defend our country from the foreign invaders.

England's first game was against the Swiss and, although they have a few problems over there and the likes of Basel and Zurich have been known to travel, they were not one of the countries who we thought would bring a troublesome following over, which proved to be the case. The Germans were different, though, and their first match at Old Trafford against the Czech Republic was earmarked as a must attend game for all the lads.

A meet was sorted at the Old Cock in Mills Hill, as we were told that the Germans were turning out a firm in Manchester at the game and, given their reputation, there were high hopes that they would. Seventy Oldham were joined by Carlisle, Shrewsbury, West Brom, Villa, Newcastle and Stockport, and we put together a massive firm 100 per cent convinced that the Germans would be there. United were also mobbed up but they wanted to do their own thing and were not keen on the joint-force idea; as it was their patch, it was their call so nobody bothered about them until later on.

After a few false alarms, we went bowling down the road, as, for the umpteenth time, some cock said the Germans had shown; it was a set-up, though, and we bounced straight into a huge firm of football intelligence police, who had their counterparts from Berlin, Hamburg and Munich with them. We were split up and given a hard time and that set the tone for the complete tournament; it was a few weeks of false alarms and police harassment. And, although I'm no lover of the police, during that tournament they did their job well; it was a massive operation and fuck knows how much it cost, but they kept things under wraps.

It was all to do with keeping the family atmosphere going; the massive media attention it all got was reader friendly and gave England the chance of winning the race to hold the 2006 World Cup Finals. What they didn't bank on was that, as soon as we went abroad again, we caused murder and fucked it all up anyway!

The no-show by the Germans was a major let-down, mobs

split up and, as usual after a day on the beer, it ended up with everyone falling out and the biggest brawl was when United had it with Carlisle in Deansgate, and it was a proper set-to. United were looking for City and bumped into Carlisle who were right up for it. That was not what we had hoped for and, if the Germans were not going to turn out at a game that was played over the weekend, then who else was? The next game for us was Scotland, so we were still upbeat that weeks of plotting and organising would not go to waste!

For the Scotland game, I sorted a meet with the Jocks in Cockfosters; we were good mates with the Hibs lads, so it was easy to arrange and we knew that, unlike the Germans, they would defiantly turn up. It was well organised but the police got on to it and it was yet another major let-down.

The firm we assembled was quality, mostly Northern, as, like United in Manchester, a lot of the Cockney mobs were doing their own thing on their own patch. Once I knew we had more than enough to sort this private battle of Britain out, I drove over with some Grimsby lads to see if the Jocks were there and there was a good 200 of them so we went back to Cockfosters to get the lads ready and the scene that met us was unbelievable.

The whole area was cordoned off with the biggest police presence I have ever seen in my life. It was a massive operation and there must have been a grass in the camp, as, if they had stumbled on to us, they wouldn't have got that amount of back-up there in that time. They were stopping and searching cars and we had to park up, just dump the motor and escape through gardens, as they were trying to nick the people who had set it up and I knew my name would be in the hat due to my connections with the Hibs lads.

The biggest fight of the day that was reported was when the Cockney firm bumped into the Jocks at Trafalgar Square, that was just a load of barmies and a few firm, the Scottish National Firm, all Scotland's top lads, saw very little all day. In fact, the biggest battle was Carlisle again who had it with Spurs – those lads were nuts and didn't care who called it on, they always obliged!

After that day, people lost interest, we had taken it to the Germans and the Jocks and both times the only people fighting were fucking Carlisle! Euro '96 captured the hearts of the normal fans, the song by those pair of twats Baddiel and Skinner and the marketing of the whole tournament got the whole country jumping on the Euro '96 bandwagon, and with the police so well informed the hooligan element had a hard time of things.

The Wolves lads who were always well represented on the international scene were also left disappointed at the Scotland game.

ABBO, WOLVES:
It was a game we had looked forward to for some time. The whole nation wanted to beat the Jocks, the Auld Enemy on and off the pitch! About 50 of us set off from Wolves and got on the early train to Euston, including two of our lads who turned up late and had to be pulled on board through the windows as the automatic doors were locked and the train was starting to pull off.

When we got there, half of the lads decided to go to the Phoenix pub to meet some Chelsea; the other half of us decided to hang fire around the station. The police numbers was unbelievable so we eventually moved on to the Phoenix but, when we got there, half of London's Met had surrounded the place filming everyone. If you had a match ticket, you could leave after giving all your details, those without were kept in the pub until halfway through the game.

Later that evening, we managed to get down to Trafalgar Square where all the Jocks were playing up, before seeing the need to hide behind barriers and Old Bill. Somehow, we managed to get through and for a couple of minutes bottles, glasses and cans of beer were flying at them before the Old

Bill landed and they soon drew their batons and waded into us all. A police dog jumped on my back, ripping into me and I was screaming for the copper to get him off. I looked up and our lads were pissing themselves laughing, while this fucking German Shepherd was feasting on me.

The handler managed to get him off and I was nicked but the dog latched on to another lad, so I made a run for it and managed to get 300 yards up the road when the Old Bill pulled me by McDonalds. I looked like Steve McQueen in *The Great Escape*, although mine was not very great or half as spectacular, as I was stood there, hands on my head, loads of media taking pictures, top ripped, with blood pissing out of my back as a *Sky News* crew filmed me getting rearrested. I complained to a copper with pips on his shoulders and started to show the photographers my bite marks when the Old Bill main man tells me I can go, which was a right result.

Day over, we headed back to Euston for the train home and bumped into a load of Birmingham, which meant that the day was back on and that the journey home was going to be lively. One of their mouthpieces walked up to my brother and asked him who he thought the top firm in Brum was. I mean there are only two clubs in it, and our kid says, 'It isn't you, it's Villa.'

The Transport Police see that things are not going well during this informal chat and put the Blues mob on one end of the train and us on the other. Three Villa lads joined us who we knew from the raves and that was it for the Blues. There was a bit of a scuffle near the buffet, so the handful of Transport Police called for back-up and by the time we got to New Street there were about 100 Old Bill waiting on the platform for us and we were sent home and not allowed to join the Blues for a night out in their town!

The day did not bring the violence that many of the lads anticipated but Mark, an Arsenal fan from Bristol, was involved in a brawl near Wembley with some unusual opponents!

MARK, ARSENAL:

I left Bristol about four in the morning and got as far as Swindon when I got stopped and done by the police for drink-driving, so that was a bad start to the day. But I was let out after a few hours and was still at Wembley at 9.30am, where I met up with four lads from North London, along with four lads from Bristol in the Green Mann pub near the famous old ground. We had a few beers, the atmosphere was good and we even had a laugh and a joke with a few Scots we'd got talking to inside.

We took the walk down Wembley Way with plenty of Scots and it was all good-natured banter even in the ground where Paul Gascoigne's wonder goal made it the perfect day. There were a few Jocks mixed in with us but there was no trouble and the day seemed to be a quiet one until we came out of the game and went to head back to the Green Mann. As we got near the boozer, about 15 women in their fifties started yelling in broad Scottish accents, 'Oi, you English niggers, let's have a fight, we wanna fight you!'

We looked at each other and they were indeed shouting to the four black lads in our company. Initially, we thought they were joking, but it turned out they were right up for it because, as we were standing there, laughing at the state of them, they came over throwing empty beer cans at us!

I turned around to them and said to one of them, 'Listen, my love, you are old enough to be my mum, so fucking behave yourselves.'

I half-expected the old birds to piss off but it made them worse and the main mouthpiece shouted back, 'I don't fucking give a flying fuck, you English niggers, come on, let's fight!'

This tirade went on for about five minutes and we were absolutely stunned and didn't know what to do, so we walked off, leaving them yelling the racial abuse. But, instead of pissing off, they have only gone and fucking followed us towards Wembley Way. As we got around the corner, they have come behind us with about 30 Scottish blokes and it's gone bang off!

It was madness, there were police everywhere and this bus load of blokes and their pissed-up wives are flying into us, mainly after the black lads. There was not much damage getting done and a few Old Bill were standing by, letting it go on – it was like a comedy sketch! Then the main police geezer stood on the wall with a tannoy, and his exact words were: 'If you lot of numpty idiots don't break it up, you are going to get arrested!'

As quickly as it started, it finished and the Scottish lot pissed off back to their bus while we went back to the Green Mann stunned.

Back in the pub, we even saw one of the Jocks who had been fighting with us and he was with a really old bloke who was probably his father. It was one of them unbelievable situations and proved how mad the Scots are when they have too much drink inside them!

A few days later, England played their final group game against Holland, after two previous no-shows by the Dutch, who by now were claiming bizarrely they did not follow the national side! Hopes were not high they would turn out a firm for this game and, true to form, they didn't!

On the field, Holland were destroyed and, with Alan Shearer scoring at will and Terry Venables's side playing quality football, the country was gripped by football fever and the nation began to believe that this could be England's year.

A penalty shoot-out win the following Saturday set up a semi-final date with Germany and, although they brought a reasonable following, what lads they did bring were kept well under wraps and didn't have enough interest in trying to break the protective police blanket that was placed around them. It was a sensible decision.

Yet another penalty shoot-out defeat meant that the carnival mood, the 'Coming Home' tune and the foam hands were replaced by anger, police sirens and boots and fists, as an orgy of violence erupted all over the country.

The media, who were probably under government advice to

do so, had kept a positive approach during the tournament, but the night of violence could not be brushed under the carpet and they were forced to report the news that the FA had dreaded, as they still harboured high hopes of clinching the World Cup bid.

The *Mirror* called it a 'NIGHT OF TERROR' and reported, 'Over 200 England fans were arrested last night in London after yobs went on the rampage in Trafalgar Square after England crashed out of the European Championships 6–5 on penalties to rivals West Germany. Over 2,000 England fans converged on Trafalgar Square, 25 policemen were injured, 40 vehicles damaged, six overturned and two set alight. Seven buildings were also set alight in what was described as the worst scenes since the poll tax riots in 1990.'

It made grim reading for everyone who had hoped that the behaviour of the fans over the previous three weeks would be good enough to convince FIFA and UEFA delegates that hooliganism in England was on the decline. However, it was not just in London where trouble erupted, and the *Mirror* report confirmed that hooliganism was alive and kicking all over the country: 'In Brighton, a Russian student was stabbed five times; the English yobs demanded to know whether or not he was German. The crazed mob attacked many foreigners.

'Three hundred fans looted shops and rampaged through Bedford, leaving damage estimated to be in the thousands.

'In Thames Valley, hundreds of youths rampaged through the town centre and clashed with police causing mayhem in their wake.

'Five policemen were injured in Bradford as England fans went on a rampage of wanton destruction.

'Another five police officers were hurt as a mob of 60 youths went on the rampage in Newport, Shropshire.'

There were a total of 942 football-related arrests made during Euro '96 and the reports of outbreaks of violence in most towns and cities in England was proof enough that, although football had indeed come home, the violence that goes hand in hand with it in this country had not gone away!

CHAPTER TWENTY-ONE

WHEN IN ROME
ITALY '97

In October 1997, England, under the stewardship of Glen Hoddle, travelled out to Rome for the final qualifier, knowing just one point would secure the side an automatic place in the World Cup Finals. If you said it fast enough, it sounded easy enough but, given the quality of the opposition, it was never going to be an easy task. Italy had already won the away game at Wembley 1–0 thanks to keeper Ian Walker giving Gianfranco Zola far too much of the net to aim at and the fact that they had not dropped a point at the venue in Rome for 15 matches.

In the weeks leading up to the game, talk of the actual football match took second stage to the possibility of trouble and many felt it would be the behaviour of the fans that would see England eliminated not the performance of the players.

The FA had recently set up an England Members Club, which was launched in response to the growing interest in following England abroad. It had two aims, to distribute tickets on the basis of loyalty, and to stop known troublemakers following the national side. Initially, it was a partial success. Fans that had followed every step of England's 1998 World Cup-qualifying campaign were rewarded with one of 7,000 tickets England were allocated for the crunch match.

That was all well and good, and the FA thought at first that a massive weight had been lifted from their shoulders, but that was until an even bigger weight was dropped from a great height through the roof of the FA Headquarters at Soho Square!

It emerged that over 3,000 tickets for the Italian end of the stadium were on sale in England and in Rome to anybody who was prepared to pay a little bit over the odds. There was talk of tickets costing £200 each but, in fact, as little as £60 could secure you a seat in the ground if you were not too fussy who you were sitting next to!

The FA and authorities had every right to be alarmed and intelligence reports were for once accurate, as literally hundreds of lads from all over England were snapping up tickets knowing that they would have to face a gauntlet of abuse and possible violence once inside the ground. In a nutshell, the game was too big to miss, they knew they would have decent numbers in there and quite bluntly they didn't give a fuck!

Det Chief Inspector Bryan Drew, the head of the strategic and specialist intelligence branch at the NCIS, was a very worried man and said officers had been gathering information about the biggest ever exodus of football fans going abroad to support England, adding that, due to the amount of 'rogue' tickets in the hands of Englishmen, there was an increased chance of trouble!

He even described known hooligans as 'soccer criminals' and warned Italians that hundreds of these criminals would be going to Rome. When his Italian counterparts asked why these criminals were being allowed to descend upon the ancient city, DCI Drew's answer was probably lost in translation!

However, Drew did reassure the nervous Italians that every port and airport and the Eurostar terminals would be monitored. Then he played his ace card – although some thought it was a Joker – by announcing that Special Branch and other units had all received comprehensive briefings!

In fairness to Drew, in 1997, there were much fewer banning orders than there are today, but his talk did seem cheap and the Italians had every reason to be worried. The day of the match could not be worse for policing, as it was on a Saturday, allowing more fans to travel to Italy, and the kick-off time of 8.45pm in Rome gave the lads a great day on the beer!

His Italian counterpart warned the travelling army that the Italian Police and riot troops had adopted the best practices in crowd control from other countries in Europe and that his men had been briefed to confiscate anything that could be used as a missile – loose change, cigarette lighters and belt buckles, he said, would all be taken from supporters.

Away from the ground, there were more pressing concerns about the behaviour of the English in Rome itself. Mario de Mecco of the Rome Prefecture said, 'We will be drawing up special plans to ensure that the centre of town is well patrolled, and will probably ensure some kind of alcohol ban, and will most definitely clamp down heavily on any English supporters leering at or touching any of our women.'

Had he arrested his own countrymen for the same offences, Mario would have made the country bankrupt, trying to fund hundreds of new prisons to house the guilty hot-blooded Italians!

Paul from Hull wrote about his memorable trip to Italy in *City Psychos*.

PAUL, HULL CITY:

We went out on a Northern Holidays trip by coach for the ridiculously low price of £160. After paying the money, you try to put to the back of your mind the two mind- and arse-numbing days' trip there and back again; but this was a big game so was deemed worth it. The holiday company was bringing three coach loads over and we were to be billeted in three different hotels just outside Rome. There were 40-plus from Hull on our coach and we made up the largest contingent.

Once in our hotel, it was shower then out on the town and we met up with a lot of the lads from the other coaches and settled down for a good night's session. We had a good drink, sang a few songs and basically let the locals know we were there – and they did!

They started gathering on the edge of the square, watching and waiting, as did the police, and eventually a couple of Hull lads, along with myself, walked through the line of Old Bill and wandered in amongst the locals. We weren't being demonstrative but we kept on goading the Italians in hushed tones: 'Come on, we're here, let's have it.'

All we got back was: 'No, no, in the stadium, we will fight in the stadium.'

'Fuck the stadium, let's have it now!'

They weren't interested, but it would all change later. I don't know what sparked it off, maybe a chance remark or someone had strayed too close to the other side; no matter, it was what we were waiting for.

Bottles, stools and tables rained down on the Italians and our lads were soon in amongst them, chasing them back to the edge of the square. We didn't know it but a couple of undercover police were in amongst us and one of them made a grab for a Hull lad called Jay just as he let fly with a bottle. He stood there, hitting Jay with this truncheon with no back-up to help him, he must have been crazy. A couple of lads realised what was happening and went for him, he was lashing out at them and didn't see one of the Brummies running up with a chair, but he felt it. Jay was hurried away and in time-honoured tradition was given a different top to hide his identity.

It was now time to board the coach for Rome; within 20 minutes, we'd been pulled over by the police who proceeded to empty the coaches of all our beer. They gave us an option of staying with the mini mountain of cans and bottles or continuing on to Rome in a dry bus, so we continued on our journey. We were dropped off and walked towards the ground, and our presence seemed to be noticed immediately, countless Italians on scooters kept driving by, giving us the old cutthroat sign. It didn't take us long to find bits of rubble and debris and hurl them down the road at the departing Vespas. It was like a duck shoot; they drove by, so we aimed to knock them off, yet we stopped if they had a girl on the back – true English decorum prevailed.

As the street rounded a bend, we could see where the riders had been heading, a square complete with ornate fountains was heaving with people as well as the Vespa boys. We didn't need an invite, a roar went up and we steamed down the narrow street and met the Italians head on. Panic ensued, as we encountered the first few; they were pushing and pulling each other to get out the way as we motored on through. A few of ours got a bit carried away and were called back, experience told you not to drift too far away, not when you're up against these ambushing blade merchants.

Our little jaunt had left us with the need for liquid refreshment, so the Italians were forgotten, as we headed for two little bars opposite each other, down a small side street just off the square where there was the odd skirmish and police attack just to let us know we were in Italy!

We soon moved on and hit a main road and slowed down, we still didn't know our whereabouts and we expected the police to quickly round us up or end up ambushed by the Italians. Paranoia now begins to set in, we've just scattered 400 locals and had it with the Old Bill, yet here we are left on our own. We thought, Aye, aye, were heading for the lion's den, surely, they must be planning something. A few lads began flagging down taxis, but I and a couple of other England fans rounded on them and more or less threatened them, the last thing we could afford now was smaller numbers and we told them in no uncertain terms what would happen to them later if they didn't get out the cabs. They sheepishly got out and rejoined the ranks. We marched on, ever wary. We had bottles stuffed down trousers, up jumpers and in our hands, imagining every corner would have hundreds of Italians lying in wait. The streets seemed quieter, shop windows were shuttered, bars were closed, and it was obvious we were heading the right way, yet we still hadn't seen any other England supporters. A bar was found and we all piled in; I was gagging for a drink, I'd listened to some idiot who said the day's forecast was poor, so I'd spent the day sweating my bollocks off in a heavy coat. I just wanted to find the ground.

The outer perimeter of the stadium was now filling up with fans from both sides, from our advantage point on the bridge, we could see wave upon wave of Italians being directed over the busy road beneath us. The traffic would start up till the next group were ready and they then crossed, moving down the stadium concourse. Whispers began, the next wave of fans was their boys (Lazio Ultras) and, as they came over, we steamed into them and it was obvious what was coming next; lo and behold, within minutes, the riot police arrived. Tear-gas canisters rained down on us, we all tried to cover our faces (luckily I had my coat); lads were shouting for us to stand and the canisters were hurtled back at the approaching line of police.

Once inside, we were hit with a barrage of plastic seats, bottles and stones. The police idly stood by as young Ultras ran up and let fly with all manner of weaponry over the so-called safety screen; it didn't surprise me, these actions are par for the course in these places. We could see it going off at the other end, with England fans battling with the baton-wielding police, but it wasn't till I got home and watched a re-run before I realised what they actually had to put up with throughout the match.

The players did us proud, a heroic draw had seen us through, and the feeling was euphoric.

Like Paul said, he didn't fancy his chances in the Italian end and was lucky enough to bunk into the English section. Tommy Robinson from Luton, who wrote the excellent book *MIG Down*, was not so lucky and had to chance his hand in the section reserved for Italian supporters.

TOMMY, LUTON:
As we boarded the flight to Nice on the morning of 10 October 1997, I felt a tingle of apprehension. I had just spent

the past few hours discussing, with Sick Nick and Flower, some of the worrying reports in the tabloids that week.

It would seem that, as Europe awaited the outcome of a titanic clash between two of the world's great football nations, the Italian authorities were bracing themselves for probably the biggest invasion of visiting supporters in their history.

This do-or-die encounter was to take place in the famed Olympic Stadium, home of the two Roman clubs Lazio and Roma. The prize was automatic qualification for the following year's World Cup and so avoiding the much-dreaded play-off matches.

For England, the omens weren't great. We had already lost to the Azzuri at Wembley, the home of football, some months earlier. We also had the less than convincing Glen Hoddle as manager, who I certainly had little faith in being able to motivate the troops for a match of this magnitude. However, we had beaten Italy 2–0 in Le Tournoi, across the Channel in France, during a World Cup warm-up competition and had played some pretty decent stuff. This was all very good but the Italian football authorities had chosen the Stadio Olympico for a good reason. They hadn't lost a game in Rome in 15 previous internationals; to be precise, they hadn't dropped one single point.

These same authorities had a particular concern with the herds of Englishmen now en route. It seemed that there could be a large batch of tickets, set aside for home supporters, now in the hands of English touts, and that these same tickets might very easily find their way on to English hooligans. The English FA had received an official allocation of 7,000 tickets and these had been sent out to the vetted members of the England Travel Club. These members had supposedly had their backgrounds checked out by the FA and, with no record of violence held on file by the police, were expected to offer no real threat of crowd disorder. If the Carabinieri were, indeed, already concerned with controlling an influx of so many English fans into Rome, then the added threat of up to 3,000 undesirables armed with tickets for sections containing home supporters turning up raised the stakes to an alarming level.

But had these rogue tickets found their way into the hands of known hardened English football thugs? Well, all I knew was that I had one in my pocket and around 15 of the Mig Crew had them too!

That night was a strange night. When returning from a much-needed shower, Nick informed me that the Carabinieri had turned up outside the hotel and were talking to some very irate taxi drivers; he had also heard some doors slamming on our landing, but further along the gothic-style hallway. As I rested in the double bed, lying next to the ex-Special Forces commando, I felt very uncomfortable. It wasn't the bed, the bed was fine and, yes, it was big enough to park a bus between the pair of our fine bodies. But, for some strange reason, the only thing that Sick Nick could find to watch on the portable TV was an Italian porn film. Second to this, outside our hotel-room door, on our landing, all that could be heard was the sound of Italian OB smashing on some poor cunt's door and shouting in angry voices: 'Police! Come out, English!'

I lay there in that darkened room, in bed with my mate of many years, and watched as some incredibly well-hung African knocked the back out of a screaming nympho with tits the size of my head, and all that I could do was guess at what the OB might think if they chose to smash our door in and found us two with hard dicks in bed together watching porn! I can only say there was a weird atmosphere in that fucking room that night and that I was getting more nervous with every sound that drifted in from outside, as the police continued their search.

'Turn the fucking volume down, for fuck's sake, Nick!'

'Why? This is quality,' he laughed back at me.

I gave up and went to sleep with my pillow tucked firmly between my legs.

The following day, we set up shop across the road from the gladiator's arena and even took a time out from necking some lovely Italian beer to pop inside the ancient Roman site.

Inside, we found a sight we hadn't expected on paying our hefty entrance fee – the flag of St George draped from many of the balconies that seemed to go on forever. I felt the mighty Caesar would have turned in his grave had he beheld the spectacle of a visiting army's banner hanging on the walls of such hallowed ground.

As the day wore on, the numbers of Englishmen crowding into the streets simply drank bar after bar dry. This had the effect of causing people to simply head off into the tight surrounding streets in search of new watering-holes. I had been to a number of England away games before this, but had never seen this sort of support on the streets; it was also good-humoured support I was witnessing. I never witnessed any violence apart from a brief bit of bottle and glass throwing at the OB outside one of the train stations that I cannot name, as I was, by then, pissed.

By the time we eventually reached the Olympic Stadium, we had linked up with other Migs including Big Cliff who was in a right state and I couldn't help laughing as he wrapped his arms around my shoulders and with heavy alcoholic breath started to slur his belief in an England victory to the tune of three goals.

If only, I thought to myself. In fact, a draw was all that was needed, as we spearheaded the group and it was Italy who needed the win.

Once in the ground, the immediate thing that came to my attention was the fact that we were indeed in amongst the huge Italian support. I was one of the first English lads to walk out on to the vast corner of the ground that the majority of the rogue tickets were printed for. I had jumped the barrier set up to corral English fans into a bottleneck so their belts and, in some cases, shoe laces, could be confiscated. The OB had been too slow to catch me and soon gave up the chase as

I leaped through the turnstile while throwing my match ticket at the startled senior citizen sat behind the screen. As the pre-match entertainment, in the form of a rock band, whipped up the carnival atmosphere inside the ground, outside things were getting heated as the numbers of English turning up close to kick-off started to try and force their way past the OB and tempers flared, as one or two of the vastly outnumbered Carabinieri drew batons but this was only to be a taster of things to come.

By kick-off time, over 81,000 fans had packed the incredible stadium and amongst this crowd there had to be nearly 15,000 English fans, although by the time Dutchman Mario Van Der Ende blew his whistle and signalled for the game to commence I may well have been seeing double!

While millions at home were watching the game unfold, another clash was taking place as, at almost the precise moment the game kicked off, a group of Italians in the section of the ground immediately to my right began to unfurl an Irish flag. OK, that's incitement enough for many England football supporters, I thought to myself ... but written across the middle of this banner was 'IRA'!

That was enough for a small party of Northern English lads to jump into action. They responded by trying to smash the Perspex panel separating themselves from the Italian aggravators, while other English supporters amongst the 1,500 now positioned in the same section as me, in this Italian area of the stadium, remonstrated with the Italian Police to confiscate the offending flag.

The police response was shocking and out of order as they drew their heavy batons and proceeded to assault the handful of English closest to the Italian fans. The response from around 300 of us Englishmen was immediate and we clambered down into the area where the action was taking place; in the process, the Italian OB drew back, seemingly knowing they were in danger of receiving the same punishment they were gleefully handing out. For a few moments, all became calm again and I looked around to find Sick Nick, Big Cliff, Flower and Tony Baloney close to where I now found myself. I started to listen to the voices of those around and soon everyone was establishing just what clubs were being represented in this part of the ground. In my opinion, Sunderland provided the most troops but there was also big firms from Leeds, Stockport and Cockney, plus Brummie voices were clearly heard.

Across from us, you could hear a continuous beat that was being struck up in the corner opposite where our unwelcome invasion had taken place. This rhythm section was being motivated by a band who I was told came from Sheffield. They were backed by around 8,000–9,000 official supporters drawn mainly from the England Travel Club but even some of these 'model' fans were now engaging the locals in a missile-throwing contest.

Then, as the band played on, *they* came.

I guess we had known all along that there was no way the Italian OB were going to let us get away with putting them on the back foot and forcing them to retreat, as we had done in the defence of our countrymen. At first, they just lined up to our right, putting themselves between us and the Perspex wall that prevented us from getting anywhere near the Italian fans, now throwing missiles at our densely packed mob. Once they had deployed around 50 of their best shiny blue-helmet brigade, they formed up into a nice and neat formation three ranks deep.

I along with many around me stopped watching the football at this point and instead focused all my attention on the movements of the Carabinieri and what now happened gave me cause for concern. Many of the shiny blue helmets were removed and the former owners quickly started to tie bandannas around their faces as though to cover their identities. Then the shiny blue helmets placed back on the heads of the now more menacing-looking troopers. We knew then that we were about to be attacked by Italian OB in an act of revenge for chasing their pals out of our section of the Stadio Olympico. All around me, lads started to get nervous and many started to put some space between themselves and this new threat dressed in facemasks and shiny blue crash helmets. I have to admit I too was concerned, as the batons this Roman legion were now waving threateningly at us looked like they could easily fracture a man's skull with one blow.

Suddenly, one of the Sunderland group stepped out towards the Italian legionnaires and said simply, 'Remember the old saying, lads … When in Rome!'

At this precise moment, I made my decision to stand and face the Roman legion. I would be proud to get my skull smashed standing alongside fellow men whose roots lay in the kingdom of Britannia and, more importantly, who weren't prepared to be intimidated by Romans with big sticks and shiny blue hats. The onslaught came in the form of wave after wave of violent baton charges that caused injury after injury to our ranks. Head injuries were particularly common and blood was everywhere to be seen. The Italians didn't have it all their own way though as at one point we battered them back and forced them against the Perspex wall. At this point in the battle, reinforcements arrived dressed in green combat fatigues and drove in against the body of our resistance from higher ground. As one of the Carabinieri riot squad was being stretchered out from the scene of carnage, I along with dozens of others became trapped on the floor by the fresh Italian war party.

We were beaten … quite literally.

The performance of Glen Hoddle's England gained better rewards that evening than our efforts in the stands. By the time Di Livio had been red-carded and four other Azzuri players had been booked, England's finest had broken the Italians' spirit – so much so that, when the magnificent Ian Wright burst past a tired-looking Peruzzi and missed a sitter by his standards, we didn't care. It seemed as though Vieri also sensed the day was England's when he headed the ball over the bar when it seemed easier to bury it in the crisp white netting in the final minutes.

So the following morning as I washed in the fountains in the grounds that surrounded the famous Leaning Tower of Pisa and nursed my beaten black and blue body, Sick Nick read a quote from England's Paul Ince that he had made to the press in the minutes immediately following the game.

'It was just amazing. We planned so hard for this game and we were fantastic in all the pressure.'

I couldn't have put it better myself, Paul!

So the result confirmed Glenn Hoddle's side's qualification for the tournament and many claimed that the FA's decision to give fans 'official' status made for a better atmosphere, which greatly helped the players secure the point they needed. In fairness, that night was probably the night that saw the birth of the football equivalent of the 'Barmy Army' who so passionately follow England's cricketers around the world. The fact, however, was overlooked that, even though many peaceful fans were able to attend one of English football's great nights, the pre-match problems indicated that even supporters given the thumbs-up to travel by the FA and authorities were capable of engaging in football-related violence.

Some sections of the media preferred to concentrate on the trouble in the ground rather than the performance of the players, and amazingly there were calls for the game to be replayed and even for England to face expulsion from the World Cup Finals. With the latter causing major concern, the FA released a statement claiming that the Italian Police were guilty of 'deliberate intimidation' of England fans and that the stadium's authorities lacked proper stewarding.

It therefore came as a great relief to the FA when world governing body FIFA agreed with the English Football Association that the crowd trouble at the game was mainly the fault of the Roman authorities when in an official statement they said, 'We acknowledge that there were lessons to be learned with regard to better control of tickets through unauthorised channels.' Which translates to something along the lines of 'If the Italian FA had had their house in order with respect to the sale of tickets in the same way the English FA had, there would not have been problems in the stadium'!

Still, some members of our fine media fraternity were unimpressed. Below is an extract from an article written by journalist Simon Gleave after the match. It is a scathing attack on the people who were in Rome that night including many who were beaten senseless in the stands while Gleave watched on from the safety of the press box. 'Unsurprisingly, there has been a lot of talk about the violence at the Italy versus England on Saturday. It does not look (for a change) as though my delightful countrymen did not deserve the beating that they took from the Italian Police. People can complain on this newsgroup that the Italian Police were out of order but the fact is their actions are completely understandable and justified.

'The initial problem is that England supporters have a reputation. This was built up over many years as thugs went on rampages all over Europe whenever England played. Unfortunately, this is perpetuated by some of the supporters who visit. They spend the day (or days) before a match drinking heavily, behaving in a boorish manner and generally pissing off the local inhabitants.

'As the police tend to also be young men from the host country, many of them are probably not averse to weighing in with the odd baton charge given the provocation. In fact, it warmed the cockles of my heart to see them doing so against the vermin who think they represent my country.

'Back in my hotel in Rome that night, many of my fellow journalists toasted the Italian Police for a job well done!'

There will be many reading this book who disagree with Mr Gleave.

CHAPTER TWENTY-TWO

THE GOOD, THE BAD AND THE UGLY
FRANCE '98, PART 1

The World Cup in France was a recipe for disaster; easy access, cheap travel and strong lager were the main ingredients. All it needed was thousands of English fans to help get the pot simmering, add a few locals, opposing fans or immigrants and the pot would boil over for sure. It didn't need the clever fellas at Leicester University or the so-called intelligence officers from various police forces to tell you that France '98 would turn nasty, everyone knew it would. If the bookies had been taking bets on the chances of mass disorder occurring, they would have been bankrupt!

What nobody could have predicted, though, was that the English fans would be involved in some of the most violent football hooligan clashes for 20 years before a ball had even been kicked in their group!

It was also a tournament that England were expected to do well at on the pitch. Despite losing at home to Italy in an early qualifier, they won the group after holding the Italians to a draw in the return and having beaten Moldova, Georgia and Poland home and away. Things were looking good, Glen Hoddle had done well since replacing Terry Venables who was sacked despite losing just one game against Brazil – well, one and a quarter if you count the abandoned match in Dublin! The memory of the Graham Taylor years had long been forgotten, as the likes of Beckham, Scholes, Campbell and a young Michael Owen replaced the aging old guard, meaning past greats such as Stuart Pearce, David Platt and Paul Gascoigne were thrown on the international scrapheap. Platt and Pearce retired gracefully, while Gazza didn't take the news quite so well and smashed up Hoddle's hotel room when he was told he was the unlucky squad member who would not be making the trip to France!

The first game was against Tunisia in Marseille and, while on paper it seemed to be a good opener, on and off the pitch many overlooked the fact that the French city housed hundreds of Arabs. While the hatred between the English and the Arabs was nowhere near as fierce as that between them and the Turks, it was still a bad mix. The local immigrants do not take kindly to having their daily routines spoiled by hundreds of marauding drunken football hooligans, but even the most clued-up experts and most seasoned England travellers could not have expected the scale of violence that erupted in the days leading up to the match. By the time the battle of the beach took place during the game, it was too late and many had been seriously injured and scores arrested.

Once again, England hooligan followers had shamed the nation but there is a darker side to what went on in Marseille, and the English at times came off worse as knife gangs and riot police took great pleasure in handing out the kind of punishment that many were not used to.

Gary Walker lives near Blackburn and is a loyal Man United supporter, He is one of many England fans who will remember France '98 for something other than Owen's wonder goal or Beckham's sending off shame against Argentina.

GARY, MAN UNITED:
I have been going to watch United for over 35 years and have travelled all over Europe following them and England, taking in the 1982 World Cup in Spain as well as the France 1998 tournament. As you do when you travel extensively abroad,

you fall victim to overzealous police many times, and I have been tear gassed several times and attacked with batons, I have also had the misfortune to have been shot at in Porto by the Portuguese cops who used steel pellets, not rice, etc that many people think hits you. I know this as my mate got shot in the leg and still has the fuckers in a jar at home!

I recall being tear gassed in Luxembourg, Norway and Sweden, while watching England and it is not all fun and games watching either your club or country abroad. Despite having had my share of bad experiences, nothing compared to what happened in Marseille when I got my neck slashed by a local Arab. It happened on the Sunday evening, the day before England's first game versus Tunisia, the riots that day and night were according to many the very worst football-related riots of all time and, unfortunately, me and my mates got caught up in them.

I had seen an advert in the *Lancashire Evening Telegraph* advertising a coach trip to Marseille for England's first game, so me, my brother Ray and a few mates booked on this coach, which picked up lads from Preston, Blackburn, Burnley and Wigan setting off early Saturday, and it arrived in Marseille on Sunday morning. We booked into a hotel facing the main station and, on arrival, we saw that hundreds of England fans were already in town. Four of us had a stroll around the harbour and there was a large police presence, as it had kicked off with the Tunisians the night before.

In the afternoon, we had settled in a small bar when it kicked off big time with the England fans and the Tunisians again. The barman pulled the shutters down and we had a lock-in for the next four hours, which suited us fine; we didn't want to get involved in all the trouble and just wanted a good booze-up, we were oblivious to all the mayhem going on outside. Don't get me wrong, we were prepared to have a go if it went; any lads our age had to grow up on the terraces and at times you had to fight fire with fire, but we were not thugs and if we could get away without the bovver we did.

There was about 20 of us in this bar and at 10pm we set off back to our hotel but decided on taking the back streets to avoid the rioting, there were now four of us, me, my brother Ray and a couple of mates, but, as we were walking down this hill I heard a lad, an England fan, shouting at us from this balcony high up to watch ourselves, as there was an Arab roaming about brandishing a bottle. He was a bit late with his warning, as in no time I was assaulted by this Arab, who punched me in the neck. To tell you the truth, it didn't hurt and we chased him down the hill. As we were running after him, blood was bouncing off the walls and into my eyes. I then realised that my neck was spurting blood and soon knew it was serious. I have first-aid experience so I lay down and got my brother to put pressure on the gaping wound.

Back on the streets, my mate was snapping and drop-kicked a French lad off his motorbike; he went flying off, but came back and waded in, smashing him over the head with his crash helmet, leaving him with a fractured skull. There were still fights breaking out all around the streets and one England fan saw the state of me and shouted to his mates, 'This one's dying!'

That is the last thing you want to hear and I politely told him to fuck off! I felt a bit dizzy but I certainly didn't feel I was dying, but in hindsight I probably would have done if the ambulance had not arrived pronto, as Ray had run to a copper who called an ambulance on his radio. Ray came with me to the hospital, and my mate with the busted skull was also in the same ambulance, but our other mate had to hide under a car for a couple of hours as big mobs of Tunisians were hunting down England fans. Finally, a local couple told him the coast was clear and he made his way back to what he hoped would be the safety of the hotel. That was not the case and he had only been in there a few minutes when Tunisians or whatever they were tried storming it. All the England fans, the hotel staff, our tour operator and cleaners fought the Arabs off and stopped them from getting into the hotel and at the English; it took an age according to my mate but eventually the cops finally turned up and restored order.

I had an emergency operation and stitches in the neck wound, and I released myself the next day and went to the match against Tunisia, which we won 2–0. I felt a bit groggy and my neck was stiff, and everybody stared at me because I had this big bandage wrapped around my neck. From what I saw there was no trouble at the game or even outside the stadium, but we later learned that it kicked off big time on the beach where the local authorities had erected a big screen where all those without tickets could watch the game. The French cops had wised up to the fact that, as well as the usual loons being the aggressors, the English were actually victims of attacks and, give them credit, they did a good job at the ground and it must have been their busiest ever weekend.

The next day we set off back to England and half of our coach was empty, lads had either been nicked or flew back home to get away from the trouble. One of the lads on our coach had his leg broken in the fights, my mate had his skull fractured, I had my neck slashed and others were sporting cuts and bruises.

We arrived home and the press was full of the usual nonsense about the nation's shame and how once again English thugs had ruined the World Cup for the majority of peace-loving football fans. I was disgusted by it all, not the fighting but by the attitude of the British press and government. I nearly got fucking murdered out there and not once did the reporters get our side of the story. Quite simply, people are not interested in the casualties, the reputation of our hooligans sells papers not the fact that a football fan from the North West of England was minutes away from death, and I find that fucking strange!

Regardless of all that, England won, I saw the match and, more importantly, lived to tell the tale so all in all it was an eventful three-day trip that's for sure!

While Gary Walker unsuccessfully did his best to stay away from the trouble, there were plenty who wanted in on it; one was Alan Williams, a Chelsea fan.

ALAN, CHELSEA:

I am a Chelsea fan, even though I was born and raised in Oldham. Ever since I can remember as a little boy back in the 1960s, Chelsea were my team, and when I was a teenager in the 1970s I followed them home and away. I had been really looking forward to the France World Cup, having missed out on USA '94. With it being so close, I just knew there would be thousands of England fans there, as the press had hyped it up too much and every lunatic was going or so it seemed.

Four of us were due to drive through France on the Saturday in preparation for the Tunisia game on the Monday, the game was being held in Marseille, famous for its gangsters and huge North African immigrant population. We just knew that these Arabs would be up for it, but on the news on Friday evening it told of street brawls already kicking off with the non-French locals and the first wave of England fans. Our lads were heavily outnumbered, so we took the decision to set off right away like a cavalry – as did hundreds of other English hooligans. It was like Wacky Races, as we flew down the M6 then the M1 for Dover and the ferry crossing. It was great seeing loads of vans and cars with England fans speeding down the motorways, desperate to help out our comrades in their time of need, even though it would take the best part of 24 hours to get to Marseille!

Saturday morning came and the race was on again heading for the coast. We had hours driving ahead of us, and we were knackered but excited and it was a heart-warming sight seeing so many England fans heading to Marseille, various flags in the back windows of cars and minibuses.

We finally landed in Marseille at about 6.30pm and it was a war zone, riot cops everywhere, most of the shops and cafes were shut down, and there were big mobs of Arabs marauding about, many of them carrying big sticks and the place looked eerie. We parked up and booked into our hotel, got showered and then headed for the marina, where apparently all the England lads were. When we arrived, the cops had all the England fans boxed off in a few bars. We got a booze and just listened to England fans' stories about what had been happening. They told us how the Moroccans were sniping English lads out on their own, cutting them up, etc, how they were driving past on mopeds doubled up and the Arabs on the back would be swinging poles and hitting English lads across the head, etc. Every time the English fought back, the French cops would set their dogs loose and they were arresting loads. It was relatively peaceful by now but still the cops were firing tear gas and it stung like fuck, in fact, the air was full of this tear gas.

At about 10pm, a mob of 50-odd led by some Leeds fans broke away and went looking for trouble and they never had to look hard, as they came well unstuck when they were ambushed by a mob of 200 Arabs, with a few getting cut to fuck. They came back to the square with their tails between their legs like war wounded. By now, the English lads were livid and getting really wound up, and they decided to take the cops on and break through the police lines; there must have been 500 English lads in this mob, half of them were just straight members, but sick at what was going on. A big fat fella seemed to be taking charge of the situation, telling us all to stick together, use chairs and bottles for weapons and to follow him when he steams the French cops, all stirring stuff.

We all mobbed up and the cops prepared themselves, because they knew we were going to have it with them. All of a sudden, this big Lincoln City fan rips his shirt off and with a 10ft pole in his hand starts to charge at the police lines. Half the fucking French coppers ran, many dragging their dogs with them! We all followed Lincoln and charged the cops, it was fucking great, piling into the cops; we didn't give a fuck and we soon broke through the police lines then across the harbour and towards the Moroccans, who also fled en masse.

By now, the English fans were rampaging, smashing shop windows, overturning cars, it was so exciting, and felt right. A few brave Moroccans stood for the battle but got twatted all over the gaff, and, for the next half-hour or so, the English lads had control of the whole harbour area, many ransacking the closed bars for a free booze.

The French cops soon regrouped and had many more reinforcements and regained control, and they really gave it to any English lads they caught. We eventually had to flee, because they were just nicking anybody and word had it that the French were jailing English hooligans for 10 months but, as the news was spread, it had risen to 10 years! I didn't want to be languishing in a French nick for 10 fucking years, so we got off and somehow got back to our hotel without getting 'sniped' off them sneaky fucking Arabs. What a night that was but I was glad to be out of it, as good as it felt at the time.

The next morning, Sunday, was a strange scenario. We walked down to the harbour, it was about 10am, and, although there were loads of England fans about, there was very little police presence and no Moroccans; it was if last night's riots never happened, all the smashed-up shops were back trading with new windows and the overturned cars were just not there, all the cafes and bars were open and it was just like a normal day.

During the next few hours more and more England fans began arriving and getting drunk; it was a scorching day, but the atmosphere was friendly, many lads talking about the previous night's riots. At about 4pm, a couple of Moroccans came flying past, and they whizzed bottles at a group of England fans eating at an outside restaurant before they sped off. It was ignored, but, over the next hour or so, these two Moroccans would do the same but to different sets of lads each time, they must have come past five times before four Notts Forest fans whacked them off their mopeds with big sticks. The Moroccans came flying off and a crew of young England Casuals put the boot in to rousing cheers; their shitty little mopeds also got trashed. A couple of French coppers came over and just separated the young English lads from the stricken Arabs.

The atmosphere began to change rapidly, big mobs of England thugs came into the harbour area, all the main English firms seemed to be here now plus all the smaller clubs each with mobs of 30-plus, there must have been 1,000-plus lads mobbing up. We could see in the distant hills large groups of Moroccans mobbing up as well, and only a couple of hundred yards away the French riot cops in all their gear began to mob up. It was going off very soon, there was no doubt about it.

I felt a mixture of fear and pride, but I knew I had to stay put, Marseille would be a very dangerous place for a lone Englishman. The French riot cops approached the big England mob, clattering their big sticks on to their shields in a pathetic attempt to scare us – it didn't work. The English began the war chants, 'No surrender!', etc, I felt like I was at Rorke's Drift, in the film *Zulu*, as by now there were hundreds of Moroccans inching their way towards the harbour. The setting was perfect as the sun began to go down, and many England fans armed themselves with bottles and chair legs.

The Moroccans got within 50 yards or so and began hurling rocks and bottles over the police lines into us, we threw them back, and approached the cops, in one big huge snarling angry mob. I could see the fear in a lot of the young French coppers' eyes, and they were literally shitting themselves. With an almighty roar, we charged as one into the cops, they naturally split, and about a quarter of the England fans broke through. The cops let their dogs go and many lads got bit and wrenched to the ground by the much braver dogs. Other English lads were booting the dogs as they ran past; I saw one big Chelsea fan lift a dog up above his head and throw it into the harbour. To be fair, the Moroccans came piling down the hill and into the England fans and a mass brawl broke out; many of the Moroccans were brandishing knives and blades and quite a few England fans got carved up. The battle lasted for what seemed like 20 minutes, but it was probably five, and then the riot police finally got a grip of the situation.

On Monday morning, we were up bright and early and watched *Sky News* reporting about all these riots that we had seen and been involved in. There were reports of stabbings and the news was true that a lad's throat had been slashed which had us all a bit worried to say the least, it really had gone haywire! Also, thousands more England fans were pouring into Marseille, no wonder the French cops were shitting themselves! The good news was that the Marseille council had decided to put up a big screen on the beach for all those who didn't have tickets, which included us. We agreed that we would not spend more than £100 on any game and we still hoped to get tickets for the game for less than that but we knew that was highly unlikely.

We went down to the harbour area at lunchtime and it was even more full with England fans, many already pissed up and chanting. The cops were once again keeping a low profile and the mood was good and there were no Moroccans about. When the vast majority of England fans headed up to the stadium, the few hundred of us left headed towards the beach to watch it on the big screen and, when we arrived, there were hundreds of Tunisians, Moroccans or whatever all mobbed up. It was uneasy but calm for half an hour or so but, when England scored, the Arabs started and began launching all sorts of debris over at us. The England fans, though heavily outnumbered, stood their ground and threw the debris back; there was a stand-off, a no man's land of about 50 yards or so. In the middle of this no man's land, I saw one of the most incredible but stirring patriotic scenes in my life, an England fan, stripped to his waist, stood there alone with a small drum around his neck and he was drumming away while both mobs were launching all these bottles, bricks and lumps of concrete at each other, he didn't flinch! What a hero! There were very few cops to break up this beach battle and England finally ran the Arab coalition, and they fled, many into the sea. It was once again stirring stuff. We then went back to watch us win 2–0.

Having been everywhere watching England that was one game we would never forget. It was a mad crazy weekend.

It wasn't all violence and rioting, though. Tony Cronshaw was one of many who stayed in Spain and decided to travel through to France on the day of the games. But even that was not all plain sailing!

TONY, SHEFFIELD WEDNESDAY:

Knowing how packed France would be, we based ourselves on the Costa Brava with the intention of travelling by road to the games in Marseille and Toulouse. Our party consisted of a dozen Blades and me and our kid who were Owls. Football rivalry was never a question with our group, we were on the piss and loved our football so all this who rules the Steel City nonsense that seems to have the riot squad out in town every weekend was not an issue. We were English and proud – thumping your mates could wait till Derby day!

We arrived late on the Saturday night and were well organised on the accommodation front. One of the Blades turned into our very own Judith Charmers and had us a nice hotel booked, so it was crash out and first thing Sunday go in search of hire cars or a minibus. Our transport organiser was not in the same league as Judith was on the accommodation front, in fact, he was not on the same planet and, after searching all day, we gave up, finally realising that the lazy Spanish bastards didn't work on the Sabbath. The best the rep could offer was to ring the hire place on the Monday when it opened at 10am. Plan A was a non-starter, as it was a fair trek to our first game in Marseille which was kicking off at half-one in the afternoon. After a few lagers we hatched Plan B, it was a day on the piss and watch the game in a bar for us come match day!

Where we were based on the Costa Brava, like most resorts at that time of the year, it was heaving with English fans and the bars were full as the news filtered through that the battle had commenced and before a ball had been kicked England were on the rampage. Many people remember France '98 for the introduction of Michael Owen and his wonder goal against Argentina, but just as many remember it for three days of running battles and a lone English drummer standing his ground and rallying the troops as bottles whizzed over his head from both sides!

The game went well and Shearer and Scholes got us off to a flyer. We had cars sorted for Toulouse so it was time to relax for a few days and enjoy the sun and a few days on the piss without worrying about knife-wielding Moroccans and Turks stabbing you in the arse when you were wandering back to the hotel worse for the wear.

The trip to Toulouse was not as straightforward as we had hoped for, thanks to Alec our personal chauffeur, who provided us with his navigational skills. He informed us that he was avoiding the tolls (you know what they say about Yorkshiremen!) and we were taking the B-roads to save money.

We'd not been on the road for 20 minutes when he spotted a sign for Francia, so we quickly turned off the main road and proceeded to follow the signs. Now my geography is to say the least questionable but we were now leaving the thin layer of tarmac and hitting a dirt track. He was adamant that he knew what he was doing, and who were we to question this intrepid explorer? We went with the flow and shut the fuck up but the destination soon became clear when we entered a massive car park that fronted what can only be described as a restaurant cum brothel. As we did a quick three-point turn, we managed to get a quick flash of tit and arse from the fine ladies sat on chairs showing off all their assets. The road to France had turned out to be the road to the HOTEL FRANCIA!

We eventually hit Toulouse but how Alec carried on after

the stick he got was amazing, he had the piss taken out of him every mile of the way and still has not lived it down to this day. We were ticketless but enjoyed shite beer that was a bit overpriced and had a run in with a slimy journalist who offered cash if anyone was foolish enough to throw bottles at the mass ranks of coppers that spanned the bridge. He and his photographer were slapped and some loon threw his bag of expensive equipment into the river.

The capacity of the grounds for England's games was a disgrace and there were thousands locked out, and we gave up hoping to get in long before kick-off. As it approached, we headed for the boozer and the police could not have been more helpful and even allowed tables and chairs to be brought out into the street because the place was heaving. I am not a lover of police at football but these boys showed us great respect and, in return, it was repaid as the lads behaved themselves despite a shock 2–1 defeat to the Romanians and at one stage they even diverted the traffic away from us because people were edging closer to the road.

It was a long journey back as we travelled through the night back to the Costa only to briefly stop at a service station on the France–Spanish border. As happens all over the world, when football meets motorway service area, it's a free-for-all. Basically, we had been ripped off all day and it was payback time. We had enough food to feed a small army and everyone was tucking in except our kid who was missing. I thought he'd been nicked but, as I rushed back inside, the boy was stood in an orderly queue with a sandwich and biscuits in one hand and his money in the other, wondering where we all had gone.

In the meantime, Glynn was on a coach that carried Brazilian supporters and he was after the massive flag in the back window. In broken English, he was telling them that he was going to leave them his tiny England one in return but the driver collared him and he left empty-handed. We must have looked a sorry bunch when we returned in the small hours but this didn't stop us going on the piss until the sun came up.

I have never been one for watching England abroad but will always say I went to see them at the 1998 World Cup. The truth is I watched two games in bars, one of them hundreds of miles away from the ground in another country but I still felt that I had been part of it all. It's like that when you are abroad watching your team, it doesn't matter that you are not in the ground, it's strange and unless you are a football fan you will never understand. Being there is everything, regardless if you get in or not!

Trevor Tanner was by now a seasoned campaigner on the England circuit and was another who went to France '98 and came home having not seen a ball kicked since setting foot out of England.

TREVOR, SPURS:

I went over for the game against Romania, but it was never going to be about the Romanians, it was more about the build-up as, if we got through these, we were going to have the Argentineans in the next round and everyone knows what that was all about. The tournament had been going on for about a week and I thought to myself, With England you can't take your chances that they're going to get through to the knock-out stages so off I pop.

We were contemplating going all sorts of daft ways like into Holland and come across up Czechoslovakia and come back down again through Russia and all that bollocks but in the end I thought, No, I'll just go from Waterloo and get on the fucking Eurostar. I went there with a couple of sensible bods – well, sort of sensible – and a couple of my Palace pals, same little firm that I've always been away with. I met them on the Eurostar, we had the tickets all booked and were dressed nicely, all Armani'd up – Armani sandals, Armani shorts and all that carry on. We kept away from all the fucking boneheads and all the idiots waving their flags and screaming and shouting and mingled in with all the families and all the foreigners that are going on holiday. And as we come through the Eurostar, as we come into Lille, got off the other end and jumped out. I've done a right and again I scanned the station here to go up the escalators and I could see plain-clothes Old Bill everywhere and they were just like grabbing people out, but as luck had it I made it through OK.

I hadn't long been out of jail for doing a three for Chelsea and a couple of other lads who were banged up with me were also out there. I've gone into this bar and I see a couple of my ex-cellmates and a few of my other bods and I just looked at them, and we just sat there together and just pissed ourselves laughing that we were in the back streets of fucking Lille and we'd made it out there in one piece and we're all in there together!

As we were in there laughing and having a beer, it was kicking off outside and the riot police were letting off the canisters, and every now and again a tear-gas canister could come flying into the front of the boozer and one of the boys would just boot it out the window and we'd just carry on talking. It was like something out of a fucking war film and this nutty French geezer behind the bar just kept shutting the shutters now and again. One time the silly bastard shut the shutters down with the gas canister still in the bar and I said, 'I know we're fucking Yids but he's taking the piss, the cunt, he's trying to gas us.'

This was going on all night, but we didn't want to draw attention to ourselves because we had no ill grudge with the Brummics and all that, and they knew who we were and left us to our own devices. I just didn't want to get kicked out after coming here, which sounded a great plan at the time.

We separated to go back to our hotel to get our bags, and little did I realise that was the last time I'd actually see all my boys properly. Our little place where we were staying was just outside Lille in a typical little French town, a funny little place, but it was clean, and we dumped our bags down and we went to a bar. We nearly had a little bit of an altercation with some bods on scooters and little French bods outside this bar, but I put a stop to it because, I mean, I was with a couple of naughty bods, young bods who were really eager and straining at the leash, but there were times and a place for doing it, and there weren't no point in it. We were going to get back on the train system but I didn't want to go back through the stations as they were overrun with Old Bill and I didn't really want to fancy my chances of getting through if I got caught, so we got a taxi back into Lille and now the fun and games were properly starting.

The English were going into the riot police in the centre. I bumped into a few Tottenham and they were roaming around and we had a little go at the Old Bill, but, again, there's no mileage in it really, it's not really our thing; we wanted it with another little firm and we got separated again. It was coming up towards the game, so we were looking for somewhere to watch the game. We've ended up going towards the Arab quarter, which is a naughty gaff to go to really, by all accounts, and we've ended up going down a road. There was me and a couple of my pals with me – and they will remember this – a geezer came driving past on a scooter with a whip or something in his hand and he's gone to whip it out; one of the boys grabbed hold of him and fucking pulled the cunt off the scooter and he just got the shit kicked out all round the road. He'll not be doing that again, I thought, that's the last time he'll try to take someone's fucking head off with whatever he had in his hand.

Soon after, we were sitting outside at this table and one of my pals has gone, 'Come here and look,' and there was about 30 of them running up the road, like bouncing all over the fucking cars and jumping over them, as they're coming towards us and they were hollering and shouting, and one of them had a pair of nunchukas. The one in the middle was just standing in the road with the nunchukas, so I jumped up from the table, picked the table up and just ran towards this

"The Caesars of Rome would have turned in their graves had they had to behold the spectacle of a blanket of visiting armie's banners hanging on the walls of such hallowed ground."

Above: England and Tunisian fans clash on the streets of Marseille (*middle*) French riot police arrest a supporter in Marseilles Vieux port area (*bottom*) French police tackle up-turned vechile during trouble.

Above: A fan is kicked as trouble erupts between rival supporters in Marseille.

Left: 'A decent bloke really'.

Below: An injured English fan is helped away by French police.

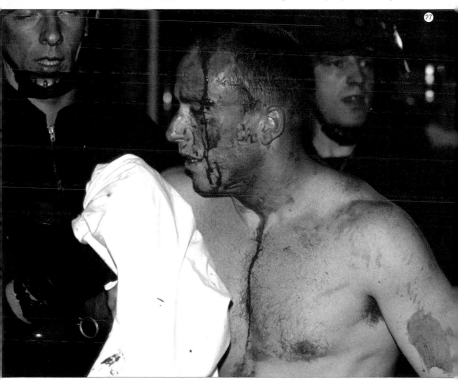

Mad Poles: Very few European mobs have been able to live with the kind of firms that the English have assembled: Only the Polish mob have been really interested in a proper "toe to toe".

"Here we go, here we go" for Euro 2000 and Charleroi and another meeting with the old enemy Germany. Once again the fans excelled themselves while the team disappointed when they finished third in their group even after beating the Germans 1-0.

Above: Tear gassed.

Below: England fans' defiant gesture to the police as they are forced back by a water cannon.

Above: Trouble explodes in Charleroi's main square before the match against Germany.

Left: A German fan is led away in Charleroi square ahead of the game.

Below: England fans chant their battle cry "No surrender" and launch missiles in the square in Charleroi.

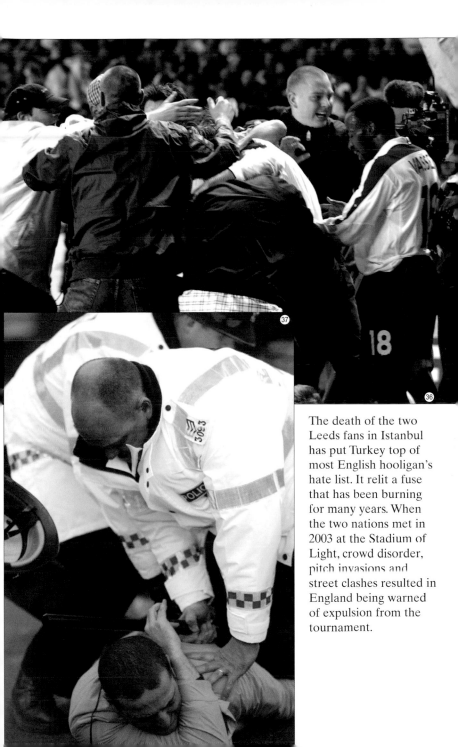

The death of the two Leeds fans in Istanbul has put Turkey top of most English hooligan's hate list. It relit a fuse that has been burning for many years. When the two nations met in 2003 at the Stadium of Light, crowd disorder, pitch invasions and street clashes resulted in England being warned of expulsion from the tournament.

Proud to be an Englishman.

fucker with the nunchukas and put my head down and didn't stop. I was getting closer and closer and closer to him and I could see his eyes thinking, What the fuck's going on with this cunt, is he going to keep going? And I just kept going and going and I smashed the table straight over his head and he just went down like a sack of shit, so this metal-top table has gone Boom! And this Arab bod has dropped and all the others with him just went, 'Fuck, this weren't supposed to happen!' And a couple of my pals have gone into the others and one got bottled badly.

The geezer who owned the bar said, 'Look, you'd better fucking get out of here now because there's going to be hundreds of the cunts after you soon,' so we walked up to this other gaff. We walked into this bar and I'm in this bar having a drink and trying to watch the game, when this little fucker's come up to me and he said to me, 'I'm fucking Carlisle.'

And I went, 'Yeah? It ain't a fucking very big place looking at you,' which is a stupid thing to say, as he was only a short little geezer.

And he said, 'Who are you?'

I said, 'Tottenham. You know who I am, you little cunt. I've got all our firm here, if you want it we'll have it any time.' Well, I didn't tell my boys that – there was only about fucking eight of us and I didn't realise the whole fucking other side of the bar was like full of them. I said to Blue, 'You're going to have to come outside and we're going to have to have it with them as they come out the door.'

So we've come outside and we've got hold of a skip and we've just fucking unloaded this skip and grabbed hold of anything, and every time they come out the door we just fucking bombarded the door; there were loads of them trying to get out and then we fucked off. I bet to this day they probably think Tottenham had about 100 outside not just the eight of us! If they'd got out, they would have annihilated us, I hold my hands up, but they didn't and that's the thing about thinking on your feet and being a bit tactical.

The next thing I know I got a fucking tap on the shoulder and was asked politely to leave France, and I was on my way home by Eurostar. At the end of the day, I'd overstayed my welcome and we had Argentina a couple of days later, but thank fuck I was safe at home because, to be honest, the way I was at that time I don't think I'd have fancied my chances of getting through the game because I fucking hate the Argentineans as well, proper hate them. There was also the Arabs, Carlisle, Chelsea and a few others on my case so it was probably for the best that I got thrown out there and then!

So France '98 had been a mixture of the good, the bad and the ugly, but, as well as the slashings, rioting and rampaging, there were also stories of injustice and, as the likes of Tony, Gary and Trevor carried on with their lives back home, one was still unfolding in Marseille.

CHAPTER TWENTY-THREE

AN ENGLISHMAN ABROAD
FRANCE '98, PART 2

While there have been many harrowing reports about the treatment of England fans on foreign soil over the years, the story of Martin Kerr is one of the most disturbing. Martin wrote a book about his experiences in France during the World Cup *An Englishman Abroad*. He has kindly let us use these extracts from the book.

MARTIN, PORTSMOUTH:

It was a balmy morning on 15 June 1998 as I waited at Sete railway station in the South of France, watching as hundreds of travelling England fans arrived from nearby campsites for the early-morning train along the coast to France's second city, Marseille. A huge poster on the opposite side of the track proclaimed the 'Coupe de Monde' would be the finest ever football tournament. Little did I know then, as I waited in anticipation of the first game against unfancied Tunisia, that the French would go on to win the World Cup, and that it would be a holiday I would never forget.

I had travelled to the South of France without a ticket, like thousands of other fans, just wanting to be part of the unique atmosphere of such a prestigious occasion. As a lifelong Pompey fan, this would be my only chance of watching football abroad, unless the Anglo-Italian Cup was reinstated, as our chances of playing in Europe were as unlikely as the Scummers bringing a crew to Fratton Park.

Later that morning, after being put on coaches from Marseille train station down to the coast, we saw the huge screen that had been erected in a park and decided that if we didn't get a ticket we would watch the game there. I made my way to the ground with a bunch of lads from the same campsite as myself, where I had left my partner at the time and her six-year-old son earlier that morning.

The atmosphere that had been so calm and tranquil suddenly changed when objects were thrown by the Africans at innocent England fans drinking in the bars on the far side of the tree-lined boulevard. After a few minutes, some of the England fans retaliated and started returning the missiles in the direction of the African hordes. Several skirmishes broke out as both groups charged and counter-charged up and down the road in full view of the French authorities, who seemed quite happy to let it continue.

All of a sudden from the far end of the road armed riot police wielding guns and batons started charging about like men possessed trying in vain to quell the fracas 10 minutes or so after they had stood by watching it all start.

It became clear from where I stood that the riot police were now marching behind the baying African mob armed with knives and sticks who were now getting closer to where I was standing. I decided to take refuge across the road in one of the bars. I had hardly broke stride when an object hit me in the calf causing me to lose my footing, my trailing foot hit the kerb and I hit the concrete very hard and undignified. Before I had a chance to get up, I felt the first of many blows to the back of my head. I struggled to pull myself up on to my knees, as, at this time, I thought the Africans had caught me and I was about to have my throat slit.

I didn't get a chance to see my attackers for another few

minutes, as another blow cracked me across the face, while kicks and fists rained blows on my prostrate body. In all the commotion, I could hear screams from a crowd of onlookers who were pleading to deaf ears for them to stop. I then felt my legs being spread apart and felt the weight of someone on my back, pushing my face further down on the scorching concrete. Suddenly, my arms were pulled back behind me and my hands cuffed. It was only then that I realised it wasn't the mob, but plain-clothes police. As I looked around for my baseball cap that had come off during the attack, I was still lying face down when I saw a young guy with a video camera filming me. As he turned to go, two of the plain-clothes officers took the camera from him and pushed him away. At that moment, I saw my cap in the gutter at the same time as one of the officers did; he bent down, picked it up and stuffed it inside his open jacket, then carried on pushing the onlookers away.

In hindsight, it was all very well planned; the police vehicles and paparazzi all camped out at the top of the road, the African gangs allowed to run riot in front of them while the police stood back and watched the trouble unfurl. Then, when the England fans retaliated, they moved in their special plain-clothes snatch squads to arrest any easy targets they could find. One of them was me, already lying on the ground. It seemed all too well planned right in front of the world's press, gaining themselves valuable brownie points and further fuelling the propaganda value of England's badly stained reputation abroad.

The van then set off at breakneck speed through the busy streets until we came to a halt inside a compound surrounded by high concrete walls. Myself and one other England fan I later came to know as Steff were led out and into the back door of a huge building. We were separated at the top of the stairs. I was taken to a room and interrogated by the French authorities who spoke no English – or chose not to.

When they did find someone who I could understand, they wanted to know if I had a firearms licence and wanted to know why I had injured one of their officers. They then produced a guy the size of Napoleon who held out his arm as if he had just been shot. I had never seen this man before in my life. A few hours later, they came to my cell and made me sign a statement to say they would hold me overnight and let me go in the morning. It was then that I made a big mistake. Still tired and still aching from the beating, I signed the paper, which was written in French, under duress.

I later found out that what I had actually signed was not the release papers as I was told, but a charge sheet listing my alleged offences: resisting arrest, throwing a bottle and injuring a policeman, all of which were a complete fabrication of the truth. Oh, how I wish I had kept up the French lessons in school. After a restless night in the cells with no food, water or even a bed to sleep on, I was joined by six others all arrested during yesterday or later in the evening. After being left in the cells for hours, we were led into the yard and cuffed to each other before being thrown in the back of a van. Twenty minutes later, we were in a holding cell in a building we later found out to be the old city's grand courthouse. Later that evening, we were told that an impromptu court hearing had been arranged for 10pm. We were also informed that a local interpreter would be found. When she did arrive, she had some stark news for us – we would not be allowed to have any legal support and would be sentenced that night. Whatever happened to being innocent before being proven guilty? We were led in one by one handcuffed to a guard to be faced by four judges. The one woman judge looked scornfully at my bloodstained England shirt and started shouting at the top of her voice. Our interpreter was not allowed to enter the courtroom, which was handy for them but not for me, as I couldn't understand a single word she screamed. When I did try to speak, I had a butt of a police rifle shoved into the lower part of my back, which had the desired effect. After a few more minutes, I was pushed out of the courtroom. My interpreter spoke in French to my guard and then told me I had been sent to the local jail, a hellhole called Les Baumettes penitentiary, where I would stay until another court date was arranged.

I sat in silence, pondering what I had been told. It felt like a bad dream, the only trouble was I was awake, and this was happening. I was absolutely gutted. I had no legal assistance, I hadn't even been able to tell them my side of the story, and my partner and six-year-old son was stuck at the campsite, still not knowing why I hadn't returned to the campsite 36 hours ago. I couldn't help thinking about the statement in the front of my passport that read that British citizens be allowed 'to pass freely without let or hindrance and to afford the bearer such assistance and protection as be necessary'.

This had obviously been amended to exclude England football fans, and an innocent one at that. It was after midnight when we were driven a few miles across the city to the old jail that was used by the Gestapo in the war. After being strip-searched and having been given soap, a carton of orange and a condom, we were escorted through the dark corridors up a spiral staircase on to the third floor past several inmates who were stood in the shadows. We were finally pushed into three cells at the end of the long passageway; I was sharing with Alan, an Everton fan from Watford (work that one out!). The room was tiny; an open toilet stood just inside the door, a three-tier bunk bed stood against one wall, a rusty sink and a tiny fridge was on the other, and at the far end of the room was a small window with three metal bars. I walked across to the window and looked down on the litter-strewn yard. It was lit up brightly by the floodlights that were placed in all four corners around the massive prison. The block opposite was several floors high and stretched away in both directions for as far as I could see. I guessed our block was the same size. We sat looking at each other wondering what the coming days would bring. I was still in shock at being given a condom! The guard had told Tall Paul the Fulham fan that he was in an Arab jail now and may need one.

At 6am the next morning, we were woken by the jangling of keys at our door. An ugly character we named Egor stood sweating in his stained apron at the door before throwing two bread rolls on to the floor. I was starving and, despite nearly losing three teeth, ate the whole thing in a few minutes. I walked to the window to get some fresh air, only to be greeted by a welcoming party down below in the exercise. Hundreds of inmates all gathered against the fencing of their exercise yard shouting and pointing broken glass and bottles at us, suggesting we should all fuck our mothers, while giving us the cutthroat sign. Later that day, another eight England fans joined us. They had all been to court that morning. An hour later, the guards led all 15 of us down through the dark corridors inside the prison to the commander's office where he told us that we had best behave or we'd be left to our own devices amongst the hundreds of immigrants!

The next few weeks took on a familiar boring existence: inedible prison food, three hours a day spent sunbathing and playing footie with a ball given to us by three Algerians who had been caught trying to blow up the French Embassy in Marseille. They too were given a small yard next to ours away from the other inmates. The evenings were spent playing battleships and watching the footie on a French sports channel on an old TV we had in our cell. My partner had eventually been found by my mates who were camping down the coast in Agde. They spent two days driving round every campsite until they found my car parked outside the tent that I had only spent one night in. They drove my partner to the prison and finally arranged a visit.

She was only allowed to bring in shorts, T-shirts, socks and underwear, but most importantly money, which now meant we could buy fruit, chocolate, crisps and fruit juice. I was struggling to eat the awful food and felt tired, so now I could supplement my diet.

We decided to contact a local lawyer as we had heard that the Marseille authorities were looking to throw the book at us and make us scapegoats for all the troubles that had gone on in the city over the last week. She had been told they were looking at three-year prison sentences, which cheered me up no end!

When I eventually met my lawyer, she was very sympathetic to my cause; she also inferred that the French authorities were keeping us as a deterrent in a joint venture with the British government. She did, however, want me to understand the serious offences that I had been falsely charged with, which could carry big sentences, especially in this part of France where they had their own rules and regulations. However, she was confident that, once they got hold of witness statements and footage that Sky TV had shown on their news bulletins back home, she would be able to prove my innocence. It was 15 minutes of footage showing the scene before the disturbances and then the police brutality during my arrest. She also asked what I was wearing on the day. I told her a white England shirt, black shorts with a Pompey crest, a blue baseball cap and white trainers. She said that the statement from the police described the man they saw throwing a bottle and he wasn't wearing a cap! I told her that I remember losing it during the arrest and a policeman picking it up and hiding it inside his jacket.

Two days before my court case, my lawyer surprisingly arrived at the prison. I once again had to be handcuffed, taken through the prison, dodging the inmates, to a small room where I was strip-searched before being allowed to see her. She had bad news; the film that my partner, who was now back in Portsmouth, had managed to purchase for £300 and send by DHL courier had arrived in Marseille, but, when she went to pick it up, the package had been opened and the film had gone. I asked how the hell that had happened. She whispered in my ear that the authorities here in Marseille must have intercepted the package.

The court case went ahead as planned, and we all met in the exercise yard the morning before we were driven to the courthouse in the centre of Marseille. None of us felt confident that we would be released and we all expected to be back in our cells playing battleships that evening. I was handcuffed to a toothless African in the back of a caged police van, while the other lads travelled in similar comfort in our little convoy that sped through the streets towards the courthouse. I caught sight of my partner who had travelled over in the courtroom which was packed with journalists and a large gathering of local Tunisian youths, who cheered and clapped as the female judge shouted and pointed at myself and my defence lawyer. When my lawyer did get a chance to speak, she was told by the judge in no uncertain terms to shut up as 'she didn't wish to hear any more for the defence, after all we don't want to make this the trial of the year'. A few minutes later, we were ushered out of the courtroom.

I asked my lawyer what had happened, as once again the whole trial had been spoken in French. She told me they would not listen to anything she had said and anyway the decision that I was guilty was made at a pre-trial meeting; all she was trying to do was lessen my sentence. I was given three months. My lawyer thought it was a good result considering the circumstances. So would I, if I were guilty. We were all sent back to the prison; some of us had been given three-month sentences, others including Yeoy, my Leicester cellmate, were given four months. We settled into a routine out in the yard and in our cells, writing letters home and watching the World Cup.

The whole prison were against us when England played, they were all leaning out of their windows shouting abuse at us; all of the cells opposite ours were shining glass mirrors into our cells trying to blind us; others above were throwing bags of urine and shit in plastic bags trying to get them into our cells. We all stood leaning out of the five cell windows singing the national anthem. The whole place went mad, screaming and whistling, trying to put us off watching the game. We were all gutted when we missed that last penalty against Argentina and the Arabs had the last laugh, celebrating long into the night.

I had one more visit before my release and received many letters from friends back home, many arriving from my football mates in the Wicor Mill pub in Portchester. They were a godsend and really cheered you up when you were feeling low. I received a letter from my bosses back home where I worked for the Provident Credit Company. They were suspending me from work until an inquiry was held, after shareholders had complained at the bad press my case had evoked in the national papers, not helped by Tony Blair's statement to 'sack the yobs'.

On 1 August, I was told I would be free to go home the next day and when it arrived I was handcuffed with my arms behind my back as tightly as they could. I was flanked in the back seat by two CRS policemen with machine guns, in the front was a driver who drove like a madman, and his partner in crime who sat staring at me while reading my charges from my personnel file. I could see pictures of my arrest and knew that he was reading the account of the arrest and, according to the charges, I had injured one of their colleagues. I was sweating as the car drove round the streets of Marseille at six in the morning. We drove past the sign for the airport and I thought, Surely, they are not driving me across France to the ferry port. Then they stopped in a side street. I was getting worried by now, there was no one about and they all sat staring at me. The driver pointed at the picture of me in the file, the guy to the right of me dug the butt of his gun into my side. By then I could feel the cuffs had cut into my wrist and I could feel blood on my arm. They kept staring, trying to provoke a reaction. I just stared back, trying to look out the window. I thought any minute they were going to lay into me, but, after what seemed like an age, he sped off past the railway station and out towards the airport.

When we eventually arrived, a skinny man in a suit walked to the car and introduced himself as Alain, he would be my escort home to Heathrow via Charles de Gaulle in Paris. He gestured to one of the guards to take off my cuffs and said something to one of them when he saw my wrists. They escorted us into the packed airport; I felt like a fugitive. Alain asked if they had hurt me, I told him I was fine. He told me that the CRS thugs were renowned for giving private beatings but because of the press coverage of the trial had not done so.

I was put on the flight home to Heathrow and handcuffed as we took off but when we passed over the channel they were removed and Alain told me I was now free to go and they ordered us a beer. When we arrived at Heathrow, we were met by English Old Bill who took us separately into interview rooms. They asked me about the trouble in Marseille: who did I know inside, who did I meet in Marseille, did I know any of the 657 Pompey crew? Cheeky bastards. All I wanted to do was go home and yet these twats wanted to have me indulge in a 30-minute question and answer session.

Eventually, after I said nothing and they knew I wasn't going to talk, they let me go. I was met by my partner and friends and drove home – 46 days after my first day in the prison, it was nice to be back home. In the months that followed, I had several meetings with my employers and even spent a day at the Sky TV studios where we watched the footage that wasn't shown in court. The two managers that went to watch the film on behalf of the firm's directors said that it was conclusive evidence and that I should be reinstated to my position as account manager.

I had been instructed to use a solicitor who was also an advocate and was also in touch with my lawyer back in Marseille. He was based in Leeds and in the weeks leading up to the appeal he told me he was worried, as, although the footage showed that I did nothing in the 15 minutes leading to my arrest, my company's solicitors were saying it didn't prove I hadn't done anything earlier in the day, even though that was irrelevant to us. The police charges stated they saw me throw a bottle (no mention of me wearing a baseball cap), then immediately arrested me, and then somehow I allegedly injured a policeman while resisting arrest lying face down in the dirt.

A few weeks after the trip to the Sky TV studios, I was told my disciplinary hearing would be held at our regional office in Aldershot. I would be allowed to take a member of staff, although my lawyer was not allowed to attend. I took Malcolm, a manager of our local office and also a union representative. I had been briefed by my lawyer that if things went wrong we would have the right to appeal, but he was confident I would be reinstated.

Within the first half an hour, it became clear that they had made their mind up, and, within 20 minutes of our return after they adjourned for lunch, they gave their decision. Apparently, even though, after seeing the Sky TV footage and reading the many eyewitness reports and numerous other statements, they admitted that I took a very harsh beating, nevertheless they somehow decided that they had to believe the court's findings, as my evidence only proved I did nothing half an hour before my arrest but not for the three hours prior to that. And to add insult to injury, my TV footage and witness accounts were omitted from court!

The bloke in charge of the fiasco went on to say he would recommend to head office I be summarily dismissed for my personal behaviour detrimental to my position. I would have a right to appeal, but I should hand my keys and ID card to my boss. I was gobsmacked and Malcolm took me out of the office before I said something that could go against me at the appeal. Over the following weeks, we planned the appeal which was to be held in Bradford on 22 September. My lawyer was quietly confident we could overturn the verdict before we met the employee relations officers and the deputy managing director of my company, which at the time was one of the largest credit companies in the country.

On the day, they listened intently as my solicitor explained the facts of how the kangaroo court had been set up and that it was well known in France that the judicial system in Marseille was a law unto itself, having himself worked in the city for five years and having read an affidavit from my French lawyer who openly admitted this problem did exist. We were asked to wait outside for a few minutes. My solicitor was not happy; he had watched the facial expressions and mannerisms of the director and said he thought he was paying us lip service and just going through the legal motions.

He was correct. The director told me he was not prepared to regard the French decision as unsafe and was satisfied I was properly represented by legal counsel throughout the criminal process. He said I had signed to admit the crime and was not at liberty to do so. That was it, I was dismissed!

I eventually found another job, despite being labelled a capital C hooligan and having been banned from France for two years, which was not a punishment in my eyes. I also gained a nickname from my mates in the pub after a picture of one of my fellow inmates appeared on the front of the *News of the World* showing Big Jim beating his chest in Marseille. The headline proclaimed him as the 'Pig of Marseille'. I was then named the 'Piglet of Marseille' – very witty – and it stuck over the years.

Two years later, while writing my memoirs of what happened in June 1998, I returned to Marseille and found it a completely different place from the ugly city it became that day in June when England came to town. I still don't blame the Africans, as we invaded their turf, it was their city and they knew they could do anything they liked, as the police would only arrest the England fans. I blame whoever's bright and very naive idea it was of choosing Marseille to be the venue for England's first game against an African nation in a city where over 300,000 young unemployed Africans, mainly Tunisians, lived in ghetto-like conditions; it was a recipe for disaster and proved to be so.

UEFA and FIFA have learned nothing from those events in 1998 and still blame the England fans, and always will, I guess. After all, we do take the most support to any competition and are fanatical about our team. Yes, at times we cause trouble, but nine times out of 10 only under provocation. But one thing we haven't resorted to is stabbing anything that moves; you don't see the authorities cracking down on the Turks, do you? I can only tell it as it was that day from what I witnessed first-hand. Maybe I should not have run across the road, maybe I should have stayed at home and not travelled without a ticket (God forbid), but then again, hindsight is a wonderful thing!

Wrong place, wrong time, wrong shirt – that just about sums up what happened to an Englishman abroad that sunny day in June.

CHAPTER TWENTY-FOUR

THE PLASTIC CHAIR BRIGADE
EURO 2000

If medals were given out for panic policing towards English fans' behaviour, this tournament would have seen the Belgian force win gold! When around 500 people are deported and nearly 1,000 arrested, there has usually been a mass riot or mini war. The 2000 European Championships saw neither, yet those were the shocking statistics which led to UEFA threatening to throw England out of the tournament after just two games.

In reality, what went on in Belgium was old hat; there were the now customary street brawls with Turkish or Arab immigrants and the familiar sight of drunken youths throwing plastic chairs at anyone who did not know the words to 'No surrender to the IRA'.

Apart from that, there was no mass rioting, as was the case in Sweden in '92 and France in '98; there was no terrace violence as there was in Italy in 1980 and Spain 82; nobody was killed and very few were injured. The statistics were purely a sign that the world football authorities and the police were sick and tired of England's new-wave hooligans' boorish behaviour.

They were not alone, as the seasoned campaigners who had made England a fighting force over 25 years were also sickened by the new-style hooligan, who complete with Stone Island or checked something, peaked cap and plastic chair were not fit to wipe their predecessors' arses.

Once Scotland were beaten in the play-offs, a massive police operation was set up to deter thugs from spoiling the summer finals. It was never going to be easy, as Holland and Belgium were easily accessible and although a midweek game in Eindhoven against Portugal was unlikely to see much trouble the following Saturday, Germany being the opponents in Charleroi did have hooligan potential.

Early indications were accurate and the game in Eindhoven saw little trouble, even after England threw away a 2–0 lead, going on to lose 3–2. While PSV, who are the club side in the city, have minor problems with their fans domestically, the venue was far less hostile than Rotterdam or Amsterdam, and, while English fans made up the majority of the 33,000 crowd, the hooligan element was conspicuous by its absence. In the town, a carnival atmosphere was reported and 3,000 Portuguese fans mixed and drank in harmony with the Dutch and English, although the locals were the only ones to notice that the beer on sale tasted different, as it was not announced at the time that bar owners were ordered by the police to only sell the weaker 2.5 per cent-strength brew on the day England were in town!

Nobody was daft enough to think that the success of the Portugal game, off the field, would be carried on to the weekend's match with the Germans, and again it was a good call as, by the time the eve of the game drew to a close, over 500 England fans were imprisoned in Brussels!

As hundreds of English arrived in the Belgian capital, immigrant gangs attacked and running street battles saw many visitors stabbed and slashed, as the Turkish and Arab youths set about doing what they do best. That came as no surprise but the brutality of the police force did, as ordinary fans were systematically arrested and beaten for basically being in the wrong place at the wrong time. This excuse does wear thin, and there is no doubt that, over the years, members of England's following have brought shame to the country and deserved the odd baton across the back, cuffing and early plane home. But Brussels was different. As had happened in Marseille during the 1998 World

Cup Finals, local police worked under the zero-tolerance banner, and a large percentage of those arrested and beaten were innocent supporters with no previous involvement in football violence.

As hundreds were held without charge in rundown police cells, more and more England fans arrived in Charleroi and, unfortunately, the numbers included the plastic chair brigade.

The German support was poor but, once the lager flowed and temperatures rose, so did temperaments, and, when a large group of German fans began chanting outside a bar near to where hundreds of English were also drinking, the lot went!

The images of water cannons blasting yobs and plastic chairs flying through the air were transmitted all over the world and, a few hours before the game, UEFA admitted that they were considering expelling England from the tournament. Hundreds more were detained, as once again the zero-tolerance stance was enforced, although, unlike the night before, many could not complain, as hundreds did willingly participate in the ritual plastic-chair-chucking championships!

At the actual football match, the security operation was once again a success and a 1–0 England win sent most of the fans home happy. Those deported on old military Hercules planes had cause to complain, as their belongings were still in hotels; they landed in airports hundreds of miles from their preferred destinations and the in-flight entertainment and duty-frees were non-existent!

Away from the game there was the usual in-house differences and fights with the immigrant population. Much of it was handbags at dawn but Nick from Forest witnessed an incident which haunts him to this day.

NICK, NOTTINGHAM FOREST:

I flew out on my own hoping to get into Brussels for midday, have a few beers then get off to Charleroi for some action, but the plane was delayed for four hours, so, by the time I got to Brussels, it was dead. I got on the next train to Charleroi and was met by hundreds of OB at the station, as it had been going off all day.

There were plenty of lads about who told me that it was not the feared Headhunters, Red Army or ICF who were running riot but the new firm the PCB (Plastic Chair Brigade) and they had brought it on top with their fucking daftness, as the police by now had the right hump!

We were escorted to the ground and I was with about 30 fans who looked like they would be up for it if it went. I spotted about 15 Germans stood on a corner who looked tasty enough, so I bounced across the road expecting my new mates to follow me. I threw a punch and the strangest thing happened as, rather than having a go back, the Germans held up their hands as if to say please no trouble! To make matters worse, I looked around and the lads who were with me were just shaking their heads in disgust, while I stood there looking a right twat. To make it even worse, the fella I had lumped turned out to be a slightly disabled chap, but how was I to know?

I found a quiet bar away from the crowds and all the Forest lads were in there, but outside you could hear sirens going off and the lads were saying that the OB were in a right mood and had took to whacking everyone who looked remotely English, so we decided to clear off back to Brussels. Near the station, we plotted up in a bar with a load of Wolves lads while we waited for the next train out of there and suddenly loads of coppers were charging down the road towards us. I thought they were going to some bother further down the road, when they just came straight at us!

There was not one bit of trouble in that bar, they were well out of order and were once again just whacking everyone. A few ashtrays headed towards them, which didn't help the cause, as straight away tear gas was fired inside the bar and everyone was ordered to sit on the floor outside. There were lads being sick and everyone's eyes were streaming but, before we got ourselves sorted, a coach pulled up and the first 30-odd got strapped and taken away. I couldn't believe this was happening. Fair enough, if you'd cracked someone on the jaw or threw someone through a shop window, then, yeah, nick us, by all means, but for simply drinking a beer quietly in some bar with not one hint of trouble? Fuck that! Another coach, another 30 gone and we were next when, out of the blue, the OB told us to get up and fuck off, warning us that large groups of Turks were out for English blood.

We decided to take his advice and got taxis to another train station out of the city centre. Most of the lads were going back to Amsterdam, meaning I had to hang around through the night which was dodgy as the station we went to was in a right shady area but more English arrived and plenty were in the same boat as me so we had enough dossing about if it came on top. I tried to get some kip but couldn't sleep, so stupidly decided to go for a walk on my own, unaware that I was about to see the worst thing I'd ever witnessed in my life.

I strolled into the nearest kebab shop and got chatting to four lads, two of which were Spurs and the other two were either Boro or Sunderland. They were sound with me and we went for a stroll eating our snack and talking about previous offs with each other, which was sound. We were walking nowhere in particular, so we decided to walk back to the station when, out of the blue, a shit-heap of a car screeched up beside us and I knew straight away that we were in serious trouble, and my instincts told me whoever was in the car was not about to offer us a lift so I tried to whip my belt off sharpish.

Four Turks, each carrying a blade, jumped out and everyone froze against the wall, shocked not moving. I stared at one of them and edged forward, waving my belt furiously in front of me, and, looking back, I think, if we had all done the same thing, they would have left it. But they turned their attention to the four startled boys trapped against the wall and, in a flash, one lunged forward and lashed out at one lad's face. The scream he let out was gut churning and the Turks turned to run back to the car. The lad was slashed from one side of his face to the other, straight through his eyebrows and blood was pouring down his face.

Three of the Turks got in the car, which still had the engine running, but the fourth tripped and I swung my belt with all my strength and caught him right across the face and he went down like a sack of spuds. I could not believe what happened next, as his supposed mates drove off and left him with us lads on him like fucking vultures, volleying him all over the floor.

One of the lads sat his mate up in the doorway and was close to tears but he turned to the Spurs boys and said, 'Bring that cunt over here.'

The fella was spark out and they dragged him to the doorway and put him next to the fucked-up Englishman. His mate searched the Turk's jacket and pulled out the same knife he had used earlier and I knew what was coming next and there was no way to stop it. The rage in the bloke's eyes was mental and he put the knife in his mate's hand, who couldn't see fuck all because of the blood and began to slash the Turk across the face.

I began to panic that the locals would come back, and told the bloke with the blade that he had done what he had to do and to get the fuck out of here before we all got murdered. The fella who got cut was surprisingly with it and walked quite normally and I bought a bottle of water to clean the blood off his face. His forehead was wide open and a huge flap of skin was drooped over his eyes, so, while we went back to the station, the injured lad and his mate went to the hospital. I decided to chance Brussels central and got there in one piece and sat in the station going over what had happened. I learned that night to show no fear to the Turks, as, if you do, they'll swarm all over you and cut you.

I'd only been there one day and had seen more than some people see in a lifetime and that's what it's like following England – it's fucking great!

A total of 945 England fans were arrested in Belgium and UEFA threatened to expel Keegan's side from the tournament. Predictably, the press had a field day.

The *Daily Mail*'s headline 'HOW THE MOB BROUGHT MAYHEM' was the most accurate and its follow up of 'HAMMER ATTACKS, BOMBS AND WATER CANNON: LIFE WITH THE ENGLAND FANS', although slightly exaggerated, was what the millions at home wanted to read.

The paper reported that the people of Brussels and Charleroi were counting the cost of the violence, which saw Belgian riot police using tear gas and water cannons to disperse fighting fans, with hundreds of arrests made and 60 people injured.

Back home, the trouble sparked a war of words in the House of Commons when Home Secretary Jack Straw blamed the Tories for the trouble by English fans in Belgium, saying, 'They scuppered tougher legislation.' The Tories claimed that Labour simply lacked the determination to act.

Sir Norman Fowler suggested a new law be introduced through the House of Commons, called the 'Football Banning Order, FBO', and that it needed to be added to the government's Crime and Disorder bill.

Sports Minister Kate Hoey agreed that new legislation was required but that the time was not right, obviously she had more pressing matters to attend to that night!

Mr Straw complained that some of the English fans sent back included barristers and engineers, who back in the UK are apparently law-abiding citizens living respectable lives and commented, 'We can target those we know about but it is much more difficult to target those who have never come to the attention of the police back in the UK.'

Meanwhile, the mayor of Brussels, Francois Xavier de Donnea, said, 'Too many dangerous hooligans have reached the continent, screening in Britain was not what we expected it to be.'

Many nationalists in England agreed 100 per cent with the mayor, but their concerns were with the screening of thousands of illegal immigrants arriving in Britain from Eastern Europe, not the hooligans leaving in the opposite direction!

Alarm bells were ringing in the England camp when UEFA President Lennart Johanson declared that the fans' behaviour would 'kill football' adding, 'We cannot have people afraid to walk the streets and afraid to walk to and from the stadia; this is unacceptable and we have to do something about it, we cannot take on the responsibility that people are going to get killed.'

Johanson further condemned the English thugs as a 'disgrace' and warned, 'This can't go on! The world expects us to take a stand. If this happens again, as it did the last two days, it's over for England.'

However, despite scoring five goals in three games England still finished third in the group behind Portugal and Romania. During Keegan's short reign as England manager, his side conceded just nine goals in 16 games, but, when it mattered, they conceded six in two which meant that, despite the PCB's antics, there was no need for UEFA to get involved, as Keegan's tactical frailties meant that we were going home early anyway!

CHAPTER TWENTY-FIVE

5–1
GERMANY 2001

By the time England played Germany in Munich, there was mutual respect for each other's mob, as the Germans were one of the few firms to arrive in England and have a go, as Fat Pat recalls.

FAT PAT, CHELSEA:
I always liked a good international, as the whole day was a buzz, meeting up with lads from all over, but in September '91 the game against Germany had a bit of extra spice to it, as we had it on good authority that their mob was going to show in London for the first time ever!

There has long been a history between our country and the Germans, our parents and grandparents fought for their lives to defend Britain against the Germans in two World Wars. The last thing we wanted was German hooligans in our capital city taking the piss – it could not happen and would not happen. They had to be repelled, it was our duty as Brits, and one that I felt duty bound to carry out. It was political and it was very important.

In the morning, we went down to Victoria, walked through the concourse at the station and I noticed about 300 geezers there. My mate turned around to me and asked who Crystal Palace were playing but I knew right from the off that these geezers were not Londoners, as they were all big bastards and, as soon as we walked through, they all clocked us, and I thought, Fuck me, they're here, they're taking the piss, what we going to do?

People were still working and we couldn't get everyone to come out together, but already it was coming on top, as the Old Bill started turning up, nicking loads of them, as they had bum bags on and when they were searching them they were finding flares and gas. Later, when it went to court, I read that all the Germans said it's legal to carry it in Germany and they didn't know they were breaking the law, so the judge apologised to them and released them! Fair play to them, even though they were Germans, we're all hooligans, and I wouldn't like to see anybody get nicked and would have loved to have seen the Old Bill's face when that happened.

Anyway, my pal went into the station and about 10 Germans were around him, and the conversation went something like this:

'You English?'

'Yeah.'

'Where are your hooligans?'

'Well, I'm not being funny, mate but no one really expected you, but we're trying to round people up.'

'That's your problem. We're here!' He went on to say that, by three o'clock, they were going up to Piccadilly Circus and meeting up there, so get our boys together!

By this time, my mate was frothing from the mouth, and he went away pulling his hair out when the cheeky bastard finished off by saying, 'We have done our bit and, as you say in English, we're taking the piss now!'

We were up for doing fucking suicide attacks by then, three or four of us, just to do something, but brains took over and we got a meet together in the Hog and the Pound in Bond Street. Everyone was running around, getting everyone together and we had about 60–70 when a few decided to go and have a nose to see if what we were saying was true. I told this little firm to wait and that I knew that what I had seen was not a fucking mirage, but they took no notice and off they went. Soon after, I got a phone call saying that, at the top of Carnaby Street, there was 150 German in the Blue Post and there was no Old Bill with them, which was a gift! I warned the lad to make sure nobody did anything to pot it up and to give us time to get there and give it to them proper.

We walked down the back streets and, as we were getting parallel to Regent Street, you could hear all the Old Bill in the distance and I saw a Villa geezer running up the road towards us with his shirt all ripped down the side. I asked him what had happened and he said that, while they were waiting for us, a few of them had got a bit pissed and said, 'Fuck them, they're only Germans,' and then gone down and attacked them on Carnaby Street, but the fucking whole pub's piled out with gas, flares and everything, and all you could hear was 'Deutschland hooligan!' as they were getting chased. I thought he was joking but he told me it was all on top, so I asked him why they didn't wait. He went on about 'You know what it's like, the lager went down and we were getting more and angry and we're English and didn't expect to get fucking chased off by them fucking idiots!'

A few of us went up to the game and it kicked off under the stands and England done them – the Germans admit it, as I was speaking to a German geezer years later, and they said they done us before the game but in the ground England did them under the stand.

After the game, the meet was back at Victoria and there was 200–300 England there now and loads of Old Bill, and they got the Germans up through the Underground and entered the concourse when about 20 of them slipped down the side exit and they got caught. And one of them got plunged, which is a bit out of order, but then again, after what the Villa geezer said about them firing flares at head fucking height, they can't really expect people to be too fucking upset if one of them gets brought in!

Ten years later, the Germans were again the visitors and it was a sad day for traditionalists, as the game was the final one under the twin towers and, weeks later, the bulldozers knocked the famous old ground down. It was the day that the 2002 World Cup-qualifying campaign got off to a poor start when England were beaten 1–0 by group favourites Germany. It was the end of the road for manager Kevin Keegan, who, after taking some flak on the long walk back to the dressing room, took the coward's way out and resigned moments later. He did the nation a favour!

As a player, he won the hearts of millions with his cheeky good looks and trendy perm, but will be remembered by many of his fans as one of the first so-called superstars who left the English game and joined the money-grabbing gravy train to Europe. As a person, Keegan was detested by hundreds of supporters who followed the national side abroad, as he was always the first to slate the fans' behaviour and was never approachable when on the odd occasion he was spotted in a bar or airport lounge by the people who were effectively paying his wages.

In a nutshell, Kevin was out for Kevin; he made a fantastic living as an average player and carried his luck into management, where his record at club level somehow convinced the bigwigs at Lancaster Gate that he was the man to try and emulate Sir Alf Ramsey's achievements.

His luck ran out and, having won just seven of his 18 games in charge, he resigned and walked away from football, hopefully for good!

The FA came up with a master plan to steady the ship while they searched for a successor to Keegan, and appointed Harold Wilkinson as caretaker manager. The decision further hindered our hopes of qualifying for the finals in Japan, as Wilkinson's negative approach saw more points dropped when minnows Finland held us to a goalless draw in Helsinki a few days after Keegan had left the country in the mire.

Peter Taylor was promoted from the Under-21 set-up and replaced Wilkinson, only to lose his one and only game in charge at a friendly in Italy. Then, in a blaze of publicity, much of it negative due to his non-British passport, Sven-Göran Eriksson was appointed as the man to salvage any hope of England making the finals. His track record was good, although not spectacular, but in his favour was the fact that most had already written off England's chances of making Japan.

Sven got off to a flyer and won his first five games in charge, including three Championship qualifiers, before losing a friendly at White Hart Lane against a decent Dutch side. Next up were Germany and defeat would mean automatic qualification was not possible, but buoyed by recent results, hopes were high that England could get the win they needed and thousands made the trip to Munich, while millions watched at home to see if Sven really did have the Midas touch!

TERRY, WEST HAM:
What an absolute blinding, unbelievable night!

We'd booked into the Holiday Inn and on the day of the game I went down for some breakfast and, as 20 of our lot were moaning about the lack of Wall's sausage, Danish bacon and HP Sauce, the phone went and it was the rest of the West Ham firm who had just arrived in Munich, telling us to get our arses over to the centre, as England were mobbing up and things were getting lively. After the reply of 'Bollocks, you come down to us, we're West Ham and we're going on our own' was received loud and clear, we got back to the continental meats and whatever and soon were greeted by the sight of 30-odd lads that were proper old school giving us a tasty mob of 50.

In the hotel bar, we had a look round and noticed about 30 other geezers who were lumps, fit-looking geezers that you could tell had done a bit, they all had a bit of the boxing appearance about them and you could tell straight away that they were Londoners. It was now a case of finding out who they were, and an elimination process took place and we agreed that they were not Yids, as they looked our age and Tottenham's firm were all a lot younger. We knew they were not

Chelsea, as they wouldn't even be sitting near us in this hotel bar as it was claimed by us and regarded as 'ours', which left the possibility of them being Millwall, which we thought was highly unlikely, or a mixture of lumps from the smaller clubs who had joined up in case they needed to be firm-handed.

We had a good afternoon, looking across at these lumps with the odd smile and pleasantry exchanged, when 50–60 Northerners came in the bar, all good geezers, who came over and asked if they could tag along with us, as they heard we were walking to the ground, as we always do, and they had been fucked off by the other mob who had just left.

It was turning into a great day; there we all were, in a decent hotel, leather seats, waitress service having a ball, all we needed now was a bit of a rumble, a good win for the lads and it would be the complete trip! Our lot had got into wearing the first Longshanks coats that had just been brought out, and I put the cap on and zipped up my coat and said, 'Come on, we're going!'

I got outside and turned right and looked behind me, and it was an impressive sight, as 130 geezers, a proper firm, all marched behind me, including a good few of the lumps who were in the bar earlier!

There were all sorts of rumours that the Germans are going to be here or there or every fucking where, and this and that is going to happen but I told our lot not to listen to all that bollocks and that, if we all stuck together as one firm, not just West Ham, no this and no that, just simply this one firm that we had assembled, then no one was gonna come through us, and that was pure fact!

Anyway, you know how it is, someone said chuck a left and we're in a road that's a dual carriageway and, because we're all walking in the road, we'd closed it off and brought the traffic to as standstill. So the German Old Bill have tried to get us off the road, we've told them to fuck off, but the problem was nobody knew where we were going, so we agreed to move on, once they pointed us in the right direction!

Eventually, we got to a hill leading to the ground and there was a firm of Germans right at the top with a firm of English towards the bottom. We'd done no more than started walking up the hill, no shouting or nonsense, just a nice steady pace, spread nice and even across the road, and the Germans were just gone in seconds, they were even joined by some of the English who were not sure who we were, so scattered too!

We were the first firm of the day to get up the ground and the Germans must have thought they were in for a rough old night as the first lot they had come across were 130 organised old-school lumps! Nobody would come near us, so, with nothing really to report home about, we decided to go in. Our man with the tickets gets them out and tells our little group that we have got the best tickets in the house, which was true but the downside of it was that they were in the German fucking end!

Picture it, 13 West Ham in the German end with thousands of English sitting across the fucking pitch from us! Our seats were in line with the penalty area but there was no segregation at all, we'd got 11 in the front, and me and a mate in the row behind, and you ain't got a seat to sit in, it was the small plastic piece on the concrete steps kind of number, which means the geezer sitting behind you has his knees in the back of your head all game which added to the danger. We were sitting there amongst thousands upon thousands of Germans laughing about what would happen if 13 Germans were sitting in the England end at Wembley! Which, although funny, was never going to happen.

So I am sitting looking all round me, thinking, We are absolutely fucked here, absolutely fucked, when suddenly they've scored, 1–0, and the Germans are all up and they're looking at us because we're the only fucking geezers who have not got up. Nothing happened, so, when Owen scored for England, we went for it and were all up jumping about while all the Germans are sitting there looking at us like we should be sectioned or something! Just before half-time, Gerrard's scored and the natural reaction was the same, so up we jump, fuck it, you're gonna get done anyway, so you might as well celebrate a bit, still nothing!

It got better, the teams come out and the third goal goes in, then the fourth and then the fifth. When the last one went in, I looked at the scoreboard and thought, Yeah this is worth getting a dig for! The truth of the matter was that you were never going to see a score like that again, never ever see one like the one that was lit up across the pitch from us, not in your lifetime; it was a one-off and we knew it. There we were in the Munich stadium and that big black board was saying Deutschland 1 England 5, so we looked at each other and just started singing 'Chim-chimney, Chim-chimney, Chim Chim Cheroo, We are those bastards in claret and blue!' Nothing to do with England but the point was, if we were going to go down, we were going to go down as West Ham and we were going to go down fighting!

Still nothing! All you could hear was the band in the England end playing out *The Dam Busters* tune over and over again. The final whistle had gone and the England section was going delirious, but I had got my head together and was just thinking of the walk out of there.

We got up and all thought the same, we knew that the chances were that we were going to get done, because we have just watched England batter them and, to be truthful, we had taken the piss a bit ourselves, so, if it was going to happen, we were ready for it. We sussed out that we could walk all the way around the stadium on the inside, so we set off towards the England end, looking about thinking, Who are the mugs who could try to do us? We stayed close together and were ready for whatever, but inside we were heartened as all you could hear was that bloody band playing *The Great Escape* tune. As we were trying to get from our end to as near as possible to the England end, this band is getting louder and louder, and we're thinking the nearer we get we might have a bit of help if it all comes on top.

We made it to the final section but found ourselves segregated from the England fans, but, as we'd come round, the gates had opened and there's just thousands of Englishmen piling out singing and dancing. We all just looked at each other and thought, How the fuck did we get away with that?

Even today, I still think about that night, and I remember when England equalised I felt a tap on the shoulder and I turned around to job him and this German bloke said, 'Michael Owen! Great player.'

Looking back on that walk back to get to the English side, it was all Germans we were passing, German skinheads, big lumps, and we was taking all the phone calls from our people that knew we were there, and all I can think of was the Germans were maybe too shell-shocked from the result to think about us. The end of that game will always live with me, that giant scoreboard showing 5–1, Owen, Gerrard and Heskey, that and us in the German end.

A funny thing occurred when everyone was all back together in the bar of the Holiday Inn hotel after. I had gone up some stairs to find the khazi and, in doing so, I heard one of the London geezers speaking into his mobile phone and heard him say, 'Oh, mate, it's one of the best games I've ever been to and you ain't going to believe this, but so-and-so is over here with his firm and we've gone to an England game with fucking West Ham! And, worse still, you won't believe it but they are proper decent fellows.'

We were walking back to the bar and I chipped in with: 'Who are you, mate?'

And the geezer goes, 'Millwall!'

We went on about what a great result it was and shook hands and we ended up all together buying each other beer; it had been a great day and was capped off with West Ham and Millwall together! The result had gone to everyone's fucking heads!

About a year ago, one of ours from the gym was over

South London amongst the boxing fraternity when the conversation switched to football. This geezer had gone up to him and said, 'Do you remember that 5–1 game?'

Our man's nodded and said he was there, and the Millwall geezer has asked him, 'Do you know that cunt Terry?'

Our man has told him that he does and the Millwall bloke has said, 'Well, I had a drink with him after the game, but we were a bit influenced after the result and all that, so you tell the West Ham cunt, never again!'

It's a funny old game!

That match went down in history as one of England's greatest ever performances and Eriksson was a national hero and his Swedish passport was no longer a problem. Another major plus to come out of the game was that there was very little trouble reported. There were outbreaks of fighting, a Northern firm were gassed on the underground and the night before the game there were problems in quite a few of the major German cities but, given the importance of the game, it passed off relatively peacefully.

England were now favourites to qualify for the finals, yet still they came very close to making a cat's arse of things in their final two home games against Albania and Greece. Having beaten the Albanians, albeit unconvincingly in Tirana, where three goals in the final 17 minutes gave Sven's men a hard-earned victory, the return game at St James' Park was in the balance until the final minute when Robbie Fowler added to Michael Owen's late first-half strike.

England now needed to beat Greece at Old Trafford to gain automatic qualification for the finals and, once again, they did their very best to cock things up! Germany were hosting Finland but an England win would make the score in Germany irrelevant; however, an early goal for the Greeks left the home crowd silenced. An equaliser from Sheringham lifted the nation's hopes, briefly, as the Greeks scored minutes later to put the Germans back to the top of the group. With a minute remaining, a fairytale ending was needed or the 5–1 win in Munich would have been in vain, and David Beckham supplied it when he curled home a magnificent free-kick to send the crowd delirious and Sven's men to Japan, as the Germans had only managed a draw themselves, which left them having to qualify via the play-offs.

Outside Old Trafford and all over the country, fans celebrated long into the night and Manchester was awash with face-painted, flag-waving nationals enjoying a carnival atmosphere. But it had not been like that prior to the match, as street fighting between home fans saw scores arrested, including some main Man United faces following an attack on known Stoke hooligans shortly before the match kicked off.

Eriksson's team continued to impress and, once again, there were high hopes that the long wait for a trophy could be drawing to a close. Despite Japan not being very accessible or cheap to get to, the authorities set about ensuring that England's support over there would follow the 'Barmy Army'-style cricket fans and hundreds of banning orders were dished out to prevent known hooligans leaving the country during the tournament.

In Japan itself, a ferry boat called the *Sunflower Tomakomai*, which was used to transport lorries from Tokyo to Hokkaidol was converted into a floating prison capable of holding 630 people. Nicknamed the 'Fuurigan Maru' – 'the Good Ship Hooligan!' – the boat was afloat off the island of Hokkaido and a Ministry of Justice spokesman in Japan warned English fans that the boat had been converted especially for them and that, if arrested, they would be locked on the ship before being taken on a 20-hour voyage to a detention centre in Tokyo, where, under Japanese law, they could be held for up to 27 days without being charged.

The threats from the Japanese were enough to deter potential troublemakers from travelling or causing problems during the competition. In Japan, England were well represented and there were little or no reports of any hooliganism. Many of the lads out there made Japan a working holiday and, in between games, trips to Bangkok were frequent and counterfeit football shirts and merchandise made many thousands of pounds, as the locals were gripped by the World Cup bug!

Back in England, there were reports throughout the finals of violence erupting in pubs and towns on days when England were playing, and, after one incident in Stoke-on-Trent, four men were jailed following violence in Hanley city centre after fans watched England beat Denmark 3–0. The courts even managed to hand out football banning orders of up to six years to the men found guilty, as they claimed the fighting was football related. It was a sign of the times that the authorities could now convict people for football-violence offences even when they were watching the game on TV thousands of miles away from the actual game. Whatever next? Undercover police officers infiltrating pubs when *Match of the Day* is on and handing out section 60s!

On the field, it was the same old story and England crashed out in the quarter-finals against eventual winners Brazil. It had been an eventful campaign and one that will always be remembered for that night in Munich and the now famous picture of the scoreboard displaying the huge Deutschland: England 1–5 image.

CHAPTER TWENTY-SIX

WHO CARES?
LIECHTENSTEIN 2003

There are many games over the years that have made national and even world news headlines due to the behaviour of the hooligan problem which exists at England games. The likes of the Dublin, Rimini, Charleroi, Marseille and Rotterdam riots have seen coverage usually reserved for outbreaks of war, royal family deaths and the assassination of dignitaries.

On 29 March 2003, England played a European Championship qualifier in Liechtenstein. It was the first time the countries had ever met and many England fans had to get the atlas out to even find out where the place was! Many decided to stay in Zurich in the days leading up to the match, and those that did predictably became involved in skirmishes with locals and general mayhem. During this disorder, five Englishmen ended up in hospital, two with stab wounds and the other three having been shot!

Some papers covered the incident briefly, there was a mention of it on the news and that was about it! It is a game where many of the English who travelled via Zurich claim that, once again, they were treated badly by the police and authorities both home and abroad. However, their biggest grievance was with the press and media bosses who seemed unconcerned that England fans had been the victims of shootings and knifings.

Ian Bailey, along with Jaffa, from Hartlepool has followed

England on numerous occasions and this is one of the games they will never forget.

IAN AND JAFFA, HARTLEPOOL:

Five of us from Hartlepool flew out on the Tuesday morning ahead of Saturday's match. Like the majority of England fans, we headed for Zurich as Liechtenstein is that small getting anywhere to stay was always going to be difficult, and, with Zurich only about an hour's train journey away, it seemed a perfect stopover destination. We arrived in Zurich on the Thursday night, put our bags in the room and went straight to a nightclub next door to our hotel. We decided we were going to have a quiet one but, a few pints later, three of us headed up towards the old town, where there were not many English around or locals for that matter, but, as you do, we still ended up having bother with a few lads from the Swiss Army after we slagged them off for not backing the British boys up in Iraq. That set the tone for the trip – our general feeling was, if you can get a fight with the Swiss Army idiots, it wouldn't be hard to get one with the hundreds of local immigrants who seemed to dwell in large parts of the city!

We awoke that morning buzzing; it's always exciting on the day before a game, as you know hundreds will be arriving and that the day will be eventful – it's a lad's thing! We headed for one of those cafe bars that most foreign cities have and just sat outside drinking strong but heavily overpriced beer and watched in awe as the invasion began and scores of English lads arrived. It was obvious that everyone had the same idea about using Zurich as a base; there were faces turning up who would never be allowed into Liechtenstein and we knew that that night was going to be naughty.

Around teatime, we'd made our way up to the area where we'd been drinking the night before, but it was like being on a different planet! The previous night it was all quiet and relaxing, 24 hours later there were groups of English lads everywhere you looked and all had the same agenda – get pissed and have it with anyone who looked like they wanted it, whether that be locals or the Old Bill.

We were walking about when we noticed there was a Stone Island shop in a side street just off the main strip, everyone agreed that, when the inevitable trouble started, we would make a beeline to this shop and basically loot it, knowing we would have to be quick, as other English lads would have the same idea. A few more Hartlepool lads arrived and told us that the in-house cancer had kicked in, as they had only been in the city an hour and already they had been fighting with a firm from Carlisle.

That is the downside with following England today, there is too much of this club rivalry, which spills over on to the international scene. It can only take a small incident to spark it off and the lot can go, as was the case in Zurich. We were talking to some Man City lads when three Swiss blokes walked past; one of them looked a bit suspect in the sexuality stakes and we gave him a bit of grief, in return he gave us one of those gay dirtiest looks, so one of our lads shot a pint glass straight at him. They turned and ran, as we gave chase but were getting punched and kicked by other English lads as they were running. With all the shouting going on, two pubs next door to each other just emptied and a free-for-all took place between ... Stoke and Chelsea!

That is all it takes when you are abroad with England, one daft little incident can spark the lot off. The time bomb that had been ticking away for hours had been patient. 'Tick tock, have some more beer, tick tock, have a line of Charlie, tick tock, boom!' It exploded and that silly little spat with the suspected Swiss homosexual caused a riot!

The mob of lads got exactly what they had come for – violence, and plenty of it. Until that time, the police had been conspicuous by their absence but the initial sight of them sent the lads into a frenzy. The first squad to turn up didn't exactly instil the fear of God into you. They were young, the flat-cap brigade, and they looked like a poor excuse for the part-time mugs we have at home. Every country has them, the have-a-go wannabe cops who work for nothing as specials, trying to be important, having probably been bullied at school and unable to get anybody to respect them in the real world. 'Be someone, become a special!'

Unimpressed by the spotty flat caps, the English charged at them and you could see the fear in their faces and, in seconds, they crumbled and ran. If they were real Old Bill, then they were a disgrace to their profession and ran like fuck, which had us all pissing ourselves laughing. Short chase and the usual mundane chant of 'Eng-er-land, Eng-er-land, Eng-er-land' over, we all went back to the bars to carry on with our drinking, snorting and in-house squabbling, knowing full well that the embarrassed deputies would be back soon with the sheriffs, the special force, with their helmets, gas and sticks who would be a little harder to shift than the kiddie cops who had just shit themselves in their trainee-issue pants!

We remembered about the Stone Island shop and we got our little squad together and shot over there for some free togs, only to find the fucking place had been ransacked as we were chasing the Old Bill by our friends from Liverpool. By the time we got back to the bar, the thieving Scouse bastards were selling it to all the English lads!

As expected, the riot police turned up, but surprisingly kept a good distance away, while still keeping a very wary eye on the extremely pissed-up English contingent who were becoming more and more boisterous. Zurich is like every other major European city in that it has (a) McDonalds and (b) a large Turkish community! Everyone knows that, even years before those poor Leeds fans were murdered, there is no love lost between the two sets of supporters, and we also knew that it would be only a matter of time before our paths crossed in this city, particularly as we were due to play them the following Wednesday. In the meantime, the riot police had called in reinforcements to keep the English under control as by now we were splitting up into smaller groups.

We ended up with a mixed mob, about 80–100-strong who were mainly Leeds, Man City and Chelsea, boosted by scatterings of smaller club members like ourselves. The riot police were trying to push everyone inside a small boozer and we sussed out that they were trying to trap us in there, so we told a few other mates to slip off with us; they didn't listen and that was the last we saw of them for a few hours. We eventually ended up in a pub full of Bristol City lads who, although we were all English, were not too friendly. Can't remember us having any history with them but they took a dislike to the two of us, so we drank up and fucked off before things got nasty.

As we were walking down the road, we got talking to a couple of lads who had also fucked off after being shunned by the Bristol lot, when we heard a bit of a commotion. Looking down the road, there was a handful of Turks shouting at me and Jaffa; the two English lads looked at each other and, without saying a word, just ran at them. They went scurrying to wherever they came from and we started laughing amongst ourselves, when we heard a whoosh sound and a bottle smashed against a wall a few feet away. We turned around and they were back, mob-handed, predictably tooled up and, as we all know, not afraid to use them. It was a case of trying to make it back to the boozer we had just left, knowing that it was full of the moody Bristol firm who surely would prefer to help us given the opposition.

One of us made it to the bar and banged on the window, and it must be something to do with cider, as they instantly came bouncing out ready to steam into us! I brought their attention to this little gang of Turks coming up the road and, with the help of our new mates, we took off up the road after the Turks who ran straight into a kebab shop and locked the door. By this time, more English had turned up and basically laid siege to this shop. In seconds, the doors had been kicked in and the shop was ransacked, much to the dismay of the owners who by now had fucked off upstairs.

The riot squad arrived and we were forced into another boozer and the doors were locked. After a few minutes, the police then fired a CS gas canister through the pub window and the bar was like a gas chamber with everyone choking and blind with their eyes streaming. After a minute or two, they calmly opened the doors and let us all stumble outside, gasping for air; instead, we got battered, as they laid into us with batons, it was payback time and they didn't miss the opportunity to get even.

None of us are moaning about it, our lot deserved it, but there were plenty in that bar who were innocent supporters, people who probably respected the police until that night!

The attack was indiscriminate and many were arrested and beaten for basically being in the wrong place at the wrong time. A few of us managed to get away but came across a load of Turks who seemed to have been given the right to mob up, carry weapons and attack the English. It was a tight call – head back to the bar and get arrested, deported and probably arrested again on arrival and banned, or chance your hand on the streets of Zurich which may as well have been the streets of Istanbul.

We went for the street option and straight away trouble erupted. The Turks had the numbers and the blades, and, during this little battle, at least two English lads suffered knife wounds. We were chased and swearing for revenge and during a break in the trouble when we were getting our breath back, regrouping and checking each other for stab wounds, there was a more light-hearted moment.

A huge skinhead came walking over to us and told us in his best English that he was from Germany and hated the Turks more than we did. We had a laugh with him, or at him, and we told him it was impossible, winding him up but he was deadly serious. Zurich is a bit like Amsterdam with a lot of people riding around on bikes, so we challenged him to prove his hatred to the Turkish nation by picking a bike up and putting it through the only remaining window that hadn't been smashed in the kebab shop. This he duly did, which had everyone laughing their heads off, leaving the German nutcase feeling as proud as punch.

Fun over, we got our act together and we were off to find the knife-wielding Turks. Zurich has a river running through it, which means the sensible ones have to cross the little bridges to get from one side to the other. The Turks were in a bar on the other side of the river, which amused us, considering Muslims are not supposed to drink alcohol, and, as we headed there, the police had cottoned on to what was about to happen and quickly blocked the bridges off. The Turks came out of the bar, giving it the large one, thinking that we were all stranded on the other side of the river when from nowhere a mob of English lads who had it over into the same street as the Turks piled into them. All the police were holding us back and the locals were routed, forcing the police to leave us and try and control the one-sided street battle over the river. It was bedlam and it took them ages to restore order. By the time we were escorted back to our hotels, it was midnight and this had been going on for six hours.

The following day we managed to cross the border into Liechtenstein but loads got turned back. The match day was pretty uneventful after Friday's trouble, but that night back in Zurich there was the odd skirmish and, during one of them, one of our lads, Twinny was bottled by a Turk, which caused him to miss his flight home the next day.

Overall, it was a cracking weekend, which will be remembered by all who were there.

Some will remember it more than others! What Ian and Jaffa didn't know was that, during the many disturbances involving the Turkish population in Zurich, three Englishmen were shot!

One of them was a Bristol City fan nicknamed Scooter.

SCOOTER, BRISTOL CITY:

Following England away was supposed to be a bit of fun and the last thing you would expect is to come home on crutches with bullet holes in yer legs. That was me, and this is how I ended up in that situation when, on 29 March, I flew out with 30 Bristol City from Heathrow to Zurich on our way to the England game with Liechtenstein.

After dumping our bags, we meet up with Funtime and his mob that had flew out the day before us. We all met up for a few beers and by early evening, our mob was up to 60–70-strong, with a few more lads that had got there by train, and a couple had even driven their way over. Pure CSF lads and we had always had a following on the England scene going way back with Beanie and Chewbar and his mob, but from the Italy game of '97 everyone started going in bigger numbers. With City languishing down the bottom of the lower leagues, because they were basically crap to watch with nothing to laugh and sing about, more and more of us started to go the England games just to experience the buzz in going to a game. The biggest turnout being was when we played Holland away in a friendly and we had around 120 all meet up in the Globe in Amsterdam.

In Zurich, as usual, we staked our claim to a bar we nicknamed the Bicycle Bar, due to the fact one of the Nursery Squad lads (early CSF breakaway mob) was riding a bike all round the bar and wouldn't let go of it in case somebody tried to nick it, even taking it to the toilet with him just in case and this is a bike that he had pinched himself off somebody. As the night went on, we started to go round to a few different bars, even bumping into a few good Pompey lads who we all got on well with, maybe because they are like us in the South. It was all banter and lads on the piss and nothing going on that was malicious or too bad. Not until the group I was with started to walk back to what was the CSF HQ and we witnessed a row going on in a kebab shop. We stood and watched the entertainment and decided to leave when we see the windows going through, as nobody wanted to get a tug from the Old Bill just a night before the game.

We were back in the Bicycle Bar, drinking into the night, when a few of our lads came in and said the locals, which turned out to be Turks, were getting a bit lively, due to their kebab shop getting turned over. Nobody seemed to take any notice, even with the sound of sirens and police now starting to park at the bottom of the road with the odd vehicle driving by, having a nose to see who's around. When you've been travelling with England a lot, you get used to all that, but we hadn't seen much apart from the kebab shop, and the area we were in seemed calm enough.

Suddenly, Funtime and a few of his mob had come in, saying the route they had taken back had the narrow street roads all covered in glass where the locals had took to bombarding the England fans walking from the bars with bottles and all kinds of objects. Now we had come by the same route and nothing like that happened, so we were all persuaded to go back up to take a look. Which we did and reached the square with several narrow lanes leading off it and saw the lads were right, as this little square appeared covered in glass. More concerning was the sight of a mob of locals about 20 metres away, which made us stop, as we didn't want to walk into something stupid. Same time we stopped, another mob of English entered the street from another lane who turned out to be Villa. This was purely coincidence but, obviously, to them it looked like we were a mob coming for them. So, now, the locals have come out into the street and started to gesticulate, and we've stood there and it all looks like it's going to go off. The locals broke into a charge and come running at us, throwing bottles; we've stood, even though we didn't have any weapons because we didn't expect to be attacked.

Next thing, you heard a popping sound and you just thought, Fucking hell, they're shooting at us or something, but you just assume that it's one of those BB guns or something like that. Anyway, as I went to turn because we were getting hit by all these bottles and we didn't have anything to throw back at them, the back of my leg felt like it had been hit by a cricket bat or something. So I am hobbling along shouting to my mates, 'Fucking hell, I think I've been shot here.' They went, 'You what? No, can't be!' Then, next minute, I went down on the ground, as I got hit in the other leg then. So I was down on the ground and it was absolute mayhem around me. I couldn't get up and your thoughts change to one of preservation then, so I managed to crawl to a café which had a number of plastic chairs, and I just scrambled myself underneath them and made a makeshift barrier with them. I can't remember what went on from there but what I was told by the other lads, who remember it clearly and say they've never seen anything quite like it. What it was, there was these locals came running down the street with their two gunmen that were firing and they got one lad, stabbed him in the back and they shot him. Another got a permanent groove in the top of his head, which had blood pouring out when he got caught by a ricochet. Someone had a nasty hand injury from a rubber bullet when the police waded in to try to break it all up.

The police that were around were at first slow to react and the locals that did the charge stayed on the run and disappeared down various alleys. News travels fast, and soon reached our other lads in other bars. One of them, Beanie, said it was like World War I because, as lads were coming in injured, other lads were going out to try to engage the locals in revenge missions.

I remember Magic and another lad Navy, they came and grabbed me, then picked me up and ran me back up to the bar and laid me back down on the ground. Luckily, the lad Navy was on stand-by at the time for the Gulf War and was there taking charge and telling everybody what to do and to get the pressure on and everything else, and made the barman phone a ambulance, etc, etc. By then, I was drifting in and out of consciousness, when they wrapped me up in the old silver foil and put me in an ambulance. Those lads were tops and I remember my legs were saturated with blood, with blood pumping out of me, particularly the leg with the three in-and-out bullet wounds. They were putting pressure on my groin to stem the flow of blood, unaware that was where wound number four was as well. I was screaming at them to get off me leg and I could hear Navy going, 'No, don't do it, keep the pressure on.' There's me: 'Fucking get off me leg,' but I was drifting in and out and he stuck to his guns. I don't think he was too impressed because he had a white Rockport coat on that, by now, was red and white.

The other injured lads got picked up in the square by police ambulance and taken to the university hospital, while I got taken to a different one. I still thought about getting to the game even if patched up, without realising that, when I came round in hospital, I had lost a day and a half and the game was over in Liechtenstein. Some of the boys came in to see me and asked how I was and good old morphine had taken hold of me, as I turned round and said, 'I'm all right I'll be out of here later.' With not being able to feel any pain, I didn't know how bad I really was. The boys were quite funny, as they wheeled in a wheelchair and said, 'Come on, we're taking you home.'

Five days later, I was still in hospital with open wounds and being kept on a drip with tubes, which is a bit heartbreaking when you watch all your mates leave one by one and you're sat there, thousands of miles away, all on yer own.

I ended up being shot four times, one in the right leg and three in the left leg. A total of three lads got shot and another two got stabbed. I was lucky to get myself out of the direct line of fire, even though I didn't realise I'd got hit so many times. One of the bullets went through the top of my groin and come out through the base of me bum, which was pure luck because it wasn't far away from my main artery. One went through the back of my right knee and out through the side of the patella muscle, one went off me shin and down my left shin and out again, and the one that did the most damage was the one that went through my left leg and straight through and ripped through my hamstring and tore it all apart. Even now, three years later and after extensive physiotherapy treatment, I have lost 30 per cent of my strength in that particular one leg. The left leg is still numb from where the bullet went through on my shin because it severed the ligament nerves. So, it is all basically numb and tingly from my shin down to the ankle, because the damage a bullet does is that it's not like a cut that tears, as you can't find the nerve ends to be able to stitch them back together again.

The hospital looked after me quite well and another thing I didn't realise was I had been made a Ward of Court and they had taken my passport away. The police were treating it as attempted murder and said I was in the wrong place at the wrong time and that I had been rather lucky, as I had been shot with a 9mm Koschler and it was lucky that the bullets bounced off me shin rather than shatter the bone. The police showed me these photos of the square, which showed all these plastic cones dotted around. I said what's with the cones, and they said that's to mark all the shell casings. The police did the usual interview and took statements, which didn't mean anything to me, to be honest, as I had never seen these blokes before and was likely never to see again. The last dealing with the police was when I had to hobble down to the police station to collect my stuff and have my photograph taken. There was this inspector there who asked me what I was going to do now, if they gave me my passport back. I was kind of dumbfounded and looked at them before replying that I was going home, and they said now you are not going to go back into the town and look for this man for retribution. I've gone, 'No, you've got no chance, I'm here on crutches, can hardly fucking walk and I'm on me own in a foreign town!'

So they gave me back my passport there on the spot, upon

which I was supposed to go back up to the hospital but I went straight out the police station, jumped into a taxi to take me to the airport and got on the first British Airways flight back home.

One of the few papers to report the horrific goings-on was the *Observer*, whose sports news correspondent Dennis Campbell wrote, 'Three England fans were shot, and two others stabbed, amid violent clashes in Zurich yesterday in which police fired tear gas and rubber bullets to quell the disturbances.

'All five were taken to hospital early yesterday after unrest in the Swiss city's old town involving around 100 supporters who were attending last night's game in nearby Liechtenstein. The three shot fans were aged 32, 37 and 38, all underwent surgery.

'It was unclear who shot them. Swiss Police denied responsibility and said that they only fired rubber bullets. One report said they were shot by locals after England fans had smashed up a snack bar.

'Twenty-five England fans were arrested in total after bottles were thrown at police and shop windows were smashed at the end of an evening's heavy drinking. The stabbed victims were aged 38 and 42, but none of the five victims had been named.'

The reports are vivid to say the least but what is interesting is the age of the victims. The majority of the 'lads' who follow England and go about rampaging, as was the case in Zurich, are in their early to mid-twenties; you would think that, among five hospitalised victims, at least one of them might come from within this age group. That alone suggests that at least some of the victims could have been law-abiding supporters, who were either shot or stabbed indiscriminately.

The other point of interest is the lack of press coverage given to the shootings particularly. Imagine the uproar and level of media coverage had the incident occurred at an England home game, and the victims were away supporters.

Recent trouble in Manchester, after England's game with Wales – which, in reality, was a bit of running around with probably a dozen punches thrown in a two-hour period – saw CCTV footage played during peak-hour news bulletins. A total of 41 men were convicted after a nationwide appeal to help track down the culprits, and the majority of them have since been sent to prison. There were no reports of anyone being injured or treated in hospital during the violence.

The men shot and stabbed in Zurich in March 2003 undoubtedly watched the footage and read the front-page headlines from Manchester with more than a tinge of resentment towards the British media and the way they report trouble at England games!

CHAPTER TWENTY-SEVEN

BANNED
TURKEY 2003

On 11 October 2003, England played Turkey, needing a draw to qualify for the European Championships the following summer in Portugal. Usually, thousands of fans would make the trip, however, at the game there were maybe 20 England fans in the crowd of 42,000. This was down to the decision made by the English FA not to accept any of the 4,000 tickets their Turkish counterparts were offering.

With hindsight, it was probably the correct decision, but there were many fans who were disgusted by it and there were also a few who swore to take no notice of the ban. As always, the press had a field day and, in the lead-up to the game, all sorts of reports were being bandied about that the game would still turn into a bloodbath. Mac worked for an established TV network at the time and he was one of those who were glad he didn't have to go. For weeks before the game, which saw predictions of deaths if any English fans dared make the trip to 'Hell', the papers were happy to get the views of fans, police, social experts and even Turkish gangs who promised to kill and maim any English who dared show up.

In the end, a football match was played and nobody was killed, England qualified and everyone was happy – apart from the Turks. It was probably the biggest police overkill in the history of football and the biggest anti-climax for those who were expecting a bloodbath.

MAC:

It is not easy being a member of the press, or the enemy, as we are also known to the majority of the lads who follow England. I've experiences of some who hate us almost as much as the police. It is even harder for me, as, for years, I was an Old Trafford regular and, believe it or not, got into plenty of scrapes during the 80s when I was studying at Manchester University. I am not a lover of many of the people who I have to work with when covering England games, but it is my job and a career I enjoy, so I do my best to get as much out of it as I can. This does not mean I stoop as low as some who work alongside me.

What many people will not realise is that there are plenty of journalists like myself who also despise the people who give our profession a bad name, and, yes, there are one or two out there guilty of that. We see first-hand the goings-on and it's not just the foreign press lads who offer inducements to lads to kick off or throw a bottle or plastic chair 'to get things going'. The problem we have is that we are often told that, if we value our jobs, then we have to turn a blind eye to such underhand goings-on. Word gets about and, if you are seen as an objector to the way some respond to the competition and deadline pressures of work, you soon find yourself struggling for work.

In all my time working for various agencies and directly for the media I have been to scores of England games and witnessed some crazy things happen and also been scared shitless more than once. I must admit, though, to being a little bit happy when the news was announced that the game in Turkey was strictly 'No Go!'

It was months before the game was played that the press first got wind that the FA might not take up the allocation on offer. Just days after, England played Turkey at the Stadium of Light when racial taunts were hurled at Turkish players and fans and the pitch was invaded by fans following each goal in England's 2–0 win. There was a genuine hatred towards the Turkish that night but, then again, the FA were foolish if they thought it would be any different. Most of the lads were surprised that the game was held so close to Leeds and that the away-ticket allocation even left FA headquarters, given that in April 2000 two Leeds fans died in Istanbul during street brawls ahead of a UEFA Cup semi-final match with Galatasaray.

In an attempt to offset any major punishment, FA sources revealed that they were 'highly unlikely' to take any of the 4,000–5,000 tickets they were entitled to for the volatile match in Turkey, a match the FA and police chiefs feared could spark violent clashes between rival supporters.

Details of the FA's stance emerged as they waited to hear how UEFA would punish the pitch invasions and racist chants, which had marred the 2–0 win over Turkey. It was feared that UEFA could make them play the qualifier on 11 June against Slovakia in Middlesbrough behind closed doors, given that they had dealt with Slovakia and Georgia in a similar way for racist abuse and object-throwing by their fans during games against England and the Republic of Ireland. The outcome was far more lenient, though, and the English FA were fined the sum of £68,000, at the same time warning anybody who had not heard it said so many times before that England could face expulsion from the tournament if there were any repeat scenes.

It was Assistant Chief Constable Ron Hogg of Durham Police, the officer in charge of policing England's away games, who advised the FA not to take any fans to Turkey, and it was a decision that was met with a mixed reaction from supporters.

Kevin Miles, the Football Supporters Federation's director of international affairs, said that, despite their claims to the contrary, the FA's decision ignored representations made by fans last week. We met with the FA last week and expressly said that we thought they should take tickets. No one is questioning that it will be dangerous but there are decent fans who are not interested in trouble, who will travel, regardless of whether they have tickets or not.

'These are people who have been travelling to England games for 20 years, before David Davies and others arrived at the FA, and they want to go. But by not taking an allocation there will be no segregation, no stewarding, and it will be more dangerous.

'The way to drive the far right and the louts out of the game is to marginalise them. Unfortunately, many of the FA's initiatives push in the other direction.'

Other fans felt that, while they would have liked to travel to Istanbul, the decision was probably the right one. Vernon Powell, who has followed England for 25 years, said, 'I agree with the decision not to take our allocation. The best-case scenario is that it would be a cracking match, with England fans getting to enjoy Istanbul. The worst-case scenario is that we get a repeat of what happened when Leeds played Galatasaray and England fans get loads of bad press.'

The government then got involved and made a lame attempt to appease millions of non-Sky viewers by asking BSkyB to share live coverage of the match with a terrestrial broadcaster, claiming it might dissuade fans from travelling to the match!

Sports Minister Richard Caborn said it would act as a further deterrent for fans travelling to Istanbul without tickets, although the fact that you would be wandering around the dangerous Turkish city with no ticket and in small numbers probably acted as a better deterrent to many!

The argument that English hooligans would travel to Turkey anyway, thus causing more problems as they would not be segregated or under any supervision, did not really wash with many, as one paper was quick to point out: 'Part of the attraction of these trips is the large official travelling England contingent and the policing and paraphernalia that is now, depressingly, part and parcel of these events. Without "official" England fans, a trip to "Hell" would be far too dangerous and unattractive a prospect for English fans.'

They had a point and only the most hardcore hooligans would

dream of showing, and they were all on a database that would make it virtually impossible to leave the country, let alone slip into Turkey.

It was reported that the tightest security operation for a sporting event was mounted for the game and British Police questioned all those boarding flights for Istanbul in London and Manchester, warning British nationals they were likely to be turned back if the Turkish authorities believed they intended to go to the game. Two men were detained on arrival in Istanbul, where British police spotters were in operation.

On the eve of the game, Istanbul's Taksim Square, scene of the fatal stabbing of two Leeds United supporters three years earlier showed not a trace of menace, while reporters and cameramen were hard pressed to spot a single England fan, as the country closed its borders to anyone arriving from Britain hoping to circumvent the Football Association's ticket ban and travel to the Sukru Saracoglu Stadium for the match.

Another paper reported, 'The usual xenophobic songs were conspicuous by their absence and most of the noise came from the calls to prayer from the minarets and Turkish fans sounding their horns, as they made their way through the chaotic traffic to Fenerbahce's ground on the city's Asian side.'

Fortunately, most England fans had heeded the warnings from the FA and the government to not even attempt the journey, and those that did found themselves detained at the city's Ataturk Airport and sent back home on the first available flight.

Sky News were quick to report that 45 supporters had been refused admission and that most were members of the England Travel Club. The unsympathetic FA confirmed that all would have their membership revoked. Other non-members were identified as England fans simply by checking the stamps in their passports against the dates of previous away matches. Just two of them were subject to banning orders after previous misdemeanours and were promptly arrested.

David Swift, Deputy Chief Constable of Staffordshire Police and the man in charge of the British Police operation, estimated that around 200 supporters might have evaded the checks and made it to Istanbul, mostly by entering the country earlier in the week, but those who had been intercepted had accepted their fate.

All were men aged between 22 and 35 who, according to Swift, were 'the usual stereotypes'. He gave credit to some of the fans who tried to make it to the game, though, and said that some were more inventive than others. 'Two insisted they were travelling to visit the war graves at Gallipoli, they just happened to be arriving on Thursday and had return tickets for Sunday, but no onward flights booked,' said Swift.

Another took out a letter explaining that he had won a prize of a weekend in Istanbul paid for by Miss World Promotions as a reward for judging a beauty contest. The spotters were unimpressed and escorted him to a holding room.

One fan discovered in the city said he had evaded the net by arriving in a sharp suit and claiming that he had a business meeting in Ankara, but even he faced a further even tougher challenge in getting to the stadium, as, although black-market tickets appeared to be plentiful, Turkish Police had set up three concentric security rings around the ground at which all supporters were asked to show their identity cards, with any non-Turkish citizens being turned away. Even if that proved no barrier – a highly unlikely scenario – any England fans spotted inside the ground faced being sent to a secure room to watch the game on television and this is what happened to two enterprising England fans dressed in Turkish shirts who were arrested outside the ground a few hours before the kick-off.

The operation was mounted by the Turkish Police with the full co-operation of the English authorities, and, once again, chief of the British operation Swift was keen to get his name in the papers, saying, 'The most obvious way to reduce the threat of disorder is to ensure that the two sets of supporters do not come in contact with each other.' (The man is clearly a genius.) He added, 'Had we not taken these measures, there probably would have been 15,000 travelling to this game.'

Meanwhile, Turkish football fans had warned that any

England fan who defied the FA's pleas and slipped the security net should show respect for the Turkish country and flag, or be done for!

'Turkish fans are ready to counter any revenge planned by England fans for the killing of Leeds United supporters Chris Loftus and Kevin Speight after a UEFA Cup game against Galatasaray of Istanbul in 2000, and previous clashes with Man United fans,' ran the story in one tabloid.

'A special summit meeting between the highly organised "Ultra" gangs supporting Istanbul rivals Galatasaray and Fenerbahce was called last weekend at a restaurant high above the city to discuss unity against England and any English fans who might provoke them at the fixture.'

The leader of the Galatasaray pack, Sabahattin Sabin, and a man called Sefa, his counterpart at Fenerbahce, stressed that their gangs would not start trouble against England fans, but that insults to Turkey and the Turkish flag in particular would 'be punished'.

'What we are saying is this,' concluded Turkish fan Oguz Altay, 'we will not attack, but, if the English mock our country and our flag, we won't be too gentle in our response.'

In the Istanbul suburb of Umraniye, professed members of a Galatasaray gang called 'Stay Out All Night' that supposedly carried out the attack on the Leeds supporters were more overt in their threats. Willing to admit that they all carry knives, one of the number, Ekrem Altayh, said, 'We are faster because the English are always drunk. If you abuse this country like Leeds did, you die again.'

It was a chilling threat but, as the team arrived in Istanbul, the welcome was lukewarm by the often fiery standards Turkish supporters reserve for English teams. Previously, visiting teams have been subjected to a hostile reception, most notably when Man United and Chelsea were greeted with banners reading 'Welcome to Hell', but there was a heavy police presence which ensured that no hostile fans could get near the team. There were more than 50 security guards, local police and several British

Police officers providing protection but most of the noise came from young girls screaming at David Beckham.

MAC:
So the lucky or unlucky few were given permission to attend the game, those who were either very brave or stupid went over to keep an eye on the crowds. I did neither and watched the game on television, in the safety of my own home. I probably could have got a trip there out of some agency if I had tried hard enough, but, to be honest, having been over there reporting at Man United's games and speaking to lads who were there when the Leeds supporters were murdered, I didn't fancy it one little bit!

There were no doubt many fans who did the same as Mac, but a few did not! John, who is a legend at his home club Portsmouth but has also been a regular and genuine England follower for many years, decided to see if the ban was breakable!

JOHN, PORTSMOUTH:
We had booked flights and accommodation months before the advice not to travel to Turkey, advice, which was then followed up with the ban. Regardless of what the FA and police were saying, we decided to travel as we were not doing anything illegal and felt strongly that more would be done for the loyal fans that follow the England team by the FA and government – some chance!

I drove up to Bolton on the Thursday straight from work at about 6pm, arriving at about 11pm, and stayed with my mate Fernie (who is now sadly dead). We were up early the next morning as we had to catch a plane at 10am from Manchester to Istanbul and, as soon as we got to the airport, the police spotters pulled Fernie but not myself. Although they told him he could fly out, they warned him that there was little if any chance that he would be allowed into the country. We still decided to go, even knowing that once we had left we would not get a refund on the flight. We arrived in Istanbul that afternoon and were immediately stopped at Customs by British police intelligence officers and were detained and had our passports confiscated. It was a total farce, the English Police blamed the Turkish Customs for not allowing us into the country and the Turkish Customs blamed the English Police!

Regardless of who was to blame, we were told we were not getting into Turkey and were then locked up for two hours with other English fans. (They said we were being detained but there was no difference, we could not leave a small room and were given no food or drink.) At about 6pm, we were all put on a flight back to London, despite telling them we were going back to Manchester, and we arrived in Gatwick late that night. I got a train to Euston and managed to get a National Express coach back to Bolton where I picked my car up at 8am, and drove back to Portsmouth in time to watch the game live on the telly in the Newcom Arms with my mates!

I had been travelling for two days solid and spent hundreds of pounds just to watch the game back where I started from!

Sometimes you wonder about your sanity when you follow football!

Obviously, John had not used the most imaginative route to try to breach the security operation surrounding the game. Will, a Man City fan, was more determined and used his vast experience of European travel and work contacts to his advantage in an attempt to see the game. This is his experience of being a lone Englishman in a stadium full of hostile Turks.

WILL, MAN CITY:
Working abroad for a living sometimes brings unexpected bonuses like the one on the 11 October 2003. England were playing at the Sukru Saracoglu Stadium, home of Fenerbahce who, in one of Man City's darkest moments, kicked us out of the European Cup in 1968, so making Malcolm Allison look

and sound ridiculous as his (stupid) statement of we'll terrify Europe came back to haunt him and many others at the time! He was right, though, as, a couple of years later, we won the Cup Winners Cup.

I was working as a contractor with a Turkish airline and managed to put off travelling to Istanbul until the Monday before the game. By now, the security operation was in full swing and it was a case of 'Shit they've taken my passport away', which they don't usually do. No worries, back comes the tart with the nose and, although I feared the worst, it was OK. No problems with the football police, the local immigration just wanted to know why I had been spending so much time in the place over the last couple of years. I smiled and told them I was a highly skilled aircraft engineer, who was responsible for keeping their fleet of aircraft in the sky.

I was in! And it was time for a beer, as I waited for the shuttle to appear for the Polat Renaissance hotel. All week, the local TV was full of reports of lads being turned back at airports, ports and borders.

By Tuesday morning, I had four tickets in hand – one for me, one for a mate who was working in Bodrum, but whose missus wouldn't let him come after he made the silly mistake of telling her he was going to the match. Another was my 'get into the game' banker and was for my tour guide, my direct boss at Turkish Air, Altug, who was going to pull strings at the checkpoints like a puppeteer. My (by now) best mate Altug wanted to go to the game; it was far too early and we decided to commence a pub crawl from the dock to the ground. By now, I was starting to feel like ET, as every Turk popped their head out to look at the alien!

Altug insisted that I had to wear a red and white band round my head which I went along with, as, although it was a bit gay, I pointed out that it was England's colours. So armed with Turkish Airlines jacket, pass and various cards and other crap picked up from my time working in the

States, the Turk boss and his 'alleged' Boeing rep make their way into the ground.

First checkpoint, no problem – Got a ticket? OK then. Second checkpoint, we got the 'You don't look Turkish', so leave all the talking to Altug, who explained how I've never been to a 'soccer' match and really wanted to attend a big one – like the Superbowl!

Now for the big one, at the gate, ticket taken, and I'm fucking only in! Joy was short-lived as they are mob-handed, the full *Midnight Express* police lookalikes all waiting at the other side. I was searched and questioned and my camera was taken off me, as Altug was given the hard treatment now, and one of the things he was told was that, if I did kick off, he's responsible — now I'm not the most intelligent bloke around, but one against 41,999 did not sound good odds although I let him explain it better than that.

I was in the ground far too early for my liking and I stood out like the proverbial sore thumb. One look around the ground was enough to see it was not a wise move to play up; there were some lovely greetings from the natives, 'you will drown in the Bosporus' being a particular favourite!

The game kicked off and, like the anthem, I can't remember much about it, to be honest, a combination of the ale and a desire for self-preservation kicked in. I do remember shouting out loud something like 'you fucking wanker' to that overrated twat, as he skied a penalty (not for the last time), and the way he looked at the pitch as though it was the grass's fault! At half-time, 0 0 was fine, that'll do. There was a bit of a squabble between the players as they were going off. I think it was Alpay saying something to Beckham that started it, but who really cares, I was not going to join in.

During the break, the cops saw fit to give me my own personal police guard and my camera back, and one sat next to me for the entire second half, which came and went in a flash. It was by no means a classic but we got the right result and, as the players danced on the pitch, making the locals even more irate, I was left with the big problem of 'How do I get out of here in one piece?'

The memories of Leeds were there, as I walked to the gates, which were only a few yards away from our exit point. I walked over to them, looking as if I knew the place as well as the locals and understood the signs, only to soon make a total twat of myself, when the gates were locked and everyone turned to see me shaking them as my guide shook his head and pointed towards the far exit worryingly.

It was the longest walk of my life and then the relief was there, as I spotted the road! I was off, bollocks to Altug, he'd served his purpose. I was a top sprinter now, Carl Lewis on speed couldn't have caught me. More luck, a free taxi! In I dived, locked the doors, skulked down in the seat and we were off across the Bosporus – stick your flag, you Turkish twats. This 16-stone lump of English rump is not drowning here boys!

I got back to Champions, a massive sports bar at the Polat, lashed a few strong ones down and, getting a bit braver than an hour before, was half hoping that it'd have a few sad Turks to laugh at – not a one – not good losers that lot, they never even had the footie on the telly, so it was a case of drink more beer and order some bird wings and off to bed shit-faced but happy and dreaming of Portuguese beaches – if we're not banned! Although, after the night I had just had, it was a case of: 'It would be easier than this, so fuck them I'll go anyway!'

I flew home a day later and can say hand on heart that I never, in the whole time I was over there, saw another English person. I have since met a few who did go and also more than a few who *claimed* to have been there but who I believe to be cowshitters. It has since been confirmed that a few of the Chelsea lads and a West Ham bird were there, so reports of no one being there were lies – there was at least six of us!

Will was one of only a handful who saw the match from inside the ground. Police reported that over 50 supporters had been detained and sent home with only two of them suspected troublemakers.

The detained fans complained that they were in a group of 20 that were held in a room for 16 hours without food and water and one, Clive Adams said they were 'treated like dirt'.

Another fan, builder Rick Farmary, 31, from Nottingham, who arrived back at Heathrow, said he was with three friends who wanted to watch the match at a Turkish hotel and had arranged to meet Turkish friends in Istanbul because he had paid for the flights before the ban was imposed. 'I've spent a lot of money for this and I am gutted. We were warned but not told that we were not able to go and we were treated like animals.'

Other returning fans at Heathrow had a different story. Micky Fuller, a plasterer from Banstead, Surrey, who spent £250 on his return flight, said he had been treated well and had no complaints. Some British consular officials had even bought supporters burgers and chips at the airport, he said.

He said he would have tried to buy tickets in Istanbul for the match and admitted it was 'his own fault' for ignoring official warnings. 'We were told that there would be a 99.9 per cent chance that we would be turned back but if they give us 0.1 per cent then we were going to try.

'At the end of the day it is your own fault but it was unfair that well-behaved fans like me who were not subject to travel restrictions should be banned.'

So, despite a few getting through the tight security ring and around 50 being sent home, the match passed off peacefully, England qualified and Turkey didn't make the finals. Security-wise, it was probably a good thing, as, despite over 2,000 hooligans being banned from the finals, there were thousands more who would have found it a lot easier to get into Portugal than it was to enter Turkey, and, in many of the Englishmen's eyes, there was still unfinished business to attend to!

CHAPTER TWENTY-EIGHT

A JOB WELL DONE?
EURO 2004

England arrived in Portugal on a crest of a wave, they had topped a difficult group having won six and drawn two of their eight games and were regarded as one of the Championship favourites. Under the stewardship of super Sven, the nation's hopes were high, although much of the optimism was generated by wonder kid Wayne 'Once a Blue, always a Blue, soon to be a Red' Rooney, who had blasted himself on to the world stage with some breathtaking displays for club and county in the lead-up to Euro 2004.

There was even optimism off the field, as domestically football violence was in decline and banning orders had been secured on a total of 2,188 fans, although, with an estimated 200,000 English tourists expected in Portugal during the tournament, 50,000 of whom were there solely for the football, the Portuguese authorities rightly had to be prepared for the worst, and they did!

A week before the opening game, the host's police force took great delight in unveiling their operation plans, and it was an impressive, if somewhat over-the-top, propaganda exercise, obviously intended to deter potential troublemakers from travelling or misbehaving.

Besides the 50,000 law enforcers in Portugal, made up of the gendarmerie and state police, the Portuguese government had spent some €16.5 million on new police equipment, which included more than 150 new police cars and the country's first water-cannon vehicles, while some 20,000 police officers were to be equipped with truncheons, riot gear, pepper spray and police dogs, while a select group would be armed with rifles that would fortunately only fire rubber bullets, which had locals wondering if it was a football championship or a war they were staging!

The announcement also gave detailed information of how they planned to police the event with the Portuguese authorities opting for a 'three-tier plan' to combat any violence, with highly visible cops on the beat, 'intervention officers' who would handle trouble on the spot immediately and forces on permanent alert. The announcement concluded that: 'Of particular concern is the Algarve, where many of England's 50,000 supporters are expected to stay, in the resort town of Albufeira.'

Organisers then switched the venues for two first-phase matches involving England to Lisbon, where policing of troublemakers would be easier, and cancelled all police holiday leave during the finals and pledged to hire another 2,000 officers to beef up security. Where the officers would be hired from remained a mystery, although there were fears that many of those 'hired' were just vigilante groups who were prone to brutality once given a sheriff's badge and baton for a month!

General Leonel Carvalho, who headed the police security at the Championships, said that his policy was one of 'gradually increasing response'! He added chillingly, 'It goes from softly softly to half-soft, to hard and then aggressive!'

Amongst all this nonsense, there was football to be played, and thousands descended on the coastal resorts in Portugal as predicted. Glenroy, a Birmingham City fan, was one of them:

GLENROY, BIRMINGHAM CITY:
I am not your typical England fan, mainly because I am black, but that has never put me off and I have rode the storm, as, over the years, the likes of my good self have been in the minority when following our national team abroad. I

say 'our' with pride, as I was born in England, have lived here all my life, so, despite what some of the confused bigots from Chelsea and the Villa think, I am, believe it or not, English!

I first went away with England in 1982 for the World Cup and was probably the first black face on the scene, so much so that, over there, I hardly had to buy a drink as everyone thought I was a Brazilian! The *Observer* were so shocked by my appearance that they even paid for me to stay in a plush hotel in return for a story of what it was like following England. I obliged but could not understand what all the fuss was about as I was not an alien, for fuck's sake!

Over the years, I have had my ups and downs, plenty of ups as the Zulu Army have always been well represented on the international scene, but also the odd down when the NF and C18 brigade have turned on us, usually when we were alone or in a small group. Lots of people will think that the England following are all racist but a lot of them just play up for the cameras with the Nazi salutes and 'There ain't no black in the Union Jack' bollocks, as most of the time the majority are fine and in some cases large gangs of white blokes have backed us up when the 'Master Race!' have called it on, the most famous instance being at the infamous Dublin riot when one group of well-known racists were sent packing with their tails between their legs!

Black and white, the Zulus decided that we were going to go to Portugal for the first three games, but our problem was getting there, as banning orders and people with plenty of convictions were plentiful in our group. There are certain people that nobody wants to travel with because the straight blokes think they will get stopped due to the company they are keeping, and, of the 30 of us who was going from Birmingham, I was one of the ones that nobody wanted to travel with, partly because I have got plenty of previous convictions and had a banning order from 2000, so nobody thought that I'd get through.

So, while everyone was looking forward to the trip, I was

left on my own half-expecting to get a tug at the airport, especially when I got to Birmingham Airport and saw the police operation that was in full swing.

I got through check in, got rid of my luggage and thought I was breezing it, until I got to passport control where I was greeted by about 20 coppers and they were all standing there, holding clipboards, looking at you. I was thinking, Fuck this, I'm not even going to look at faces, so I just walked through, give them my passport and my ticket and got through all right. I got a few nods and the odd smile but I didn't acknowledge them, as I thought that any second they were going to pull me over, as, to be truthful, it was all too easy. I just walked through head down and carried on walking and ... nothing! Not one question. And, when I met all the guys in the departure lounge, they were amazed and we sat down, had a few beers and caught the plane. One killjoy cheered me up by saying that they were letting me through before fucking dragging me off again, but they didn't and everything was sweet!

We flew into Faro and then jumped a taxi to Albufeira, as a few were going to the game in Lisbon and some of us were going straight to the resort on a bit of a football holiday, as I had tickets for the rest of the games but not the first one. I was bunking with four other geezers who weren't fighters or anything like that, and, on the first night, we came out of the apartment at about midnight and headed for the strip, which we ended up calling Kosovo because it was just proper mad.

At the top of the road leading to the strip there were hundreds of England fans singing 'No surrender', and it was echoing. It was not a football firm as such, just a load of lads with no tops on and all pissed up, but they had bottles and glasses in their hands and it didn't take an expert to know that it was all going to go off. As we had walked up, we saw the riot police down a side road by the hotel, so from the strip you couldn't see them but they were ready and looked like they were itching to go, all kitted out in their brand-new visors and jackets with their bats drawn ready to roll!

I thought we are going to have to watch ourselves, because, for one, the geezers I was with were not hooligans and, two, there were no black faces about, and I knew that, if I was spotted, the one black face would get nicked. The blokes I was with said they were getting off to a place called the Blues Bar where all the guys were meeting, but my heart ruled my head and my heart said, 'Stay and have a watch!' It's daft but it's in you – you know deep down you should fuck off but just can't, so I've stayed back and waited for it to get going!

It took less than a minute, and all it took was one bottle. Once one pissed-up lad decided to throw one, hundreds followed and the English piled down the hill throwing glasses and bottles at the police who started to bash a few people who were nearest them but who had done nothing wrong. That was it and the sky filled with missiles as the horses came round, which caused total mayhem; it was just a running battle in the street and I thought, Fucking hell, it's getting brilliant!

The English at first were doing all right because there was not that many coppers but the brave few who were getting carried away had not seen what I had on the way up and panic set in when the reinforcements came! It turned into a free-for-all, and the thing that was funny about the Portuguese with batons was that they seemed to be people who may not be police but who had been given a fluorescent jacket and became officers for the night, ordinary Portuguese folk who were well up for it and basically they've steamed in and were bashing England fans all over the place.

It was time to back off and I went upstairs into Lineker's bar and they shut the doors, and all you could see was the Old Bill steaming into the English and there were geezers trying to get into the pub but the doors were locked and they're getting killed outside for about 30 minutes. It was non-stop battling up and down the whole street, which in the end was just cleared.

That first night was just a taster and the next night it really went off big time because obviously the first night's goings-on have done the rounds all day, so later the firm that was about 500 is now about 1,000. But, for every extra England fan or tourist who wanted a bit of excitement, there were two more coppers and it started off the same as the night before with a bit of a stand-off between the police and the English.

We went to the Blues Bar and some of the young guys who came over with us had had an argument with three mad Russians who had steamed over and said we're going to have it with the English, but who had turned round and steamed into the coppers before running into this bar for cover with all our lot. It was stupid, as these loons were sitting there and on their black T-shirts they've got 'Russian Hooligans' written on the back. The gaffer of the bar had a phone call, saying that the police were going to raid the bar because they had a spotter who had seen an English hooligan who was leading or orchestrating all the violence outside come into the bar, and that they were going to come and get him.

The bloke was spot on and told us to go out the back door, so 20 of us got out the back door and set off across this mad field, which had a huge drop down on to some little side streets. As we're walking down this little side street away from the town and looking in the distance, there were lights coming up the road and moments later these 4x4 came flying past us, jammed his brakes on, the four doors have flown open and all these geezers dressed in black have come steaming towards us and everyone's shot their hands up.

As I have put my hands up, they've shone a torch in my face and said in broken English something about me being black, and 'You're not what we're looking for.' One of my mates, Gary, did a runner and they chased, caught him and battered him, basically kicking the fuck out of him. The rest of us were allowed to get away but they arrested Gary and we never saw him again until he went to court.

The following day, we went there and the obvious thing happened – you go in there, they don't want to speak English, and all the ones they'd arrested the night before and the previous night were all in the court at the same fucking time, which makes it look worse and Gary was given a two-year prison sentence. He was gobsmacked and thought he was going to prison, but they stuck him on a plane and sent him home. The funny thing about it was that, on the second night, I took my camera out and I took photographs of everyone in the pub and he never left the pub. All the pictures I'd taken had all the times and dates on them so, when he went to court, the time they were saying he was orchestrating all the violence, he was actually in the pub!

He got off the plane and, because they didn't send him down over there, he was rearrested and they tried to jail him in England, but their efforts failed and eventually they had to release him. It was crazy, as it was proved in Portugal that he was not guilty but, because they gave him jail then sent him home, the blind Home Secretary at the time called him a flaming hooligan after learning about him being arrested and charged, and called for him to do his time in England. Now this fella was in England at the time, cannot see the pictures I had taken and still wants the geezer to go to jail?! I'm all for equal rights but surely a bloke who needs a dog to help him across the fucking road should not be making calls like that one?

Blues fan Gary made the headlines and, as Glenroy said, there was uproar when he was sent home, having served just one night of a two-year sentence. But many fans who were caught up in the trouble in the Algarve claimed that they were innocent and, thankfully, David Blunkett did not have a say when it came to punishing them!

Apart from the two nights of rioting, the group stages passed peacefully enough and even the press were quick to praise England fans' behaviour and raised claims that the Portuguese Police had been heavy-handed in their treatment of many.

One paper reported, 'Two men from Manchester were among those who appeared in court in Portugal after being arrested in

violent clashes in Albufeira. The 12 England fans arrested
following the first night of fighting were led into the Albufeira
courthouse in handcuffs and among them were Paul Donohue
aged 21 from Heath Road, Manchester, and Jason Boyle aged 22
from Peter Wood Gardens, Stretford, Manchester. One of the 12
said, 'I'm innocent,' as he was led into the courthouse in Albufeira.
The men were arrested along with a Russian and a Portuguese
man after fighting broke out near the La Bamba bar in Albufeira
and one of them arrived in court wearing shorts covered in
bloodstains and had his arm in a cast.'

There was no defending the behaviour of hundreds in the
resort who, after a day's drinking, decided to call it on with the
local police and vigilantes, but some fans, however, said the
Portuguese Police were a little too aggressive in stopping potential
troublemakers.

English fans told reporters that the situation in Albufeira only
got out of hand because police officers were jittery. Paul Donahue,
who was among those deported, said that he suffered broken ribs
and other injuries from police brutality even though he wasn't
doing anything wrong. 'We just feel like we've been made
scapegoats,' Donahue told the BBC.

Portuguese Police denied they did anything wrong and
confirmed that they would stick to the methods employed
throughout the tournament. Captain Carlos Pereira of the GNR
Military Police said, 'My officers acted within the law following
outbreaks of violence and the detention of more than 40 England
supporters in the resort of Albufeira.'

His comments followed claims that his men had used batons
indiscriminately, hitting innocent bystanders as they dealt with
those throwing bottles, glasses and chairs, an allegation he denied
or seemed to justify!

'If they were not making trouble, they should not have been
there,' said Pereira. 'If they were there, then they have some risk –
the force was used only when necessary. This kind of
phenomenon, with 300 or 400 people together to commit violent
acts, is completely new to us.'

And he was scathing of those parents who had taken young children out to an area where trouble had been taking place. 'If people are there with children, they should take them home and protect them. I am surprised at how many are out late at night.'

He had a point, as, rightly or wrongly, who in their right mind would book a family holiday in a resort where thousands of football fans will be staying during a major tournament?

Despite the problems in Albufeira, officials were pleased with the operation and the Interior Ministry claimed that just 64 fans had been deported, a figure which included only 41 English. 'If we compare the figures to previous tournaments, I thought the numbers of arrests for public disorders would be relatively higher,' said Paolo Gomes, the deputy head of the committee responsible for tournament security. 'There is already talk of a new fan culture in Europe ... where people are concentrating on the soccer itself, on living the moment, on enjoying themselves.'

Mr Gomes was talking sense but, days later, his words would count for nothing, as an English fan was murdered in Lisbon.

Stephen John Smith from Wolverhampton was not a hooligan but a decent bloke who loved football and enjoyed travelling, and he was killed in a senseless stabbing. The 28-year-old England fan was stabbed to death in Lisbon by a local immigrant after trying to intervene as the pickpocket targeted fans celebrating England's 4–2 win over Croatia. A Ukrainian national was arrested and charged with Stephen's murder.

Superintendent Mick Treble of West Midlands Police, who revealed Mr Smith's identity after speaking to his parents, said at the time, 'I must emphasise that this is not a football-related incident. This is a tragic incident in which a young man who was fulfilling his dream of travelling the world has died.'

A Foreign Office spokesman earlier said it had been 'completely peaceful' overnight and there were no reported arrests of any England fans.

Superintendent Treble's comments were true, the incident was not football-related, but, as Man United fan Eddie Beef says, the press were not happy about that.

EDDIE, MAN UNITED:

Portugal had not gone well for me. I had jibbed it over but on the way to the first game was in a car smash and I had bust myself up, with my ribs and chest all over the place. With a few beers, I got by, as you do, and was a lot better after a week and was enjoying the football as England were doing well and, like most of the fools out there, thought we may even win the thing!

After the Croatia game, we were all on the lash and it was a party mood, daft congas and plenty of the face-painted fans not shy in getting a round in, which was just as well as I was skint! We were all in a square, a couple of hundred, and no trouble at all. I have been to loads of these things and can say, hand on heart, that Portugal was the friendliest of them all, by a mile.

Every big city has got its share of pains in the arse – fuck me, Manchester is one of the worst, with your bag heads and *Big Issue* sellers, it is hard to keep your cool at times – and this place had plenty of pests, mainly tramps and beggars, but one bloke was particularly annoying and was trying to blag and rob people all night and was told dozens of times to fuck off before he got filled in.

I was sitting with a few lads from various places and we were having a good laugh and, all of a sudden, this bloke came back and stabbed the young Wolves bloke for nothing; there was uproar and the police were there in minutes and dragged the bloke away, while the stabbed lad was taken to hospital where he was pronounced dead on arrival.

We were all stunned and it was a sad time, so, in the morning, a few of us went back there and some put flowers down where he had died and someone else put an England shirt there as a mark of respect. It was all dignified, until the press turned up. I'm no lover of them at the best of times, but that morning they deserved a kicking. They were offering money and drinks to people if they could give details of 'the fight'! What fucking fight?! There was no fight, it was a cowardly attack on an innocent bloke trying to enjoy himself.

I had little money left but would not take a drink from the scum, as that is all they were and eventually they got wise and pissed off before somebody put one on them. When I got home, I contacted the lad's family and was invited to his funeral and attended what was a truly great send-off. I have been in some problems at the football over the years and am no angel, but that day made me realise how senseless it all is. You go away to watch a game of football and you expect to come home alive; that lad never and I will always be sad for his family because they were real decent people, and, try as they could, the press could not slant that any other way.

England stayed on in Lisbon and were knocked out by hosts Portugal in yet another penalty shoot-out defeat. The fans' good behaviour continued and there were reports that fans on both sides shook hands and exchanged compliments. On the streets of Lisbon, euphoric Portuguese, flags wrapped around their waists, consoled sullen English fans, their faces still painted with St George crosses.

'Everybody wants to be a winner, but in this game there are also losers,' said Steve Collins, who had driven 34 hours from Manchester with his son just to see the game. 'You have to be gallant when you lose.'

That sentiment was evidence of what analysts say is a new fan culture to emerge from the tournament in Portugal, and hooliganism, the bane of tournaments both in Europe and on the world stage in the past, made only small appearances at the European Championships.

Back home, it was a different story and there was widespread disorder all over the country following England's elimination. A total of 14 arrests were made in Jersey, whose population is around 10 per cent Portuguese, after police in riot gear had to use CS gas to disperse crowds, as trouble flared after England's defeat. A crowd of Portuguese fans were pelted with cans, bottles and coins in St Helier after the match when around 1,500 England fans brought Minden Place to a standstill. The situation was eventually brought under control and Mitch Couriard from St Helier's Honorary Police said, 'It was shocking. There's been nothing like this in Jersey in living memory.'

It was a similar story in towns and cities across England and it was reported that police and community leaders in Thetford, Norfolk, were meeting after the attack on the Red Lion pub, which was filled with around 80 Portuguese fans and 40 English friends when more than 100 English fans surrounded the pub and some tried to force their way in, as police attempted to hold them back. Police said 15 people were arrested on suspicion of disorder offences, a number of which were released on police bail without charge pending further enquiries.

Jorge Pascoal, 37, who works as a press officer for the Red Lion and is an adviser to Portuguese immigrants arriving in Britain, said the bill to repair the damage would run into thousands of pounds. 'Basically, everything is devastated. It was shaming.'

In Liverpool, a 24-year-old man needed surgery after his ear was cut off in a fight following England's defeat. The victim was taken to hospital after the disturbance in the city centre, while seven people were arrested in Boston, Lincs, and there were also 17 arrests in Hertfordshire, following scenes of public disorder.

Ironically, police in Lisbon said England supporters were well behaved after the defeat. 'The English fans since they have been here have known both defeat and victory and in each case they have behaved in a very civilised way,' a Portuguese Police spokesman said.

It seemed that the Portuguese approach to the visiting fans had worked and, while the police forces from both countries were busy congratulating themselves on a job well done, let's hope they shared a thought for the Smith family in Wolverhampton.

CONCLUSION
THEY THINK IT'S ALL OVER!

Since Euro 2004, there had been a feel-good factor about following England. The new-style supporter, complete with painted face, replica shirt and musical instrument, had replaced the Stone Island warriors with their plastic chairs, who, in turn, took over from the 80s-style Casuals with their own identification which was usually Lacoste and a Stanley knife!

The banning orders which a few years ago were dished out more frequently than school dinners all but decimated England's hardcore hooligan following, although there were plenty of lads who had completed bans or had yet to receive them still on the scene, and only a fool would have considered that the hooligan problem that had blighted England games for 30 years was over.

What nobody will deny, though, is the fact that the police all over the world and especially in Europe had the English taped, and scenes that filled newspapers over the years of rampaging mobs fighting all-comers were much harder to produce. The ingredients were still there, as was the recipe for violence, but our national game was running short of cooks, hence the decline in what was always regarded as an English disease.

High-profile games a couple of seasons ago against Wales, which were supposed to see wide-scale organised mass disorder, passed relatively peacefully. Yes, there were problems, but, once again, most of them were the in-house disagreements that have been a cancer on the International scene since the early days, when, as has become clear, there was England and there was West Ham England!

It is a problem that has never gone away and, following the street battles in Manchester involving mainly Stoke fans, many were tracked down and jailed, adding scores more to the undesirables list that police hoped and prayed would result in a peaceful World Cup in Germany 2006.

It was a commendable stance that the NCIS and the FBOA took, but many thought it would need more than just the English authorities to set an example to keep the peace. As the host nation, the Poles, and even the likes of the Swiss and the Serbs, said they would be out there in force trying to win the world number-one title amongst the thugs, and – whisper it quietly – but even the Dutch threatened to show when they read how many troublesome England thugs had been prevented from making the trip!

In fairness, the authorities pulled it off and the little trouble that did occur throughout the showpiece was quickly dealt with; it turned out to be nothing worse than what happens every weekend in major towns and cities all over the country when too many lads congregate in one place with too much ale in their bellies!

The lack of trouble had to be credited to the intelligence gathered by the authorities, although it was made relatively easy for them with the new set of rules and laws granted by the courts at home and in Germany, as they had even given the go-ahead for police to be accompanied by prosecutors able to build legal cases against hooligans, after British courts refused to impose banning orders based solely on convictions in Portugal at the 2004 European Championships.

In Germany, British Police with experience at securing banning orders worked with official prosecutors gathering evidence that could be used in English courts. Just days before the finals, Nick Hawkins, the Chief Crown Prosecutor for soccer issues, said, 'We will use evidence collected in Germany to make sure any English fans who cause trouble there will receive a football banning order when they return home. This initiative solves the legal complications which prevented action being taken against troublemakers returning from previous tournaments abroad.'

Nearly 80 British police officers attended the tournament and then British Home Secretary Charles Clarke said negotiations with German authorities on security during the tournament had begun two years earlier in a bid to ensure there was no repeat of the violence England fans caused at the 2000 European Championships in Belgium and the Netherlands.

'I have formally agreed key areas of co-operation with my German counterpart, including the role of British uniformed police officers, as part of a package of measures to provide maximum support to the home nation,' said Clarke. 'These are unprecedented measures that reflect the government's commitment to ensuring that this year's World Cup is a positive experience for the anticipated 10,000 travelling England fans and for the host nation.'

Well, if the government believed that only 10,000 fans were going over, they were lucky that their source of information was not responsible for dealing with hooligan intelligence, as that figure was way off the mark and probably reflected the amount of fans with tickets purchased via the FA.

German Police confirmed that English officers would be sworn in as auxiliary police officers, although their powers would be limited to the railway system and the airports, while, in return, a small team of German officers would police British ports and airports, as England fans headed to the tournament.

Clarke said the reputation of England fans, once considered the worst in the world, had improved since 2000, largely due to court orders that ban hooligans from travelling, and boasted that more than 3,200 people were to be banned from travelling to Germany; he also warned that Hitler salutes and other gestures from Germany's Nazi past would not be tolerated.

'We want a celebration of football and an expression of the

modern relationship between our countries,' he said. 'I would say to anyone who thinks it's amusing to get involved in this kind of thing, it's not. It's deeply insulting and wrong.'

It was a typical out-of-touch statement, when there were far more pressing concerns, like thousands of Poles, Germans and immigrant gangs who were after English blood for instance, instead of the relatively trivial matter of people making Nazi salutes!

A voice that seemed to know the score far better than Mr Clarke was Assistant Chief Constable of Greater Manchester Police, Steven Thomas, who asked his German counterparts to 'police the English because of their behaviour and not because of their reputation', and added, 'English fans are now often in fear of other countries starting trouble and the "spotter" operation is not just to look at our fans, but what's going on around them too.'

Away from the fear of football violence, there was also a terrorist threat hanging over the competition, which was a major concern for England in particular, as, of the 32 teams competing, England and the United States were seen as the most likely potential terrorist targets, with both high on al-Qaeda's list of enemies.

In the main, the Germans were hoping for a trouble-free tournament, which would give the police a chance to present a welcoming face, in keeping with the official World Cup slogan: 'A time to make friends'.

However, they still warned England fans that they were considering arrest for fans who performed the theme from *The Dam Busters*, meaning that, during the competition, as well as the potential threat from the Germans, the Poles, machete-wielding kebab-shop workers and al-Qaeda, our lads had to take great care that, after a few light ales, they didn't forget the new rule as they could have been the first fans ever deported for whistling the popular tune!

Thankfully, there were no reported arrests – for that offence anyway! – and overall the authorities were pleased that the tournament passed reasonably peacefully. There were isolated incidents involving the English, the main one occurring in Cologne after the Sweden game when hundreds of Germans attacked ticketless England fans in one of the areas set up for them to watch the game. They were dispatched with relative ease as the Germans did not bank on the English having similar numbers prepared to have a go. It was a mistake and, while hundreds of law-abiding fans were on their way back from the ground, lads from most clubs in the country united and let it be known that they were still alive and literally kicking!

Earlier that day, the Germans had even teamed up with a mob of Swedes to have a go at the English but were not prepared to come looking for it and any potential major disturbance was quelled by local police intelligence and local hooligan lack of bottle!

It is an amazing statistic that, in the first week of the World Cup, there were more violence-related arrests at Royal Ascot than there were in Germany. So, either horseracing has become the new thugs' pastime or the police have nipped our football problem in the bud! A *Panorama* documentary seemed to prove that the main culprits causing trouble were an embarrassment to the hooligans as well as to the country as a whole, and scenes of drunken yobs swilling beer over tourists and passers-by were frowned upon by all.

An England return to Wembley saw the Germans arrive mob-handed but once again they failed to impress; and away games in Estonia, Israel, Croatia, Macedonia and Andorra in the main saw the fans turn their anger against the team and boss Steve McClaren rather than the local support. Then came Russia!

Regarded by many as 15 years too late, the Russians still needed sorting! They now believe themselves to be number one in the world of football violence and, having previously dispatched the Soul Crew of Cardiff with ease, they awaited the English arrival with glee as soon as the draw was made, even mocking on one hooligan show, 'The English are finished; all they want to do is drink Guinness and take drugs!'

But they underestimated their task and, although small groups of England fans and hooligan mobs were beaten up regularly over the few days they were there, on the day of the game a rejuvenated

England mob, led by many semi-retired thugs who had completed football banning orders, passed the main test with flying colours. One who wishes to remain anonymous said,

Moscow, for many, was the first time we had been abroad with England for years. Top lads from all the major firms were represented and, although we never really got it together before the game, after it was like the good old days. Basically, everyone was fed up of the Russians' bullying antics, picking off small groups and normal fans, so we decided to do something about it. All we had heard all day was that they wanted to meet us here or meet us there, and, there is no doubt about it, they had fantastic numbers about the city, but when push came to shove they did not have the experience or the quality. It was OK when 100 of them ambushed about 30 Leeds on the underground, Leeds were as game as fuck by the way; word has it that, after the beating they took, the Russians stood on the platform and applauded them! Well, we were not so impressed with them, as they were with Leeds after!

We had hundreds in a well-known hotel they said they planned to attack and, as soon as they tried it on, we were out amongst them and, to cut a long story short, they were done, and done proper. The myth that they stand toe to toe until death is bollocks and they run like the rest of Europe when the English get it together, and after the match that is exactly what we did. Nobody would get near us that night and it goes to prove that anyone who thinks we are a spent force needs to have a long hard think again. We were back that night. Back to stay? Who knows, but, with banning orders coming to an end left right and centre, it seems a lot of the older lads quite simply can't keep away!

After so much hard work went into nearly eradicating the problem, the trouble in Moscow has made the authorities sit up and take notice, and as the lad in the thick of things in Moscow mocked, 'They think it's all over … Is it now?'

THE GENERAL OF TERROR

While bringing this book to a conclusion, we contemplated asking a professor from Leicester University, one of the so-called 'hooligan experts', to give his views on the problems that have blighted England games for 30 years, believing they are the specialists in the field and would give an unbiased angle on what you have just – hopefully! – found fascinating reading.

Then a name was thrown into the hat, a name which continually cropped up in interviews for this publication, a name which not one person had a bad word to say about: Steven Hickmott. It was a good call – why bother chasing men who were never even in the back ranks, never mind the frontline when the things you have just read about took place?

Hickey is more of an expert on the subject than all the so-called hooligan professors put together, in fact, for years he was Mr England, so much so that the press named him 'the General of Terror'. He never asked for such a title and he never asked for the England firms over the years to look up to him – they just did, because Hickey was a general in the hooligan armies that were assembled over three decades and his reputation and charisma made him the number-one hooligan this country has ever produced.

Steve 'Hickey' Hickmott was the Wayne Rooney of the terraces!

HICKEY, CHELSEA:
It all began for me when Scotland used to come down in the

mid-70s, and they absolutely decimated us. In Central London, at Wembley, they took the piss, properly took the piss, and that really did it for me, boys. Scotland were good at the time, there's no doubt about it, but I got it into my head that we had to get them back and it took years, but, in the end, we turned the situation completely around and, by the time the games were scrapped, the Scots knew that when they played England they could take the piss no more! At the time, it hurt watching them take Wembley and parts of London to bits, but with hindsight we have to thank them for it, as that is what got us all together, and England – on most occasions anyway – were as one!

Of course there were in-house disagreements, West Ham were always West Ham, they didn't like mixing, still don't to this day. But they will admit there were times when they had to if they were to survive, and this is where I came into the fold, as I always wanted England to be England. It took time, in 1980 in Switzerland, West Ham were fighting Chelsea, as we were the main two firms out there; Man United were the only other major mob to travel in those days. There were never many Scousers with us, as, for one, they were hated and many of their lads gave the trips a wide one, and, secondly, the red lot were always in Europe anyway. We never had a fucking week in Europe with Chelsea and nor did West Ham as such, so we all started going to England games in the late 70s and early 80s and that's where all that skirmishing started. But I always preferred it when we all got together and said, 'Fuck all this, we're England!'

Again, it was not an overnight thing, but eventually I think most people agreed with what I was trying to do.

Our first big one was Spain '82. Myself and all the boys from Tunbridge Wells who were not all Chelsea got together, went down to Plymouth and got the boat over to San Sebastian. I think it was about £40 at the time. Once we got there into Spain, most of the lads were there, living it up in seafront hotels, while all the official supporters were in a campsite up on the hill. Even in the early days, the official tours were a rip-off! That campsite full of clowns and FA cronies had its uses, though, as every time we caused any grief or aggravation in town – such as the time when Chelsea legend Micky Greenaway nicked a local donkey, and rode it into the disco bar chanting his trademark 'Zigger-Zagger' – the police immediately headed towards the campsite and smashed all the geezers up!

From there, it was on to Bilbao. More and more fans latched on to our firm and we had quite an entourage by the time we arrived in the old city ready for the first game, so much so that the police blocked off a bridge to stop us getting into the main town. Tanks, armoured cars, you name it, they were there, so hundreds of England followed our firm and just walked straight towards them. We walked between their tanks, round their armoured cars and a few of the madder members climbed over the top! No problem.

Inside the ground was fantastic, we were still smashing into the French when Brian Robson scored in less than a minute. That was the start of a great holiday and everyone had a superb time in San Sebastian. It was all done in the name of fun. A proper good holiday, probably one of the best holidays I've ever had and ever will have, and I've been a lot of places in my time.

We went on to Madrid for the other two and, as soon as we arrived, there were stories of knifings and beatings, so we made our way up to the main area where the ground was and where normal England fans had been getting battered. If it wasn't the local Spanish boys, it was the Old Bill doing the battering; it was so bad we even let some good German skinheads come with us that time. A great battleground was an area called Sol; it went on night after night after night. Every night, we were beaten by the police after we had smashed the locals who were always obliging.

Eventually, England were knocked out after drawing two games 0–0 and we were all at the airport when we bumped into Kevin Keegan; we were really polite to him but he could see we were not the usual flag-waving supporters and the cunt looked at us and said, 'We don't want your type here.'

I thought, What the fuck am I following these twats about for, spending all my money while they're living in nice hotels?! It was typical of the fucking players at the time, they didn't appreciate our support, and that is one thing that hasn't changed over the years, as most of the overpaid wankers are the same today!

Little spats like Keegan's were never going to deter us, though, and after the World Cup we rarely missed a game. Later that year, we played Denmark and all met up in the area where all the sex shops are, in a boozer called the Spunk Bar. All the boys will remember that one as it was the trip when one bloke called Baddy Dave went out and got himself a bird, but, as well as getting his hole, he also got robbed when he left his fucking trousers on the floor, while he had a shower. When he came back and told us, that was it; we did every pimp in the street and half the brasses, we just slapped the fucking lot of them all over the place.

It was the same at the game and it went off for the duration – Denmark was just one long fight! A big smoke grenade and tear gas went off in the ground, fighting broke out everywhere and a lot of people saw it on the TV, as it made big news. Some clips showed me being bundled out of the crowd all the way down to the front and being punched in by a couple of plain-clothes policeman at the bottom; they gave me a good hiding, but we done all right, I was never one to moan if I took a slap. Outside the ground, the Danes put up a good fight, we took the piss really but they did put up a fucking good fight in fairness to them!

There were bad days, as you have read, and I'll agree that one of the most terrifying was Greece. We always used to take in the Under-21 games, which were usually the night before. They were low-key matches but, in Athens, the amount of people that turned out and the hatred shown towards us was unbelievable. We formed our fucking group, maybe 200 of us in the ground, and Ted Croker came by with his entourage of wankers from the FA and give it the old: 'We told you people not to come, you're not welcome here and you're a disgrace to those shirts.'

Someone replied, 'Well, you fucking sold them to us and you get the profit out of it, you cunt.'

Anyway, he ignored it and, as he made his way back down the terracing towards the open gate that he'd come through, the Greeks cut him off and he took a few digs; it was wonderful and, no, we didn't help the cunt!

After the game, we left the ground in armoured buses, after they kept us locked in for an hour and they dropped us off at a place called Piraeus Port, where it's like bringing people out of Chelsea's ground and dropping them off where everyone's waiting. The doors of the vans opened and they were there, fucking hundreds of Greeks and they absolutely terrified us. That was a proper fight in retreat and anyone who was there will remember it, scary but yet another great day out!

The next day, we went up to Salonika, me and my boys, maybe 150 of us on three coaches, and anywhere else that would have been enough to take liberties – well, it was not enough out there and we had to fight our way to the ground. As we got in there, it was an impossible task to get the lads on to the terracing, the Greeks were everywhere, and they battered us back out. We backed off across the road, still fighting, and there was a huge hill outside the ground, which we went up, and we held that hill from hundreds of Greeks who didn't get in the ground like ourselves.

They continually attacked it throughout the game and we were forced to roll boulders down at them and so on. West Ham's crowd, about 70 lads, and a few Northerners did get in and I saw pictures in the Greek papers the next day of them being escorted on to the pitch for their own safety, the Greeks really did put up a fucking proper good fight that day.

Another fantastic trip was Hungary in '83 – that was one of the greatest battles, but I would call it a fighting retreat really! Other people might see it a bit differently but in the stadium we stood our ground, and we held it – just, but when we came out, it was really on top down in the underground when the Hungarians attacked the trains and put the windows in. We came off of the trains and we're giving it the old 'Ooo, ooo, ooo' and we went into them and they backed off, up the stairs, and as they were going down the set of stairs on the other side, they all fell down on top of each other, literally hundreds, fell down on top of each other. Well, that was a result for us, but, from where they'd fallen down, the police were charging along that platform and, instead of helping them up, the Old Bill stamped on them, beat them and smashed them, as they climbed over them, fucking people with broken bones and all sorts!

We were back on our toes and got on a different train and we were all thinking we'd had a result here, until we pulled into the next station which was full of Old Bill. The doors stayed closed and they calmly pulled the little slide windows open and sprayed tear gas inside the train, so we had to break our way out through the windows and the Old Bill backed off, and we had them outside the station, it was mental and got better when the Hungarians came again. This was when we had to do a fighting retreat, all the way round some square – to this day, I can't remember the name of the square but it was non-stop for maybe an hour that night. I'd say that was one of the best nights I've had in my entire life, and, even though a few boys got hurt, very few got nicked, and that's what it was all about, we all stuck together for England!

As the years went by, more and more lads started to watch England, there was a lot of Chelsea and West Ham going. The ICF were in their prime and they wanted to go on their own and prove they were a bit more tasty than us and Man United. I always tried to keep the lads together, tried to keep them part of England, fuck Chelsea, fuck Man United, fuck West Ham, we were England. I got sick of saying it all the time but believe me you needed to be all together in places like Greece and Hungary. Once or twice, West Ham found this out, when they were stuck on their own in some places they didn't have the numbers and things came on top, so in the end they joined up again and we all went together and it was great.

There were some legendary battles, too many to remember, but ones which will never be forgotten were France, Luxembourg, Romania and Turkey, all mad trips and all fantastic memories. In Paris, I was with Scarrott and we'd come on to the terracing and they had called in the CRS riot squad due to the problems we were causing. We were facing them and they were sizing us up and, to be honest, it didn't look too good. They fired the first couple of canisters over, so I ran forward, picked up one of them as it was spinning and slung it back at them. There were 50–60 riot police and the guy in charge of them was the only one without the full riot gear on, he had his stick and his flat cap marshalling his troops and it was just my fucking luck that it hit him straight on the peak of his hat. Well, that was it, they came into us and I got one of the worst beatings of my life.

Somehow I squeezed under one of those seats that are eight or nine inches off the concrete, but I got stuck and they beat me and fucking dragged me from there and threw me down into a moat and, although I didn't realise it at the time, I broke my wrist in the fall. They then dragged me out of the moat and kicked me all the way round the pitch until I got to an area where they put us into vans, where, much to my delight, we were taken out an hour after the game and were given a trip through the main fucking street in Paris where everything had been smashed to pieces! It was absolutely wonderful knowing the boys had carried on what we had started.

We went to Romania and it was full of old gypsy people and they were quite simply horrible cunts. In the ground, we fought for ages and managed to get ourselves a bit of space and they could not get near us. The normal fans were giving us grief, saying we were a disgrace to our country and loads of other nonsense but, if we had let the locals in, they would have been destroyed as the Romanians were not bothered who they were attacking. Ken Bailey, the old England mascot, who people say turned out to be a wrong one, was walking round the pitch so they attacked him, tried to drag him through the fence, had his top hat off, pulled his fucking tailcoat and kicked the daft old bloke all over. The supporters' club people were saying, 'Help him, help him!' And we're going, 'Fuck off, you didn't want us in here half an hour ago, you go and fucking help him!'

Outside the ground, the Romanians didn't put up too much of a fight, but it was another absolutely wonderful trip.

Luxembourg, well, what can you say? We absolutely sacked the place. West Ham were fighting with Man United, Chelsea were supposed to be fighting with West Ham, all sorts of things like that. Everything went fucking through windows. I saw a geezer I know with a fox-fur coat and matching hat – worth about £5,000, I'd imagine – running down a street. Everyone had their new Lacoste jumpers or whatever the fashion was in those days. In a nutshell, England nicked everything and absolutely destroyed the place. It was all a bit of fun, the same thing we have been doing for the last 500 years, march into their country, take the piss, drink all their beer, shag some of their women, and do what we do best – fight people. It was fucking wonderful!

Turkey was the game where the photograph of me in the goggles appeared because we got there a few days before and we'd been down to the place where you buy all World War II bits and pieces in Istanbul, and I'd bought those goggles for a laugh. The next day we went to the game and we fronted the Turk; there were only 50 of us that night and we came across the car park, having it with them, when all of a sudden the door opened by the ground and the official said, 'Are you the England party?'

'Fucking right we are!'

'This way, please, gentleman!'

The soft bastard thought we were the Under-21 team, led us into the ground and put us in a VIP area, so we're there and some press bloke has taken a picture of all the dignitaries and I'm there with these daft goggles on sitting with important-looking Turkish people and the British ambassador. His wife and daughter were there, but didn't like our language so they fucked off sharpish.

A short while later, the England Under-21 team come in and we're all in their seats. That's when I had the row with Barry Venison who said, 'I think you're in my seat.'

I said, 'Fuck off and, if you're going to stand there, you'll get it as well!'

So the England team moved over and we had their seats for the game. We won 8–0 and the Turks were so disgruntled that they were setting light to these small cushions that they bring with them to sit on the terraces and they started hurling them at us. Inside these cushions were thousands of small feathers and all these feathers were on fire in mid-air, the sky was alight with these feathers and smoke and you couldn't see a yard in front of you!

We came outside and there was the official England supporters club and us lot. Well, I'll never forget the guy in charge saying, 'You must stand together here.'

Just then, the Turks rained bottles, bricks, everything, down on us so we knew we would have to get out of there, so we broke forward, 30–40 of us, giving it the old chant and we done those Turks all the way up the road. We never stopped chasing them, absolutely annihilated them everywhere, another fantastic, absolutely wonderful time.

I went away in '86, it was a daft jail sentence to stop me going to the World Cup in Mexico, but after I got out of nick it didn't take me long to get back into the swing of things. There was Italy '90 and, right from the off, right from day one, it went off, we had the Deutschland Hooligans, the Germans, fancying themselves and everywhere we went the Italians would want to fight us, as per usual the cowardly Italian Police would arrest innocent bystanders and never ever seemed to nick any of their geezers, but over the years we got used to that type of thing.

Through the 90s, I didn't go to quite as many games, because the Old Bill and press were on to me and they made it hard for me to travel. I went to Norway a week before England were playing them and got deported, even though I wasn't going to the game. I was in a hotel three days before, when the police kicked in the door, took me away and then put me on the TV the day before the game, saying I'd been deported from Norway! I happened to be working a Bruce Springsteen tour selling shirts at the time!

Times were changing and I picked my games carefully. One you could not miss was the World Cup qualifier in Rome in '97 and, by this time, England had a lot of what I would call family supporters, and they were getting treated like shit. Anyway, we turned up and were involved in skirmishes all the way to the ground and I ended up getting stabbed in the shoulder with a screwdriver, nothing too serious, but it bled for a fucking day and a half.

I had heard about this area, the East Curve, where their boys were supposed to be, so I'm now inside the ground and the police and Italians are properly giving it to the straight goers and all the family supporters in the official section and I've noticed the sign saying Ost Curve, or whatever it is in Italian. So we went up there and, as we went in, they were about 300–400 Italians taunting the English straight goers in the next two sections. We went into those cunts and they fled; they went so far they took the whole Perspex barricade, which was 8–10ft high, with them as they smashed through it to get away from us. Well, after that lot had fucked off, there was the Old Bill and they came into us and there's many pictures in the newspapers of me with the caption 'GENERAL OF TERROR'.

After the game, they were trying to keep the England fans in, but we came off the East Curve, maybe 300 of us, and we broke out of the ground and were straight into the Italians who were waiting to attack all the true supporters. Inside the ground, the police were doing the job well enough and were generally beating, smashing and taking the piss out of the straight guys.

They knew they wouldn't have a go back; that section was full of wankers saying, 'Oh I'm going to report you to my MP!'

I've got one very good souvenir – apart from the stab wound from that night – which is a beret from one of the police officers there. He'd taken it off and was trying to get his riot helmet on, as he got a right-hander. I've got the beret hanging up in pride in a pub that a lot of people know in South East Asia in Thailand. Outside, it was hand-to-hand all the way for two hours afterwards, while the main firm of England, maybe 4,000–5,000 were kept in that ground till two-thirty in the morning. We were out straight away and we did our country proud that night!

Apart from the games, there were the characters, people like Scarrott from Nottingham, a wonderful geezer, no fear whatsoever but he was so stupid. We loved the geezer, but we'd be plotted up, we'd be right where we want to be, 100 of us in the pub, and he'd have to break into the machines. He always had his screwdriver handy and never had any money! He tried to throw a French bloke off the second tier in Paris in '84, he was totally mad but he always stood with you. You didn't need to look around, you knew he was there; he was never going backwards and, even though he got some severe beatings, he always came back for more. Unfortunately, he died a few years ago in Barcelona, which was sad, as he was a true terrace legend, in the days when you had to fight to earn the title.

There are some other great lads out there, the Bin Man, he was Man City, Kenny Salford, he was Chelsea but came from that area, and they would always turn up. Aston Villa Kevin, he was a great bloke and we would all meet up at Victoria Station and head off to wherever with those moody Inter-Rail things.

There were times when it was scary. And anyone who says they weren't scared and weren't terrified, I can honestly say they weren't fucking there because our firm were usually outnumbered; apart from places like Luxembourg, it was fucking coming on top all the time.

But we came through it and I don't believe lads from any

other country in the world could have kept it together like the English did during those years, when we all stayed tight. Even today, when the likes of the Poles and Croats think they are fit to wipe our arses, we would swot them like flies if we stuck together; the problem is England don't, and it will be their downfall. We have been in this situation before and, unless we are as one, we will come unstuck.

Not so long ago in Poland, I was in a hotel and Wolves wanted to fight Oldham and Chelsea wanted to fight West Ham and I had to turn round and say, 'Right, you cunts, we're fucking leaving this hotel in 10 minutes and we're England. Anyone who wants to be West Ham, Chelsea, Arsenal or Man United can fuck off! When I walk out of the fucking door, we're England, it's four miles to the ground and we're walking. All the wankers who want to go in a taxi fuck off now because I have got the key to a back door to the Katowice hotel and England will be leaving via that door!'

Some geezers might have thought I was a wanker but I didn't give a fuck because we walked out of the back door and, while all the Old Bill were out the front, we walked all the way to the ground. It was brilliant and we had some fantastic battles on the way that night and that was England, true England!

The words from Hickey may ring true in relation to the long history of the once-feared England fan but it shouldn't be seen like a battle cry to those lads heading out to Austria for the 2008 European Championships, a tournament that may see the English number-one hooligans title come under threat.

With so many banning orders in place, England's support is likely to be made up of thousands of family-type supporters who are out there for all the right reasons – the football and to have a good time. The problem is that the reputation built over the years by England's hooligan army may mean that the followers of our national side, who have so long been regarded as the hunters, may well become the hunted.

CONTRIBUTING AUTHORS ALSO WROTE:

Top Boys: True Stories from all the football firm's main faces,
Cass Pennant £7.99 Blake ISBN7659781844542

Hooligans: The M–Z of Britain's Football Gangs vol 2, Nick Lowles,
Andy Nicholls £14.99 Milo ISBN1093854512

Tottenham Massive: One of football's most uncompromising firms,
Trevor Tanner £17.99 Blake ISBN1844541819

It's Only A Game: Notorious Chelsea Headhunter Jason Marriner lifts the lid on his trial by television case that got him six years, Jason Marriner £16.99 Mainland GB Publishing ISBN0955268206

The Town Where I Was Born: Football-mad lad growing up in Oldham,
Carl H Spiers £9.99 Chas Promotions

Mig Crew: The story of Luton's Mig Crew as told from the sharp end of football's frontline, Tommy Robinson £10.99 Pennant Books
ISBN9781906015008

Sex, Drugs and Football Thugs: On the road with the Naughty Forty,
Mark Chester £9.99 Milo ISBN190385444X

Hooligans: The A–L of Britain's Football Thugs vol 1,
Nick Lowles, Andy Nicholls £14.99 Milo ISBN1903854415

Gilly: Running with a Pack of Wolves,
Gilroy Shaw, Martin King £9.99 Head-Hunter ISBN0954854217

Inside the 'Forest Executive Crew': Memoirs of the Forest main lad,
Gary 'Boatsy' Clarke, Martin King £19.99 Head-Hunter ISBN0954854233

Good Afternoon Gentlemen, The Name's Bill Gardner:
Autobiography of West Ham's top man, Bill Gardner, Cass Pennant £17.99
Blake ISBN9781844542611

Terrace Legends: Confessional interviews with the legends who ruled the football terraces and beyond, Cass Pennant, Martin King £7.99 Blake
ISBN9781844540921

Grafters: The inside story of the Wide Awake Firm, Europe's
most prolific sneak thieves, Colin Blaney £7.99 Milo ISBN1903854288

Scally: The shocking confessions of a category C football hooligan
who followed Everton, Andy Nicholls £6.99 Milo ISBN1903854253

Naughty: The story of Stoke City's hooligan gang, Mark Chester £7.99
Milo ISBN1903854261

Rolling with the 657 Crew: The true story of Pompey's legendary
football fans, Rob Silvester, Cass Pennant, £7.99 Blake ISBN9781844540723

A Casual Look: A photo diary of football firms 1980s to 2001, Lorne Brown, Nick Harvey £15.00 FootballCultureUK

Congratulations You Have Just Met the I.C.F.: West Ham's notorious Inter-City Firm, Cass Pennant £7.99 Blake ISBN9781904034858

We Are The Famous Football Hooligans: Carl H Spiers £9.99 Chas Promotions

Wednesday Rucks & Rock 'n' Roll: Lively tales and memories from the Sheffield Wednesday boys, Anthony Cronshaw £8.95 ISBN0954422600

Want Some Aggro?: The true story of West Ham's first guv'nors, Micky Smith, Cass Pennant £7.99 Blake ISBN9781844544035

City Psychos: The era and time of the notorious Hull City mob, Shaun Tordoff £7.99 Milo ISBN190385413X

Blades Business Crew: The violent exploits of Sheffield United's BBC, Steve Cowens £7.99 Milo ISBN0953084787

An Englishman Abroad: A harrowing account and story of an innocent fan, Martin Kerr £8.99 S.T. Publishing ISBN0953592065

Armed for the Match: The troubles and trial of the Chelsea Headhunters, Colin Ward, Steve 'Hickey' Hickmott £7.99 Headline Books ISBN0747262926

Cass: The bestselling biography that's now a motion picture, Cass Pennant £5.99 Blake 9781903402900

Divide of the Steel City: The history behind the hostility between United and Wednesday fans, Steve Cowens, Anthony Cronshaw £17.99 Pennant Books ISBN9781906015015

Home Fans Only!: The away supporters' pub guide, Martin Kerr £10.99 ISBN9789060150467